FIRST CORINTHIANS

BIBLE STUDY TEXTBOOK SERIES

STUDIES IN
FIRST CORINTHIANS

by
Paul T. Butler

College Press Publishing Company, Joplin, Missouri

Copyright © 1985
College Press Publishing Company
Second Printing 1992

Printed and Bound in the
United States of America
All Rights Reserved

Library of Congress Catalog Card Number: 84-072-347
International Standard Book Number: 0-89900-063-0

This volume is dedicated
to
Lakin Paul Lankford
and
Deker Kyle Lankford
my cherished grandsons

in the hope that they will follow in the
steps of the great apostle to the Gentiles
and
preach the gospel of Christ
wherever they go.

Table of Contents

Introduction 1

First Corinthians   *Page*
Chapter

One	The Problem of Schism	8
Two	The Problem of Revelation	32
Three	The Problem of Ministry	48
Four	The Problem of Favoritism and Conceit	64
Five	The Problem of Church Discipline	81
Six	The Problem of Baseness and Brotherhood	97
Seven	The Problems of Sexuality and Marriage	118
Eight	The Problem of Conscience	148
Nine	The Problem of Freedom	161
Ten	The Problem of Presumptuousness	179
Eleven	The Problem of Disorderly Worship	199
Twelve	The Problem of Maintaining Unity in the Midst of Diversity	222

Special Study: Gifts, Miracles 240

Special Study: Paul's Power to Give Charismatic Power 249

Special Study: Is the Church An Organization or An Organism? 260

Thirteen	The Problem of Maintaining Love in the Midst of Diversity	278

Special Study: Love Is A Many Splendored Thing 291

Special Study: The Christian Syndrome 298

FIRST CORINTHIANS

First Corinthians Chapter		*Page*
Fourteen	The Problem of Edification in the Midst of Diversity	302
Fifteen	The Problem of the Resurrection	320
Special Study: On Cloud Nine		349
Special Study: The Existential/Neo-Orthodox Philosophy of History		358
Sixteen	The Problem of Aiding Christian Brethren	376
Index of Scriptures		393
Index of Places		409
Index of Subjects		410
Index of People		413
Index of Organizations		416

INTRODUCTION

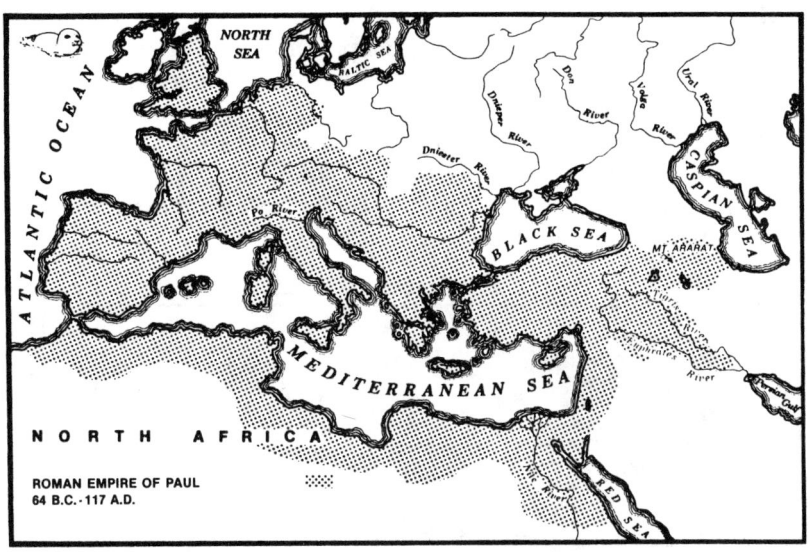

Historical Background:

Corinth: in Greek language, *Korinthos,* meaning, "ornament."

In Paul's day, Corinth was the capital of the Roman province called by them, Achaia, and the most important city in Greece (even more important from the Roman viewpoint than Athens).

Athens was the intellectual center of Greece; Corinth was the commercial center.

Corinth occupied a strategic geographical position. It was the southern gate on the isthmus into Greece.

It was built on the side or at the foot of the 2000 ft. Mount Acrocorinthus.

The acropolis of Corinth was atop this mountain. On a clear day you could see from this acropolis 40 miles northeast to the city of Athens. Corinth had three harbors.

Ancient seafaring men so dreaded having to make the 200 mile voyage around the southern capes of the Peloponnesus, they would tie ropes to their ships, put logs under them and drag them across the isthmus. Large ships were unloaded, dragged across, the cargo carried across, put back on board and then they would sail on across the Mediterranean Sea.

FIRST CORINTHIANS

Many attempts were made to build a canal across the isthmus in ancient times; the most notable attempt being that of Nero (about 15 years after Paul established the Christian church there), in 66 A.D.

The Romans declared Greece and Corinth "free" in 196 B.C. But a Greek rebellion in 146 B.C. caused the Romans to destroy Corinth totally; its famous art treasures were taken to Rome as booty.

Julius Caesar rebuilt Corinth as a Roman colony and made it the capital of Achaia in 46 B.C.

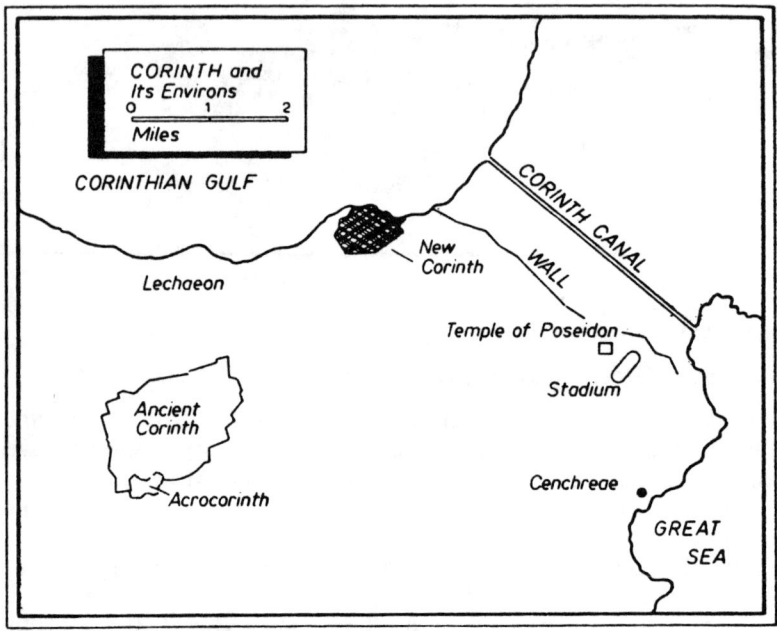

At the height of its power, Corinth probably had a population of 200,000 free born Greek citizens and 500,000 slaves. . . . about the population density of St. Louis, Missouri.

Its population consisted of descendants of the Roman colonists who came in 46 B.C. (100 years before Paul)—many Romans who came for business from Italy—a large Greek population—many strangers from different nationalities—and the inevitable Jewish community with its synagogues.

INTRODUCTION

A broken lintel (part of a door) discovered by archaeologists bears a Greek inscription, "synagogue of Hebrews."

The canal at Corinth, connecting the Ionian Sea with the Agean was begun in 66 A.D. by Nero. The present canal, begun in 1881, shortens the distance from the Aegean Sea to Athens by 202 miles for ships able to navigate its 69-foot width and 26-foot depth.

Paul undoubtedly chose Corinth for a missionary "base" because of its itinerant and cosmopolitan population. Anyone who could make his voice heard in Corinth was addressing a spectrum of people from all over the known civilized world, many of whom would be sure to go all over the world and possibly carry with them what they had heard.

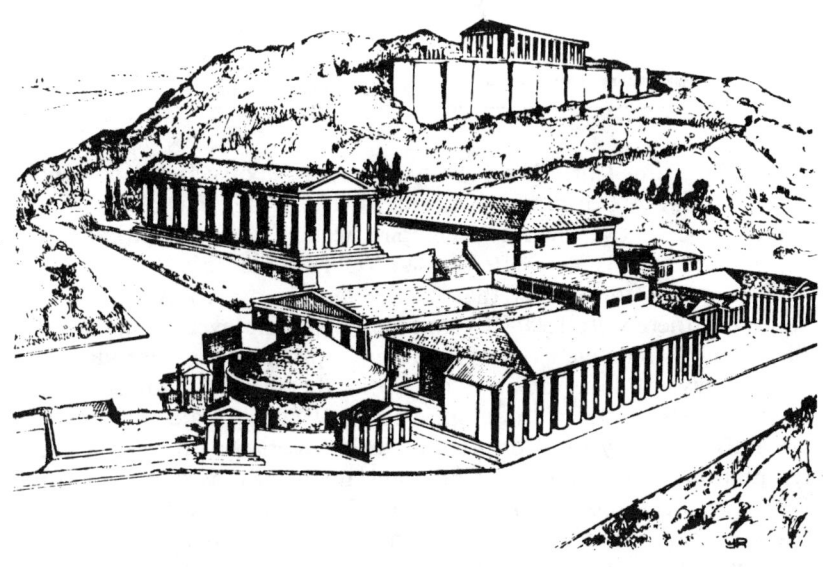

This is probably what Corinth looked like in Paul's day (up-town). The acropolis had the pantheon upon it where their gods were housed. Poseidon, god of the sea, was their chief god. The Isthmian Games were held there every two years, second only to the Olympic Games in Athens. The agora (market place and public buildings) is in the foreground. What the remainder of the city looked like is not pictured.

FIRST CORINTHIANS

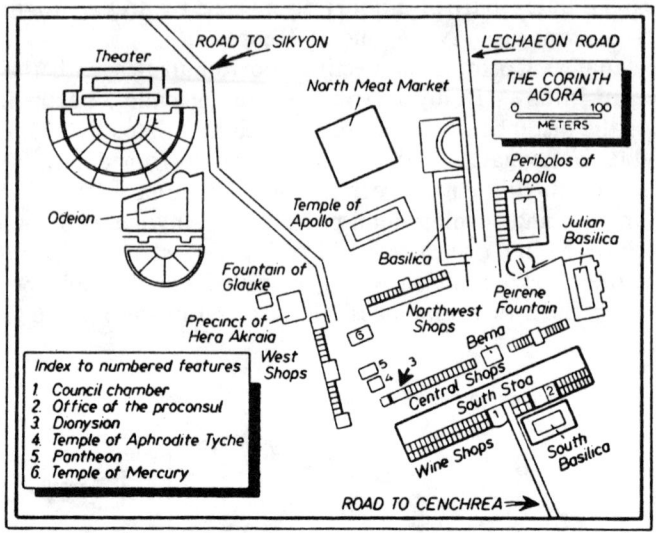

In Paul's time Corinth was a city of wealth, luxury and immorality! To "live like a Corinthian" meant to live a life of profligacy and debauchery. All over the Roman empire, women who were promiscuous or of loose morals were often called "Corinthian girls."

The reason for this is that at the temple of Aphrodite on the Acropolis there were 1000 "Corinthian girls" employed as *hierodouloi* (lit. "temple maiden servants"), actually prostitutes. Aphrodite was the goddess of love (*eros*). Worship at the temple involved sexual intercourse with one of these "priestesses." Young male homosexuals were also used by the Corinthians. This "worship" formed a great temptation, even to the new Christians at Corinth, as evidenced from Paul's exhortations against it (I Cor. 5:1ff., 6:9-19). This attracted "worshipers" from all over the Roman world. To become "corinthianized" meant a person was living the most licentious, debauched life possible. It was customary in a stage play in the theater for a Corinthian actor to come on the scene drunk. Much drunkenness, homosexuality, fornication, robbery, thievery, idolatry and immorality of all kinds went on here. Strabo quoted the proverb, "All the people of Corinth gorge themselves." Corinth had many important industries, its pottery and brass and marble for building columns were famous all over the world.

INTRODUCTION

Sex crazy, sports crazy, affluent and cynical, citizens and visitors of Corinth liked to tell of the notorious priestesses of Aphrodite, whose studded sandals spelled out in the dust of the street, "Follow me!" Every shop in the city had a deep, spring-fed well in which to cool containers of wine.

Alciphro wrote: "I did not enter Corinth after all; for I learned in a short time the sordidness of the rich there and the misery of the poor." Aristophanes coined the word "corinthianize" to denote debauchery.

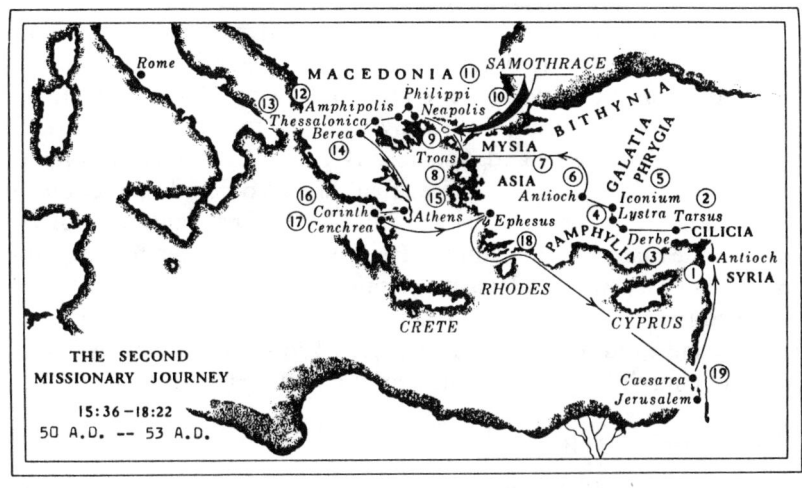

Date of the Epistle:

Paul visited Corinth for the first time on his second missionary journey (Acts 18) about 50-51 A.D. Claudius was emperor of Rome at that time. He had just been to Athens where he was not well received

FIRST CORINTHIANS

so he came to Corinth hesitantly ("in much weakness, fear and trembling," 2:3). The Lord told Paul He had much people in the city. He became acquainted with Aquila and Priscilla, tent-makers like he was. During his stay of 1-1/2 years he resided in their home. Soon after his arrival, Silas and Timothy joined him with news from Thessalonica. Every sabbath Paul preached in the synagogue of the Jews; he met with strong opposition and gave the rest of his stay in Corinth to the Gentiles (Acts 18:6). Titus Justus, Crispus, Gaius and Stephanas were some of Paul's first converts. During Paul's stay, Gallio, the elder brother of the Roman philosopher Seneca came to his rescue when the Jews tried to have him imprisoned.

Paul seems to have visited Corinth again, during his third missionary journey when he was headquartered at Ephesus (II Cor. 12:14, 13:1). While at Ephesus, Paul wrote an earlier letter to the Corinthians (I Cor. 5:9) which has been lost. Paul wrote our present First Corinthians from the city of Ephesus about 56 or 57 A.D. in answer to a letter from Corinth (probably brought to him from there by Stephanas, Fortunatus and Achaicus (I Cor. 16:17) relating some of the problems in the church there. Paul had also heard of factions in the church from the servants of Chloe (1:11), probably one of the women members of the church. Paul wrote this letter to deal with these *problems*, which plagued the saints.

Of course "the church" at Corinth was probably composed of many small groups of Christians meeting in different homes. There were no church buildings as such until about 200 A.D.

The Purpose of This Epistle:

Problems, problems, problems; every church has them. Even the first century churches were beset with problems. The Holy Spirit guided Paul in the composition of this letter that divine wisdom might be delineated for dealing with these enigmas and abberations. There are nine or ten distinct problems dealt with: factionalism and schism; spiritual maturation; immorality; Christian integrity; marriage and divorce; liberties in Christ; order and decorum in worship; communion in Christ; abuse and misuse of miraculous gifts; probability of life after death (the resurrection from the dead); collections made for the saints. This book reads like a modern, twentieth century, "Report on the State of the Church of Christ."

INTRODUCTION

The church today faces, essentially, the same problems. The problems do not change because human nature is the same in every generation. Human beings are either in the process of regeneration through the power of the word of God growing in them, or they are in the process of degeneration through the power of the word of the devil developing in them. The Holy Spirit's purpose through the pen of the apostle Paul was to produce a holy growth in the "saints" at Corinth. It will be evident as one studies this epistle that these Christians had much growing to do. But so do we all if we are to reach "mature manhood, to the measure of the stature of the fulness of Christ" (Eph. 4:13). God wished the Christians at Corinth to know that he loved them with an eternal love as they were growing into the persons for which he had created them. There could never, after the Cross, be any question about the faithfulness of God's love. The question was, then, whether the Corinthians would choose the growth he desired for them. That is still the question for the church today.

Chapter One

THE PROBLEM OF SCHISM
(1:1-31)

IDEAS TO INVESTIGATE:

1. How could Paul address people with so many spiritual failures as "saints" and "sanctified"? (1:2)
2. Do Christians have to all agree on everything and think alike? (1:10)
3. If Christ did not send Paul to baptize, is baptism then not essential to salvation? (1:17)
4. Does Paul's denunciation of the "wisdom of the wise" mean Christians should reject all human knowledge? (1:20-25)

SECTION 1

Unity Originates in the Character of God (1:1-17)

1 Paul, called by the will of God to be an apostle of Christ Jesus, and our brother Sosthenes,

2 To the church of God which is at Corinth, to those sanctified in Christ Jesus, called to be saints together with all those who in every place call on the name of our Lord Jesus Christ, both their Lord and ours:

3 Grace to you and peace from God our Father and the Lord Jesus Christ.

4 I give thanks to God always for you because of the grace of God which was given you in Christ Jesus, 5that in every way you were enriched in him with all speech and all knowledge— 6even as the testimony to Christ was confirmed among you— 7so that you are not lacking in any spiritual gift, as you wait for the revealing of our Lord Jesus Christ; 8who will sustain you to the end, guiltless in the day of our Lord Jesus Christ. 9God is faithful, by whom you were called into the fellowship of his Son, Jesus Christ our Lord.

10 I appeal to you, brethren, by the name of our Lord Jesus Christ, that all of you agree and that there be no dissensions among you, but that you be united in the same mind and the same judgment. 11For it has been reported to me by Chloe's people that there is quarreling among you, my brethren. 12What

CHAPTER 1   FIRST CORINTHIANS 1:1-17

I mean is that each one of you says, "I belong to Paul," or "I belong to Apollos," or "I belong to Cephas," or "I belong to Christ." 13Is Christ divided? Was Paul crucified for you? Or were you baptized in the name of Paul? 14I am thankful that I baptized none of you except Crispus and Gaius; 15lest any one should say that you were baptized in my name. 16(I did baptize also the household of Stephanas. Beyond that, I do not know whether I baptized any one else.) 17For Christ did not send me to baptize but to preach the gospel, and not with eloquent wisdom, lest the cross of Christ be emptied of its power.

1:1-3 Consecration: Paul, whose Hebrew name was Saul, was born near the beginning of the first century in the busy Graeco-Roman city of Tarsus in Cilicia at the northeast corner of the Mediterranean Sea. He was born with Roman citizenship (Acts 22:28); the son of a Pharisee and a Pharisee himself (Acts 23:6), he could have boasted of the purest Hebrew background (Phil. 3:5). As a young Jewish patriot and fledgling rabbi he persecuted the Christians with zeal (Acts 7:58—8:3; 9:1-2; 26:9-11; I Tim. 1:13) until his conversion on the road to Damascus (Acts 9:1-31; 22:1-21). Calling himself "chief of sinners" (I Tim. 1:15), he forever after attributed the change in his life to the overflowing grace of the Lord toward him (I Tim. 1:12-17). Paul studied at the feet of the famous Hebrew rabbi Gamaliel (Acts 22:3; 26:4-5). He was well educated in the literature of the Greeks (Acts 17:28) and was a world traveler with a cosmopolitan attitude (I Cor. 9:19-23). The authenticity and historicity of this epistle is beyond question.

Paul begins by stating that he was *called* (Gr. *kletos,* means more than "invited"—it has the connotation of being *uniquely chosen*) by the *will* of God to be an apostle. Paul is declaring that he is in the service of God not by any merit of his own but by the sovereign call of God's grace. When Paul wrote to churches where his authority as an apostle was unchallenged, he did not assert his apostolic title (Phil. 1:1; I Thess. 1:1; Philemon 1); but when he corresponded with a church or churches where his apostolic authority might be questioned, he always declared his office in the salutation and sometimes presented the evidence for his apostleship (Rom. 1:1; Gal. 1:1; Col. 1:1; II Cor. 1:1).

On his first missionary journey (45-48 A.D.) Paul established churches in Asia Minor (modern Turkey) (Acts 13:1—15:35). On his

FIRST CORINTHIANS

second missionary journey (Acts 15:36—18:22) he established churches in Macedonia and Achaia (modern Greece) (51-54 A.D.). It was during this second journey that Paul established the church in Corinth.

The third missionary journey took three years (54-58 A.D.) and, after spending three months in Achaia (Acts 20:3), he stopped in Ephesus for about two or three years. It was from this residence in Ephesus he received communication from Corinth and wrote back to them this epistle. A Christian named *Sosthenes* was with him in Ephesus. That this is Sosthenes, the ruler of the synagogue in Corinth (Acts 18:17), is doubtful. Sosthenes, the ruler of the synagogue, seems to have been an enemy of Paul.

Paul addressed the Christians in Corinth as "the church of God." The Greek word for church is *ekklesia* (related to the same word Paul used to describe his "call" to apostleship). *Ekklesia* means literally "the called out ones." It was used in the Greek world to denote the convening of the assembly of all the citizens of a particular city to fulfill the functions necessary for the maintenance of their social structure; a "town-meeting." Paul adapts the word to the church for the very same purpose. William Barclay says: "In essence, therefore, the Church, the *ekklesia,* is a body of people, not so much assembling because they have chosen to come together, but assembling because God has called them to Himself; not so much assembling to share their own thoughts and opinions, but assembling to listen to the voice of God." The word *ekklesia* as it is used in the New Testament certainly connotes those who have been *called out* of a life conformed to this wicked world order unto a life transformed into the image of God's Son, Jesus Christ.

Paul emphasizes the fact that those addressed are a "church" of God because God had *sanctified* them. The Greek words *hegiasmenois* (sanctified) and *hagiois* (saints) mean literally "to set apart, to consecrate, to separate for a specific use." Vine's *Expository Dictionary of New Testament Words* declares these words do not denote some ethical attainment but rather define the state into which God, through the grace merited by Christ, has made available membership in his kingdom (the church) and all the attendant blessings of salvation. Sanctification is the separation of the believer from evil things and ways. This is God's will for the believer (I Thess. 4:3); it must be learned from God as he teaches it by his Word (I Thess. 4:4; John 17:17, 19; Ps. 17:4; 119:9) and it must be pursued by the believer, earnestly and undeviatingly (I Tim. 2:15; Heb. 12:14). Men must

CHAPTER 1　　　　　　　　　　　　FIRST CORINTHIANS 1:1-17

deliberately choose the sanctification which the Lord provides and promises. They must pursue it through the directions and instrumentalities which are authorized exclusively in the revealed Word of God.

At first, reading only the salutation, the idea that a church of Christ might exist in Corinth would present no problem. That Paul addresses the members of that church as "those called to be saints," would be initially acceptable also. By the time one has read to the end of this epistle, however, he may find it difficult to believe that a church could ever have been formed in such surroundings and, once formed, that it could have survived. When Paul wrote this letter, the church was not much over six years old. It should give twentieth-century Christians pause to note that the condition of the Corinthian church is a specific example of our Lord's parables insisting that the growth of the kingdom is slow and difficult (cf. Matt. 13:1-53; Mark 4:1-34; Luke 8:4-18) and the devil is always sowing tares in the same field in which God's servants are sowing good seed. Christians today should learn from this that no matter how spiritually immature a member of the Lord's church might be, he is called by God to be a saint and is a brother in Christ if he is willing to be taught the word of God and is willing to conform his mind and life to that Word. No matter how wrong some of these Corinthians were about doctrine and practices, so long as they were willing to receive his divinely-inspired instruction and grow toward it, he said they were "sanctified in Christ Jesus." We can do no less today! Of course, a brother who blatantly defies apostolic doctrine (such as the man in I Cor. 5:1ff.) and refuses to repent must be "delivered unto Satan" for the destruction of the fleshly mind. Once such a brother repents, however, the church is to forgive him (see II Cor. 2:5-17). A congregation of Christians is not sanctified in Christ because it has reached a pre-determined level of spirituality, but because every member is constantly struggling and growing into the image of God's beloved Son (cf. Rom. 8:29; II Cor. 3:18; II Peter 1:3-21).

Paul reminds the Corinthian Christians that they belong to a universal brotherhood of saints—all who in every place call on the name of Jesus as Lord and Savior. This reminder is to have its impact on the whole situation at Corinth. Paul wants them to understand they are a part of a whole body of Christians. When they have divisions, immoralities, jealousies and other disorders, the whole body of Christ throughout the world will be affected, one way or another. No congregation is an island! Every saint in every congregation is

FIRST CORINTHIANS

called *together* with all those who in every place call on the name of Jesus as Lord.

So, as Paul salutes the Christians at Corinth, he begins his argument against the factionalism in the church there. He salutes them as "those sanctified . . . called to be saints" and they are thus *because* the God who called them and to whom they profess allegiance is "sanctified." That is, God is holy! There is absolutely no falsehood or wickedness in God's nature, nor was any manifested in God's Incarnate Son, Jesus Christ. Those who call upon the name of Jesus Christ as Lord (God) must be holy. Division and schism are unholy. God does not divide himself and fight himself. He is not jealous of his Son's glory nor is his Son jealous of the Father's glory. They glorify one another. Christians cannot love one another "earnestly from the heart" unless they aspire to and act in *imitation* of the holiness of God (see I Peter 1:13-25). Those who destroy God's "holy temple" (the church) by division and partyism are trying to destroy God—and they will be destroyed (I Cor. 3:16-17). Christians are called to be members of the "sanctified" (holy) body of Christ throughout the world. Disunity, factionalism and jealousy make a mockery of the call of God for sanctification. The congregation that is constantly bickering and separating one brother from another is not holy—it is carnal and no different than the strife-filled, discriminatory, cliquey "clubs" of unregenerate men.

Unity has its origin or source in the nature and character of God. Unity cannot exist without holiness and sanctified living. Jesus' longest recorded prayer is for the unity of his followers through sanctification (holiness) in the truth (see John 17:13-26).

Grace and peace are part of God's holy nature. The word *grace* is from the Greek word *charis,* and means "something granted, a favor given, a gift." We get the English word *charisma* from it. Paul is reminding the Corinthian Christians that their santification is only by the favor granted them by God through Jesus Christ. They did not earn the right to be sanctified—it was by the grace of God. Therefore, the love of Christ should have constrained them to dwell together in unity. If *all* Christians are sanctified by the grace of God and by no merit of their own one has no right to esteem himself above another and no cause for jealousy and division. Peace in Hebrew is *shalom* and means wholeness or well-being. The Greek word for peace, *eirene,* was often used in the same way. It means health, harmony and integrated wholeness. God, in Christ, has called men to peace (unity, harmony). The church is God's kingdom of peace, God's holy habitation of peace (see Eph. 2:11-22). God, by the vicarious atonement of Christ's death, has declared himself at peace with rebellious man. Those who accept the peace Christ earned for them must practice peace with all other men (Rom. 12:14-21). In fact, the peace of Christ must be allowed to *arbitrate* (Col. 3:15, Gr. *brabeueto,* rule) in the hearts of men. All decisions a Christian makes are to be decided on the basis of the meaning and application of the peace Christ has wrought for him. When this is so, there is no schism in the kingdom of God.

1:4-9 Constancy: God is gracious. And God is also constant. He is faithful. What God promises, he will fulfill. Christ's body, the church, finds both *motive* and *source* of unity in God's faithfulness. Paul was always *giving thanks* (Gr. *eucharisto,* present tense verb, continuing action) for God's faithfulness and grace to the Corinthians. The Corinthian Christians had been made rich (Gr. *eploutisthete,* aorist) when they answered the call to be set apart (sanctified) unto Christ. Christ had seen fit to bless the Corinthian church with many miraculous gifts (cf. I Cor. 12:1—14:40). Paul mentions two of those miraculous gifts, "speech" and "knowledge." The Greek word for "speech" is *logos* and is usually translated "word." This probably means the miracle of declaring divine revelation. It is translated "utterance" in II Corinthians 8:7. *Knowledge* in Greek is *gnosis* (from which the English word *gnostic* comes) and refers, in this context, to a miraculous understanding of the miraculous revelation.

The testimony to Christ's faithfulness to fulfill his promises was *confirmed.* Paul uses the Greek word *ebebaiothe,* a word found frequently in Greek papyri to describe the confirmation of a business transaction. God settled the issue of his faithfulness to the Corinthians by extending a special measure of grace to them, making them *excel* (II Cor. 8:7) in miraculous gifts. The Corinthian church was second to none in experiencing Christ's faithfulness to confirm the gospel by miraculous gifts (cf. Heb. 2:4; II Cor. 12:12; Eph. 4:7, etc.). They were by no means *lacking* (Gr. *hustereisthai,* last, lagging behind). Christ had kept his word. They had all they needed while they waited in daily expectation for his return. There was no lack that could justify their jealousies and factionalisms. They should not have divided up to follow other leaders as if to find in such division something *more* to sustain them against the judgment day. Christ alone gives the revelation and knowledge necessary for that. No other leader has anything to say about salvation worth hearing! If that be true, there is no reason in heaven or on earth for Christians to divide over human leaders or institutions. The unity of God's kingdom has its source in this characteristic of God and his Son, Jesus Christ—absolute faithfulness!

The sentence in the Greek text (v. 9) begins literally, "Faithful, the God through whom you were called . . ." It stresses God's faithfulness. *Faithful* is the very name of God. And if *he* called the Corinthians into communion (Gr. *koinonian,* fellowship, sharing) with his Son, he is certainly able by himself to sustain them. They need not divide up, compete with one another, or follow other leaders. Factionalism would make the world believe the God of the Corinthian Christians was impotent, unfaithful and less than absolute. And that is precisely what division in Christendom does in the twentieth century!

The grace of God had made it possible for these Corinthians to have the saving work of Christ imputed to them. God saw to it that they were second to none in possessing miraculous gifts. They had advantages other Christians did not have. Their disgraceful conduct (division, immorality in the church, disorderly worship, vanity, pride, and misapprehension of true doctrine) was not because God supplied them insufficiently with divine direction or that God was unfaithful toward them. It was due to their own spiritual immaturity and refusal to grow.

1:10-17 Completeness: "Is Christ divided?" Paul appeals for a mentality and practice of Christian unity in the Corinthian church on the basis of the oneness of God. "Hear, O Israel, the Lord our God is one!" (Deut. 6:4). God is *one* in character, in purpose and in action. There is no variation in him (James 1:17). Jesus declared that he and the Father and the Holy Spirit were one and the same person (cf. John 1:1-18; 14:1-11; 14:18-24; 8:25-30, etc.). Paul clearly taught that Jesus was God when he wrote, "For in him (Christ) the whole fulness of the Godhead dwells bodily . . ." (Col. 2:9; see also II Cor. 5:19; Col. 1:19; Gal. 3:20). Even the prophet Isaiah declared the triune oneness of God (Isa. 48:16). Jesus claimed he *always* agreed with and did perfectly the works of God because he *was* God (cf. John 5:17-46; 6:45; 8:28-30; 8:58; 10:22-39; 15:7-11; 16:15; 17:1-5, etc.). That Jesus was God in the flesh is certainly a verifiable proposition. His deity was established historically by the signs and wonders he did in the presence of men (cf. Acts 2:22; 26:26). The "Shema" (Deut. 6:4) means more than simply enumerating Jehovah as the only God there is. It means that he is one integrally—that is, he is perfectly unified, totally single in purpose, objective and goal. God may manifest himself in three persons, but his mind, his will, his heart, his actions and his purpose are absolutely undivided. God is not man

CHAPTER 1   **FIRST CORINTHIANS 1:1-17**

that he should change or be divided (Num. 23:19; I Sam. 15:29; Isa. 40:8; 55:11).

Paul appealed (Gr. *parakalo,* "called upon") to the Christians at Corinth on the basis of the name, or authority, of the one Lord of all Christians, Jesus Christ. His appeal was that they all *agree* (Gr. lit. *hina to auto legete pantes,* "that the one thing you may be saying, all."). The KJV translates it, ". . . that ye all speak the same thing . . ." In the present context, this unquestionably means Paul is directing them to all say one thing (all agree on one thing) which is: there is only one church of God—one body of Christians—over which Jesus Christ alone is the head. Paul is not here insisting that all Christians must agree on every issue of life—especially those issues not expressly commanded or clearly enjoined in the New Testament. All Christians are free, in Christ, to have opinions which may differ from other Christians in matters where the New Testament gives no specified direction. But even our opinions must be subordinated to the authoritative commands of the New Testament for brotherly love, peace, doctrinal purity, unity of the church and edification of one's brother. *Agreement,* in this context, applies primarily to the fundamental New Testament doctrine of the *oneness* of the body of Christ. There are not many *different* churches, separated according to differing teachings of human leaders, constituting *the* church of Christ. If the church of Christ is *essentially* one, as Thomas Campbell said in his Declaration and Address, then to speak of a divided church is a contradiction of terms. If it is *intentionally* one, to divide it is to disobey the intentions of Christ. If it is *constitutionally* one, it implies conformity to a plan or constitutional (Biblical) organization which must be inherent in the revealed will of its Head.

Paul considered himself free to exercise his own opinions about cultural preferences, evangelistic methods, and marital status so long as the Lord Jesus had not plainly commanded otherwise. But Paul had also committed himself so completely to the law of love he would relinquish his freedom to exercise personal opinion if opinion caused a brother to sin (see I Corinthians, chapters 8, 9, 10, and Romans, chapter 14). Paul would not divide the body of Christ over one of his own opinions. He certainly would not allow any attempt to divide it over human personalities to go unrebuked.

The Corinthian Christians are exhorted to refrain from *dissension.* The Greek word is stronger than that—it is *schizmata,* meaning, to rend, to split, to break. In non-biblical Greek the word was used to describe "cleaving the head with an axe," or "a ship breaking to pieces in the sea." Greek cultic religions punished members for

FIRST CORINTHIANS

schizmata (division) in the same manner they punished someone for stealing from or deceiving a member of their cult. Cancer cells within the human body are physical *schizmata*. Division within the church is destructive. The Greek word *schizo* is used as a prefix to many English words used in psychology to describe the mental disorder sometimes referred to as "split-personality." *Schizophrenia* is "a type of psychosis characterized by loss of contact with (withdrawal from) environment (reality) and by disintegration of personality." That is an apt description of a divided Christendom! Modern Christendom has a spiritual sickness (psychosis) characterized by loss of contact with (withdrawal from) its real unity in Christ and evidences a disintegrated personality to a lost world! Dividing the church of God is a *sin*. It is called a "work of the flesh" (Gal. 5:19-21). There the words are *dichostasiai,* from which we get the English word *dichotomy* (stand apart), and *haireseis,* from which we have the English word *heresy* (to defect, to divide). James wrote that the *contention* which causes division (Gr. *eritheian,* from *Eris,* goddess of strife and fighting) is *demonical*! Indeed, the devil is the master designer of all division in the church. The devil is an anarchist, a divider, a liar and a murderer from Eden until now. Those who deliberately practice and cherish dividing the church of Jesus Christ into opposing, unbelieving, unloving factions are children of the devil.

The apostle urges these Christians to "be *united* in the same mind and the same judgment." The Greek word *katertismenoi* translated *united* means, "be repaired" or "be restored." It is used in Matt. 4:21; Mark 1:19 to describe the "folding together" of the fishermen's nets. In II Cor. 13:11 Paul tells the Corinthians to "mend" their ways. The idea is to restore or repair something that has been disordered to its proper order so that it will be fit for productive use. Christian unity is not something which originates from man—it originates from God. At the time a human being becomes a Christian God joins that new-born being to the body of Christ. We *are* joined—we do not join. Once we are joined to Christ's body (the church) we must "give diligence to keep the unity of the Spirit in the bond of peace" (Eph. 4:3). There are times when Christians may sin and promote division, but they must repent and be diligent to "repair and restore" that unity by surrendering to the will of Christ for their lives.

Paul insisted that unity would not come until these Christians were "restored" (united) in the *same* (Gr. *auto,* one, only, same) mind and same *judgment* (Gr. *gnome,* understanding, means of knowing). Some commentators insist that the Corinthian Christians were not

CHAPTER 1   FIRST CORINTHIANS 1:1-17

dividing over central or doctrinal issues, but over diverse opinions. Consider the following issues over which there seemed to be not only differences but *divisions:*

   a. The issue as to whether *who* baptized a person was more crucial than the doctrine of the cross (I Cor. 1).
   b. The issue of divine revelation and apostolic inspiration and inerrancy (I Cor. 2).
   c. The issue of sanctification and church discipline (I Cor. 5 & 6).
   d. The issue of marriage and divorce (I Cor. 7).
   e. The issues of idolatrous associations; of Christian liberty; of apostolic rights (I Cor. 8, 9, 10).
   f. The issue of who is the Lord's body and of judging others and improper observance of the Lord's Supper (I Cor. 11).
   g. The issue of immaturity; of misuse of spiritual gifts; of indecency and disorder in worship (I Cor. 12, 13, 14).
   h. The issue as to whether there can be a resurrection from the dead or not—perhaps even belief in the bodily resurrection of Christ an issue! (I Cor. 15).

Most of these are more crucial than differences of opinion. They are doctrinal issues. We believe the Lord intends his church to be of the same mentality, knowing the same revelation of his will and understanding his will the same way. We believe that is the reason the Holy Spirit inspired Paul to write this epistle to the Corinthian Christians. The Lord intended the church at Corinth to come to the same understanding, to think the same and act the same way in all the matters to which Paul gave instruction in this epistle.

Is it possible for Christians to all understand the Bible alike? Of course it is! God wrote his book in human language. That is what Paul clearly says in chapter two of this epistle. The Bible is to be understood by using the same principles of understanding human language one would use in understanding any other book. There are some fundamental guidelines used by every one who reads in order to understand what another person has written:

   a. The correct and true interpretation of any written communication is what the *author intended* to say—*not* what the reader *wants* the author to say.
   b. God intended only one ultimate meaning in every word he has written in the Bible—not many conflicting meanings for each word.

FIRST CORINTHIANS

    c. God is certainly able to say what he intends to say and he knows to whom he speaks. God expects men to be *able* to understand his message to them and insists they *must* if they are to be saved.

    d. To understand a communication from another person we must investigate how he uses words. To do, that we must take into account grammatical structure, context, historical usage, historical circumstances, parallel passages, etc.

This is why Paul states emphatically in I Corinthians 2:13 that the mind of God has been imparted to mankind (through the apostles) in *words*—human language. No human being could have known the mind (will) of God had it *not* been delivered through words (human language). God wants all men to know and understand his will. And God wants all men to understand it alike! Paul repeated this appeal many times (cf. Rom. 15:5-6; II Cor. 13:11; Phil. 1:27; 2:2) and so did Peter (I Peter 3:8).

As long as Christians have different levels of scriptural *knowledge,* there will exist differences in spiritual mentality and judgment. One of the major functions for which the church was established was to bring all followers of Christ to "the unity of the faith and of the knowledge of the Son of God, to *mature* manhood, to the measure of the stature of the fulness of Christ . . ." (Eph. 4:13). Bringing all Christians to the same (unified) faith and knowledge in *mature* (Gr. *teleion,* perfected, attained the goal) manhood to the *stature* (Gr. *helikias,* adulthood, grown up) of Christ is the purpose of ministry. The very fact that some Christians are content to be deficient in the knowledge of God's word gives the devil fertile ground in which to produce division! The church must not neglect the imperative ministry of edifying every member in the scriptures. A *primary goal* for the church is to bring all members to the same level of knowledge of God's word. Until it gives priority to that goal it is *not* giving diligence to keep the unity of the Spirit in the bond of peace. Bible study must have *top* priority in the church!

A woman member of the Corinthian church named Chloe had apparently visited Paul in Ephesus, with members of her household (people), and they had informed Paul of the divisions and quarreling (Gr. *erides,* strife) among the Christians. Practically every Christian ("each one of you") in Corinth was involved in the strife. Christians were forming certain doctrinal and/or non-doctrinal stands opposing one another and striving against one another. Beyond that they were trying to make out that they followed divinely-appointed leaders of

CHAPTER 1   FIRST CORINTHIANS 1:1-17

Christianity who also opposed one another in these differences of doctrine and opinion. Some had even attempted to portray Paul, Peter and Apollos as opposing Christ and Christ opposing these leaders. Satan still dupes theologians and religious leaders today with the same sophistry—alleged doctrinal differences between Paul and Peter and Christ. It is absurd to think that the absolute, almighty, inerrant Holy Spirit of God would contradict himself as he spoke through these. But the biggest lie the devil perpetrates is that these men were not divinely inspired and inerrant instruments of the Holy Spirit. They were, according to many modern theologians, fallible and often mistaken in what they wrote. Before unity in the church is ever "repaired" or "restored" the issue of the infallibility and inerrancy of the Bible must be settled.

What the attraction was that polarized these Christians toward certain human leaders we do not know for certain. Perhaps it was "seniority" or the "successes" which the parties claimed for their superiority over one another. Peter was one of the first called to be an apostle and was recognized spokesman for the twelve a number of times. Paul, on the other hand, had demonstrated phenomenal success with evangelism and missionary endeavors to the whole Gentile world. Apollos was a man noted by many in the Roman world for his eloquence (for which neither Paul nor Peter was noted). Paul's question, "Or were you baptized in the name of Paul?" means divisions were being made according to who the baptizer might have been. There is no historical evidence whatever that Peter was ever in Corinth. There might have been some people in the Corinthian church who had been baptized by Peter in Palestine on the Day of Pentecost (or later) who then returned to Corinth. The divisions were probably more according to *alleged* differences in doctrine than anything else. There is only one name in which Christians are baptized—the name of Jesus Christ (cf. Matt. 28:19; Acts 2:38; 10:48; 22:16; Acts 4:12). Men are not to be baptized in the name of the church.

Paul was thankful that he had not baptized many at Corinth with his own hands lest some glory in the fact they had been immersed by the great apostle Paul. Paul would not have his name used by these factions to set themselves apart from others. Paul had immersed Crispus, ruler of a synagogue in Corinth (Acts 18:8), and Gaius (identity unknown), and the household of Stephanas, first convert of Achaia (I Cor. 16:15). He could remember no others. Paul would have a difficult time understanding some preachers today who take great pains to advertise the number of baptisms they perform. Paul's statement that he was not sent by Christ to baptize but to preach the gospel must not be taken to mean that Paul considered baptism unessential or of little importance. Baptism was and is an essential part of the gospel message of salvation. Paul submitted to baptism himself as necessary to washing away his sins (Acts 22:16). He stated in his writings that it was the act of obedient faith which brought penitent believers *into* covenant participation in Christ's death and resurrection (Rom. 6:1-11). He implies that only as many as are baptized into Christ have "put on Christ" and are sons of God, Abraham's spiritual offspring, heirs according to the messianic promise (Gal. 3:25-29). Paul taught people to be *baptized* (Gr. *baptizo,* immerse, plunge, dip) when he preached or there would never have been any question raised about some claiming to have been baptized in Paul's name! We have documented proof that people were baptized as a consequence of Paul's having preached what to *do* to be saved (Acts 16:14-15; 16:29-34; 18:8). When Paul preached, most often others did the baptizing. John writes in his Gospel about Jesus, "The Pharisees had heard that Jesus was making and baptizing more disciples than John—Jesus himself baptized not, but his disciples (did)," (John 4:1-2). The twelve apostles undoubtedly did not, with their own hands, baptize each of the three thousand believers on the Day of Pentecost (Acts 2:38ff.). There is no commandment in the New Testament that only an ordained clergyman may officiate at the immersion of a believer into Christ. For the sake of propriety, it would be preferable to have someone who was already an immersed believer in Christ to immerse new believers; but it might be an elder, a deacon, a father baptizing a son, a son baptizing a father, or, most appropriate, a Christian baptizing the person he has brought to belief. There was no problem with immersion in water in obedience to the gospel covenant of salvation in the first century church; neither in mode nor purpose. The problem Paul had to deal with here is sectarianism, not gospel immersion. It is not immersion Paul is renouncing here but the argument over who immersed whom! He is disclaiming the idea that being immersed by any particular human leader makes the immersed one a member of any religious faction or party. He *is* saying it is possible to *overemphasize* baptism. Baptism is not redemption. Redemption is what Christ did on the cross and through his resurrection. Christ's command, and that of the apostles, to be immersed in water for the remission of sins (Acts 2:38, et. al.) is one of the initial covenant terms by which that redemption is to be granted. The New Testament is plain: to possess redemption requires covenant relationship and covenant relationship requires, initially, faith, repentance and immersion. But to make the person or party by whom one is immersed the central issue of redemption is to empty the cross of Christ of its power. Paul says, "*He* (Christ) is the source of our . . . redemption" (I Cor. 1:30). Being immersed into Christ is not the *source* of our redemption; Christ is the source. But we cannot receive that source without accepting the Source's terms. Immersion into Christ does not tap us into different sources—it unites us in the One and Only Source! That is what Christ sent Paul to preach. And preach it he did!

Paul declares that he was not given the commission of apostle of Christ to compete in sophisticated word-games (Gr. *sophia logou*). He wanted no one to become his disciple or trust their redemption in his eloquence or other abilities. The fact of the cross of Christ cannot apply its power when human pride gathers followers through human cleverness. Such an approach inevitably produces heresy and destroys unity in Christ.

Unity Operates Through the Instrumentality of the Gospel (1:18-25)

18 For the word of the cross is folly to those who are perishing, but to us who are being saved it is the power of God. 19For it is written,

> "I will destroy the wisdom of the
> wise,
> and the cleverness of the clever I
> will thwart."

20Where is the wise man? Where is the scribe? Where is the debater of this age? Has not God made foolish the wisdom of the world? 21For since, in the wisdom of God, the world did not know God through wisdom, it pleased God through the folly of what we preach to save those who believe. 22For Jews demand signs and Greeks seek wisdom, 23but we preach Christ crucified, a stumbling block to Jews and folly to Gentiles, 24but to those who are called, both Jews and Greeks, Christ the power of God and the wisdom of God. 25For the foolishness of God is wiser than men, and the weakness of God is stronger than men.

1:18-20 Because the Gospel is Revelational: Unification of men and women from all different strata of humankind in one brotherhood of peace and love is operative only by the instrumentality of the gospel of Christ. That is so because only the gospel of Christ is the final, complete and perfect revelation from God. It alone is the divinely-sanctioned, perfectly-delivered, and supernaturally-functional instrument for man's redemption. Paul says the *word* (Gr. *logos,* teaching, doctrine) of the cross is *foolishness* (Gr. *moria,* moronic, stupidity) to those who are continuing to perish. However, God's declaration and demonstration that in the cross (and the resurrection) of Jesus Christ he atoned for all the sins of all the world is the *dynamic* (Gr. *dunamis,* power, dynamic) of God to those who are continuing to be saved through it. The Greek prepositions *apollumenois* (perishing) and *sozomenois* (being saved) are present tense, denoting a continuing action. Those who continue willfully to perish, reject the fact and doctrine of the cross as moronic. It does not make sense, from a strictly human perspective, that someone else should suffer (or could suffer) for my sins. It does not seem reasonable; it does not seem fair. Bishop G. Bromley Oxnam, former head of the World Council of Churches, wrote the following:

> We hear much of the substitutionary theory of the atonement. This theory to me is immoral. If Jesus paid it all, or if He is the substitute for me, or if He is the sacrifice for all the sin of the world, then why discuss forgiveness? The books are closed. Another has paid the debt, borne the penalty. I owe nothing. I am absolved. I cannot see forgiveness as predicated upon the act of some one else. It is my sin. I must atone. (*A Testament of the Faith,* 1958, pg. 144)

That is precisely why the doctrine of the substitutionary, vicarious atonement of Jesus Christ on the cross at Calvary must be established on the basis of the historically-verified resurrection of Jesus Christ from the dead. It is a doctrine that is unacceptable to human pride. It is a doctrine that must be accepted on the basis of faith (a faith based on verification). It is a doctrine *revealed.* Jesus teaches that man's willingness to accept revelation from God is *primary* in the matter of kingdom citizenship (see comments on Matt. 11:1-30, *The Gospel of Matthew, Vol. II,* pp. 426-594, by Harold Fowler, College Press). So long as there are those claiming citizenship in the kingdom of God unwilling to let God give arbitrary, indisputable, seemingly-irrational revelations, there will be division. No nation can have a dependable, unified army if it has no final authority—the commander-in-chief.

Verse 19 is a quotation of Isaiah 29:14 as God's prophecy that he would, in the messianic era, deliver a divine revelation which would destroy dependence upon human pride and wisdom for salvation.

CHAPTER 1   **FIRST CORINTHIANS 1:18-25**

The student should study both Isaiah chapters 28 and 29 in their entirety. Isaiah is predicting the messianic kingdom to come as one in which men would humble themselves and let God teach them by revelation rather than presumptuously thinking they knew all they needed to know through their own wisdom. Isaiah has a great deal to say (and so do all the prophets) about the fact that God is aiming to build in the messianic age (the church) a kingdom filled with people willingly surrendered to total guidance, in every area of life, under the revealed word of his Messiah. That is a fundamental issue of the prophets; "they shall all be taught by God" (see Isa. 54:13; John 6:45). Through thousands of years of history God allowed one human philosophy, religion, and political system after another to come and go. They each repeated themselves, so that even in Solomon's day he could say, "There is nothing new under the sun."

God is one—he is not divided. His mind, will and purpose are all united. The unity of God's revealed will (the Bible) may be thoroughly demonstrated by simply comparing it with the pronouncements and writings of the "scribes and debaters" of the ages. Philosophers, theologians, scientists, teachers and sages have contradicted and negated one another consistently since the world began. Their inability to find unity in human tenets has been the cause of men dividing themselves from one another and from God. But the Bible, because it is a divine revelation of the One Unified Being, God, produces unity when every proud obstacle to the knowledge of God is destroyed by the gospel and every human thought is taken captive to obey Christ (cf. II Cor. 10:3-5). The power of the gospel to change wicked, idolatrous pagans into loving, believing, hoping people demonstrated the utter foolishness of the alleged "wisdom" of the ancient philosophies and philosophers. Claiming to be wise, the ancient philosophers exchanged the truth of God for a lie, and became fools (see Rom. 1:18-32). That was not simply theoretical—that was demonstrated in life! It still is today! Human unity operates through the instrumentality of the gospel, or it doesn't operate at all!

1:21-23 Because The Gospel is Reportable: The gospel is real. It is history. It is not theoretical or ephemeral. Human beings make theories. God does things in history and in reality. God was wise enough to give men the freedom to theorize if they choose. In this freedom God is able to demonstrate vividly the finitude of man. Since man without God is able only to theorize he should acknowledge his limitations. Man should welcome an Absolute Being with absolute wisdom—especially since such a Being has revealed Himself in history. When God decided that man's inability to redeem himself had been sufficiently established in the demonstration of the foolishness of human theories, the Son of God was sent to the world to establish historically and experientially the absolute wisdom of God.

The KJV translation of verse 21 is unfortunate. Paul is *not* saying that preaching is foolishness, or that the world will be saved by the foolishness of preaching. Many people preach. Politicians preach; philosophers and moralists preach; terrorists and anarchists preach, so it is not the methodology of preaching that the world calls "foolish." The RSV is much clearer when it translates, ". . . through the folly of *what* we preach to save. . . ." The world calls the Christian *message,* the gospel of the cross, foolish. But, clearly, it is the message of the gospel that saves human beings from lawlessness and wickedness. The Greek phrase, *tou kerugmatos* clearly intends the reader to understand that it is the *thing* preached (the message) which the world calls foolish. But that message is of the accomplished redemption of Christ and God has chosen to save through it. This redemption was wrought upon the cross and verified by the resurrection of Jesus Christ from the dead. Its proclamation and acceptance saves men unto the glorious destiny for which God created them. T. R. Applebury wrote: "While the basic facts of the gospel are the death, burial, and resurrection of Christ, the gospel is not limited to these facts, for it takes the whole Bible to tell the whole story of the whole counsel of God about salvation through His Son. In the Old Testament it is seen in prophecy, promise, and type. In the New Testament it is seen in the facts of the life of Christ; in the history of conversion to Christ; in the explanation of the essentials of righteousness; in the application of the gospel to daily life; and, finally, in the prophecy of the victory of Christ and of those who accept His gospel." (*Studies in First and Second Corinthians,* by T. R. Applebury, p. 23, College Press, 1963). If the Christian message (*kerugmatos*) was *only* of a crucified, dead Messiah, it would be foolishness. Any claim to atone for the sins of the whole world by someone who had no power to conquer death would be an absurd, abortive claim. But the Christian message, authenticated by eyewitnesses, friends and enemies alike, is of a Messiah who conquered death. Therefore his claims of atonement are trustworthy and will transform or regenerate those who continue to believe him. God transforms the minds and personalities of sinners through the word of his Son's redemptive program, the gospel. But man must believe that. God created man with the capability to believe and respond to God's promises and commands. So Paul says, God was pleased to save men through the agency and instrumentality of his word. Paul uses the Greek present tense when he writes the word

CHAPTER 1   FIRST CORINTHIANS 1:18-25

believe (Gr. *pisteuontas*) indicating that those who are being saved (see comments, v. 18) are those who are *continuing* to believe.

While those continuing to believe the facts of the gospel are being saved, those continuing to demand signs and continuing to seek wisdom from some source other than the gospel are being lost! The Jews continually demanded signs. Paul uses the present tense Greek verb here, *aitousi,* indicating that the Jews were not satisfied with the signs Jesus gave of his Messiahship, but continued demanding them. Jesus called these Jews, "an evil and adulterous generation" for continually demanding signs (Matt. 12:38ff.) when sufficient signs were already promised (Jesus' miracles and his resurrection from the dead). God is not pleased with people who continually put him to the test, asking for signs, when sufficient signs have been given (cf. Exod. 17:1-7; Num. 14:22; Deut. 18:18-19; Luke 16:30-31). Elevating spiritual (miraculous) gifts above teaching and preaching the word "line upon line and precept upon precept" is a clear indication of spiritual immaturity (cf. Isa. 28:7-13; I Cor. 14:20ff.). The Jews were even demanding a sign from Jesus when he was hanging on the cross (Matt. 27:41-44). Jesus pronounced condemnation on whole cities (cf. Matt. 11:20-24; Luke 10:1-20) for demanding signs and then not repenting when many signs were done. It is not one's proximity to supernatural demonstrations or even persons which saves, but faith in the deity and divine work of Jesus. Jesus said some at the judgment would claim proximity to his fleshly presence as merit for salvation (cf. Luke 13:22-30) but to no avail. It is not the possession of supernatural gifts which signified the salvation of the Christians at Corinth (for they came behind no other in such gifts). That which saves is faith in the reportable, reliable redemptive work of Christ on the cross and at the empty tomb. Without the word being preached there can be no faith (Rom. 10:17); without the "seed" (Word) being sown, there can be no fruit produced (Luke 8:11ff.).

1:24-25 Because the Gospel is Reliable: Unity operates through the instrumentality of the Gospel because the Gospel is the only source of power available to man to break down barriers of racial, cultural, and religious divisions. It is reliable *first,* of course, because it is authenticated by miracles and signs and fulfilled prophecies (Heb. 2:3-4). But the world should now acknowledge its reliability because it has been demonstrated through 2000 years as the only workable instrument of true spiritual unity for the human race. Producing human spiritual unity in love and peace through universal human philosophy, culture and government was tried for 700 years by four successive world empires (Babylon, Persia, Greece and Rome). That did not produce! In fact, it produced the opposite—slavery, hatred, war and wickedness. Only the righteousness of God in the redemptive work of Christ (which the world calls "foolishness") is powerful enough to effect the unity of the human race under the constraints of love, peace, justice and righteousness. That is what is taking place in the church of the Lord Jesus Christ because that is where redemption is made available. The church, dwelling place of the living word of God, is the living organism in the world, kept alive by God's Spirit, where men may be redeemed. The church is the only place where men do not lift up sword against one another and where they learn war against one another no more. In the world are the lawless. For them only a superficial form of unity and temporary restraint against wickedness is maintained by enforcement of law (cf. I Tim. 1:8-11; Rom. 13:1-7). But for the citizen of God's kingdom, all arbitration is done peaceably and with love by the power of the Spirit of Christ in their minds and hearts (cf. Col. 3:1-24).

The Gospel is the only reliable dynamic for bringing about spiritual oneness between man and God and man and man. Christ proved it by the supernatural verification of his redemptive plan; history had proven it by experience. It is imperative that all those who profess to be followers of Christ focus all their energies to the proclamation of that message.

Unity Occasions Glory to God Alone (1:26-31)

26 For consider your call, brethren, not many of you were wise according to worldly standards, not many were powerful, not many of noble birth; 27 but God chose what is foolish in the world to shame the wise, God chose what is weak in the world to shame the strong, 28 God chose what is low and despised in the world, even things that are not, to bring to nothing things that are, 29 so that no human being might boast in the presence of God. 30 He is the source of your life in Christ Jesus, whom God made our wisdom, our righteousness and sanctification and redemption; 31 therefore, as it is written, "Let him who boasts, boast of the Lord."

1:26 Their deficiency: The very fact that there existed in Corinth a body of believers, immature and struggling, but united in the love and peace of Christ, proved that whatever unity they had achieved was to be credited to God the Father and Christ the son, for there was no other such body of human beings in Corinth like them. The

CHAPTER 1   FIRST CORINTHIANS 1:26-31

philosophers and politicians had not produced such a fellowship. These Christians certainly had not come to their fellowship through wisdom according to worldly standards. Paul reminds them to *take a look at* (Gr. *blepete,* see, look) their condition at the time they answered the call to the Gospel. Not many of them were *sophisticates* (Gr. *sophoi,* wise) as judged by *worldly* (Gr. *sarka,* fleshly, human) standards. Not many were *powerful* as the world would estimate power; nor were many of *noble birth* (Gr. *eugeneis,* well-born).

God actually chose what the sophisticates, the powerful and the nobility would call "foolishness" to form a society in Corinth of loving, caring, righteous-living people. They were called Christians. This put all the philosophies and other human attempts of man to create his own Utopia, by his own wisdom, to shame. The faith and righteousness of Christians became, as it were, a condemnation of all the humanism of their society, just as Noah's obedience to God thousands of years earlier (cf. Heb. 11:7).

The apostle's enunciation of the former lack of worldly prestige of these Corinthians is mild compared to his reminder of what a few others had been before becoming Christians (cf. I Cor. 6:9-11). The gospel not only has the power to create a kingdom of love and peace and goodness out of the unsophisticated and powerless people of the world, it also has divine power to bring into this same kingdom, by conversion, people who were formerly the dregs of humanity. Its power is operative, however, only when human beings acknowledge they have no sufficiency in anything that is human and surrender to the revelation of God's redemptive plan for their lives.

1:27-28 Their dynamic: When one considers the tools God chose to use in his redemptive program and the end result he produced, one must admit divine power as the source. God chose what the world, in all its accumulated expertise, calls "foolishness" (Gr. *mora,* moronic, stupid), to demonstrably put to shame the sophistication of worldly-wisdom. The world, with all its science, philosophy and psychology has never done what the gospel has done. God chose the *weak* things (Gr. *asthene,* no strength, sick, impotent) in order to expose the shame of what the world calls strong and powerful. The world calls the vicarious atonement of Christ "sick." But the change wrought in the lives of those who believe Christ proves that the world is wrong in what it depends on for power.

God chose to use what the world calls "low" and "despised" (Gr. *agene,* inconsequential, unknown; and *exouthenemena,* contemptible, rejected) to *abolish* (Gr. *katargese,* nullify, destroy) the things which the world in rebellion against God considers effective. Paul is not the first God uses to reveal this. The Old Testament Prophets warned their people that God was going to accomplish man's redemption by a despised and rejected Messiah, one in whom was no "comeliness" and who would not be "esteemed" (cf. Isa. 52:13—53:12). Jesus warned in his parables that the kingdom would start as small and insignificantly as a "mustard seed" but would grow to be huge (Matt. 13:31-32). Righteousness, love, self-control, humility and faith are things the world calls weaknesses. Wealth, fame, self-sufficiency, political position and skepticism are things the world calls powerful. God has demonstrated his sovereign wisdom by putting everything the world calls powerful to shame through the power of the redemptive work of Christ. Only the gospel of Christ produces the society of people transformed into loving, hoping, trustworthy, faithful, peaceful servants of God. Wealth, fame and political power all combined has never done it and never shall.

God chose the betrothed of a lowly Jewish carpenter as the mother for the Savior of the world. He decided this Savior was to be born in a cattle-shed. This Savior's friends would be harlots and hated publicans. He would select as his intimate co-workers fisherman, publicans and women. But these "low born" and "rejects" would, with the divine message of God's reconciling grace through the cross of Christ, turn the world "upside down" (cf. Acts 17:6) showing that philosophies of men were totally inadequate while the word of God changed people and society for the best.

It is through this word that human beings may be born again (cf. I Peter 1:22-25). Through these promises human beings may partake of the divine nature (II Peter 1:3-4). Through this, human beings receive power to be transformed and purified (cf. Rom. 12:1-2; I John 3:1-3). And the word of God is the *only* instrument chosen by God to accomplish this in the world. The world thinks otherwise because it has believed the devil's lie told in Eden (Gen. 3:1-7) that to trust, depend upon and obey God is weakness, while independence from and resistance to God brings power.

1:29-31 Their declaration: God deliberately gave salvation to mankind as a gift so that no human being might boast. He chose to effect man's salvation through what the world called weaknesses so that man would not be able to glorify himself or any of his finite schemes. Salvation is absolutely by faith in the redemptive deeds done by God in Christ—not by any merit of man. Salvation is appropriated (or accepted) by man's believing obedience to the covenant terms decreed by God in his New Testament. But man, by accepting salvation, never

CHAPTER 1   FIRST CORINTHIANS 1:26-31

merits it. His sins were paid for by Christ's death—finally and completely. When finite and sinful man compares himself with other finite and sinful men, he is inclined to find someone who, in his estimation, is worse than himself. He then resolves to trust in his own self-righteousness and his own glory, (cf. II Cor. 10:12). But when man, by belief in the divine record (the Bible) honestly compares himself with the infinite and absolutely righteous God (and his Son), he finds nothing in himself to trust—not even his own feelings (Jer. 17:5-10, esp. v. 9, 10; Mark 7:21-23; Eph. 4:22; Eccl. 9:3; Isa. 6:5). Jeremiah, tempted to follow his own feelings and desires, surrendered to the word of God burning in his "bones" (cf. Jer. 20:7-12), and preached to turn man's trust in the Lord.

    The KJV is nearer a literal translation of the Greek text in verse 30. The Greek phrase is: *ex autou de humeis este en Christo Iesou.* Literally that would be translated: *but out from him you are in Christ Jesus.* The RSV gives the meaning in its translation: "He is the source of your life in Christ Jesus. . . ." Christ is the *source* of our salvation because he *became* (Gr. *egenethe,* 3rd aorist, sing. passive—he was both *made* and willingly *became*) our wisdom, righteousness, sanctification and redemption. God was in Christ on the cross, reconciling the world to himself. God decreed (made) Christ to be sin for us and righteousness for us (cf. II Cor. 5:11-21). At the same time, Christ, the Son, willingly became sin for us (Heb. 10:5-10). God decided on the substitutionary atonement by his Anointed One from the foundation of the world (cf. I Peter 1:19-20; Isa. 53:1-12, etc.). The Son of man knew he had come into the world as a vicarious *ransom* for the sins of the whole world (Matt. 20:28; 26:28). He knew that it was only by his perfect sacrifice men would be able to be set apart (sanctified) to God (cf. Heb. 10:5-10; John 17:13-26). Christ is the *source* of our sanctification. We could never be good enough on our own to be set apart unto God! If we are sanctified for God at all it is because we trust completely in the merit of Christ's perfect sacrifice. Of course, we must choose to accept his sanctification for us. And our choosing must conform to his revealed will. The same concepts apply to any claims we may have to *wisdom* or *redemption.* Christ alone is the source. We choose whether we want what he offers or not on his terms.

    Verse 31 is a quotation of Jeremiah 9:24. Jeremiah faced the same problem with God's covenant people 600 years before Paul. Men basked in their own self-glory. The glory of other men was what they thought was the ultimate meaning of life (Jer. 9:23). As a result they conducted their lives on the bases of falsehood, hypocrisy, treachery, slander and deceit (Jer. 9:1ff.). But Jeremiah poured out his life in

FIRST CORINTHIANS

ministry of the Word to turn them to glorying in the Lord (Jer. 9:24) and in what the Lord determines is righteousness.

Paul wrote a great deal about "boasting" and "glorying" to the Corinthians. The Corinthians apparently assumed that anyone with the office of apostle would automatically be boastful, proud and arrogant. Paul did not behave like that (see I Cor. 3:18-23; 4:1-13; II Cor. 11:1-33; 12:1-21). Paul made it plain that Christians have nothing to boast about except the grace of God (Rom. 3:27-28; Gal. 6:14; Phil. 3:3-7; II Cor. 12:9). And who can boast in self when all one is or has or hopes to be is by the grace of Christ?

Since *all* Christians are thus joined and united to Christ by *grace alone,* such unity must give occasion to glorifying only Christ. Whatever results from the regenerative work going on in the church on earth, whether through spiritual leaders or those being led, it all redounds to God's glory and not man's. Man works, God gives the increase. Unless God gives the increase, there will be none of any value or permanence at all, no matter how hard and expertly man works.

APPREHENSION AND APPLICATION:

1. Why do you think the apostle Paul left his home country and wandered all over the Roman empire preaching Christ? Could anyone do that?
2. Would the city of Corinth, for its time, be comparable to a large American city? Could people be sanctified to God in New York? San Francisco? How?
3. What is a saint? Which work of grace sanctifies people?
4. Why does Christian unity have as its basis the character of God?
5. May Christians be united with those who impugn the character of God?
6. How important is God's faithfulness to you? Could not all religious people unite without all believing in the absolute faithfulness of God?
7. What does the Bible mean by saying God is "One"?
8. Is it possible for all Christians to "be of the same mind" and "united in the same judgment"? *How*?
9. Why are the principles of interpreting human language so important to Christian unity?
10. Why do people divide the church over human leaders? Do leaders sometimes contribute to division? Why didn't Paul?
11. Did Paul infer that baptism was unessential or unimportant? Why didn't he baptize those he converted? Who is authorized to baptize people?

CHAPTER 1　　　　　　　　　　FIRST CORINTHIANS 1:26-31

12. What is the instrument with power sufficient to unite all men in God?
13. What is a revelation? Why must we accept the atonement of Christ for our sins as a revelation?
14. Why is the acceptance of revelation necessary to Christian unity?
15. What has the historicity of the gospel to do with unity? Should Christians seek unity with those who deny the historicity of the Bible? On what basis?
16. Is preaching foolishness? Why does the world consider the cross foolish?
17. Is there anything wrong in seeking signs? Is there too much of that today?
18. Can there be faith without the Word of God being preached? In what?
19. In what two ways may we prove the Word of God is reliable to produce Christian unity? Have you discussed this with other believers lately?
20. Should Christians keep reminding themselves of what they were before being saved? What has that to do with unity in Christ?
21. Do Christians have anything about which they may boast? Nothing at all? Why not?

Chapter Two

THE PROBLEM OF REVELATION
(2:1-16)

IDEAS TO INVESTIGATE:

1. Why is revelation a problem? Why is it a problem to Christians?
2. How is the apostolic message different from the philosophies of men?
3. What vehicle or instrumentality did God utilize in revealing the apostolic message to man?
4. Why can't man discover God's will and plan for his life?
5. How spiritual does a person have to be to understand the apostolic message?

SECTION 1

Unsophisticated but Dynamic (2:1-5)

2 When I came to you, brethren, I did not come proclaiming to you the testimony of God in lofty words or wisdom. ²For I decided to know nothing among you except Jesus Christ and him crucified. ³And I was with you in weakness and in much fear and trembling; ⁴and my speech and my message were not in plausible words of wisdom, but in demonstration of the Spirit and of power, ⁵that your faith might not rest in the wisdom of men but in the power of God.

2:1-2 Plain Words: The Greek love for sophisticated philippic and techniques of argumentation colored their concept of the worth of the apostolic gospel. The heroes of the Greek culture were the philosophers who spent all their time debating philosophies (see Acts 17:16-21) and displaying their expertise in eloquent use of language. "The speaking was the thing" with them—not the reality of what was being said. William Barclay says:

> The Greek sought wisdom. Originally the Greek word *sophist* meant *a wise man* in the good sense; but it came to mean a man with a clever mind and cunning tongue, a mental acrobat, a man who with glittering and persuasive rhetoric could make the worse appear the better reason. It meant a man who would spend endless hours discussing hair-splitting trifles, a man who

CHAPTER 2　　　　　　　　　　　FIRST CORINTHIANS 2:1-5

had no real interest in solutions but who simply gloried in the stimulus of "the mental Hike." . . . It is impossible to exaggerate the almost fantastic mastery that the silver-tongued rhetorician held in Greece. Plutarch says, "They made their voices sweet with musical cadences and modulations of tone and echoed resonances." They thought not of what they were saying, but of how they were saying it. Their thought might be poisonous so long as it was enveloped in honeyed words. Philostratus tells us that Adrian, the sophist, had such a reputation in Rome, that when his messenger appeared with a notice that he was to lecture, the senate emptied and even the people at the games abandoned them to flock to hear him.

The Greeks were intoxicated with rhetoric and eloquence. They would look on Paul's preaching of the cross and resurrection of Jesus Christ in simple, direct words testifying to plain historical facts as crude and uncultured. Paul says literally, "And I coming to you brethren, came not according to over-hanging (high, superior) word or sophistry." Paul might have had the background to have attempted competition with the Greek sophists. He had studied for years from the most famous rabbis of Israel. He knew Greek poetry (cf. Acts 17:28). But he was not interested in eloquence.

Paul determined to speak nothing among the Greeks but Jesus Christ and this One having been crucified. He could do nothing else and be true to the gospel. That is what the gospel is—the redemptive work of Christ. The gospel is not what man must do—the gospel is what God, in Christ, has done. We know Paul included the resurrection of Christ in his preaching to the Greeks for we have a record of his having done so (cf. Acts 17:30-31; I Cor. 15:1-11). Paul preached that the fulfillment of the Old Testament was the death and resurrection of Jesus accomplishing atonement and reconciliation of man to God, available through faith and baptism into Christ. Paul had no time for irrelevancies; not even for the peripheral things of life. There was only one issue for him and he determined everywhere he went, to everyone who would give him attention, he would preach the facts of the good news—Christ crucified and risen again commanding all men everywhere to repent. Without this everything else in life *is* irrelevant (see I Cor. 15:12-19). Without this all of life is *bad* news. Without this all mankind is guilty before the Absolute God and sentenced to eternal damnation. No wonder Paul had no time to talk about innane and trivial matters. Not Christianity, but

FIRST CORINTHIANS

Christ; not a system, but the Savior; every Christian who would be faithful to God must live by the same determination (cf. Col. 1:27-29).

Unlike many modern theologians who want to present Christ as a great teacher, the founder of a great religion, or a great example of humanity at its apex of goodness, Paul preached Christ *crucified.* The Greek word Paul uses, *estauromenon,* is a perfect participle, meaning a thing completed with a continuing result. Christ's death on the cross is unlike all other deaths in this world—it continues to be efficacious for all who will make it theirs by faith.

2:3-5 Powerful Witness: When Paul went to Corinth, he was vividly aware of his weaknesses as a human being, (see Acts 18:9). His weaknesses would include his "thorn in the flesh" (II Cor. 12:7), his poor personal appearance (II Cor. 10:10) whatever that was, and what the Corinthians thought was an inadequate speaking ability (II Cor. 10:10). The power of Paul's address before the philosophers in Athens would seem to refute the accusation of the Corinthians about his inability to speak. That sermon on Mar's Hill is irrefutable in its logic, clear in its simplicity, and persuasive in its appeal. If Paul had any inability in speaking it must have been some physical impairment in his voice.

What were the fears and tremblings Paul had? He certainly did not fear for his life. Neither did he fear that the gospel was inadequate. Paul was apparently overwhelmed, at his first glimpse of Corinth, and the enormity of the task before him, (Acts 18:9). He was afraid people, with their prejudices and superficialities, would focus on his human inadequacies and not give ear to his message in which the power resided to transform them.

Realizing this, says Paul, "my *word* (Gr. *logos*) and my *message* (Gr. *kerugma*) were not in *enticing* (Gr. *peithos,* sometimes translated *plausible* or *persuasive*) words of human *sophistry* (Gr. *sophias*)." Paul did not seek to entice, trick, seduce, or "psych" people into faith in Christ. He would not be a "peddler" of God's Word (II Cor. 2:17). He would not use disgraceful and underhanded ways, practice cunning, or tamper with God's Word (II Cor. 4:2). He openly stated the truth. And that truth was Jesus Christ crucified and risen from the dead. There were no public relations "advance-men," paid exorbitant salaries to create an "image" for Paul. There were no huge musical ensembles, with their amplifiers, microphones, spot-lighting, and staging accompanying Paul (desensitizing men's minds so they could not *think* about what Paul was preaching).

His message was fact, not sophistry. Paul uses a number of Greek words in this text which emphasizes the legal and scientific nature of

CHAPTER 2 — FIRST CORINTHIANS 2:6-16

his message. Paul's message is historical and demonstrable as opposed to the specious theories and equivocations of the philosophers and sophists. For example, the Greek word *apodeixe* (translated *demonstration* 2:4) is a word used to describe the examining of witnesses in trials testifying to eyewitnessed evidence, or to describe the testing of ore in a crucible to provide evidence of its identity. Not only was Paul's message based on eyewitnessed proofs of the life, death and resurrection of Jesus Christ (see I Cor. 15:1ff.), it was also confirmed by the powerful demonstration of the Holy Spirit in the miracles done by Paul himself (see II Cor. 12:12).

God never intended that man's faith should be based on speculations and feelings. The life, death and resurrection of Jesus Christ is not speculation—it is history. What we believe about God and his promises, we believe on the basis of these supernatural deeds done in time and space, in this historical frame in which we exist. The Christian's faith rests on the power of God—and that is not a power about which we theorize, but a power demonstrated in history!

All God's word needs is to be preached. It will produce faith in the mind and heart of anyone who will allow it (cf. Rom. 10:1ff.). The word of God does not need the sophistries of psychology, theology, philosophy or politics to make it relevant and powerful. It has power in itself. It is a "living seed" and will produce of itself (see Mark 4:26-29; Isa. 55:10-11). It simply needs to be sown.

SECTION 2

Undiscoverable but Understandable (2:6-16)

6 Yet among the mature we do impart wisdom, although it is not a wisdom of this age or of the rulers of this age, who are doomed to pass away. 7 But we impart a secret and hidden wisdom of God, which God decreed before the ages for our glorification. 8 None of the rulers of this age understood this; for if they had, they would not have crucified the Lord of glory. 9 But, as it is written,

"What no eye has seen, nor ear heard, nor the heart of man conceived,
what God has prepared for those who love him,"

10 God has revealed to us through the Spirit. For the Spirit searches everything, even the depths of God. 11 For what person knows a man's thoughts except the spirit of the man which is

in him? So also no one comprehends the thoughts of God except the Spirit of God. ¹²Now we have received not the spirit of the world, but the Spirit which is from God, that we might understand the gifts bestowed on us by God. ¹³And we impart this in words not taught by human wisdom but taught by the Spirit, interpreting spiritual truths to those who possess the Spirit.

14 The unspiritual man does not receive the gifts of the Spirit of God, for they are folly to him, and he is not able to understand them because they are spiritually discerned. ¹⁵The spiritual man judges all things, but is himself to be judged by no one. ¹⁶"For who has known the mind of the Lord so as to instruct him?" But we have the mind of Christ.

2:6-8 Perfected: The understanding of this whole chapter hinges upon two major premises: (1) clearly, the antecedent to the repeated pronoun "we" and "us" all the way through this chapter is Paul and the other supernaturally endowed apostles, the only persons Christ ever said would be "led into all truth" (cf. Jn. 16:13); (2) contextually, the subject is divinely *revealed* truth as opposed to the limits of finite knowledge. The context is *not* dealing with different levels of understanding or even with ability to comprehend. It is dealing with the impossibility of knowing the mind of God until God decides to reveal His mind to certain individuals so they might pass it on through human langauge (words). Whatever Paul is saying, it must conform to these two fundamental rules of understanding what someone else has written.

Notice the clear indication that Paul is speaking of the *relevational* aspect of the apostolic message of the cross by the continuity of the antecedent:

    a. "When I came to you . . ." (2:1)
    b. "For I decided to know . . ." (2:2)
    c. "And I was with you . . ." (2:3)
    d. ". . . and my message . . ." (2:3)
    e. ". . . Yet among the mature we do impart . . ." (2:6)
    f. "But we impart a secret and hidden wisdom . . ." (2:7)
    g. "God has revealed to us through the Spirit . . ." (2:10)
    h. "Now we have received. . . ." (2:12)
    i. ". . . that we might understand . . ." (2:12)
    j. "And we impart this in words. . . ." (2:13)
    k. "But we have the mind of Christ" (2:16)

CHAPTER 2   FIRST CORINTHIANS 2:6-16

Paul's shift from the first person to the third person means only that he is including the other apostles as those who have received the "mind of Christ" by revelation—it does not include all Christians.

Who are the "mature"? The Greek word used in verse 6 is *teleiois*, and is often translated, *perfect,* or, *whole.* Lenski says, "*teleios* is the one who has reached the goal. The context invariably determines the goal referred to and the sense in which the term is employed. The present context speaks of only two classes of people: such as accept the gospel in faith and such as spurn the gospel and prefer their own wisdom. No reference has been made to undeveloped Christians."

We believe the context forces us to look back to I Corinthians 1:18-25 for the definition of the "mature ones." The *mature* are those who receive the gospel message in honest, virtuous, unbiased and logical minds. They accept the message as the revelation of God on the basis of the evidence presented. The *immature* are those who are prejudiced and dishonest and who deliberately refuse to acknowledge that there is an Absolute Being existing outside the empirical knowledge of this world who may *reveal* knowledge man may not otherwise discover by his own human resources.

The *immature* are:

  a. ". . . like children sitting in the market places. . . ." (Matt. 11:16-19)
  b. "the wise and understanding" (Matt. 11:25-30)
  c. ". . . those who receive glory from one another . . ." (John 5:44)
  d. those in whom the word of Christ finds no place (John 8:37)
  e. those who cannot bear to hear Christ's word (John 8:43-47)
  f. those who say, "We see . . ." (John 9:35-41)
  g. those who love the praise of men more than the praise of God (John 12:37-43)
  h. those who think that the Deity is like gold, or silver. . . . a representation by the art and imagination of man (Acts 17:22-23)
  i. those who claim to be wise and exchange glory of the immortal God for images. . . . who exchange the truth of God for a lie. . . . who do not see fit to acknowledge God (Rom. 1:18-32)
  j. those who refuse to love the truth . . . those who do not believe the truth but take pleasure in unrighteousness (II Thess. 2:9-12)
  k. those who will listen to anybody and can never arrive at the truth (II Tim. 3:6-7)
  l. those who deliberately ignore the facts (II Peter 3:1-7)

The *mature* are:

  a. those who, hearing the word, hold it fast in an honest and good heart, and bring forth fruit with patience (Luke 8:15)

FIRST CORINTHIANS

  b. those who do what is true and come to the light (John 3:21)
  c. those who are babes and are willing to take Christ's yoke upon them and learn of him (Matt. 11:25-30)
  d. those who acknowledge they are blind without the apostolic revelation (John 9:39-41)
  e. those willing to be guided by divine revelation (Acts 8:31)
  f. those who accept the apostolic message of the cross as the revelation of God for salvation (I Cor. 1:18-25)
  g. those who accept the word of the apostles as the word of God revealed for salvation (I Thess. 2:13)

When the gospel message of the cross and the apostolic message explaining the doctrine of the cross (and resurrection) is proclaimed, those with honest and good hearts will accept it as a revelation—something man could not know without God telling him. The revelation of God concerning eternal life is totally outside the experience of mortal man. It is not a wisdom of this age nor of any of the greatest human minds of this age. All man can know on his own is that in his present existence everything is passing away, even man himself. Man may know from the creation around him that there is an Eternal Deity (cf. Rom. 1:18-22). Man may know from his conscience that he incurs guilt and deserves judgment. But man *cannot* know from anything within him or around him that God atoned for his guilt in the death of Christ and that salvation may be his by faithful convenant relationship to Christ. That is known only by *revelation*!

The apostles *impart* (Gr. *laloumen,* speak) a secret and hidden wisdom of God. Actually the Greek word translated *secret* is *musterio* which would be literally, *mystery*. A mystery was *not* something that could not be explained or understood, but something unrevealed and unknown. A mystery, in the New Testament usage of the word, could be known when it was revealed. Paul's use of the word *mystery* may be seen in Ephesians 1:1-23; Colossians 1:24-29; Romans 16:25-27. For man to know the *mystery* of God's will for salvation requires only that the apostles (who have the mind of Christ by supernatural gift) reveal it in human language. It does not require some additional illumination or miraculous empowering of our minds to understand it.

God speaks his eternal wisdom (his plan of redemption and salvation) through human messengers, in human language. God is certainly capable of making himself understood in human language. All that is needed for man to understand God is that God, by signs and wonders, delineate and authenticate those who are his chosen messengers, and that man listen with an honest and unbiased mind.

CHAPTER 2   FIRST CORINTHIANS 2:6-16

None of the rulers of this world understood this. Actually, the Greek word *egnoken* may be translated either *known* or *understood*. The proper translation, according to the context, would be *known*. It is something they refused to know because they refused to surrender to the fact that God *revealed* himself *incarnately* in Jesus Christ. They did *not want* to know it. They *chose* to be ignorant (cf. Luke 23:34; John 15:21; Acts 3:17; 13:27; 17:30; Eph. 4:18; I Tim. 1:13). Had they wanted to know this hidden wisdom of God they could have known it because God revealed it in his incarnate Son, Jesus Christ. Many others knew it. Had the rulers been *willing* to know it, they *would* have known it and would not have crucified the Lord of glory (cf. John 7:17). T. R. Applebury puts it succinctly: "Are we to say that the natural or uninspired man cannot understand the message revealed by the Holy Spirit? Some do take this position. But are we to say that God who created man, an intelligent being capable of communicating his thoughts through language, could not speak to His creatures in a manner so as to be understood? But, of course, man by his own experience and observation could never know God's mind. The only way he could know it was by the revelation through the apostles and prophets."

2:9-11 Private: God predicted his redemptive promises to the human race as far back as the Garden of Eden (Gen. 3:15), but the exact manner in which it would be accomplished was kept *private* in his own mind until he revealed it in Christ and subsequently through the Holy Spirit to the apostles. Until God decided to let it be known, no human being could know it.

Verse 9 does *not* refer to man's future state in heaven. It refers to the apostolic message of redemption through the vicarious atonement of Jesus Christ. That divine program was not conceived by man. It never occurred to man that God would save him by grace. That is evidenced by all the religions of the world, except Christianity, attempting to attain reconciliation with God through works. Man, in his pride and arrogance, refuses to acknowledge he must be saved by grace. He could never even imagine the way God would accomplish salvation. If God had chosen to keep his redemptive plan privately hidden in his own mind forever, man would never have discovered it with his own finite and limited human knowledge.

But God chose to reveal his redemptive program to the whole world through the apostles ("us," v. 10) through his Holy Spirit. The Holy Spirit is the third person of the Godhead, but he is the same person as the Father and the Son. Jesus plainly declared that he and the Holy Spirit were one and the same person (see John 14:15-23).

FIRST CORINTHIANS

The Holy Spirit of God knows everything God knows—even the deepest recesses of God's mind and heart. Everything God wanted to be revealed concerning his prepared redemption the Holy Spirit was fully capable of revealing. Therefore, Paul is saying, everything we apostles have declared to you to be God's redemptive plan is all there is. Men do not need to expect any revelation of God's redemptive program beyond what the apostles have written! There is no "latter day revelation" to be expected. Salvation is found by reading, believing and obeying the apostolic doctrine—not in some subjective, extra-Biblical, experience. What the apostles wrote is everything the Spirit searched from the Father's mind—even the *depths*.

One person can never know the mind of another person unless that person communicates his mind. Minds really never communicate until they do so by words (language). Events and deeds cannot bring about the personal encounter which the genius of language alone accomplishes. By means of the sense of hearing, as the receiver of verbal communication, one mind can make contact with the mental world of another mind and can be influenced by that inaccessible and mysterious realm of thought. But until one person decides to tell another person what is on his mind, his thoughts are inaccessible to everyone but his own spirit. This is what Paul is saying about God's mind in verse 11. Without the voluntary communication (that is, without revelation) of one person's thoughts to another by words, there is an impenetrable boundary to personal encounter. The mind of a man sitting next to you may be quite inaccessible to you, while at that very moment a friend some thousand miles away may be allowing you, by means of a letter, to learn something of what is beyond this boundary. The act of crossing this boundary (through a revelation in words) is one of the most remarkable phenomena of our experience.

No one but the Spirit of God could know what was on God's mind. God chose to cross that boundary for man so he gave his Spirit to the apostles who spoke the mind of God in human words.

2:12-13 Published: One of the big problems with this Corinthian church had to do with Paul's presentation of the gospel. Apparently, his presentation did not compare favorably with the eloquence of the philosophers and "preachers" of the pagan mystery cults in cosmopolitan Corinth. Some Christians in the church were probably being tempted to turn away from the gospel and classify it as not divine because it was not colored by the sophistries and verbiage of the silver-tongued orators of Greece. It just did not sound divine. It did not thrill them emotionally—it was not artistic—it was not entertaining.

CHAPTER 2   FIRST CORINTHIANS 2:6-16

The apostles received the Spirit which is from God so they might know the mind of God and Christ. Christ promised them the Holy Spirit for this purpose (see John, chapters 14, 15, 16 and 17, and 20:22). They claimed to be speaking by the direct inspiration or revelation of the Holy Spirit (cf. Acts 2:14-21; I Cor. 2:12-13; II Peter 1:16-21). Their claims to divine inspiration or revelation were authenticated by the signs and wonders done by their hands (cf. II Cor. 12:12; Heb. 2:1-4). No one but the apostles were promised this revelation of the mind of Christ as his *direct* agents to communicate it to the rest of mankind. The apostle John makes it clear that whoever listens to the apostles listens to God, and whoever does not listen to the apostles does not listen to God (I John 4:1-6). The only possible way to distinguish between the spirit of truth and the spirit of error is to accept the teachings of the apostles as the final and completed teaching from God!

The Bible leaves us in no doubt whatever that the vehicle of revelation is language (words). The construction of the Greek sentence in verse 13 emphasizes *words* as the vehicle of imparting God's mind to the world. The sentence reads literally, "which things we speak, not in teaching of human wisdom words, but in teaching of the Holy Spirit." Paul, in putting *words* at the end of the phrase, emphasizes that the agency of apostolic revelation is not in emotions, feelings or any other subjective experience, but in human language. Language is versatile. It is unique in the reception and transmission of knowledge. It is the only means which possesses such potentiality. Mystical or subjective communication, in which the intellect is in abeyance and the object of the participant is to merge himself by a non-verbal process in the Godhead, is excluded by a word often on the lips of the writers of the Old Testament. The word is *shema,* translated "to hear," and signifies not only to hear, but "to understand" and even "to obey" what is said. There are literally thousands of references in both Old Testament and New Testament representing God as "speaking" *words* (cf. Exod. 20:1; Deut. 1:6; Ps. 33:9; Jer. 7:13; 14:14; John 6:63; Matt. 24:35; John 17:14, 17). Language is the only conceivable means of communicating non-empirical places, things or concepts. It has the ability to cross dimensional limits of time and space and communicate by verbal deputies (figures of speech, analogies, etc.) the non-experienceable.

So the apostles spoke the mind of God and Christ in human words, but not in human teachings. There is a difference in the two! The devil is able to take human words and proclaim demonic teaching (see James 3:13-18). The apostles were taught what was on God's

FIRST CORINTHIANS

mind about redemption by the Spirit of God in human language. They, in turn, teach all who will listen to them in human language also. When a man listens to the teaching of the apostles and obeys it, he is being taught by the Holy Spirit of God. If the apostles were "led into *all* truth" (see John 16:13) and if the faith is "once for all time delivered unto the saints" (see Jude 3), then there is nothing more the Holy Spirit intends to say to mankind (this side of heaven) about redemption. The apostles have said it all!

Verse 13 reads literally, ". . . with spiritual things, spiritual things comparing . . ." The RSV translation which reads, ". . . interpeting spiritual truths to those who possess the Spirit," is not a good translation. Paul is not dealing with those *receiving* the apostolic message— he is dealing with those *giving* the apostolic message. This is Paul's way of saying here that the apostles spoke the revelation of the Spirit ("spiritual things") in *terms* or words ("comparables") which the Spirit directed them to use. In other words, the apostles spoke and wrote the very message, in the very terminology, the Spirit of God desired it to be written. As Peter explained it, "men spoke as they were *borne along* by the Holy Spirit" (II Peter 1:20-21). The Greek word *sunkrinontes* is translated *comparing* but means, more precisely, "combining, fitly joining together." It means "to adapt the language to the subject." This does *not* mean that the Holy Spirit spoke to the apostles in some "unknown tongue" or that the Bible is in some heavenly language that cannot be understood by the same rules of human language used in all other communications. It simply means that the Holy Spirit guided the apostles in selecting exactly the right words in the Greek language (for the New Testament) to communicate exactly the mind of God concerning redemption.

2:14-16 Privileged: Only the apostles (in the New Testament) were privileged to receive the mind of God through the Holy Spirit. And they received it as a gift from God because *no man* can know the mind of God unless God decides to give it. The natural man may know God's mind only if he is "borne along by the Spirit" (II Peter 1:20-21) because "no prophecy ever came by the impulse of man."

The Greek word *psychikos* is translated *unspiritual* in the RSV, but means the *physical* man, i.e., the natural man without the supernatural guidance of the Holy Spirit. The natural man, limited to natural faculties, cannot know the will of God unless it is revealed to him by the Spirit. God's will for man's salvation must be revealed before any man can know it. This is precisely what Paul has already said: "For since, in the wisdom of God, the world did not know God through wisdom, it pleased God through the folly of *what* (the revealed

CHAPTER 2   FIRST CORINTHIANS 2:6-16

message) *we* (the apostles) preach to save those who believe" (I Cor. 1:21). It certainly does *not* mean every human being must have his mind illuminated *separately* from the apostolic word before he can understand the Bible.

There is no need for extra-Biblical illumination or revelation for man today. As a matter of fact, the New Testament clearly teaches that a cessation of the miraculous gifts of prophecy and discerning prophecy, etc., would come soon after the first generation of Christians passed away (see our comments on I Corinthians, chapters 12, 13, 14).

The Greek words *ou dunatai gnonai,* in verse 14, mean literally that the physical man *is not able to know* (unless the Spirit of God reveals) the mind of God. Until God's Spirit reveals God's mind, the physical man is like a *moron* (Gr. *moria,* foolishness)—he is unable to know. God's redemptive work in the world, without the Spirit's revelation of God's mind about redemption, is folly (or moronic) to the physical man. This may be illustrated by all the ancient (and modern) pagan attempts to explain history and nature without the propositional revelation (the Bible) of God. One poet said of history without divine revelation, ". . . it is a tale told by idiots, full of sound and fury, signifying nothing. . . ." Ancient philosophers grew cynical, depressed and despairing when they tried to explain life without a direct, spoken revelation from God.

But with God's Spirit searching the deep things of God's mind and revealing them as "gifts" through the apostles, everything necessary for the redemption and salvation of man becomes discernable. Nothing really makes sense in this world without the cross and resurrection of Jesus Christ. Without that, it would all be vanity (see Ecclesiastes). The physical man is not able to discover by investigation (Gr. *anakrinetai,* discern, critique) the deep things of God because they are discovered (Gr. *anakrinetai,* discerned) by God's spirit. Verses 14-16 and verses 11-13 mean exactly the same thing—". . . So also no one comprehends the thoughts of God except the Spirit of God. Now we (apostles) have received not the spirit of the world (physical), but the Spirit which is from God, that we (apostles) might understand the gifts bestowed on us by God." Paul, in verses 14-16, is simply restating what he said in verses 11-13.

The Spirit-filled one (Gr. *pneumatikos*), the *apostle* (remember the continuity of antecedents) discerns and discriminates *what* the mind of God is and *how* God wants it taught, and teaches all things as God's Spirit chooses to reveal them. The apostles, borne along by the Spirit of God, examined and discerned the deep things of the mind of God and then spoke them in language that could be understood by the human mind.

FIRST CORINTHIANS

The Spirit-filled apostles were, in their capacity as *revealers* of God's word, not to be judged by any one about the veracity of their message. This would not apply to the actions or life-style of the apostles. But when it came to what they preached, no one could say it was not from God. The apostolic message became the touchstone by which all other preaching was judged. The apostles proved they alone revealed the mind of the Spirit by the miracles they wrought. It was the miraculous baptism in the Holy Spirit that endowed the apostles to determine whether any teaching was from God or not (see I John 4:1-6). The man of the Spirit, the apostle (not the Christian), was not to be contradicted or disobeyed when he spoke God's revealed mind. In the first century, before the New Testament revelation reached its completion in written form, only an apostle (or someone upon whom the apostles had laid hands) could judge whether a purported "revelation" was a God-given revelation or not. Now that we have the completed revelation of God in written form, all truth purporting to be from God is to be tested as to its conformity by the written revelation of the apostles.

In verse 16 Paul summarizes this whole discussion of the problem of revelation versus the wisdom of the world. The RSV translates the first sentence, "For who has known the mind of the Lord so as to *instruct* him? Actually, the word *instruct* is a translation of the Greek word *sumbibase*. That is the only place in the New Testament where *sumbibase* is translated *instruct*. Everywhere else in the New Testament it is translated *knit* (see Eph. 4:16; Col. 2:2; 2:19) or *proving* (see Acts 9:22; 16:10). The word *sumbibase* really means, "to understand or know or conclude so as to be *joined* together with God." Thus, Paul is saying, "We inspired apostles so have the mind of God through the revelation of the Spirit that we are united in Him teaching His will as no uninspired ("natural") man could ever do." The second sentence of this verse leaves no doubt that Paul's subject here is divine revelation, not spiritual maturity. The Greek is constructed: *hemeis de noun Christou echomen,* literally, "we indeed, the mind of Christ are having." The syntax puts strong emphasis on *we* (the apostles). That is the subject—what the *apostles* have as a supernatural gift and *not* what every Christian has by faith.

Now it should be clear to even the most cursory reader of this letter to the Corinthian church why Paul deals with this subject of apostolic revelation at the very outset of the letter. He must establish beyond contradiction the source of his authority. He is going to have to deal with very sensitive and controversial issues in both the corporate life of the church and the private lives of its members.

CHAPTER 2   FIRST CORINTHIANS 2:6-16

What he will say *must* be accepted as direct revelation from the mind of God to the church and not simply human opinion. Divine revelation is the only absolute wisdom, and the deeply spiritual problems besetting the Corinthian church will not be solved with anything less.

APPLICATIONS:

1. The apostolic message was demonstrated to be the mind of the Holy Spirit. The written apostolic message in the books of the New Testament is as true, as authentic, as powerful now as it was then. It needs no futher demonstrations any more than a fact that has been once established in court needs reestablishing (Heb. 2:3-4).

    The apostolic message needs to be preached. Edward John Carnell said, "If it is true that Jesus Christ died on the cross to save sinners, have we any right to say that we love sinners if we fail to confront them with this truth? And where can we find a divinely validated account of this truth apart from Scripture? In sum, we can express no higher love to lost humanity than to preach the gospel in the precise form in which God has been pleased to reveal it.

2. If the apostolic message did not need humanly-limited wisdom to make it powerful (relevant) then, it does not need it today. The Gospel is relevant and applicable to all of man's problems today!

    In fact, it is the only wisdom that is relevant.
    By obeying it we can purify our souls (I Peter 1:22).
    By believing and obeying it we can be born anew (I Peter 1:23-25).
    By knowing and believing it we can know ourselves as God knows us (Heb. 4:11-13).
    By knowing, believing and obeying we can have His Spirit living in us (John 14:23; I John 2:24; 3:24, etc.).

3. If the mind of God, His wisdom for man's salvation, could not be known by human speculation or human sciences then, it never could.

    All human religions which do not depend upon the revealed word of God (specifically the apostolic message in the New Testament alone) are powerless and irrelevant.

    All human religions and philosophies which contradict or oppose the revealed apostolic message are in opposition to God, because the apostolic message is *all* the mind of God which He has chosen to reveal to the world about salvation.

    If ever God wanted man to know anything, God had to tell man—man could not read God's mind. That was true in the Old Testament as well as the New Testament covenant.

FIRST CORINTHIANS

4. God chose to tell man what He wanted man to know in words—human language. Language (symbols verbalized) makes the communication of minds possible. Without it, communication (at least to the human mind) is impossible. Language makes the imposition of one will upon another possible. Thus, human language makes "personal confrontation" possible. Without it personal relationships are impossible (cf. Helen Keller).

THE WAY WE HAVE A "PERSONAL RELATIONSHIP" WITH GOD IS THROUGH HIS WORD . . . JUST LIKE WE HAVE "PERSONAL RELATIONSHIPS" WITH OTHER BEINGS!

Of course, God's personality is divine, and when you let His personality come into yours through His word, you have a Person in you. Words are "instruments" by which a part of you becomes a resident in me. The Holy Word is an Holy Instrument by which the Holy Spirit becomes a resident in you.

5. God's redemptive work in the world without the Spirit's revelation (the apostolic message) is folly to the man limited by physical only.

The man who does not believe the Bible is God's divine revelation has a very limited knowledge of what life is all about. Eating, drinking, relief from all the pain possible, and vainly hoping not to die is about all he sees in life.

Why was I born?
Why do I work?
Why do I get money and spend it?
Why have children?
Why think?
Why help anyone?
Why even live?

This, in fact, is where many people end it all today when they are taught and believe that there is no divinely revealed message from a Heavenly Father.

6. The apostolic message (the written word of the New Testament) is the final and complete mind of God for man's salvation (cf. II Tim. 3:16-17). It is all that is needed to make a man of God complete, thoroughly equipped for every good work.

Every preacher, teacher, book, program or lifestyle must be tested by that apostolic revelation. If it does not conform in principle and precept it must not be followed.

CHAPTER 2　　　　　　　　　FIRST CORINTHIANS 2:6-16

APPREHENSIONS:

1. Why did Paul find it necessary to defend the simplicity of his presentation of Christianity?
2. Could preachers you've heard use more simplicity?
3. Did Paul mean to say he did not want people to exercise their minds and think about Christianity? Is there nothing profound about God and Christ?
4. Did Paul limit his preaching at Corinth to only the details about the crucifixion ("Christ and him crucified")? How do you know?
5. Why can't mankind know the wisdom that comes from God on his own?
6. Is there anything man can know about God from his environment (the world in which he lives)? (See Rom. 1:18ff.) What?
7. Is creation a revelation from God? Does man need the Bible to understand creation? Why?
8. How would you illustrate that no man can know the mind of God unless God reveals it?
9. How do we know those to whom God reveals his mind?
10. Does God continue today to reveal his mind to so-called "prophets"? How do you know?
11. Why did God reveal his mind through the apostles in human words?
12. How are we to understand God's revelation in human words—what rules of interpretation should we use to understand the Bible?
13. Would it be necessary to use different rules of language to interpret a cookbook than to interpret the Bible?
14. Is it impossible to understand the Bible unless the Holy Spirit works directly (and extra-Biblically) on each individual to enlighten him?
15. Is God able to use human language so as to make himself understood by man without extra divine aid? How do you know?
16. Why would Paul deal with the problem of apostolic revelation at the very beginning of his letter to Corinth?
17. Is the problem of apostolic revelation a current problem in Christendom today?
18. Do you believe the New Testament is the final, full and perfect revelation of God to man in all things that pertain to life and godliness?

Chapter Three

THE PROBLEM OF MINISTRY
(3:1-23)

IDEAS TO INVESTIGATE:

1. Why is ministry a problem with Christians?
2. How can Paul address these jealous and strife-minded Christians as "brethren"?
3. Why does the discussion of survival or destruction of works arise here?
4. What is God's temple?
5. How does one become wise by becoming a fool?

SECTION 1

Commence With Spiritual Feeding (3:1-4)

3 But I, brethren, could not address you as spiritual men, but as men of the flesh, as babes in Christ. ²I fed you with milk, not solid food; for you were not ready for it; and even yet you are not ready, ³for you are still of the flesh. For while there is jealousy and strife among you, are you not of the flesh, and behaving like ordinary men? ⁴For when one says, "I belong to Paul," and another, "I belong to Apollos," are you not merely men?

3:1-3a Babyish: It is of first importance to note that while in chapter two the contrast is between uninspired human beings (or *psychikos*, physical, finite man) and the inspired apostles (or pneumatikos, spirit-guided one), the contrast in chapter three is between Christians who are carnal or fleshly-minded (Gr. *sarkikois*) and the spiritual maturity they should have attained (*pneumatikois*). Chapter two deals with divine revelation *given* by God to some and not to others. Chapter three deals with spiritual maturation which all Christians may *attain* through study and practice of the written word of God. The use of different Greek words in the two chapters makes the difference apparent.

There is, course, an essential connection between the two chapters. Paul is connecting his claim (in chapters one and two) for the divinely inspired authority of his teaching to the spiritual problem (in chapter

CHAPTER 3   FIRST CORINTHIANS 3:1-4

three) of the Christians in Corinth. Had they fed themselves on apostolic revelation more than on Greek sophistries, they would not have the problems of immature, fleshly-minded attitudes toward Christian ministry.

There was something wrong with the "feeding" the Corinthian church was getting. "We are what we eat . . ." is an adage some apply to the physical person. The same principle holds true in the spiritual person. Jesus stated this principle very clearly in his great sermon on the Bread of Life (John 6:25-71). Unless a man feeds on the Bread of Life he will have no spirituality in him, and Jesus plainly said that his words were spirit and life (John 6:63). Jesus said his own "food" was to do the will of the Father who sent him (John 4:31-34). If Jesus found it necessary to feed his mind and life on the will of God, so must we! The explicit work of the Christian ministry is the feeding of the flock of God (see Acts 20:28-32; John 21:15-19; I Peter 5:2) to bring it to spiritual maturity (see Eph. 4:1-16; Col. 1:24-29; Heb. 5:11-13).

What is spirituality? Paul clearly defines spirituality as "setting the mind on the things of the Spirit" (see Rom. 8:5-8). Spirituality is *not* emotionalism. Spirituality is *not* measured by quantity of good deeds. Spirituality is fundamentally a *mind-set*. No matter how emotional we may become or how many religious ceremonies we perform, if our motives or our reasons for doing them are carnal (worldly) and selfish, we are not spiritual. Jesus called the very religious Pharisees hypocrites because their reasons for being religious were self-serving (cf. Matt. 6:1-8; 23:1-39).

If spirituality is setting one's mind on the things of the Spirit, where do we find the things of the Spirit in order that we may *set* our minds on them? That is precisely what Paul is talking about in I Corinthians, chapters 1 and 2—the *things* of the *Spirit* are revealed in the *teachings* of the *apostles*. The apostles have the mind of Christ and of God because they are the ones to whom the Spirit of God has revealed them! The things of the Spirit are *not* found innately in man's heart. The heart of man is deceitful above all things and desperately corrupt (see Jer. 17:9). God has not put his mind in every man in some subjective way. God has put his mind in his Word in an objective way through the revelation given to the apostles. Now any man who wants to assimilate the mind of God into his mind may do so by assimilating the objective word of God. This assimilative process involves, of course, putting the *things* of the Spirit to practice in one's life. We cannot have Christ in us unless we *do* his commandments (I John 2:24; 3:24). But we cannot know what the will of God for us is until we read, understand and believe the revelation of God made to us in human language by the apostles.

Paul declared to the Corinthians that he had to address them as *infants* (Gr. *nepiois*) in respect to their spiritual maturation. It was clear to him that they were not *setting* their *minds* on the things of the Spirit because they were still thinking as worldly-minded people would. Paul does *not* mean that he was talking to non-Christians for he plainly calls them "brethren." He means simply that having made their initial commitment to Christ and having been baptized into him (cf. Acts 18:8), they did not feed themselves on God's word enough to bring them to a state of spiritual growth commensurate with their opportunities and privileges. They had not trained their faculties by practice and study of the apostolic message to be able to distinguish good from evil as well as they should (see Heb. 5:11-14). They were allowing their ways of thinking and living to be dominated more by the habits of their pre-Christian life than by God's will.

Do not wonder that Paul still called them brethren. Spiritual maturation comes, like physical growth, slowly. We would not throw away a baby brother in our physical family because he did not grow into physical manhood overnight. But we do insist that a baby brother eat, learn, exercise and grow. And we make all kinds of personal sacrifices to see that he does. So must we tenderly feed and strengthen our spiritual brethren, no matter what stage of spiritual growth they may manifest. All of us are spiritually deficient when we compare ourselves to Christ, our Elder Brother. The leadership of the church cannot relax its dedication to the ministry of bringing all members to spiritual maturity in Christ. There may be many causes for Christian immaturity:

   a. Inadequate study of the Bible in the corporate worship of the church; superficial sermonizing, unhermeneutical Bible studies.
   b. Low expectations for individual growth. Teachers and preachers may not expect their Bible students to be able to think deeply. Expect the most from every brother.
   c. Failure of the church leadership to provide opportunities for all members to share in the Lord's work ("each part working properly . . ." Eph. 4:16).
   d. Failure of the church leadership to accept their call from Christ to exercise firm, but gentle and merciful, moral guidance to church members.
   e. Just plain unwillingness on the part of Christians to give up thinking and doing worldly things. If any one is willing to do Christ's will, he will mature (see John 7:17).

CHAPTER 3 FIRST CORINTHIANS 3:1-4

There was something seriously deficient in the process of Christian maturation within the Corinthian church. Whether it was the fault of those charged with the "feeding" or of those being "fed" (probably both) we are not certain. It is certain that it had to do with the teaching and believing of the most fundamental Christian doctrine of all—the resurrection of Jesus Christ (cf. comments on I Cor. 15:33). They were still infantile in their thinking. They were still acting like children, apparently able to be "tossed to and fro and carried about with every wind of doctrine, by the cunning of men, by their craftiness in deceitful wiles . . ." (Eph. 4:14).

3:3b-4 Biased: The "party" spirit is a sign of spiritual immaturity. Only the carnal (worldly-minded) think of structuring the church in terms of human superiority and arrogance. Paul tells the Corinthian Christians they were behaving like "run-of-the-mill" (non-Christian) human beings who, through jealousy and strife, scheme and plot to promote their own fame and fortune.

Probably the most crucial issue Jesus had to deal with in his ministry on earth was the nature of the kingdom of God. Most people conceived of the kingdom as a place to establish worldly fame and to promote their own advancement. This involved jealousy and strife by:

a. Mary, the mother of Jesus (John 2:3-4)
b. Disciples of John the Baptist (John 4:25-30)
c. Thousands of followers (John 6:15)
d. The twelve apostles (Mark 9:38-41; Luke 9:49-50)
e. The disciples wondering who is the greatest (Matt. 18:1)
f. Jesus' own half-brothers (John 7:3-4)
g. Those dining at the Pharisee's home (Luke 14:7-14)
h. James & John (and their mother) asking Jesus for chief honors (Matt. 20:20-28; Mark 10:35-45)
i. Pharisees in their love for the places of honor in synagogue (Matt. 23:5-12)
j. Twelve apostles at the Last Supper arguing about who would be greatest among them (Luke 22:24-28)
k. Peter, refusing to let Jesus wipe his feet as a servant (John 13:5-11)

These instances do not take into account the multitude of inferences (from Acts through Revelation) that such jealousy and strife arose among the early churches. The life-style of the person whose highest hopes begin and end with this present world and a fleshly existence is one of immorality, impurity, licentiousness, idolatry, sorcery, enmity, strife, jealousy, anger, selfishness, dissension, party spirit, envy, drunkenness, carousing, and the like (see Gal. 5:19-21). Those who belong to Christ have put such a life-style to death ("crucified" it). Christians, who believe there is a higher plane on which to live than bodily functions and who believe there is another world coming, live a life-style of love, joy, peace, patience, kindness, goodness, faithfulness, gentleness, and self-control. They trust Jesus Christ that this is true and real because he lived such life-style to perfection on earth, was slain because of it, but rose from the dead to vindicate it forever.

Jesus' statement, "He who would be greatest among you, let him be the servant of all" (Matt. 20:27) is proven true by his resurrection from the dead. Those who say, "I belong to Paul," or "I belong to Apollos" are not living in the light of Christ's truth.

SECTION 2

Consists In Spiritual Work For God (3:5-17)

5 What then is Apollos? What is Paul? Servants through whom you believed, as the Lord assigned to each. 6 I planted, Apollos watered, but God gave the growth. 7 So neither he who plants nor he who waters is anything, but only God who gives the growth. 8 He who plants and he who waters are equal, and each shall receive his wages according to his labor. 9 For we are God's fellow workers; you are God's field, God's building.

10 According to the grace of God given to me, like a skilled master builder I laid a foundation, and another man is building upon it. Let each man take care how he builds upon it. 11 For no other foundation can any one lay than that which is laid, which is Jesus Christ. 12 Now if any one builds on the foundation with gold, silver, precious stones, wood, hay, straw—13 each man's work will become manifest; for the Day will disclose it, because it will be revealed with fire, and the fire will test what sort of work each one has done. 14 If the work which any man has built on the foundation survives, he will receive a reward. 15 If any man's work is burned up, he will suffer loss, though he himself will be saved, but only as through fire.

16 Do you not know that you are God's temple and that God's Spirit dwells in you? 17 If any one destroys God's temple, God will destroy him. For God's temple is holy, and that temple you are.

CHAPTER 3　　　　　　　　　　FIRST CORINTHIANS 3:5-17

3:5-9 Builders: All Christians are workers in God's field—builders on God's building. What are apostles? Workers, like every other Christian. They may have gifts from God diverse from ours to equip them for the special job to which God called them, but they are still only workers. Paul calls himself and Apollos *servants* (Gr. *diakonoi,* deacons, table-waiters). The apostles were merely messenger-boys, delivering God's revelation to mankind. They were sent into the world of the first century to serve, not to be served. Paul was a *planter* (Gr. *ephuteusa*) and Apollos was a *waterer* (Gr. *epotisen*) in God's field. God is the owner of the field and the Master of the servants. Everyone else is a planter, waterer, cultivator, or a reaper. Some are sent to sow and some to reap (John 4:36-38). Neither one is more important than the other. Since not even one apostle is superior to another, partisan loyalty to one human servant of God or another which creates jealousy and strife is senseless.

The Greek tenses in verse 6 point to an interesting emphasis. The verbs used for "planted" and "watered" are aorist tense while the Greek verb for *gathering* (*euxanen*) is imperfect. Aorist means a single action completed in the past, while imperfect shows continuous past action. It could be translated thus: At one time in the past Paul planted in Corinth, and later Apollos watered there; but God was making growth occur all along during that time. It is also of importance to notice in verse 7 that the strong adversative conjunction in Greek, the word *alla,* puts emphasis on the contrast. Verse 7 might be translated "He who plants is nothing, he who waters is nothing, *but (alla)* God who *is giving growth* (Gr. *auxanon,* present participle) *is everything.*" One planted, some watered, and each was the same as the other—nothing without God for their labors produced only because God made it to be so!

Verse 8 is a reaffirmation of what Jesus taught in the gospels. All Christian servants are equal—they are all servants. Each servant will receive his wages according to *faithfulness.* Servants do not receive wages according to amount produced for producing is God's doing—God gives the increase. The servant is responsible only to faithfully use the tools over which he has been given a stewardship. The servant is not responsible for the amount of the crop.

Paul wants to discuss with Corinth the problem of pride as a factor contributing to the schismatism in the church. The attitude of servanthood is part of the answer to division in the church. Involvement, increased work-load or busyness will *not* produce Christian unity. There can only be real unity when Christians are emptied of self and willingly take the form of servants (Phil. 2:1-11).

FIRST CORINTHIANS

3:10-11 Boss: The apostle uses two figures of speech (verse 9) to illustrate the work of ministering the gospel. It is farming and building. Paul called the Corinthian Christians God's *field* (Gr. *georgion,* from which we get the name *George,* and the word *farmer*) and he called them God's *building* (Gr. *oikodome,* house, edifice). Paul called himself a "masterbuilder" working along with his co-laborers erecting God's building, the church. The Greek word *architekton* is the word from which our English word *architect* originates. However the use of the word by the ancient Greeks indicates the word had a wider application than our English word architect. Literally the word comes from, *arche,* master, superior—and *tekton,* artificer, skilled craftsman. In the context of this chapter Paul exhorts Christians, "Let each man *take care* how he builds. . . ." The ministry of the gospel demands the best skill in selection and use of "building materials." Paul refers to his own extreme care, as if he were a master technician, using precisely and exactly the right "material" for the foundation of the church in Corinth. Paul used Jesus Christ and him crucified as the foundation.

But the main thrust of this passage is that Paul used the "material" he was told to use by the "Boss" (God). Paul writes, "According to the grace given to me, like a skilled master builder I laid a foundation. . . ." The RSV translates, "According to the commission of God given me. . . ." but the Greek word is *charin* which is translated *grace* or *gift.* Of course, Paul often refers to his being called by God to be an apostle (a builder of God's church) using the word "grace" (see Rom. 1:5; I Cor. 15:10; I Tim. 1:12-16, etc.). What Paul is stressing here is that he exercised all the skill he had to follow the orders (or instructions) of God who was gracious enough to employ him as a builder on His building.

Immature, spiritual babies were not ready to really add to the "building" of God in Corinth which Paul had begun. Paul's foundation was the sure and solid rock of God's revelation that Jesus was the Christ. That was what God told Paul to lay as a foundation for the church. Paul did not vary from the instructions of the "Boss." Ignorant (I Cor. 10:1) and unskilled (in the revelation of God) Christians must not disregard the divinely revealed Word (blueprint) of the Owner concerning the building of the church. All Christians who wish to involve themselves in building the Lord's church must train themselves (see Heb. 5:11-14), lest they attempt to lay a foundation other than Jesus as the Christ, or lest they build upon that foundation with unenduring materials.

CHAPTER 3   FIRST CORINTHIANS 3:5-17

There is only one foundation upon which the church is built—Jesus as the only Anointed of God (and all that implies as to Jesus' deity), (see Matt. 16:13-19; Eph. 2:20; I Peter 2:4-8). To try to build on any other foundation is vain (cf. Ps. 127:1). Actually, God laid (past tense) his Son, the Messiah-Servant, as the foundation of his new covenant people (the church) long before Paul was born. God laid the promises of the Servant as the foundation in the Zion of the Old Testament (see Isa. 28:16; Ps. 118:22-23; Matt. 21:42). The Jews, for the most part, rejected Jesus as the Messiah and thus rejected the foundation-stone of God. The very foundation-stone God sent became a stone of destruction falling upon those who rejected him!

3:12-17 Building: Paul had laid God's foundation. Apollos had continued to instruct the new converts. Now, some of the Christians of the congregation in Corinth were beginning to teach and lead in building the church. But it was evident to Paul that care was not being taken in their building. They were producing disciples who were jealous, indifferent to immorality in the church, bringing litigations against one another in pagan courts, careless about marriage, uncaring about weaker brethren, disrespectful in the corporate worship of the church and toward God ordained structures of human authority, both prideful and envious in the matter of supernatural gifts, teaching confusion about the bodily resurrection, and slack in matters of Christian stewardship. The teaching leadership of the Corinthian church was constructing God's building with weak and unendurable material. They were not building up Christian people who had strong, self-disciplined, servant-minded faith in Christ and his Word.

There are two classes of building materials (disciples, Christians); fireproof and flammable. Some Christians will be able to stand the scorching heat of persecution and testing while others will wither under it and die (cf. Matt. 13:5-6; 13:20-21). Paul's main concern in this exhortation is the ability of the Corinthian Christians to withstand the fiery trials which were coming upon the whole first-century world of Christendom (see I Cor. 7:26; I Peter 2:20-23; 4:12-13). John the apostle writes in the book of Revelation about the "great tribulation" coming upon the Roman Empire of the first and second centuries. Christians had been put to the "fires" of testing ever since the Day of Pentecost when the church was begun (see Acts of the Apostles). And physical or economic hardships are not the only forms of testing the Christian must prepare to meet. There is also the seductiveness of fleshly self-indulgence and the deceptiveness of false religious teaching.

A day of testing comes to every follower of Jesus, in every age. The word *hemera,* Greek for *day,* is *not* capitalized in the Greek text,

FIRST CORINTHIANS

although it is preceded by the definite article. That, however, does not necessarily mean *he hemera* ("the day") is pointing to the final Judgment Day of God. The Old and New Testament both have many references to specific, past, historical judgments of God upon the earth and use the term, "day of the Lord" or, "the day of the Lord." Many days of testing (in fact every day) are in the Christian's life. Paul is probably referring to a specific era of testing (perhaps the Neronian persecutions or those later under Domitian).

Paul was concerned from the reports he had received of conditions in the Corinthian church that many of the Christians there were "wood, hay and stubble" as far as their spiritual substance was concerned. Paul knew that Christians then faced "an impending distress." Their spirituality was about to be proven (Gr. *dokimasei,* tested) or disproven by some "fire" (Gr. *pyri*). Paul comes back to this subject of testing and temptation for the Corinthian Christians in chapter ten where he uses the tragic story of the Israelites in the wilderness as a case in point. Some of the Christians at Corinth will withstand the "impending distress" and others will be consumed.

The trials of the Christian life (whether persecution or temptation) will prove not only what the material (disciple) is, but it will also prove how careful the builder (teacher) has been with the material. The "day" will disclose each teacher's work! Temptations, trials and tests of faith are very revealing. Every preacher, Sunday School teacher, Christian parent, elder, deacon, and Bible college teacher who has ever sown the seed of God's word anywhere will have his work tested. Fires of persecution and temptation are so certain to come Peter chides Christians for being surprised, or acting as if these "fires" were something strange (I Peter 1:7; 4:12-13). It was predicted that the Messiah would bring the fires of testing to mankind (cf. Zech. 13:9; Mal. 3:1-5). Jesus himself said he came to cast testing-fire upon the earth (Luke 12:49). God will not have any person built into his church as a living stone who has not been tested. The "wood, hay, stubble" kind of disciple is illustrated by Jesus in his parable of the soils and the "rocky ground" which has "no root in itself" so when the scorching heat of tribulation or persecution arises on account of the word "immediately he falls away"; or in the "thorny ground" which lets the word be choked out by the cares of the world and the delight in riches. The gold, silver and precious stones kind of disciple is like the "good ground" of the parable or one who hears the word and holds it fast in an honest and good heart bringing forth fruit with patience (see Matt. 13:1-23; Luke 8:4-15).

Thoughtless building, using shallow and superficial "materials" (as some teachers at Corinth appear to have been doing) will program

CHAPTER 3   FIRST CORINTHIANS 3:5-17

the structure for demolition when the inevitable fires of testing come. But there will be reward for the worker in God's farm or God's building who builds with depth and discipline. Such a worker's materials will "survive" (Gr. *menei*, remain)—they will not perish in the scorching pressures of temptation and trial. Paul's reward or "crown" was seeing his converts survive (see Phil. 4:1; I Thess. 2:19-20). The apostle John expressed the same joy that his converts were remaining true to Christ (cf. II John 4; III John 3, 4). The teacher who uses superficial materials will suffer the loss of this reward but he will be saved even if his part of the building (disciples) cannot survive the fiery trials. Even the best teachers cannot be sure those whom they teach and to whom they give their best will withstand temptation and persecution. Jesus lost Judas as well as many "thousands" of disciples who left him and followed him no more (cf. John 6:66ff.). Paul lost Demas (II Tim. 4:10). John lost Diotrephes (II John 9). The seven churches of Asia Minor lost members (Rev. ch. 2-3). However, the teacher's own salvation does not depend on the faithfulness of his disciples, but on his own faithfulness to Christ. Every teacher will face trials and hardships, discouragements and heartaches. The teacher, too, must go through the fire. He will be saved only if he is built of enduring material. The teacher, also, is a part of God's building, having been built into it by someone else. Every human being will survive God's testing-fires according to his own faith. No one will be condemned for someone else's lack of faith. Some may be saved and experience joy that others they pointed to Christ were saved also. And some may be saved and experience loss that those they pointed to Christ refused to be saved.

    The honest and sincere builder (teacher) will be saved, even if some of his material (pupils) does not endure the testing. But the one who deliberately takes up the work of wrecking God's building will most certainly be destroyed. In this context, the *entire* church is being called "God's temple" (see also Eph. 2:19-22). This is *not* a reference to the individual Christian as in I Corinthians 6:19-20, and it should not be used as such. This refers to the jealous and striving brethren at Corinth who were quarreling (1:11-17) and dividing the church into separate parties following human leaders. There is no excuse for separating the local, or universal, church of Jesus Christ into factions following human leaders or using human names. Not even the name of Christ may be used to separate oneself from anyone else who is sincerely trying their best to be obedient to Christ's teachings. The only reason by which a Christian may justify separating himself from one who claims to be a follower of Jesus is deliberate, demonstrable, provable false teaching or licentious living. Even then such separation must have as its goal the reclamation of a brother or sister straying from Christ, (II Thess. 3:14; II Cor. 2:5-11; I Cor. 5:3-5).

God will not tolerate those who wreck his church by willful division. One must be either a builder or a wrecker. There is no middle ground. Every man or woman either gathers with Christ or scatters (Matt. 12:30). All people fall into one of two categories: either a citizen of God's kingdom making every effort to build it, or an alien enemy trying to destroy it. How terribly awesome is the sin of those who rebelliously and deliberately perpetuate divisions among believers in Christ. Division is perpetuated when unscriptural doctrine is wilfully perpetuated; when party-spirit or partiality is perpetuated; and when legalism is perpetuated. For further study of Christian unity see *Learning From Jesus,* by Seth Wilson, College Press, pgs. 412-430.

SECTION 3

Concludes With Spiritual Compensation (3:18-23)

18 Let no one deceive himself. If any one among you thinks that he is wise in this age, let him become a fool that he may become wise. 19 For the wisdom of this world is folly with God. For it is written, "He catches the wise in their craftiness," 20 and again, "The Lord knows that the thoughts of the wise are futile." 21 So let no one boast of men. For all things are yours, 22 whether Paul or Apollos or Cephas or the world or life or death or the present or the future, all are yours; 23 and you are Christ's; and Christ is God's.

3:18-20 Nothing: The man who thinks he is following the way of wisdom by dividing the church into factions striving against one another for superiority is self-deceived. The Greek word *exapatato* is intensive and means *thoroughly* deceived; it is related to the word *apatao,* meaning "to cheat." The man who is looking to glorify himself or some other man in the church is only cheating himself of the real reward from God. The wisdom of this doomed world is foolishness. The world that refuses to see through the perspective of God's revealed truth is a world that cannot know what is real and abiding. Christians do not see anything from a human standpoint of view (cf. II Cor. 4:16-18; 5:16-17). Christians are the ones who are wise; all who are not Christians are cheating themselves of God's divine wisdom. These are being blinded by the devil (II Cor. 4:3-6) and

CHAPTER 3   FIRST CORINTHIANS 3:18-23

deceived into thinking that following Christ is foolishness. It is true, "he who would be greatest in the kingdom must be the servant of all" (Mark 9:35; Luke 22:24-27).

If we are to follow Christ and have his reward we must be ready to be considered a "fool" by the worldly-wise. Those who give their money to see that the gospel is proclaimed and to minister to people's physical needs in the name of Jesus are "fools" according to the worldly-wise. The "smart" thing to do, according to the worldling, is to keep one's money and invest it for one's future security. The Christian who is willing to take the lowliest task or position, and let others receive the credit and applause, is a "fool" according to the world.

But the worldling is a fool! No human being can "out-fox" God. Paul says all wisdom in this world not focused on knowing God and doing his will is foolishness—but how many people believe that? God traps all the worldly-wise in their craftiness. The Greek word *panourgia* is translated *craftiness*. Literally, it means, "all working," that is, a "crafty" person is one who is versatile and clever in everything—he thinks! The word *panourgia* is applied to the subtlety of the devil in deceiving Eve (II Cor. 11:3) and to the methods of teachers who deceive immature Christians with false doctrines (Eph. 4:14). Christian teachers renounce the very idea that they need to practice such human cleverness (II Cor. 4:2). The Christian does not need the clever subtleties of falsehood and deception to feel secure in this world. He has the faithful, never changing word of God which makes him happy and secure. The one who lives by deceit and dishonesty is *caught* in the trap of guilt, shame, and destruction of selfhood. That is the way God governs his creation, (cf. Romans ch. 1 and 2).

3:21-23 Everything: While the non-Christian thinks the Christian is a fool and has nothing, Paul says the Christian has *everything*! Everything God has made belongs to the Christian to use to glorify God and thus be glorified by God. God has given everything to the Christian because only the child of God has surrendered his evaluation and use of everything to the revealed will of God. The Christian is the only person who knows what everything in God's creation is for! To surrender one's mind to human leaders is really a kind of self-impoverishment. Human "wisemen" who deny God understand nothing about what God has made. They will eventually use what God made for good to produce evil. But the Christian, in harmony with Christ's will, has opened up to himself the whole universe as his servant. Everything God has made is *good* (cf. Genesis, ch. 1-2; I Tim. 4:4-5). God intended his creation for man's benefit—to make

FIRST CORINTHIANS

man a spiritual partner with him and to give man enjoyment. When a man uses all that God has made to promote good, truth, purity, holiness and mercifulness, he is rewarded with glory and happiness.

All things belong to the Christian. Some in Corinth had been saying, "I belong to Paul," others, "I belong to Apollos." But the truth was that Paul and Apollos belonged to the Christians as their servants to bring them into a glorifying, enjoyable relationship with Christ. The world was theirs to use in service to God by serving men. In this they would be exalted and find satisfaction. Life was theirs to live in harmony with God's truth and holiness and in so doing find purpose and fulfillment. Even death belonged to them. Death belongs to the Christian as a release from the trials and tribulations of this world and a door opening into eternal bliss (Phil. 1:21; II Cor. 4:16—5:1). "He who did not spare his own Son but gave him up for us all, will he not also give us all things with him?" (Rom. 8:32) Christians are stewards of the whole universe. It belongs to their Father. He has given it into their hands for faithful use. He did not give it to them to be enslaved. They are to control it as men made free by Christ to enjoy and praise the name of their Master. They will be asked for an accounting when the Master returns. They will be asked only if they honestly used it to the best of their abilities according to his will.

The fact that God has given the Christian everything in his creation in no way gives the Christian room to be arrogant or boastful. With great privilege comes great responsibility. It is only by virtue that the Christian is in Christ that God gives these things. Having been united in Christ by faith and obedience the Christian has victory over death, life, present, future and everything else. Man had been given dominion over God's creation in the Garden of Eden, but man lost it by believing the devil and rejecting God. The Son of man (God incarnate) won that dominion back for man by his life of perfect faith and obedience (see Heb. 2:5-18). We share in what Christ has won for man only if we hold our faith in him firm to the end (Heb. 3:14).

To minister or not minister has been a problem with God's covenant people from the time Israel left Egypt until now. In old Israel (from Moses to Malachi) the majority of priests, prophets and kings were self-centered. There were always a few saintly exceptions. Among the thousands of Israel who assumed the offices of ministry, only a few heroic individuals really ministered God's will to God's people. There was Moses, Joshua, Samuel, Elijah and Elisha; there was David, Jehoshaphat and Hezekiah; there was Isaiah, Amos, Jeremiah and the other faithful prophets. These ministered in times of great distress, devastation and discouragement. But for the most part the whole nation of Israel defaulted on its call from God to minister to the nations around them—they begged, rather, to be ministered unto. So God said through the old prophets that he would form a new "nation" a "new Israel" out of every nation on earth who would be ministers unto him and the world (cf. Isa. 66:18-23, etc.). The church of Christ is that new nation of priests (I Peter 1:9-10). *Every Christian is called to be a minister.* Every Christian is a priest offering the sacrifices of praise and confession with the lips and of good deeds toward those in need (see Heb. 13:15-16). When every Christian is committed to ministry rather than being ministered to, the problem of division in the church will disappear.

APPLICATIONS:

1. Servanthood is learned through practice, it is not innate. Jesus had a difficult time teaching his first disciples that greatness was in serving others. He taught it primarily by his own example: "The Son of man came to minister, not to be ministered to. . . ." Jesus washed the disciples feet (John 13) and said they ought have the same attitude toward one another. Paul served the Corinthian Christians—he was not served by them. In fact he refused to take any salary from them for his ministry to them so they might have it as an example (II Cor. 11:7-9; 12:13-18).
2. Dissension and the party-spirit in a church or among Christians is a sure sign of worldly-mindedness (i.e., *not* thinking as God thinks in his word). It is usually a result of refusing to see human beings as God sees them and, rather, seeing them as the world does—objects to be exploited for one's own selfish purposes (see II Cor. 5:16-17). It is perpetuated by "comparing ourselves . . . or measuring ourselves by one another" instead of by Christ (cf. II Cor. 10:12). Christians can never make spiritual progress or come to maturity until they repent of such worldly thinking.
3. Every Christian, whether apostle, evangelist, teacher, elder, deacon, secretary, carpenter, custodian, man or woman is simply a *laborer* in God's "field" or on God's "building." Only God and his Son have authority to be "boss." Men are simply planters, waterers— God alone has the power (through his word) to produce life and growth.
4. Every laborer or worker will take care how he works on God's building if he wants his work to survive and enjoy it:

FIRST CORINTHIANS

He will build only on the One Foundation—Christ crucified and resurrected.

He will exert every effort to produce quality materials; materials that will survive the fires of temptation and testing.

He will recognize that he too is saved by the quality of fire-survival built into his own life.

5. Christians must believe that the compensations of self-serving are for fools, while the compensations of servanthood for Christ and others are for the wise.
6. God made everything good and he made it for Christians to exercise dominion over in order to praise and serve him, to enjoy and benefit from, and to use to bring others to salvation in Christ.

APPREHENSION:

1. How could Paul call these Corinthians "brethren" and, in the same breath, say they were not "spiritual men"?
2. What is a "babe" in Christ? Should we remain "babes" in Christ? How does this fit into Christ's admonition that we must "turn and become like little children" to enter the kingdom?
3. Should Christians be fed in "stages" or "phases"? Are all Christians ready to receive teaching from the scriptures on the same level?
4. What is the responsibility of the leaders of the church in this?
5. What is a *clear* manifestation of spiritual immaturity?
6. Do you find this clearly manifested in the brotherhood of Christians today?
7. Is Paul saying in this chapter we should not show respect or honor to those who teach us the scriptures? What is he saying about human teachers?
8. What is the *one* and *only* essential to church growth?
9. Where does God put his power to give growth? Are churches and Christian leaders "plugging in to" God's growing-power or relying on something else?
10. If apostles are "not anything" but planters and waterers, why did God give them powers and authority he gave to no other Christian?
11. Is God serious about Christians being careful how they build his "building"?
12. Name some practical ways we may be careful about how we build!
13. Have you seen any of your "building materials" tested in the "fire"?

CHAPTER 3   FIRST CORINTHIANS 3:18-23

14. Have any failed the test? Have any survived? What made the difference?
15. Will there be any stars in your crown when you get to heaven?
16. What will God do with those who destroy his church through division?
17. Did you realize God was that serious about Christian unity?
18. Why is it foolish for Christians to be biased in favor of some of God's servants and reject others?
19. Do you really believe that all of God's creation is yours? Are you using it?

Chapter Four

THE PROBLEM OF FAVORITISM AND CONCEIT (4:1-21)

IDEAS TO INVESTIGATE:

1. Why would Paul emphasize trustworthiness and then tell these Corinthians not to judge one another?
2. Does the admonition against favoring one another mean Christians should not feel closer to some brethren than to others?
3. What is Paul's purpose in demeaning the office of apostle?
4. Is it really all right to imitate Christian leaders like Paul—should we not rather imitate Christ?
5. What is the "power" in which the kingdom of God consists?

SECTION 1

Partiality (4:1-5)

4 This is how one should regard us, as servants of Christ and stewards of the mysteries of God. ²Moreover it is required of stewards that they be found trustworthy. ³But with me it is a very small thing that I should be judged by you or by any human court. I do not even judge myself. ⁴I am not aware of anything against myself, but I am not thereby acquitted. It is the Lord who judges me. ⁵Therefore do not pronounce judgment before the time, before the Lord comes, who will bring to light the things now hidden in darkness and will disclose the purposes of the heart. Then every man will receive his commendation from God.

4:1-4 Cause: The Corinthian Christians were showing partiality toward their favorite apostles and other leaders of the church. Partiality has no place in the kingdom of God. Partiality is defined: "To show favor to a person because of his external possessions, position or privilege; or, to accept the person instead of the cause." In the Old Testament the Hebrew words *nasha panim* are translated *partiality* and mean literally, "face-taking" (i.e. to judge on the basis of appearance). The Greek words *prosopolempsia* and *prosopolemptes* (sometimes translated, "respect of person") also mean literally, "face-taking" (see Acts 10:34; Rom. 2:11; Eph. 6:9; Col. 3:25; James 2:1, 9).

CHAPTER 4   FIRST CORINTHIANS 4:1-5

Partiality is severely condemned in the Old Testament (see Lev. 19:15; Deut. 1:17; 16:19-20; Job 13:10; Prov. 24:23; 28:21; Mal. 2:9). Jesus clearly taught that it was not to be a part of the character of the kingdom-citizen (Matt. 5:43-48). The epistles speak severely against partiality (see Col. 3:22—4:1; Rom. 2:11; Gal. 2:6; Eph. 6:9; I Tim. 5:21; James 2:9).

Partiality creates discord (Matt. 20:24; Mark 9:34; Luke 9:46f.; 22:24-27; Acts 6:1-6; I Cor. ch. 11-14); it causes denigration of God (Jer. 18:13ff.; Rom. 2:24; Gal. 2:11ff.); it defiles the conscience; it destroys the soul.

The cause for the display of partiality among the Corinthian brethren is evident to Paul. They were not evaluating apostles and other leaders by the *one and only* God-approved standard which is *faithfulness.* Paul uses two Greek words by which he categorizes *all* Christians whether they be leaders or followers. The word *servant* in Greek (*huperetas*) is the word from a mariner's vocabulary designating the "under-rower" in the ancient galley ships of the Mediterranean Sea. It came to mean "under-servant" or "underling" and was applied to anyone who took orders from someone higher. The second word, *steward,* in Greek is *oikonomos,* literally, "law of the house," meaning "house manager." Barclay calls the *oikonomos,* the *major domo.* The point Paul is stressing here is no matter what a Christian's place in the church, he is a servant. All Christians are underlings and take orders from Christ. All Christians are merely stewards taking care of the Master's goods. All Christians are to be evaluated only as to whether they have faithfully *accepted* this position as servant or not. We are not to compare one another's relationship to the Lord on the basis of skills, talents, accomplishments or any other quantitative measurement. When Jesus told the parable of the pounds (Luke 19:11-27) it is noteworthy that the nobleman did not condemn the man who had been given five pounds and came back with only five pounds more. If quantitative measurements are the criteria of God's judgments, the servant given five pounds should have been condemned for not returning ten more like the first servant. The only servant condemned was the third one who was unfaithful and distrusted the nobleman's faithfulness and fairness, (see comments, *The Gospel of Luke,* pages 420-425, by Butler, pub. College Press).

Christians must *always* think of apostles or other brethren in places of leadership as servants. To think otherwise produces favoritism and partiality and, ultimately, destructive division. Paul was emphatic! He insisted that the Corinthian Christians should *regard* the apostles as no more than underlings and stewards. The Greek word translated

FIRST CORINTHIANS

regard is *logizestho*. It is a word from the Greek world of business and finance. It means "to enter a calculation on a ledger." He wants it calculated and written down that apostles are merely servants. They are *not* Masters! The church must not enter one apostle on the "ledger" as of more account than others. The church must not show favoritism toward any church leader—they are all servants. Human judgments are always on the basis of appearances, seniority, popularity, or the like. Paul said the only thing that counted was *trustworthiness*.

The apostles were merely the first "stewards" commissioned by the Lord to dispense the "mysteries" of God. The apostles were specially gifted dispensers, to be true, but nothing more than dispensers. The Greek word *musterion*, translated "mystery" is used in the New Testament of God's redemptive program. The word *musterion* is often used by the pagan religions of the first century for doctrines and rites known by the members of their cults but kept secret from the uninitiated. The writers of the New Testament gave a new meaning to the word. God's redemptive program was symbolized and prophesied progressively but dimly in the Old Testament (Rom. 3:21; Heb. 1:1). Redemption was fully accomplished and revealed in the incarnate work of Christ and through the apostolic message which explains it and applies it.

Verse two begins with an unusual Greek phrase; *ho de loipon zeteitai en tois oikonomois*. Literally it would be translated, "As for the remaining, it is sought among stewards. . . ." What Paul means is that a certain character is sought after in *all* servants. That character is *faithfulness* (Gr. *pistos*). It is not simply sought for—it is *required!* The Greek word *zeteitai* is often translated "required, demanded" (see Luke 11:50-51; 12:48). J. B. Phillips paraphrases, "And it is a prime requisite in a trustee that he should prove worthy of his trust." Faithfulness is dependability and reliability. *All* servants of Christ (and that includes apostles) are evaluated not on the basis of giftedness but of dependability and reliability. Because some Christians may have been given miraculous powers in the first century, or even the calling as an apostle, does not mean they are to be set apart from other servants who never received miraculous gifts. Each servant is required only to be reliable and dependable with as much as Christ has given him. Jesus described the "faithful and wise steward" in Luke 12:42-43. Some classic examples of men who were faithful to earthly masters are Joseph to Potiphar, Daniel to King Darius (Dan. 6:4), and Hananiah (Neh. 7:2).

CHAPTER 4 FIRST CORINTHIANS 4:1-5

The apostles have come down to us in history as men of greatness, not because of their educational attainments or political achievements but because they were *faithful* to Christ. Being the *servants* of all, they became the *greatest* of all (see Matt. 20:20-28).

The Corinthian Christians had a problem with judging! Paul had to warn them again in his second letter that they were "comparing themselves with one another" and, in so doing, "were without understanding" (see II Cor. 10:12). Jesus evidently anticipated that all citizens of the kingdom of God would have a problem with judging. He devoted the last one-third of his Sermon on the Mount to the problems of making proper judgments (see Matt. 7:1-27). Christians are supposed to make certain judgments:

a. Christians must judge that some are "swine" and some are "dogs" and not cast pearls before them (Matt. 7:6).
b. Christians must judge what they would wish others to do to them so they may do the same to others (Matt. 7:12).
c. Christians must judge which is the narrow gate and which is the broad way (Matt. 7:13).
d. Christians must judge who are false prophets by the doctrines they teach and by the fruits they produce in their teachings (Matt. 7:15-20).
e. Christians must judge that doing the will of God is of primary importance (Matt. 7:21-23).
f. Christians must judge the proper place to build their lives (Matt. 7:24-27).
g. Christians must *not* judge by appearances, but with righteousness and justice (John 7:24).
h. Christians ought to be able to make fair and honest judgments between themselves when one has a grievance against another (I Cor. 6:1-8).
i. Christians are to test everything for its evil-quotient and abstain from every form of evil (I Thess. 5:21), especially in the matter of religious teaching (see I Cor. 14:29; I John 4:1-6).
j. Christians must be able to judge when a brother is "living in idleness" (II Thess. 3:6-15).
k. Christians must be able to judge when a brother "is overtaken in any trespass" and restore him in a spirit of gentleness (Gal. 6:1ff.; James 5:19-20, etc.).

There are many judgments Christians must make about people and situations. Why then did Paul say, "But with me it is a very small thing that I should be judged by you or by any human court"? Literally, the Greek phrase is: *de eis elachiston estin hina huph humon anakritho e hupo anthropines hemeras;* "But unto a little it is that by you I have been judged, or by the agency of a man's day." The context makes it clear Paul is saying human beings, even Christians, should not be arrogating to themselves the prerogatives of selecting the "best" apostle to follow. Christ chose the apostles. Christ alone has authority to distinguish one above another. So Paul is telling these divisive minded people that what they are doing is of no significance whatever, except that it is ruining the Christian fellowship there. Their decisions that one apostle or leader is *better* than another is ridiculous. If they were trying to decide whether Paul were actually an apostle or a false apostle, they had every right and obligation to do so. That could be decided, and should be decided, on the basis of the *signs* of an apostle (see II Cor. 12:12). But deciding as to which apostle or leader was *better* than the other, and then using such a decision to form divisions and opposing sides within the church was utterly pointless. It was worse than that! It was assuming prerogatives which belonged only to Christ.

The phrase, "or by the agency of a man's day," is an idiomatic statement referring to the indisputable limitations of the human experience to make eternal judgments. Human life is bounded by too narrow an horizon to make such judgments. The word "day" in all languages and idioms signifies judgments. The word "diet" to designate a legislative or judicial body comes from the Latin word *dies,* the word for *day.* The word "daysman" means an arbitrator. The RSV has translated the phrase to give its idiomatic meaning. There is no human *diet* (or court) with sufficient authority or expertise to divide the church over human leaders. What Paul has said here condemns *all* division in the body of Christ, and especially that division which is perpetuated by and in favor of religious leadership. Modern denominationalism with its proclivity to perpetuate the distinguishing of one Christian from another by elevation of human religious leaders (dead or alive) stands under this apostolic censure! All a Christian needs to know about a spiritual teacher and leader is whether he is faithful to the Lord's Word and the Lord's way of life. All Christians manifesting honest effort to be dependably and reliably following Christ are to love, cherish and honor one another and unite their hearts and minds in singleness of praise and service to Christ alone.

Continuing to expose the cause of so much favoritism and division, Paul implies that part of it may be the tendency of the Corinthians to misevaluate themselves. The way Paul makes this inference is to say that he does not even critique (judge) himself. Every man is predisposed to evaluate himself too highly (Rom. 12:3; Phil. 2:3). No

CHAPTER 4   FIRST CORINTHIANS 4:1-5

human being can trust self-evaluation because the heart of man is deceitful above all things, and desperately corrupt (see Jer. 17:9). Only the word of God is able to discern the thoughts and intentions of the human heart correctly (cf. Heb. 4:12-13). The Greeks placed great emphasis on the adage, "Know thyself." That is good advice if a man has in his possession the revealed word of God, the Creator, and if he will saturate his mind with that word surrendering to its divine judgments and evaluations. But by himself *no* man can know himself for he did not create himself! When men reject God's word for their own opinions, they overlook their faults and are always able to find someone else more wicked than they. Consider Jesus' parable of the two men who went to the temple to pray—one a Pharisee the other a tax collector (Luke 18:9-14), or consider the Jewish ruler's estimate of the common people (John 7:49).

We think J. B. Phillips has captured the essence of Paul's statement here in his paraphrase, "I don't even value my opinion of myself. For I might be quite ignorant of any fault in myself—but that doesn't justify me before God. My only true judge is the Lord." When Paul said he knew nothing against himself he was not claiming that he had never sinned. He was well aware of his failings (see Rom. 7:13-25; I Tim. 1:15, etc.). Paul is simply speaking hypothetically. He is saying, "For the sake of illustration, let us presume that I can't think of any wrong doing or wickedness against myself—that still does not prove infallibly there isn't any!" All it would prove is that Paul could not think of any. But what about the omniscient, omnipresent, omnipotent God? Before God *all* men are sinners—even apostles! Before God *all men saved* are men saved by grace through faith.

4:5 Cure: In the final analysis, the judgment of God is the only infallible and absolute judgment. God alone knows all the circumstances, secret thoughts, intentions and motives behind man's actions. Much that the world thinks is goodness may have been done from very wicked and self-serving motives. So Paul advocates as the cure for the problem of favoritism and conceit an awareness that honoring one Christian servant above another must be left to the judgment of God. Paul exhorts these Corinthian Christians to cease their favoritism and partiality toward spiritual servants. When Paul says, "Therefore do not pronounce *judgment* . . ." he uses the Greek verb *krinete,* in the imperative mood, which means Paul is *commanding* them to stop making such superficial judgments. Christians must not pronounce final verdicts on any person who is evidently trying to the best of his ability (and is not causing divisions in the church) to be faithful to the Lord. Christians must wait upon the Lord's return for final rewards and honors to be handed out to his servants. The Lord alone has the prerogative to hand out final commendations or condemnations. Some of these Corinthian church members were usurping the Lord's prerogative and honoring one servant of the Lord over another by their fallible, schismatic standards when they said, "I am of Paul" or, "I am of Apollos." Some of them, causing division and disorder in the church by jealousy and selfish ambition (see James 3:13-16), were collaborating with the demons of hell! One would think the elders of the Corinthian church would have recognized such schismatic persons as false teachers by the fruits (division and disorder) of their teachings (see Matt. 7:16; Acts 20:29-30).

SECTION 2

Pompousness (4:6-13)

6 I have applied all this to myself and Apollos for your benefit, brethren, that you may learn by us not to go beyond what is written, that none of you may be puffed up in favor of one against another. 7 For who sees anything different in you? What have you that you did not receive? If then you received it, why do you boast as if it were not a gift?

8 Already you are filled! Already you have become rich! Without us you have become kings! And would that you did reign, so that we might share the rule with you! 9 For I think that God has exhibited us apostles as last of all, like men sentenced to death; because we have become a spectacle to the world, to angels and to men. 10 We are fools for Christ's sake, but you are wise in Christ. We are weak, but you are strong. You are held in honor, but we in disrepute. 11 To the present hour we hunger and thirst, we are ill-clad and buffeted and homeless, 12 and we labor, working with our own hands. When reviled, we bless; when persecuted, we endure; 13 when slandered, we try to conciliate; we have become, and are now, as the refuse of the world, the offscouring of all things.

4:6-7 Egotistical: Paul had made it clear that Peter, Apollos, and he, had all *received* their stewardship to Christ by grace, not by merit. Paul insisted that whatever any apostle or leading teacher in the church might appear to be by the world's standards, they were nothing

CHAPTER 4 FIRST CORINTHIANS 4:6-13

more than servants seeking to be found faithful to their one Lord. He made it plain that no apostle or leader should be exalted above another. And all along he has been using himself and Apollos as an illustration. The Greek word translated *applied* is *meteschematisa*. It is the word from which we get the English word *schematic*, which means a sketch or a drawing. *Meteschematisa* means "to transfer by way of a figure."

Paul made himself and Apollos an illustration *for their benefit*. The Greek phrase, *di humas,* means, "for you, or, on account of you. . . ." Notice also Paul continues to call them "brethren" even though they are thinking too highly of themselves and are "puffed up." He has not "written them off" or expelled them from his fellowship. He will exert every effort, by every proper means possible, to benefit them.

The word *live* (as in the RSV) is not in the Greek text, and neither is the word *think* (as in the KJV). The literal reading from the Greek text would be, ". . . that in us you may learn not above (or beyond) what has been written. . . ." The phrase which follows shows that Paul is talking about *both* their thinking and their living. The Corinthian Christians are exhorted to learn by the example of humility and service practiced by Paul and Apollos toward one another and toward all other Christians. Paul and Apollos do not think of themselves or live toward one another in any way contrary to the *scriptures* (Gr. *gegraptai,* what is written). They are bound by the scriptures to be humble before God as much as anyone else. Paul had already quoted six Old Testament references about boasting (Ps. 33:10; Isa. 29:14; Jer. 9:24; Isa. 64:4; 65:17; Job 5:13) and there are many more (Ps. 49:6; 94:4; 17:7; Prov. 27:1; Isa. 10:15). Jesus spoke much about humility and against arrogance and conceit, and it may be that Paul is referring to the gospel documents since there is evidence that some of them may have been in existence as early as 50 A.D. The Christian must *not* be guided in his attitude toward himself and toward others by personal feelings or by any human standard. His attitudes are under the control of the mind of Christ which is revealed in the Bible (and nowhere else).

Literally, the Greek text of verse six reads, ". . . that not one over (or, beyond one you may be puffed up against the other. . . ." The Greek word *phusiousthe* is translated *puffed up* and means, "to blow up, to inflate," and is from the word *phusa*, "bellows." It is used metaphorically in the New Testament of pride (cf. I Cor. 4:6, 18, 19; 5:2; 8:1; 13:4; Col. 2:18). This does not mean we cannot feel closer to some co-workers than others. Paul had his Luke and his Timothy!

FIRST CORINTHIANS

The apostle now asks a series of questions, with just a trace of sarcasm to arrest their attention, to bring them back to a realistic view of themselves. He asks first, "Who sees anything different in you?" The Greek phrase is *tis gar see diakrinei* and literally translated would read, "For who makes you thoroughly separate or distinct?" J. B. Phillips has captured the idea in his paraphrase, "For who makes you different from somebody else?" The Corinthian Christians may have had many different functionaries (cf. I Cor. 12:4ff.), but they all had the same position or rank before God—that was *servant*. Paul is implying that their attitude of superiority toward one another was born of presumptuous conceit. Even the fact that they had chosen one apostle over another to follow did not make them superior, for apostles themselves are only servants! Their conceit was perpetuating division which in turn was destroying the temple (church) of God.

The second question, "What have you that you did not receive?" shows why their feeling of superiority was presumptuous. Everything they had they received from God. Life, salvation, spiritual gifts, the apostolic word, the Spirit of God—nothing was merited—everything was by grace (cf. I Cor. 1:26-31). All men everywhere need to be constantly reminded of this fact. Paul with the third question, "If then you *received* (Gr. *elabes*) it, why do you boast as not having received (Gr. *labon*) it?" There was simply *nothing* they could claim to have earned or originated themselves—therefore, they had no reason to boast. There was no need to elevate one apostle over another for they, too, had only what they *received* from God by grace.

4:8-13 Exploitative: These Corinthian brethren had become so egocentric, they were exploiting apostles and teachers for their own selfish purposes. They were building (they thought) their own reputations and glory at the expense of the apostles, for their divisions and partyisms hurt the apostles and brought disrepute to the name of Christ and his church. But they did not care so long as they appeared to be "wise" in their selectivity and exclusivity. Paul seeks to correct this by admonishing them through sarcasm and irony. They must be brought to see themselves as they really are—arrogant, exploitative, uncaring spiritual brats. It is a serious problem. It is destroying the church! Striking, impressive, attention-getting words must be used to solve the problem.

They considered themselves to have arrived at the goal of the Christian life—spiritual maturity—by being wiser than others. They exalted one leader or one apostle over another, thereby arrogating to themselves the stature of "spiritual giants." They thought they proved by their divisions that they alone knew which leader was the

CHAPTER 4   FIRST CORINTHIANS 4:6-13

right one for the church. Each party or group believed they alone could make superior spiritual evaluations. Each group considered the other groups immature, unqualified, and unacceptable for fellowship in the Lord. Each group considered itself the ruling group ("kings").

The apostle vividly compares their pride, egotism and superiority with the actual life and reputation of an apostle. William Barclay illustrates:

> When a Roman general won a great victory he was allowed to parade his victorious army through the streets of the city with all the trophies that he had won; the procession was called a Triumph. But at the end there came a little group of captives who were doomed to death; they were being taken to the arena to fight with the beasts and so to die. The Corinthians in their blatant pride were like the conquering general displaying the trophies of his prowess; the apostles were like the little group of captives doomed to die. To the Corinthians the Christian life meant flaunting their privileges and reckoning up their achievement; to Paul it meant humble service and a readiness to die for Christ.

The apostles never considered themselves kings. They knew there was only one King—Jesus. Paul is reminding them all followers of Jesus are merely his bondslaves and servants. Paul proceeds to tell these Corinthians, glorying in having chosen certain apostles to follow, just where apostles are in the scheme of things (especially as viewed by the worldly-minded). First, apostles were made to be spectacles. The Greek word translated *spectacle* is *theatron* from which we get the English word *theater*. What Paul means is the apostles were made public spectacles of humiliation through what they suffered. The same Greek word *theatron* is used in Hebrews 10:33 and translated "publicly exposed." There it is describing the public abuse and affliction Jewish Christians had to suffer from the unconverted Jews. Paul suffered that kind of humiliation from Jew and Gentile alike (see the book of Acts; also II Cor. 11:21-33). The Jews called him an apostate and blasphemer; Greek philosophers called him a babbler and trouble-maker; governors called him "mad." Paul had a reputation as a menace to society (Acts 17:6). Next, Paul says, the world looks upon the apostles as morons (Gr. *moroi,* fools). Paul accepted the world's evaluation, willing to be called a fool if it was for Christ's sake. He is saying to the Christians at Corinth that if they are expecting to gain a reputation from the world by dividing up and claiming to be followers of any of the apostles, their reputation will be that of fools following fools.

All through this section, Paul contrasts what the sophisticated world thought of the apostles and what the Christians at Corinth, in their naivete, thought the world should think of them. To the world the apostles (and, all of Christianity) were fools, weak, disreputable. The Corinthian Christians thought if they structured the church after worldly ways, with positions and parties of seniority and superiority by selecting the most prestigious leaders to follow, they would rule, be wise, be strong, and be honored. But the world does not see apostolic Christianity that way.

All the while the Corinthian Christians were reveling and basking in their own egotism, the apostles were suffering great privations and hardships to bring them to Christ and to strengthen them in Christ. Apostles went hungry and thirsty many times for the sake of the gospel. Paul knew how to endure hunger (Phil. 4:11-13). He knew what it meant to be beaten like a slave would be *buffeted* (Gr. *kolaphizometha,* beaten with the fist). One ancient Greek knew a man was a slave because he watched him being *kolaphizometha*—buffeted. Apostles were looked upon as itinerant wanderers (Gr. *astatoumen,* unsettled, unfixed, without a stationary place or home). They had to do *manual labor* (Gr. *kopiomen*), working for a living with their own hands (see I Cor. 9:6; Acts 18:3). Greek culture looked upon those who worked with their hands as the lowest class of society—just above slaves. Tradesmen certainly would never be classed as leaders of Greek society. Regardless of what any society or culture says, labor and work are held up throughout the Bible as character-building virtues. The sophisticates of the world, however, think otherwise. The world would see the Christians at Corinth as followers, low-class common laborers—tentmakers and fishermen.

The apostles were, by temperament, quite unlike the sophisticated Greeks. Aristotle said that the highest virtue was *megalopsuchia—with great soul;* and, he said, the virtue of the man with the great soul was that he would not endure insults. But the apostles had the Spirit of Christ in them. By Christ's love they were constrained and controlled. The Greek text is extremely terse, for the sake of impact. Paul says, literally, "Being slandered, we bless." The Greek word *loidoroumenoi* means *to be insulted* or *reviled* (see John 9:28; Acts 23:4). Paul says, "Being persecuted, we bear it; being blasphemed, we entreat, or conciliate." The pagan Greek and Roman world of Paul's day looked upon conduct such as the apostles exhibited as grovelling weakness, a character defect, and a sure mark of the lowliest class of society.

The apostles were, by reputation, the scum of the earth. The Greek word *perikatharmata,* translated *refuse,* refers to the garbage scoured or scraped off a kitchen vessel. The Greek word *peripsema,* translated *offscouring* means "to wipe the dirt off all around." In other words, the majority of the world, in that day, looked upon these apostles of the crucified Christ as garbage and dirt. And these Corinthian Christians thought their choosing one apostle over another would make them appear wise and worldly in the eyes of the pagan culture of the day. One is reminded by modern-day church people who create divisions in the body of Christ because of preacher-worship. And preachers are not exactly considered first-class citizens of modern culture. In fact, movies and television go to great lengths to portray preachers of the Bible as rabble-rousing, ignorant, self-serving menaces to society. Preachers, teachers and other leaders of the Lord's church should never be the object of a church's pride. They certainly are no reason over which to divide the church.

SECTION 3

Exasperating (4:14-21)

14 I do not write this to make you ashamed, but to admonish you as my beloved children. 15 For though you have countless guides in Christ, you do not have many fathers. For I became your father in Christ Jesus through the gospel. 16 I urge you, then, be imitators of me. 17 Therefore I sent to you Timothy, my beloved and faithful child in the Lord, to remind you of my ways in Christ, as I teach them everywhere in every church. 18 Some are arrogant, as though I were not coming to you. 19 But I will come to you soon, if the Lord wills, and I will find out not the talk of these arrogant people but their power. 20 For the kingdom of God does not consist in talk but in power. 21 What do you wish? Shall I come to you with a rod, or with love in a spirit of gentleness?

4:14-17 Misbehaving: Paul, having just written rather sarcastically, does not want the Corinthians to assume that he is bitter toward them or that he does not care for them. He *does* care for them—he loves them as a father loves his exasperating children. So he admonishes them. He does not write to destroy them with shame, but to correct them. The Greek word *noutheto,* translated *admonish,* is a compound of two Greek words, *nous,* mind, and *tithemi,* to put. Literally, it means to put into the mind as a warning some word or words. It is different from the Greek word *paideia* which stresses correction by action, although a good father uses both forms of correction (see Eph. 6:4). Paul hopes to correct their misbehavior by a word of admonition, but he will take action if necessary (see 4:18-21 below).

They are his *agapeta tekna*—beloved children—and although they may have had *thousands* (Greek, *murious,* myriads) of *teachers* (Greek, *paidagogous,* tutors, pedagogues), they have had only one spiritual father—Paul. The Greek word *paidagogous* means, literally, "a leader of the child." The Greek *pedagogue* was usually a slave who was given charge of the children of the wealthy and influential. The *pedagogue* escorted the children to school, disciplined them when they needed it, and often tutored the children when they were not in school. The *pedagogue* might do some of the work of a father and even become very intimately attached to the children, but he could never become the father. A father begets. Only one person can be the father of a child. When Paul said, ". . . you do not have many *fathers*. . . ." he used the Greek word *pateras* (from which we get the English words, paternal, patronize). But when he said, ". . . I became your *father* in Christ Jesus. . . ." he used the Greek word *egennesa* which actually means *begat.* Paul brought about their conversion to Christ personally through his preaching (see Acts 18:8; I Cor. 3:10). He laid the "foundation" of gospel work in Corinth. Paul had begotten many spiritual children in Christ Jesus; Timothy (I Tim. 1:2) and Titus (Titus 1:4) and Onesimus (Philemon 10), and hundreds of others (see I Thess. 2:11).

It is important to notice in this text that Paul says the Corinthians were begotten by Paul in Christ *through* the gospel. Spiritual birth (new birth, being born again) is through the gospel preached by the apostles. Where does one find the gospel preached by the apostles? In the book of Acts, beginning in Acts chapter two. What is the apostolic gospel through which the Corinthians were born again or anew? It is that Jesus Christ, the Son of God, was manifested in the flesh, died on a cross for the atonement of the world's sin, arose from the dead on the third day to validate that atonement; it is that men must so trust that declaration of God they will repent (change their mind) and submit to the command of the apostles to be immersed in water unto the remission of sins; it is that the Holy Spirit of Christ will take residence in the penitent and obedient believer and become to him God's down-payment on eternal life. No man,

CHAPTER 4   FIRST CORINTHIANS 4:14-21

since the redemptive work of Christ at the cross and the empty tomb, can be begotten in Christ apart from believing and obeying the apostolic gospel. Christians are begotten through the word of God, the gospel (see I Thess. 2:13; II Thess. 1:8; 2:13-15; James 1:18; I Peter 1:22-25). The word of God, the gospel, is the spiritual *seed* (Greek *sperma* or *spora,* see Luke 8:11 and I Peter 1:23) or *sperm* of God which begets the Spirit of God in man's heart but only when man believes it and obeys it. Many of the Corinthians, hearing, believed and were immersed in water (see Acts 18:8) and were thus begotten in Christ *through* the gospel!

Paul admonishes them (warns them) they are straying from the example he had given them as to how to live in Christ. He exhorts them to *mimic* his life in Christ (Greek, *mimetai,* imitate). He does not infer they should become disciples or followers of Paul or anyone else, but that they should imitate his "ways in Christ" (4:17). Paul used this exhortation frequently (see I Cor. 11:1; Acts 20:35; I Cor. 7:7; Phil. 3:17; 4:9; II Thess. 3:7; II Tim. 1:13). The Bible is full of admonitions for Christians to imitate the example of men of faith such as Abel, Enoch, Noah, Abraham, Moses, David, and countless others (see Rom. 4:1ff.; Heb. 11:1ff.). Of course, Christ is the Way, the Truth, and the Life. Jesus is the "pathfinder" or "pioneer" of our salvation (Heb. 2:10). We *follow* Jesus, but we may also imitate Paul as he follows Jesus. Like spoiled and selfish children, these Corinthian Christians were misbehaving. They certainly were not behaving as their spiritual father did.

As Paul was writing this letter, Timothy was on his way from Ephesus to Corinth. Paul had sent him (see Acts 19:22) by way of Macedonia with Erastus as his companion. Timothy was sent to remind them of how Paul lived in Christ and what he taught in Christ. Paul was no hypocrite—he lived what he taught and he taught Christ and lived Christ everywhere, in every church (see I Thess. 2:9-12; II Cor. 11:23; 12:14-18, etc.). A journey from Ephesus to Corinth, by way of Macedonia, by ancient modes of travel, facing all the dangers of the ancient traveler, might seem unnecessary in light of what might appear to be an insignificant problem in the church. But Paul knew it was not an insignificant problem. All the sacrifice and tension necessary to correct it must be made immediately. The church at Corinth was being *destroyed* by the schismatics! Timothy and Erastus must travel some 600 miles or more, the major portion of which would probably be on foot, to attempt to produce some spiritual maturity in these bickering, arguing, misbehaving "children." This will be a work that spiritual "fathers" will have to do with their "children" so long as the church remains in this world. It does not cease!

FIRST CORINTHIANS

4:18-21 Mocking: Paul had heard that some of the Christians in Corinth were not only misbehaving, they were arrogant (Greek, *ephusiothesan,* puffed up) about it. Paul wrote this epistle at Ephesus in the Spring of 57 A.D. He told the Corinthians he planned to stay in Ephesus until after Pentecost (June) (I Cor. 16:8) and then come to Corinth for a visit. But he changed his plans (II Cor. 1:15, 16, 23) and apparently the Corinthians then accused him of weakness and cowardice, so he wrote what is entitled the second epistle to defend his change of plans.

There must have been some indication at the writing of the first letter that some of the brethren at Corinth were arrogantly boasting Paul would never come to Corinth and exercise any apostolic authority. They accused him of being bold when he was away from them and meek when face to face with them (II Cor. 10:1). His sending Timothy instead of going himself as first he planned seemed to them to be justifiable cause for a bold and arrogant attitude toward the apostle.

So the apostle promises, "But I will come to you soon, if the Lord wills, . . ." and he promises to show that their mockery is all talk without any power behind it. The Greek word *gnosomai,* translated "find out," is literally, *shall know.* Paul means to settle the issue once for all with the Corinthians about the authority of his apostolic message. The Greek word *pephusiomenon* is a perfect participle meaning they had become *puffed up* in the past and were *continuing* to be puffed up. They had not repented. For some reason the teachers and leaders of the church there had not seen the error of their ways and they were getting more arrogant and bold with each passing day.

In 2:4-5 we have the antithesis of *word* and *power.* The difference there is between words of sophisticated philosophies verses the historical facts of Christ's redemptive work. The truth of God (in the gospel of Christ and his apostles) has *power* to destroy all philosophies and theories that are merely guesswork (and not even good guesses at that). The power of the Spirit of God in his word is able to cast down all *imaginations* (Gr. *logismous,* rationalizations) and bring every *thought* (Gr. *noema,* concept, purpose, device) into captivity to obedience to Christ (see II Cor. 10:3-5). Paul is talking about going to Corinth to exercise the power of truth in the apostolic message versus the boasting sophostries of the wayward and divisive Christians there. He is *not* threatening a demonstration of any physical or ecclesiastical power. None of the apostles ever assumed any papal powers.

Paul is challenging the schismatics at Corinth that when he comes to them he will put their sophisticated philosophies to the test to see if they are producing in the lives of people what his apostolic gospel is able to produce. It will be a test of spiritual strength and power. For, he says, the kingdom of God in a man's life is not demonstrated by words, but by the power of Christian living. So far, their sophistries have shown the exact *opposite* of Christian love and unity. In the kingdom of God, every thought is brought into obedience to Christ.

The choice is theirs. He will, if the Lord wills it, arrive shortly in Corinth. The question is, will they repent and bring their thinking and acting into obedience to Christ (as preached to them and written to them by Paul), or will they continue in their egotistical divisiveness? If they repent Paul will come with a gentle love. If they do *not* repent Paul will come with a chastening love. He says he will come with a *rod* (Gr. *hrabdo,* large wooden staff), but he is using the word rod as a metaphor. He does not intend to beat them physically, but to chasten them with the truth. It is by the power of the truth men are set free from enslavement to the destructive, damning lies of the devil which alienate them from God.

APPLICATIONS:

1. To extend favors or privileges to one person over another because of some outward attainment or circumstance is strictly anti-Biblical.
2. Christians have only *one* criterion by which they may judge the worth of a servant of Christ—*faithfulness*; not quantity, but quality, is the standard for stewardship.

    Today's churches would do well to remember that in evaluating a minister's or missionary's success!
3. It is when the church begins to think of itself as a "business operation" or an "institution" and compares itself with the world that it begins to judge its servants (ministers, elders, missionaries, teachers, etc.) by worldly criteria of successfulness.

    When the church does that, jealousy, arrogance, division and eventual destruction follows!
4. To really know yourself, study the Bible. No man should fall into the trap of evaluating himself apart from the Bible, for he cannot do so objectively and honestly.
5. Men and women put in places of Christian leadership must remember they are to be examples other Christians are to imitate.
6. The cure for the problem of partiality and arrogance which causes divisions in the church is to remember that *every* Christian is *only* what he is by the grace of God.
7. Schismatics in the church who exalt one leader over another are usually exploiting that leader for their own egotistical purposes.

FIRST CORINTHIANS

8. To accept insults, or to work with one's hands, for the sake of Christ, is not a sign of weakness, but of strength.
9. People are not born again through apostolic miracles, but through the apostolic gospel.
10. A faithful "spiritual father" will not shrink from chastening wayward "spiritual children" through the word of Christ, when love calls for it.

APPREHENSIONS:

1. What is a steward? What is trustworthiness? Why is this the only standard for judging a steward?
2. Are Christians to judge anything or anyone at all? What? How?
3. What are Christians *not* to judge?
4. What should a church seek foremost in a man they call to preach? Should it be personality? Speaking ability? Age? Administrative success?
5. Does the Scripture prohibit partiality? What is partiality? Are you partial?
6. Why did Paul use sarcasm about what the Corinthians thought of themselves?
7. Is it all right for Christians to use sarcasm? When? How?
8. If the apostles were held in such low esteem in their own lifetime, why are they widely venerated by the world today? How did Jesus explain this twist of human nature? (See Matt. 23:29-31.)
9. How are people "begotten" in Christ? Should those who lead others to Christ feel like a spiritual "parent"? What would that involve?
10. Do you look upon truth as powerful? What power does truth have? (See John 8:31-32.)

Chapter Five

THE PROBLEM OF CHURCH DISCIPLINE
(5:1-13)

IDEAS TO INVESTIGATE:

1. What was the immorality being practiced in this instance in the Corinthian church?
2. How could Christians be arrogant about that?
3. Wasn't Paul's instruction too severe to do any good for the sinners?
4. Does all sin in the church act like leaven?
5. What should the Christian's relationship be to immoral people outside the church?

SECTION 1

Atrocious Sin (5:1-2)

5 It is actually reported that there is immorality among you, and of a kind that is not found even among pagans; for a man is living with his father's wife. ²And you are arrogant! Ought you not rather to mourn? Let him who has done this be removed from among you.

5:1 Aberration: Abruptly Paul brings up the subject of the grossest immorality being practiced in the Corinthian brotherhood by one of the church members. It had *actually* (Gr. *holos,* most assuredly, incontrovertibly) been established and reported that there was *immorality* (Gr. *porneia,* sexual unchastity) among Christians in Corinth. The Greek word *porneia* does not indicate the specific form this immorality had taken because the word is used as a synonym for adultery (Matt. 5:32; 19:9) and for illicit sexual intercourse in the unmarried (I Cor. 6:9) while in classical Greek and the book of Revelation the word is used for prostitution (Rev. 17:2, 4; 18:3, 9). In fact, *porneia* often means, in the New Testament, illicit sexual intercourse in general. But Paul specifies the sexual immorality in Corinth as a form of *incest,* (*incest,* from Latin *incestus* and French *incastus,* meaning simply, "not chaste"). Paul does not use the word incest but simply describes the case as "a man living with his father's wife." Some commentators assume that the guilty man's father had died and the son was living with one of the father's wives. Most do not think it

FIRST CORINTHIANS

was the guilty man's own mother, but a second wife of his father after divorce or death. Other commentators think the father may have been still living and was the "one who suffered the wrong" mentioned in II Corinthians 7:12. Whatever the status of the guilty man's father, the crime of incestuous sexual intercourse is severe enough to warrant the death penalty in the Mosaic covenant (cf. Lev. 18:6-18; 20:10-21; Deut. 27:20). The possibility of genetic deformities in the offspring of incestuous relationships is not relevant to scriptural prohibition. God decrees against incest because it destroys the divinely decreed order of human hierarchy in marriage and thus is destructive of the social order itself.

Paul describes this sin with shock as, "such immorality as is not even named among the Gentiles." Paul was speaking hyperbolically to emphasize the seriousness of the crime. Incest *was* practiced among a few of the more depraved Gentiles. Some of the ancient Egyptians (Cleopatra II, with her brother, Cleopatra VII with Ptolemy XIII, her brother) practiced incest; Herod Antipas was married to Herodias, his niece-sister-in-law; some of the Roman emperors were accused by Suetonius in his *Lives of The Twelve Caesars* of practicing incest (Nero with his mother; Caligula with his sisters); Cicero, citing the case of the woman Sassia's marriage to her son-in-law, Melinus, says, "Oh, incredible wickedness, and—except in this woman's case—unheard of in all experience." There is also the case of a man named Callias, cited by Andocides in Greece in 400 B.C., who married his wife's mother! But Andocides asks whether among the Greeks such a thing had ever been done before. Even some Jews practiced incest in the days of Ezekiel (cf. Ezek. 22:11). So, even though some of the more depraved practiced it, the crime of incest was generally abhorent to the pagan. Even modern day anthropologists and sociologists find incest a crime considered immoral, aberrant and destructive in all ages and cultures:

> Cross-cultural studies of morality have typically remarked on the complexity and diversity of values to be found across time and space. One commentator has been led to conclude that "There is scarcely one norm or standard of good conduct that, in another time and place, does not serve to mark bad conduct." One possible exception to this conclusion is the universality of the incest taboo. (*Moral Development and Behavior,* pg. 70, Thomas Lickona, Editor, pub. Holt, Rinehart, Winston, 1976)

True, Corinth was Corinth—one of the fleshpots of the ancient world—but for all their obsessions with sin, the pagan Corinthians themselves had certain limits! It is hard to believe that a sin which even the pagans shunned had invaded the Church! Carnality (concentration on worldliness) plays funny tricks. It often turns truth upside down, or as Isaiah the prophet put it, "calling evil good and good evil" (Isa. 5:20).

5:2 Arrogance: The Christians in Corinth divided when they were supposed to be united—and united when they were supposed to be dividing! Is there ever a time when Christians are supposed to divide? Certainly not over song books, church buildings or human leaders, or any other frivolous matter. But immorality of any kind is never a frivolous matter. Apparently, from this text and others, God expects Christians to keep themselves separated from anyone who calls himself a brother and is continuing to practice immorality. The RSV says the guilty man was "living" with his father's wife; the Greek text uses the word *echein* which is a present infinitive and means literally, "to keep on having." This immorality was flagrant and continuous. Some of these Corinthian Christians had formerly been fornicators, adulterers, homosexuals, thieves, drunkards and robbers as well as idolaters (I Cor. 6:10) but they had overcome these sins. Even at the time this epistle was being written they were having difficulty resolving the problems of sexuality and marriage (I Cor. ch. 7). Indeed, even those called "saints" are faced with such problems. It is not a guarantee against temptation to be a Christian. Temptations are sure to come (Matt. 18:7). But Christians must not give in to temptations. Forty years later, the Christians of Asia Minor were still having problems with immorality in their congregations (see Revelation, ch. 2-3).

They were *puffed up* (Gr. *pephusiomenoi,* perfect tense verb, meaning, having been puffed up in the past, they were continuing to be puffed up). Paul was shocked about the incestuous relationship in this Christian, but he was *more shocked* at the attitude of the congregation toward it! The congregation had puffed itself up with self-importance and worldly wisdom. It was more interested in maintaining its cliques and parties and its "image" with the worldly-wise than in righteousness. They were concentrating on patterning the church after human institutions and worldly structures of leadership. Perhaps they were so puffed up about their image they did not want to admit this problem existed among them. If they took the drastic action taught by Christ and the apostles, they might be stigmatized as "prudish" by the pagan society of Corinth and their image of sophistication would be destroyed. It does not seem they were proud of the immoral conduct on the part of this brother, but their sin lay

FIRST CORINTHIANS

in the fact that they failed to do what God required and remove the immoral person from their fellowship. Perhaps the elders of the church were afraid their fellow Christians might accuse them of being "judgmental" had they taken the action required by the gospel. These are the very reasons some Christian congregations and leaders do not exercise New Testament guidance today in disciplining church members guilty of flagrant, aberrant and continuous immorality. Another reason it has become difficult today to apply discipline that would lead to repentance is the fact that a Christian disfellowshiped from one congregation may find sympathetic indulgence and reception in another congregation, often within the same city or locality.

Paul suggests that the only proper attitude for the congregation toward this disgraceful immorality is that of *mourning*. Incidentally, Paul's suggestion furnishes a classic illustration of what Jesus meant in the second Beatitude (Matt. 5:4), "Blessed are those who *mourn* for they shall be strengthened." The Bible pronounces a blessing on those who mourn over the *cause* of sin which is rebellion and disgrace toward God. Most people selfishly mourn because they are suffering the consequences of their sin—they are not concerned that sin has brought shame and hurt to God. The Greek syntax of 5:2 is instructive! Literally it would be translated, "And you, having become puffed up continue to be, rather than having mourned about this circumstance *in order that* (Gr. *hina*) the one having done this deed might be removed from among you." In other words, true Christian mourning about sin *does* something about the sin. Mourning is not satisfied simply with regret. Paul advised, "Let him who has done this be *removed* (Gr. *arthe,* be driven out) from among you."

The Corinthian congregation was not mourning—they were *boasting* (see 5:6). What had they to boast about in this situation? Obviously, they were not bragging about how immoral the congregation was. Their pride undoubtedly centered in their concept of "sophistication" or "broadmindedness." The elders and leaders of the different factions may have rationalized, "What our brother does in his private life is entirely his affair. Our obligation is to continue to love him; we dare not be judgmental toward these people." Perhaps they justified their approach to the circumstances by saying to themselves, "When you live in Corinth, you have to adapt somewhat to the culture. Besides, morals change with the times and we should feel a certain obligation to 'loosen up' ourselves, become less bigoted and more liberal." This same carnal attitude of boasting about "broadmindedness," especially in the area of sexual promiscuity, is sweeping our nation in high and low places—and even in some churches.

CHAPTER 5   FIRST CORINTHIANS 5:3-8

Whatever the excuse for their boasting, it was improper—in fact it was sinful!

SECTION 2

Apostolic Summons (5:3-8)

3 For though absent in body I am present in spirit, and as if present, I have already pronounced judgment 4 in the name of the Lord Jesus on the man who has done such a thing. When you are assembled, and my spirit is present, with the power of our Lord Jesus, 5 you are to deliver this man to Satan for the destruction of the flesh, that his spirit may be saved in the day of the Lord Jesus.

6 Your boasting is not good. Do you not know that a little leaven leavens the whole lump? 7 Cleanse out the old leaven that you may be a new lump, as you really are unleavened. For Christ, our paschal lamb, has been sacrificed. 8 Let us, therefore, celebrate the festival, not with the old leaven, the leaven of malice and evil, but with the unleavened bread of sincerity and truth.

5:3-5 Chastening: This advice that the immoral man should be expelled from the church comes with full apostolic authority. It is advice from the Holy Spirit of God speaking through the instrumentality of an apostle. There is no human guesswork involved here. Christ's bride (the church) is to keep herself sanctified, cleansed, in splendor, without spot or wrinkle, that she might be holy and without blemish (Eph. 5:21-27). Immorality and all impurity must not even be *named* among the saints (Eph. 5:3). The church is to take no part in the unfruitful works of darkness, but instead expose them, for it is a shame even to *speak* of the things that they do in secret (Eph. 5:11-12).

Although the apostle was absent from their presence, and could not be there to speak with them face to face, he had already *made judgment* from the moment he received the report (Gr. *kekrika,* perfect tense verb), and his judgment continued to be, "deliver such a one to Satan." Note the qualifying statements Paul makes about his judgment:

    a. It is in the name of (by the authority of) the Lord Jesus.
    b. It is by apostolic epistle—the apostle being absent in body.
    c. It is to be done by the assembled church.
    d. It is for the purpose of putting to death worldly-mindedness in the guilty man in order to save his spirit for God.

FIRST CORINTHIANS

Paul's bodily absence from these brethren did not mean his spirit (will) could not be present among them. His spirit would be actualized among them through his letter to them. His letter expressed his will—his spirit—his personality. As a matter of fact, it is through the written word of the Holy Spirit (the Bible) that God actualizes the Spirit of Christ in the heart and soul of every believer (see John 14:21, 23; 15:7, 10, 11; I John 2:5-6; 2:24; 3:24). And, of course, Paul's written word carried with it "the power of our Lord Jesus."

The apostolic order is to "deliver this man to Satan." The Greek word is *paradounai,* which means, "give over, abandon, deliver up." What is it to abandon someone to Satan? It is the same as, "Let him become to you as a Gentile and a publican" (Matt. 18:17); it is the same as "having nothing to do with him" (II Thess. 3:6, 14, 15). To deliver, or abandon, a church member to Satan is to declare him a non-covenant person. Those of the Old Testament dispensation who were "cut off from the congregation" were to be considered no longer members of Israel and severed from all rights and privileges of the covenant! They could not offer sacrifices at the temple, they could not associate with God's people, and they were considered unclean. They were no longer able to be reconciled to God. The same is true in the case of a Christian excommunicated from the church. Such a one is unreconciled to God, a rebel, and not a member of God's redeemed community *until* he repents and seeks forgiveness. Delivering an immoral impenitent to Satan is really only an acknowledgment by the church of that which the sinner has already done to himself! It gets the church's position straightened out on sin as much as it gets the sinner's attitude straightened out on it!

Excommunication does not mean that the church has given up on the sinner and wishes him to be lost forever. In fact, it means just the opposite. It means the church really cares that the sinner is jeopardizing his eternal salvation by continuing in his sin, and the church is jealous for his salvation and fellowship, but the church must also fear God and keep his commandments concerning "sin in the camp."

This is precisely why Paul qualified his order to deliver the man to Satan with the words, ". . . for the destruction of the flesh, that his spirit may be saved in the day of the Lord Jesus." The church was not to destroy the man, but to reclaim the man for Christ. As he was, living in contemptuous rebellion against Christ's rule over him, he was giving allegiance to Satan. The church must understand this is where the man is, admit the man belongs to Satan and not to Christ, and take unpleasant but affirmative action that might move the man to return to Christ's lordship in his life.

CHAPTER 5   FIRST CORINTHIANS 5:3-8

Satan, of course, would not personally offer any assistance to the guilty man to destroy his carnal-mindedness. Satan would use every opportunity and circumstance to deceive the man into involving himself ever deeper into carnality. God alone, through his word and Spirit in our hearts, destroys fleshly-mindedness. Paul did not mean the physical body of the man was to be destroyed—he meant the destruction of an attitude! The apostle wanted to slay a certain mind-set, a philosophy of life, which the man had accepted and allowed to turn him away from godliness. Paul himself had to fight and conquer (by God's grace) this same mind-set (cf. Rom. 7:13-25; I Cor. 9:24-27). There is this same struggle in every Christian (see Gal. 5:17).

Apparently Paul believed this man would learn something by being excommunicated and given over to some realm where Satan is allowed by God to function which might motivate the man to draw near to Christ. Paul "delivered to Satan" two of his co-workers, Hymenaeus and Alexander, that they might learn "not to blaspheme." How did he expect them to *learn* this? How did God teach Job to depend more on God's grace than on his own self-righteousness? God "delivered" Job to Satan (see Job 2:6-7). How was Paul, the apostle, taught that he should not boast in having received revelations from God that no other human had received? How did Paul learn that God's grace was sufficient and that he should not rely on himself? God "delivered" Paul to Satan and sent Paul through the school of affliction (see II Cor. 12:1-10; II Cor. 1:3-11, respectively). Jesus "delivered" Peter to Satan "to be sifted as wheat" (Luke 22:31-32). Evidently Paul believed that when this man was cast out of the brotherhood of believers, he would suffer affliction (which the devil would gladly inflict because the devil's total ambition is to hurt both God and man) which God would allow the devil to inflict, and this might produce repentance in the man. Since Satan is the great accuser, the man's torment might be such a burden of guilt he would be moved to shame (see II Thess. 3:14-15) and turn to Christ for grace and forgiveness which would demand that he "put to death the deeds done in the body." When God "gave up" the heathen society Paul wrote about in chapter one of Romans, to whom and to what did he give them up? He gave them up to the prince of darkness! When God allowed a strong delusion to come upon those who did not believe the truth but had pleasure in unrighteousness, to whom did he deliver them? He delivered them to the "activity of Satan" (II Thess. 2:1-15). We must always remember, however, that Biblical religion is not a form of dualism like the religions of ancient Babylon and Persia. God's word never presents a picture of two kingdoms (light and darkness; good and evil) with *equal* power! In the Bible we learn that Jehovah is without beginning and end and is all powerful forever. Satan has only such power as is relegated to him and is constantly subject to the control of Almighty God (see our comments on Revelation, ch. 20, in *Twenty-Six Lessons on Revelation, Part Two,* pgs. 95-121, pub. College Press).

If this guilty man, delivered to Satan, puts to death his attitude that this world and physical things are man's ultimate purpose and goal, his spirit will be saved. Paul, of course, does not mean to infer that man is only spirit and that the physical body is evil, *per se.* That was the deception taught by the Gnostics to justify their depravities. Paul was well aware that at the resurrection man will be raised with a new body. But it will be a body different from the one he inhabits in this cosmic order. Man's new body will be celestial, immortal and incorruptible (cf. I Cor. 15:35-58). Therefore, what Paul means by the saving of man's spirit is the saving of the *whole* man. Man is not whole until he is "spiritual." It is the holy spiritual essence of man that is eternal and if controlled by the love of Christ (cf. II Cor. 4:16—5:21), will be clothed with immortality at Christ's "day" (his second coming). Scandalous and impenitent immorality in any congregation must be dealt with. There is no option except discipline. It is the Lord's command. However, in view of the awesome responsibility of having to "deliver . . . a man (or woman) to Satan for the destruction of the flesh" it must be done with compassionate love, with strict adherence to the divine guidelines of the New Testament, and with reclamation of a penitent brother as its only goal. When such a case demands attention by the congregation and its leadership, it must be done with firmness, without partiality and as quickly as love allows. "Because sentence against an evil deed is not executed speedily, the heart of the sons of men is fully set to do evil" (Eccl. 8:11; see also Isa. 26:9-10). The action of delivering a member of a congregation to Satan (or excommunication) must never be done on the basis of hearsay. The evidence of immorality must be clear and actual—not merely rumored.

5:6-8 Cleansing: It seems incredible that the Corinthian Christians would be boasting about such an abhorrent sin in their midst. Perhaps they were boasting about their graciousness and tolerance in not having judged the man (see comments on verse 2). Whatever the case, the apostle is as appalled at their attitude as he is at the sin. By their tolerance of this perversion they are leaving the whole congregation to be infected with sin. Leaven (yeast) is commonly used

CHAPTER 5   FIRST CORINTHIANS 5:3-8

in the Bible to symbolize the penetrating power of a small matter so as to permeate and influence the greater, for either good or evil. The context always determines how the symbol is being used. It is clear that Paul is using leaven here as a figure of evil influence. Every one knows that just a little leaven will reproduce itself in a large lump of bread-dough. It is also true that one sin may infect a whole congregation, reproducing evil throughout the whole body. And how much more deadly would be the influence of such sin if the congregation was proud of its toleration of the evil.

    Paul commands the church to *cleanse* itself. The Greek text has the word *ekkatharate* (aorist imperative). This is an order, not a suggestion. The Greek word is a compound word with a prepositional prefix meaning, "clean out, purge out, eliminate." It is the word from which we have the English word *catharsis* which means to purify.

    Should anyone think the apostle is too severe in his demands or his language he has only to read the Old Testament law concerning punishment for sins of seemingly lesser perversion. In the law of Moses Israelites were to be put to death for rebelling against parents, for bowing down to an image, for practicing witchcraft, and many other sins. Surely Christians are never to get the idea that God is more tolerant of sin in the New dispensation (see Heb. 2:1-4; Matt. 5:27-30). Jesus cursed a fig tree and withered it simply because it gave signs of fruit but produced none. Ananias and Sapphira were struck dead by the Holy Spirit for lying about what they gave to the church; Elymas was struck blind by the Holy Spirit trying to turn Sergius Paulus away from faith in Jesus (Acts 13:8ff.). God is serious about sin!

    All the symbolism of Jewish history and God's redemptive program for man is applied here to the Christian experience. The Christian covenant is God's ultimate feast. Jesus spoke often (parabolically) of his new kingdom (the church) as a "feast." Paul is not referring to the Lord's Supper, *per se,* in these verses. He is using the same figure of speech Jesus used in his parables. Paul is likening the *whole* Christian life to a festival or holy-day. Of course, the best symbol to illustrate that is the Jewish Passover feast. The Christian's *Passover* is Christ (Gr. *pascha*). Christ is the absolute passover—the perfect passover. He is the fulfillment of that which all the Jewish feasts typified and prophesied. The Old Testament passover specifically celebrated God's redemption of Israel and sanctification or separation from bondage into a people called out for God's glory and purpose. All the festivals or holy-days ordained by God in the law of Moses were celebrations of righteousness, love, truth and goodness. They were holy dedications acknowledging man's reconciliation to the will of God through sacrificial, vicarious atonement.

At the Jewish passover, specifically, all Jewish homes had to be searched with minute care for leaven and any that was found was to be put out of the house (see Exod. 12:14-20). If anyone disobeyed this commandment they were to be "cut off" from the congregation of Israel! Leaven, in the matter of the Jewish passover, symbolized the old life of bondage in Egypt, which, in turn, symbolizes sin. In the Jewish passover the old leaven had to be thrown out before the slaying of the sacrificial lamb and the observance of the festival. In the Corinthian antitype their lamb had already been sacrificed and they were trying to celebrate the festival (the Christian's life) with the old leaven still remaining in their "house."

The whole Christian experience is said to be a festival or a feast. The Old Testament prophets often predicted the messianic age in the figure of a feast (Isa. 25:6-9; 55:1-2; Zech. 14:16-19, etc.). Jesus used the figure of a feast to predict his messianic kingdom (Luke 14:1ff.; Matt. 22:1-14; 25:1-13; John 6:35-63; Luke 15:22-32). The apostles frequently spoke of the Christian life as feasting (cf. Heb. 6:1ff.; 12:22-23; I Cor. 3:2; Heb. 5:12-14; I Peter 2:2-3; Eph. 5:18; see also John 4:34; Matt. 5:6; Isa. 65:13). So, when Paul says here, "Let us, therefore, celebrate the festival . . ." (Gr. *heortazomen,* feast) he is not limiting the need for cleansing to partaking of the Lord's Supper. The church must purge itself of the sin within it in order to be considered as being a participant of the whole Christian experience!

And the sin within the church is not only the man living with his father's wife! The translation of the Greek word *kakias* by the English word *malice* is not sufficiently precise to give the clear meaning of the sentence. The word *kakias* means "badness in quality." It may have the connotation of maliciousness if the context demands it, but that does not seem to be the case here. The word *kakias* refers more to disposition or attitude (bad attitude) than it does to deeds. The next word in the sentence, *evil* (Gr. *ponerias*), has to do with deeds. It would seem, therefore, that Paul was urging the Corinthian church to purge itself of its bad attitude or disposition (arrogance and worldly sophistication) as well as the incestuous relationship of the man with his father's wife.

So long as the church was of the attitude to see itself as sophisticated by allowing the sinful couple to continue in its fellowship, they could not possibly be living the Christian life ("keeping the festival with the unleavened bread") of sincerity and truth. The word *eilikrineias* is translated *sincerity* and is from two Greek words which mean *sun* and *judge*. The idea is that a life lived in *sincerity* is a life that is not lived in darkness or shadows, but one that is lived in the undimmed, brilliance of pure truth.

SECTION 3

Affiliations Sorted (5:9-13)

> 9 I wrote to you in my letter not to associate with immoral men; 10 not at all meaning the immoral of this world, or the greedy and robbers, or idolaters, since then you would need to go out of the world. 11 But rather I wrote to you not to associate with any one who bears the name of brother if he is guilty of immorality or greed, or is an idolater, reviler, drunkard, or robber —not even to eat with such a one. 12 For what have I to do with judging outsiders? Is it not those inside the church whom you are to judge? 13 God judges those outside. "Drive out the wicked person from among you."

5:9-10 Associating with Heathen: We learn from verse 9 that Paul wrote at least three letters to the Corinthian church. It is clear from his statement, "I wrote to you in my letter . . . ," that he had written to Corinth prior to the epistle now before us, and, of course, he wrote at least one (Second Corinthians) afterward. In the non-extant letter Paul had exhorted them "not to associate with immoral men." The Greek word *sunanamignusthai* is a compound of three words and literally means, *mix up with,* and is translated *associate with* (RSV) and *company with* (KJV). The same Greek word is used in II Thessalonians 3:14, and is translated *"have nothing to do with him."* In his previous letter Paul intended his exhortation about dissociation from immoral people to be applied in its strictest sense to any fellow Christian who was continuing, impenitently, in an immoral sexual relationship. That would probably apply specifically, as we shall observe later, to grossly impenitent and perverted sexual sinners in the heathen society as well. It seems, however, that the Corinthians inadvertently (or perhaps deliberately) misunderstood Paul. They assumed he meant they were to withdraw *completely* from *any* associations with their heathen neighbors. The RSV translation, *not at all,* of the Greek words *ou pantos* seems to make Paul mean that Christians should have no reservations *at all* about *mixing* or *mingling* with the immoral around them. Such an idea would make the inspired apostle contradict himself since in II Corinthians 6:14—7:1 Paul

FIRST CORINTHIANS

pointedly commands Christians not to share in heathen depravity! The Greek words *ou pantos* are better translated, *not meaning altogether*. Thus Paul is saying, "I wrote to you in my letter not to associate with immoral men; not meaning that you must dissociate yourself *altogether* (or completely) from the immoral of this world. . . ." The apostle categorizes the heathen into those who sin against their bodies (immoral, Gr. *pornois,* sexual sins), those who sin against society (greedy and robbers), and those who sin against God (idolaters, Gr. *eidololatrais,* image worshipers).

Since all the citizens of Corinth, except the Christians and Jews, would be idolaters, and many of them would be guilty of sexual sins and/or greedy, it would have been nearly impossible for the Christians to reject *all* associations with the heathen. They could have made no purchases in the markets, made no appeals for civil justice, visited no neighbors and relatives, and made no evangelistic contacts with the lost. The only way they could have had no associations at all, theoretically, would be to move away from the city of Corinth into the uninhabited mountains and forests and formed monasteries or communes which were completely self-sustaining and self-governing. Total dissociation would have precluded any possibility of the Corinthian Christians carrying out the Great Commission (cf. Matt. 28:18-20). Neither Jesus nor the apostles ever advocated asceticism or monasticism. New Testament Christianity is to be lived out in the midst of a sinful society so it may have a leavening (in the good sense) influence (cf. Matt. 13:33; Luke 13:20-21). Christians are the "salt of the earth" and "light of the world" (Matt. 5:13-16). Christians are to be "in the world but not of the world" (John 17:15-19). As one writer has put it, Paul's admonition here concerning the immoral of this world did not prohibit *contact,* but it did prohibit *conformity.*

But Paul's admonition concerning an impenitent, immoral person who bears the name of brother, is, "not even to eat with such a one." This does not refer to the Lord's Supper, but to dining together socially. Being a guest for dinner in another person's home was considered in the ancient world to be a sign that the host was intimately associated with the guest and that he agreed with his philosophical stand and his life-style. The Pharisees were shocked that Jesus would eat with publicans and sinners (cf. Matt. 9:10-11; 11:19; Luke 19:7). It would be dangerous to both the faithful Christian and the impenitent brother for the faithful Christian to *socialize* with the impenitent (see II Thess. 3:6, 14; Titus 3:10-11; II Peter 2:1-22; II John 10-11). First, it would give the impenitent brother the impression that he would be acceptable in the Christian fellowship whether he repented

CHAPTER 5   FIRST CORINTHIANS 5:9-13

or not; second, it would expose the faithful brother to temptations in a seductive atmosphere of geniality and acceptability; third, it would make possible certain unwarranted conclusions from both the Christian community and the pagan society that the Church was not much different than the world in the matter of immorality.

The church is not charged with the responsibility of disciplining ("judging") outsiders. Paul expected the Corinthian church to know that. As far as the unchurched sinners of society was concerned, the apostle allows for such contact as was necessary for the ongoing of life in the world. But he permitted no contact (complete withdrawal) at even the social level with a sinning brother.

On the other hand, the church is most specifically charged with the responsibility for disciplining ("judging") members of the church. For the church to fail in this *duty* is to dilute the spiritual quality of the congregation, and thus destroy its purpose as a "city set on a hill"! This does not mean that all church members must be sinless. It does not mean that every church member who commits an unwitting sin or falls into a temptation, must be excommunicated. The crucial issue is flagrant, shameful, continued sin for which there is no apparent repentance (including a change of mind issuing in a change of conduct). When such impenitence is reported and has been established by due scriptural process, discipline involving *driving out* (Gr. *exareite,* expel, take out, removed from) the *evil one* (Gr. *poneron*) from the fellowship of the church is demanded. It is the word of the Lord!

APPLICATIONS:

1. Church membership and association with Christian people does not necessarily guarantee immunity from the grossest and most perverted forms of sin.
2. There are sins so destructive of social fibre that even the heathen are appalled at them.
3. What is even more appalling is that the church may take an attitude of sophisticated arrogance or indifference toward the sins which heathens abhor!
4. The proper attitude of church members toward flagrant and perverted sin by one of its members is *not* arrogance, indifference, gossip, titillation or self-righteous apathy, but mournful discipline.
5. The spiritual authority of the apostolic revelation to guide the church in matters of discipline is as equally viable in the New Testament epistles as it would be if the apostles were present in the body.

FIRST CORINTHIANS

6. God may allow Satan to hurt those whom the church excommunicates in order to motivate them, if possible, to repent (destroy the flesh).
7. Impenitent sin is like yeast. It permeates and influences the whole community of the redeemed unless it is purged out of the church.
8. The whole Christian life is symbolized by the holy-days and feasts of the Mosaic covenant—especially by the Passover. The church could learn a great deal about its call to holiness and sanctification by studying these great Israelite festivals.
9. The Christian community cannot "celebrate" the Christian life in a manner pleasing to God if it allows flagrant, impenitent sinners to continue in its fellowship.
10. God's demand for sanctification and holiness by church members does not mean they are to withdraw completely from the world into monasteries and convents. Christians must have *contact* with the world but not *conformity* to it.
11. But toward those who are called brothers in Christ, if they continue in immorality, Christians are not even to have contact—socially or religiously!
12. While the church is not responsible to judge and punish the immoral or criminal people outside the church, it is clearly commanded by apostolic order to judge and discipline the immoral within the church.
13. The drastic measures ordered by the apostles concerning Christian discipline are designed first for the reclamation of the sinner; second for the integrity of Christ's holy church.
14. Paul was as harsh with the Corinthian church for its arrogance and apathy, as he was with the perverted immorality of the sinning man. For the church to do nothing about persistent immorality is as sinful as to do the immoral act!

APPREHENSIONS:

1. Why are sexual relationships between immediate members of a family wrong?
2. Is Paul correct in saying that incest was not even found among pagans?
3. What does Paul mean by saying the Corinthian Christians were arrogant?
4. What would Paul expect the church to do if they followed his instructions and "removed" the one who had done this sin among them?

CHAPTER 5　　　　　　　　　FIRST CORINTHIANS 5:9-13

5. How could Paul be absent from Corinth in the body but present with them in spirit to the extent that he would be judging the man?
6. Why did Paul equate excommunication with delivering someone to Satan?
7. What did Paul expect to be the result of delivering this man to Satan?
8. What is "destruction of the flesh"?
9. Why does Paul liken the Christian life to the Passover feast?
10. What is sincerity?
11. Why would Paul say it was all right for Christians to associate with the immoral men of this world and not all right to associate with immoral people who bear the name of brethren?
12. Is sexual sin the only sin demanding non-association when found in one bearing the name of a brother? What others? Does the church follow this apostolic doctrine?
13. How do you reconcile Paul's command here for Christians to judge one another, and Jesus' command (Matt. 7:1ff.) not to judge one another?

A SPECIAL BRIEF ON CHURCH DISCIPLINE

"For if the message declared by angels (the Old Testament law) was valid and every transgression or disobedience received a just retribution, how shall we escape if we neglect such a great salvation?" Heb. 2:2-3

A. Causes for discipline in the New Testament.
　1. Refusal to repent of a wrongdoing to a brother, Matt. 18:15ff.
　2. Being the instigator of dissensions and difficulties in the church, Rom. 16:17; Titus 3:10-11
　3. Laziness in personal life, II Thess. 3:6
　4. Preaching false doctrine, Rom. 16:17-18; II John 9-11
　5. Immorality in a member, I Cor. 5:1-7
　6. Anyone who is greedy, an idolater, reviler, drunkard, or thief, I Cor. 5:11 (I Cor. 6:9-10).

B. Purpose of discipline
　1. To save the sinning member, I Cor. 5:5; II Cor. 2:1-11; Gal. 6:1-10; Matt. 18:15; James 5:19-20; Jude 22
　2. To maintain the honor and authority of Jesus Christ
　3. To preserve the purity and reputation of the church before the world (not absolute, for that is impossible in this world). When the church is compared to the world, it must be *different!* The church must not tolerate flagrant, impenitent sinfulness in any member.

FIRST CORINTHIANS

C. Method of discipline
   1. By expression (teaching) and repression (disfellowshiping)
   2. First, go to the brother in personal counsel (Gal. 6:1; Rom. 15:1; Matt. 18:15). It is divisive and schismatic to go to anyone else first.
   3. This failing, take with you one or two elders so that evidence of sin and impenitence may be established by witnesses (cf. II Cor. 13:1).
   4. This failing, a meeting of the church should meditate the problem and make a decision as a congregation. If the offender refuses to comply with the congregational decision, he should be disfellowshiped, excommunicated, "driven out," not even socialized with, having nothing to do with him (I Cor. 5:2, 13; II Thess. 3:6, 14; Titus 3:10-11; II John 10-11).

D. Manner of discipline
   1. Gentleness and humility must always characterize administration of any discipline (Gal. 6:1ff.; Col. 3:12-13; I Tim. 5:22, etc.)
   2. According to the guidelines of scripture
   3. Firmly, faithfully, without partiality, steadily and constantly
   4. With wisdom and sound judgment; with clear thinking controlling one's emotions.

Chapter Six

THE PROBLEM OF BASENESS AND BROTHERHOOD (6:1-20)

IDEAS TO INVESTIGATE:

1. What kind of "grievances" would Christian brethren have against one another? 6:1
2. Why does Paul insist that they not sue one another in civil court? 6:1ff.
3. How could Paul advise Christians to accept being defrauded? 6:7
4. What has the list of depraved sinners to do with this context? 6:9-10
5. If a man joins himself to a prostitute is he married to her? 6:16

SECTION 1

Defrauders Are Not Brothers (6:1-8)

6 When one of you has a grievance against a brother, does he dare go to law before the unrighteous instead of the the saints? ²Do you not know that the saints will judge the world? And if the world is to be judged by you, are you incompetent to try trivial cases? ³Do you not know that we are to judge angels? How much more, matters pertaining to this life! ⁴If then you have such cases, why do you lay them before those who are least esteemed by the church? ⁵I say this to your shame. Can it be that there is no man among you wise enough to decide between members of the brotherhood, ⁶but brother goes to law against brother, and that before unbelievers?

7 To have lawsuits at all with one another is defeat for you. Why not rather suffer wrong? Why not rather be defrauded? ⁸But you yourselves wrong and defraud, and that even your own brethren.

6:1 Squabbles: Chapter six is very evidently continuing the train of thought from chapter five. The apostle had just dealt with judging and settling disputes which must be done *within* the kingdom of God. In chapter five the problem is sexual immorality; Christians are commanded to judge and take action to solve the problem. In chapter six the problem is Christians suing one another in pagan law-courts.

FIRST CORINTHIANS

And again, Christians are commanded to judge themselves and take the action necessary to bring about a solution.

The word *grievance* (RSV), or *matter* (KJV), is *pragma* in the Greek text. *Pragma* is the word from which we get the English words *pragmatic* and *pragmatism*. Its generic meaning is, work, deed, event, or occurrence. The word *pragma* is used frequently, however, in ancient Greek writings (Xenophon, Josephus, the payri) to denote a civil law-suit with someone. *Pragma* was the technical term for a litigation.

It is unfortunate that an arbitrary division of this context has been made by those who, centuries ago, numbered chapters and verses. Such division tends to divert attention away from the fact that Paul is still talking about the same fundamental problem. That problem is the irresponsibility of the ancient Corinthian congregation of Christians to maintain scriptural standards of righteousness, justice and mercy.

We do not know with certainty what the "grievances" were between the brethren. They were probably disputes over properties. It is doubtful that they would have taken the case of the incestuous man to the civil courts for settlement. We do know that by the middle of the first century, A.D., Rome had saturated all her subjected provinces (which included Greece) with Roman law and its procedures. Of all ancient peoples the Romans were the most prone to litigation. Any man could make himself a prosecutor in a Roman court. Each party to a litigation deposited with the magistrate a sum of money (called *sacramentum*), which was forfeited by the losing party to the state religion. The defendant also had to give bail (*vadimonium*) as security for his subsequent appearances. The magistrate then turned over the dispute to a person qualified to act as a judge. If the defendant lost, his property—sometimes his person—could be seized by the plaintiff until the judgment was satisfied. Problems of ownership, obligation, exchange, contract, and debt took up by far the largest part of Roman law. Material possession was the very life of the Roman empire, and its provinces. This would be especiallly true in cosmopolitan and commercial Corinth. Ownership of property came by inheritance or acquisition. The making of valid wills was complicated with hundreds of legal restrictions. No heir might take any part of an estate without assuming all the debts and other legal obligations of the deceased. Acquisition came by transfer, or by legal conveyance resulting from a suit at law. Transfer (*mancipatio*, "Taking in hand") was a formal gift or sale before witnesses and with scales struck by a copper ingot as token of a sale; without this ancient ritual no exchange had the sanction or protection of the law. Obligation was any compulsion by law to the performance of an act. It could arise by delict or by contract. Delicts or torts—noncontractural wrongs committed against a person or his property—were in many cases punished by an obligation to pay the injured person a sum of money in compensation. Obviously, there would be *many* "grievances" which might arise between Christian brethren engaged in the multiple vocations and businesses which would be present in the huge, sophisticated metropolis called Corinth.

6:1-6 Shamefulness: There are a number of reasons the apostle shames the Corinthians in this matter: (a) in verse one he uses the Greek word *tolma* which means presumptuous, audacious, bold (see its use in II Peter 2:10). They have *presumed against* the power of Christ to settle these disputes and have taken them to heathen judges; (b) Christians are to judge the heathen world, not vice versa—they are showing their unworthiness to be Christians by declaring their incompetence to judge their own disputes. Just how are the saints to judge the world (v. 2)? Christians living by faith in Jesus Christ in this present world are judging this world (declaring it to be condemned) by their obedience to God's Word (see Heb. 11:7). Every Christian who preaches or teaches the gospel pronounces judgment upon those who do not. There is no other way to deliver the gospel (see Rev. 14:6-7). But in a real sense, also, the resurrected saints will have some part in the eternal judgment of the lost world. Perhaps that judgment will be simply a vindication of Christian choices made on earth (cf. Luke 11:32), or maybe it will be some form of active participation with Christ as Christians *rule* with Him (see Rev. 2:26-27; 3:21) in eternity; perhaps both. Peter indicates that the godly behavior of the Christians, before their heathen contemporaries, will provide a vindication for the Christians should there be any charges made against them at the day of judgment (I Peter 2:11-12, 15). Now, if these Corinthian Christians are incapable of acting like Christians toward one another and producing justice, are they not declaring themselves to be incompetent to fulfill their destiny to judge the world with justice? Shame upon them! (c) Christians are to judge angels; Paul does not say how or when; we would speculate this refers to the angels who "left their first estate" (rebelled against God in heaven) and are being held temporarily in the "pits of nether gloom" (II Peter 2:4; Jude 6); Paul does say the manifold wisdom of God will be made known to the "principalities and powers in the heavenly places" through the church (Eph. 3:10); it may be, as T. R. Applebury wrote: ". . . the church is God's means of demonstrating to the angels that rebelled . . . that some men will serve Him out of their love for Him. The church

FIRST CORINTHIANS

is made up of those who deliberately choose to do God's will and refuse to do the bidding of Satan. If men can do this, angels certainly could have done so. The character and conduct of the saints then become a means of judging angels that sinned." (*op cit* pg. 105); if Christians are to judge these cosmic, spiritual and eternal matters, how much more are they obligated to discipline themselves to make proper judgments between themselves in this life! (d) They lay their brotherhood disputes before heathen judges who have no place in the church; Paul uses the Greek participle *exouthenemenous* which is translated by the RSV as *those who are least esteemed* but would be more properly translated as *those who are rejected or condemned by the church*—in other words the Corinthian Christians are asking judges who are alienated and opposed to the church to judge matters that would require a mentality and spirituality completely foreign to them; Shame upon them! (e) In so doing these Corinthian Christians are declaring to the world that the wisdom Christians are supposed to have is not as good as that of heathen judges; they cannot seem to find one of their own brethren wise enough to settle disputes between themselves; even brothers by natural birth are often able to settle disputes between themselves without recourse to civil law courts; but in Corinth it was *Christian* brother against *Christian* brother, and that in courts where unbelieving judges sat!

Christians should obey all the laws (which do not demand direct and certain disobedience *against* God) of their governments. All transactions requiring legal sanction by a civil government should be submitted to such sanction. And Christians are not prohibited from recourse to civil court when it is necessary to defend themselves against heathen accusers. At Philippi, Paul demanded his rights as a Roman citizen against ungodly and unjust treatment (Acts 16:37); he did the same before Festus (Acts 25:10). But Christian brethren should not have to bring civil suit against one another to obtain justice when there is a grievance. Let Christian brethren first do what is fair and honest and just; let them settle any dispute between themselves, then, if civil law requires it, let it be legally sanctioned in civil court. The law is for the ungodly—not for the godly (I Tim. 1:8). Christians should never have to resort to civil law to arrive at what is fair, honest and just between themselves. Civil law should be resorted to only as a secondary sanction of the justice already accomplished between Christian brethren! And this is to apply in every area of Christian life—transfers of property, accidental harm done, services performed, etc. In every circumstance the Christian's first concern is *not* "What will it cost me?—Will I make a profit?—Shall I accept responsibility for my error?" but, "Have I been fair, honest, and just—Have I given what my brother rightly deserves?"

6:7-8 Solutions: The apostle has already suggested (v. 5) that since it appears they cannot settle these disputes between themselves, they should select a "man among you wise enough" to decide between members of the brotherhood. That would be the first suggestion to bring a solution to their incompetency. But who, among them, would be wise enough? He should be well-trained in what the Word of God says in the areas of ethical absolutes and principles. He should know what the Scriptures say about brotherly relationships. He should be old enough to have had much practical experience in the circumstances of life and interpersonal relationships. Ordinarily, it would be the responsibility of elders and/or evangelists (see epistles to Timothy and Titus) to arbitrate and bring about reconciliation between disputing Christian brethren. But any wise Christian should be able to function in this capacity.

The second solution Paul offers is that a Christian would be much better off to allow himself to be defrauded by a brother than to quarrel over grievances to the point of bringing suit in a pagan civil court. When Christians take one another to a heathen judge, rather than being able to settle between themselves, it smacks of some underlying greed or spirit of retaliation. Whether that be the case or not, two Christians suing one another in civil court is taken by the world to mean that Christians are no different than greedy and spiteful heathen. Paul clearly states that for Christians to sue one another in pagan court is *defeating* (Gr. *hettema*, loss, detriment, overthrow)—it brings discredit on the church and the gospel. When Christians cannot settle a grievance between themselves, one of them should be willing to suffer personal abuse, injury or loss rather than let the church be defeated in its mission to bring men to Christ! That is not easy—but that is what Christ, Himself, did! Nowhere does the New Testament say the Christian cannot appeal to the civil courts for redress and justice when he is wrongfully sued by an unbeliever. In fact, a number of scriptures (the clearest being Rom. 12:14—13:7) tells the Christian that when he has done all he can to be at peace with all men. If an unbeliever persists in an unjust action, the Christian is to leave the wrath of God up to the civil authorities for execution.

But all members of the kingdom of God are expected to think and act as regenerated, reborn people. They should act toward *one another* as Jesus taught in the Sermon on The Mount. While force and law is for the ungodly, the Sermon on The Mount characterizes the citizens of God's kingdom. The kind of brotherly love that would rather accept

FIRST CORINTHIANS

being defrauded by a Christian brother than to sue him in civil court is taught in a number of New Testament passages (see Col. 3:12-13; Rom. 15:1-2; I Peter 2:20; 3:8-15; Phil. 2:3-4). This is as relevant today as it was when Paul wrote it. The word of God abides forever!

SECTION 2

Debauched Are Not Brothers (6:9-11)

9 Do you not know that the unrighteous will not inherit the kingdom of God? Do not be deceived; neither the immoral, nor idolaters, nor adulterers, nor sexual perverts, 10nor thieves, nor the greedy, nor drunkards, nor revilers, nor robbers will inherit the kingdom of God. 11 And such were some of you. But you were washed, you were sanctified, you were justified in the name of the Lord Jesus Christ and in the Spirit of our God.

6:9-10 Reprobation: Clearly, Paul is classifying those who are taking brotherhood grievances to civil courts as some of the "unrighteous" who shall not inherit the kingdom of God! The Greek word *adikoi* may be translated either *unrighteous* or *unjust*—the two English words mean the same. It is frightening to contemplate that those who would rather defraud a brother than be defrauded are categorized with the debauched but that is precisely what Paul is doing here.

Those who *defraud* are as abominable to God as the *immoral,* the *idolater,* the *homosexual,* the *effeminate,* the *thief,* the *greedy,* the *drunkard,* the *reviler,* and the *robber*. All these "unrighteous" ones (except the homosexual and the effeminate) are listed earlier by Paul as alien to the kingdom of God and unacceptable as citizens (5:9-13). The Greek word *arsenokoites* is a combination of *arsen,* male, and *koite* (Eng. *coitus*), sexual intercourse, and is translated *homosexual*. The Greek text here includes the word *malakoi,* literally meaning, "soft to the touch," but used metaphorically in the New Testament to mean male effeminacy in a practicing homosexual. The word *malakoi* was used by classical Greek writers near the first century A.D. to denote *catamites* (men and boys who allowed themselves to be misused homosexually). Homosexual behavior is not sickness—it is sin! Why would the act of suing a Christian brother in a heathen court be counted such a serious crime by the apostle? Because it is a deliberate rejection of the very essence of God's kingdom. It is a refusal of the principle of self-denial. Anyone who refuses to put self to death, allowing Christ to live in him, is not worthy of the kingdom (see Luke 12:13-31; 14:25-33; 16:10-15; John 12:20-25; 15:12-14; Gal. 2:20; 5:13; 5:24-26, etc.). It is the love of Christ which is to control every Christian. Christians are *never* to consider one another from the world's point of view (II Cor. 5:14-21). When Christians are unwilling to settle any grievance they have with one another, even if it means being defrauded, it means they are unwilling to surrender to the sovereign will of Christ and are not fit to inherit His kingdom. Paul told these Corinthian brethren they were being *led astray* (Gr. *planasthe,* wandering stars, planets), in their unmerciful, non-Christian actions of suing one another in heathen courts.

6:11 Regeneration: These straying Christians, in their present shameful, defeating, unrighteous behavior unfit for the kingdom, are reminded they do not have to remain disinherited. Some of them were once before living debauched and ungodly lives. Paul is warning them not to continue in this *fallen* condition, lest they be lost. It *is* possible to fall from grace after having once been "washed, sanctified and justified" (see Gal. 5:1-26). Paul considers them, in their present conditions, as "unrighteous" and not heirs of the kingdom. But he exhorts them (by inference) to repent and return to the state of being sanctified and justified.

It is well to note here that the *order* of the regenerative process harmonizes with what the rest of the New Testament says about it. *First,* the Corinthians believed and were baptized ("washed"), *then* they were pronounced sanctified and justified, (see Acts 2:38; 18:8; 22:16; Rom. 6:5ff.; Gal. 3:26-27; Col. 2:12-13; I Peter 1:22-25). The Greek verb *apelousasthe* is 2nd plural aorist middle, and might be literally translated "you were washed clean." The word is a combination of two Greek words, *apo* ("from") and *louo* ("washed"). The verb *louo* and its various forms are often used metaphorically for baptism (see Acts 22:16; Eph. 5:26; Titus 3:5; Heb. 10:22). The believer's obedience to Christ's command to be baptized (see Matt. 28:18-20) is the initial and fundamental act of faith through which God has chosen to judicially declare a believer both sanctified and justified. It is at this point in the believer's calling upon God that he has his sins washed away (Acts 22:16), is saved (I Peter 3:21; Titus 3:5), is made a member of Christ's church (Eph. 5:26), is joined to Christ and justified (Gal. 3:23-29), is sanctified (Eph. 5:26). Without surrender to the command of Christ and the Holy Spirit (through the apostles) to baptism there is no promise of cleansing, salvation, justification or sanctification.

FIRST CORINTHIANS

While these Corinthian Christians had previously been baptized, sanctified and justified, they were not presently considered in a sanctified and justified state of the apostle. One who is aware that he is sinning, after having been once baptized, must appeal to the grace of God by repentance and prayer (Heb. 10:19-25; I John 1:8—2:6). To be an heir of the kingdom of God *after* initial admittance through belief and baptism, one must *continue* in sanctification and justification, which is done through daily repentance and prayer. *Repentance* is from the Greek word *metanoeo* which means changing the mind and actions. *Sanctification* is from the Greek word *hagiasmos* which means, set apart unto God, or dedicated to God. Justification is from the Greek word *dikaiosis* and means, to declare right, to declare innocent, to acquit of guilt. God is able to declare sinners innocent of guilt because Christ vicariously atoned for all sin upon the cross. This is established as a fact by the historical resurrection of Jesus Christ from the dead. But God cannot declare any sinner innocent who will not accept that declaration of grace. God has decreed that any sinner who wishes this free gift of grace (declaration of innocence from all guilt) must do so by believing Christ's death paid for his sin and by submitting to the ordinance of baptism. When the sinner accepts God's offer, on God's terms, he is set apart to God's will in his life. Of course, a washed, justified, sanctified person may renounce his inheritance and return to the former state of alienation and impenitence (II Peter 2:20-22). That, says Paul, is what these Corinthians were doing by refusing to settle their grievances with one another on Christian principles.

"In the name of the Lord Jesus Christ and in the Spirit of our God" simply means these Corinthians had been previously washed, justified and sanctified under the *authority* of and by the *agency* of Christ and the Holy Spirit. That authority and that agency is the *word* of Christ in the apostolic message. There is no indication in the New Testament that the Holy Spirit operates or leads in any extra-Biblical manifestation in the matter of salvation, justification and/or sanctification. The Holy Spirit's will in these matters is contained in and operates through His revealed Word. That Word is the Bible—nothing less and nothing more! The oral teachings of Christ and the apostles were the first revelations of the Holy Spirit's will for salvation, justification and sanctification. Later, their spoken doctrines were committed to writing. These apostolic documents have the same authority and power as their oral teachings did. These written words of the apostles (and the Old Testament before them) form the completed, canonized Word of God—the will of the Spirit of Truth. They are all

CHAPTER 6 — FIRST CORINTHIANS 6:12-20

the world needs for salvation, justification and sanctification. Nothing must be taken away from these writings and nothing must be added to them. *All* things that pertain to life and godliness are in his precious promises (II Peter 1:3-5).

SECTION 3

Defilers Are Not Brothers (6:12-20)

12 "All things are lawful for me," but not all things are helpful. "All things are lawful for me," but I will not be enslaved by anything. 13 "Food is meant for the stomach and the stomach for food"—and God will destroy both one and the other. The body is not meant for immorality, but for the Lord, and the Lord for the body. 14 And God raised the Lord and will also raise us up by his power. 15 Do you not know that your bodies are members of Christ? Shall I therefore take the members of Christ and make them members of a prostitute? Never! 16 Do you not know that he who joins himself to a prostitute becomes one body with her? For, as it is written, "The two shall become one flesh." 17 But he who is united to the Lord becomes one spirit with him. 18 Shun immorality. Every other sin which a man commits is outside the body; but the immoral man sins against his own body. 19 Do you not know that your body is a temple of the Holy Spirit within you, which you have from God? You are not your own; 20 you were bought with a price. So glorify God in your body.

6:12-14 Perversion of Humanness: Brotherly love acknowledges there is a lawful purpose for all things which God has created, but using the body for immorality (including hatred, greed and unchristian lawsuits) is perverting and downgrading that which God made to be the residence of the Holy Spirit. The last section *does* connect to the beginning admonition concerning unchristian lawsuits. It teaches that Christians who become enslaved to their emotions and feelings and drag one another bodily before heathen tribunals for their ungodly purposes of greed and retaliation are "prostituting" themselves. When God created man and gave him a human body, it was intended that God's Holy Spirit would dwell with each man in that body.

The apostolic principle, "All things are lawful, but not all things are helpful . . ." must be understood in its *context*. When a Christian brother defrauds you, it is lawful (you have the right) to sue him in a civil court—but such action is not always helpful (or, edifying). Christians are to live above the plane of law in the kingdom of grace. Christians are not to seek their own good, but the good of their neighbors (I Cor. 10:24); they are not to look only to their own interest, but also to the interests of others (Phil. 2:4); they are to please their neighbors for their good, to edify them (Rom. 15:2). Therefore, the Christian has the responsibility of denying any "right" he has to build people up in Christ rather than perverting these things to destroy people.

Some ancient Greek philosophers (especially the Gnostics) held that mind and thought were spiritual and holy while material things, including the human body, were impersonal and thus amoral. These philosophers taught that the natural, physical and material processes of life had *no* moral significance. Suing one another in court over physical and material things would have no moral implications according to this philosophy. Apparently some of the "wise" Christians of Corinth had decided to practice the philosophy of the Gnostics.

Paul had twice listed ways in which material things, including the human body, might be perverted (I Cor. 5:9-11; 6:7-10) and which would cause the Christian to forfeit his spiritual inheritance. That would include greed and robbery and reviling a brother in the matter of civil law suits. And it would most definitely include sexual promiscuity, which is the first subject in the context of chapters five and six.

So, as Paul wrote about Christians suing one another in heathen courts and assuming, like the Gnostics, that they might do as they pleased with material things without sinning, his thoughts were directed back to the subject of sexual promiscuity. Sexual abandon and all forms of unnatural perversion were the norm for most of first century Greco-Roman society. This is evidenced in ancient art and literature. We quote here from William Barclay:

> The Greeks always looked down on the body. . . . That produced one of two attitudes. Either it issued in the most rigorous aceticism in which everything was done to subject and humiliate the desires and instincts of the body. Or—and in Corinth it was this second outlook which was prevalent—it was taken to mean that, since the body was of no importance, you could do what you liked with it; you could let it sate its appetites. What complicated this was the doctrine of Christian freedom which Paul preached. If the Christian man is the freest of all men, then is he not free to do what he likes, especially with this completely unimportant body of his?

CHAPTER 6 FIRST CORINTHIANS 6:12-20

So, the Corinthians argued, in a way that they thought very enlightened, let the body have its way. But what is the body's way? The stomach was made for food and food for the stomach, they went on. Food and the stomach naturally and inevitably go together. In precisely the same way the body is made for its instincts; it is made for the sexual act and the sexual act is made for it; therefore let the desires of the body have their way.

Another element in the heathen culture of Greco-Roman society Paul had to deal with was the matter of religion and human behavior. Heathen gods were what men made them. Naturally, when they disavowed the true God's revelation of his infinitely holy character and exchanged that truth for a lie (Rom. 1:18ff.) they supplied their own human characteristics to gods of their own making. Religion, to the heathen, was, and still is, a way to appease, cajole, and prevail against their gods until the gods are won over to the human's desire to do as he pleases. To the heathen, the human was relatively free to behave as he pleased so long as he did not anger the gods or the civil authorities. He could very easily appease the gods by making the right offerings and observing the superstitious rituals. So long as he paid his taxes, and did not participate in treason or revolution he could please the civil authorities. The Christian doctrine of freedom limited by morality and self-sacrifice was in absolute opposition to heathen selfishness.

Thus, Paul sets out to clarify the doctrine of Christian freedom as opposed to the philosophy and practice of heathen permissiveness. It is the teaching of Christ and his apostles that everything God has created is good (Gen. 1:10, 18, 25, 31; Acts 10:15; I Cor. 10:26; I Tim. 4:1-5) if used according to the precepts and principles revealed in God's word. There is a created purpose for the human longing for justice so long as it is not allowed to degenerate into a spirit of exploitation, hatred and retaliation. There is a God-ordained purpose for the physical appetite for food so long as it is controlled and not allowed to degenerate into gluttony. There is a God-ordained purpose for the desire for sexual intercourse as long as the desire is not permitted to deteriorate into adultery, fornication and homosexuality. Sexual intercourse was created by God but he never intended it to be casual, amoral and promiscuous. The longings and desires of the human being created for this earthly life have their limitations. They are for the present world order. They are created by God in order to test, discipline and prepare men during this earthly probation for existence in the next life.

FIRST CORINTHIANS

One of the principles under which these human longings are to be controlled is that while all things created by God are lawful, all things are not, in certain circumstances, helpful. Some things created by God, under some circumstances, are harmful. And, as Paul clearly says, whatever would enslave a person, under any circumstances, would be harmful. Food, drugs, sexuality, emotions, material possessions—all are lawful, good and helpful if controlled and limited by the revealed principles of God's word. But even these good and helpful things become harmful if man allows himself to be enslaved, possessed and obsessed by them, or when he abuses them beyond the limitations of God's directions. Paul uses the Greek word *exousiasthesomai* which is translated *enslaved* and means, more precisely, *ruled over by*. For the apostle it is Christ who rules over him—not his emotions, not food, not sexuality, and not material possessions. He is a slave to the will of Christ.

These Christians of Corinth, attempting to be sophisticated and follow popular Gnosticism, were apparently teaching that the appetite for sexual intercourse was merely a physical thing like the appetite for food. Paul makes it very clear that these two human functions do not belong in the same category. The statement, "Food is meant for the stomach and the stomach for food" is correct, so long as man is not enslaved by food and becomes a glutton. What a man eats, so long as he is not obsessed with food, has no spiritual significance. Jesus and his apostles made that clear: (a) food has no spiritual significance even if it has been sacrificed to an idol, because an idol is not god (see I Cor. 8:1—10:33); (b) food has no power in and of itself to make a man spiritually clean or unclean—it is the attitude of the heart that makes clean or unclean (cf. Matt. 15:1-20; Mark 7:14-23); (c) human opinions as to which foods may be eaten and which may not is of no spiritual significance (Rom. 14:1-4; I Tim. 4:1-4; Col. 2:20-23) until someone attempts to make abstinence or indulgence a test of Christian fellowship. It is clear a man cannot be spiritually defiled by what he eats or what he does not eat, so long as it does no physical harm to the human body. There may be one exception to this in the Christian dispensation (see Acts 15:19-20; 21:25). The human function of eating and digesting food is purely a physical process and has no spiritual significance. It is for this life only. When this life is over neither food or the human stomach, as we know them now, will continue to exist. But the "body" is different!

It must be clear that Paul is using the word *body* (Gr. *soma*) in a sense intended to mean *more* than flesh and bone and blood. The Greek word in the New Testament which most often means *flesh and*

CHAPTER 6   FIRST CORINTHIANS 6:12-20

bone is *sarx*. *Vine's Expository Dictionary* says of the New Testament usage of the word *soma,* or *body*:

> SOMA . . . is the body as a whole, the instrument of life, whether of man living, e.g., Matt. 6:22, or dead, Matt. 27:52; or in resurrection, I Cor. 15:44; or of beasts, Heb. 13:11; of grain, I Cor. 15:37, 38; of the heavenly hosts, I Cor. 15:40. In Rev. 18:13 it is translated "slaves." In its figurative uses the essential idea is preserved.
>
> Sometimes the word stands, by *synecdoche,* for the complete man, Matt. 5:29; 6:22; Rom. 12:1; James 3:6; Rev. 18:13. Sometimes the person is identified with his or her body, Acts 9:37; 13:36, and this is so even of the Lord Jesus, John 19:40 with 42. The body is not the man, for he himself can exist apart from his body, 2 Cor. 12:2, 3. The body is an essential part of the man and therefore the redeemed are not perfected till the resurrection, Heb. 11:40; no man in his final state will be without his body, John 5:28, 29; Rev. 20:13.

Soma as Paul used it here means man in his total existence in this world. Man is more than body, but he *is* body. It is through the body that the personality, the spiritual man, functions and operates in relationship to God and his fellow man. It is difficult for people of western culture to think of the body as the person. We tend to think of the body as a group of fleshly organs that will die and decompose in the grave. It is true, Paul spoke this way of the stomach, but to the Oriental (eastern) mind (including the Hebrew) the term *body* most often was associated with the *self*. So, in this section, we might correctly paraphrase the apostle by using either the word "self" or "man." Man is both body and soul (or spirit). In the New Testament *soul* describes man in his thinking, feeling, willing capacities; *body* describes man as an acting, functioning, personality living in this world in relationship to his Creator and other creatures. The body is the extension of and instrument through which the soul is expressed.

Man was not made for immorality. Man in his totality was made for the Lord. God made man to function and express self or soul in this existence through his body. Thus, the human body has, as it were, a spiritual purpose. In and through our bodies we are to serve and glorify Christ. Man, in his totality—body and soul—was made to serve and exhibit truth, purity, holiness, and goodness (the character of God). Man was *not* made with a body to abuse it in selfish, hurtful, degrading and false practices. The stomach was made for good, but man in his totality was made for God. Paul is certainly aware that some men may make their bellies their gods (Rom. 16:18; Phil. 3:19) so he is *not* saying in this text that there is no possibility of sinful abuse of the stomach and food. He *is* saying the Gnostic philosophy which says the sexual appetite is just like the appetite for food, a totally natural function, is *false.* He is saying man is *not* as free to satisfy the sexual desire as he is the desire for food.

The apostle had undoubtedly taught the Corinthians in his earlier visits that the Old Testament legislation about "sinful" foods had been fulfilled in the Gospel and they were "free" to eat anything that was not physically harmful. It is certain that he had previously taught them they were free in Christ from all opinions and superstitions of paganism. But now he sets out upon a five-chapter dissertation (ch. 6-10) concerning the limitations of Christian freedom. Clearly, the Corinthians had been twisting his earlier teaching about liberty to mean they were free to be totally abandoned to whatever fleshly appetite they might feel urged. Paul seeks to correct that by a concise and clear statement of the divine purpose for the human body.

6:15-20 Purpose of Humanness: The stomach was meant for food, but not for complete dietary abandon. Eating must be controlled. Gluttony is a perversion of the body and a sin. But in eating there is no intimate spiritual involvement with another person. Human sexual organs were meant for sexual intercourse. But they were not made to be given over to complete sexual abandon. Sexuality must be controlled. Sexual promiscuity is a perversion of the body and a sin. But there is more than mere physical function involved in sexual intercourse. In sexual intercourse two beings are spritually or psychologically *joined* or united in a mutual purpose.

Paul begins his explanation of the purpose of humanness by declaring that Christians are supposed to have given their bodies (selves, persons) to be united in mutuality with Christ. Christians are to be joined, spirit, soul and body (in totality) to Jesus Christ. They are married to him (Eph. 5:21-33). For the Christian to engage in sexual intercourse with someone to whom he or she is not married is not only unfaithfulness to the human spouse but is also unfaithfulness to Christ.

The person who joins with a prostitute (male or female) in sexual intercourse does more than perform a physical function. Two people who join in sexual intimacy undeniably unite psychologically or spiritually in a mutual purpose. Those who do so as married people are fulfilling a good spiritual purpose—the will of God. Those who do so outside the marriage bonds are fulfilling a mutual, spiritual purpose of rebellion against the will of God. If we translate (or paraphrase) Paul's use of the word *body* by using the word *person* or *self,* he would be saying, "Do you not know that he who joins himself to a prostitute becomes one *person* with her?" Sexual intercourse is the point in human relations at which two *persons* (not just fleshly bodies) are united in the *ultimate* human intimacy. There can be no other intimacy in human relations as deeply spiritual or as psychologically binding. Two thus joined become one! Legally, of course, there is more to marriage than the act of sexual intercourse. Spiritually and psychologically there is more to marriage than sexual intercourse. But both legally and spiritually, sexual intercourse is the act that *consummates* a marriage. A person who unites sexually with a prostitute (or in an act of adultery or fornication) is not legally married to the prostitute. Paul is *not* setting forth some technical law by which a person who joins in sexual intercourse to a harlot must forever after consider himself legally married to her. In fact, there are any number of persons, legally "married" having also consummated their marriage sexually, who are not "one" in other areas of marriage. Paul *is* saying here, with all the emphasis possible, that sexual intercourse is more than a physical function. Certain physical functions of the human body are instinctive and amoral. That is, when these functions operate they are neither good nor bad—man has no moral control over them one way or another. They operate whether he chooses for them to do so or not. Digestion is such an amoral physical function. With sexual intercourse that is not so. Man has been given moral choice and control over sexual intimacy. The Greek word *de* (translated "but" in verse 17) is a conjunctive particle "marking the superaddition of a clause, whether in opposition or in continuation, to what has preceded, and it may be variously rendered *but, on the other hand, and, also, now,* etc." We think verse 17 is a clause in *continuation* of what has preceded and not in opposition. Therefore, Paul is *likening* the intimateness of the Christian's relationship to Christ to that of two persons engaged in sexual intercourse. The Christian joins himself intimately to Christ by choice. So the person who joins himself intimately (sexually) to another person does so morally—by choice. A Christian who joins intimately (sexually) with a prostitute has taken the body (person) purchased by the sinless blood of Christ, which has been intimately joined to Christ and made a dwelling place of the Holy Spirit, and joined it in rebellion against the will of Christ and the desecration of his glory. God created man to glorify his Son. Man was not given a human body to use as an instrument of rebellion. So Paul exhorts these Christians to make deliberate choice and take deliberate action to keep from sinning with their bodies. Because of modern connotations, the RSV translation "Shun" for the Greek word *pheugete* in verse 18 is not strong enough. The KJV and the ASV give it the more emphatic translation, "Flee" fornication. The Greek word *porneia,* translated "fornication," may also be used generically for all immorality. No human being can begin to fulfill God's purpose for having created him until he is willing to flee from all immorality.

The statement "Every other sin which a man commits is outside the body; but the fornicator sins against his own body" must be interpreted in this context. Paul is clearly teaching these Corinthians that sexual intercourse is *more* than a mere physical action. Divine revelation teaches that sexual intercourse is an intimate, spiritual and psychological union of personalities, much like the spiritual union of a Christian to Christ (it is, indeed, a *marriage*). He is *not* saying that other sins have no spiritual causes or consequences. He is simply saying that other sins do not unite one person with another in such a life-affecting way as fornication. The student should immediately read Proverbs 5:8-11; 6:24-32; 7:24-27. The spiritual intimacy of the sexual relationship, when perverted contrary to the will of God, results in the destruction of the personality; especially is the person inhibited from the spiritual goals for which God created him. This may be documented today from the experiences and files of counseling psychiatrists and clergymen.

A physical function of the body is temporary. It is of the flesh and will perish with the flesh. The *use* of some physical functions, however, is a spiritual matter. The *use* of most physical functions is a matter of moral choice. To use any physical function contrary to the revealed will of its Creator is immoral. All sins abusing the physical organs are "outside" the most intimate part of our personality *except* sexual abuse. Sexual sin is against the deepest recesses of the person *inside*! This is a solemn warning to those sophisticates of the world today who would seduce mankind with the ancient Gnostic philosophy that sexual intercourse is merely a physical function and may be practiced without obedience to the word of God.

In some way, when a human being gives his body to sexual intimacy with another being, he gives it as a *residence* to the personality of that other person. When sexual intimacy is given contrary to the will of God the body becomes a residence of the "spirit of harlotry" and prostitution. God wants man to give his or her body for the residence of the Holy Spirit. This is what a person vows to do when becoming a Christian. The *whole* man (which is what Paul means in his use of

CHAPTER 6　　　　　　　　　　　　FIRST CORINTHIANS 6:12-20

the Greek word *soma*, or "body") is not to perish like food and the human stomach. Sexual promiscuity treats the *whole* man as if it were to perish! Sexual promiscuity destroys that which is eternal in man—love, faithfulness, honesty, orderliness, and righteousness. It is no accident that God symbolizes idolatry and unbelief as "harlotry" in the Old Testament. Sexual promiscuity and prostitution are so irresponsible, so exploitative, so degrading and dehumanizing in attitude and action. They treat the human body as a "thing." That is why Paul said every other sin which a man commits is outside the body but the sexually promiscuous person sins against his own body.

Paul's final explanation of and argument for the purpose of humanness concerns the human self or person (the whole man) as a potential residence of the Holy Spirit of God Almighty. Actually, it is presupposed by the apostle that God's Spirit had already taken residence in the bodies of these Corinthian Christians. Just what does Paul mean by the question, "Do you not know that your body is a temple of the Holy Spirit within you, which you have from God?" What is the phenomenon known as "the indwelling of the Holy Spirit"?

Let us first consider what, according to other New Testament passages, it *cannot* mean; (a) it cannot mean the power to perform miracles; that is specified in the New Testament as "the baptism of the Holy Spirit" and was promised only to apostles—passed on by the apostles to selected Christians of the first century only by the laying on of the hands of the apostles; some (e.g. John the Baptist) who were said to be "full of the Holy Spirit" *never* worked a miracle so far as we know; (b) it cannot mean supernatural illumination that enables those who have it to understand the scriptures; all men are created with the capacity to read human language and understand without divine illumination; the apostles were given, supernaturally, a revelation of the New will of God, but they delivered it to the whole human race in human language (see our comments on I Cor. 2:1ff.) and all sinners are expected to hear and read those apostolic words and believe *before* the Holy Spirit comes to abide with them; faith comes by hearing the word of Christ (Rom. 10:17); there would be no point in preaching, no point in sinners reading the Bible, no point even in printing Bibles if every non-Christian must wait until he is sure he has the Holy Spirit in him before he can understand the revealed will of God.

The coming of the Holy Spirit of God and Christ to take residence in the human being involves *more* than understanding, acknowledging and obeying the revealed will of the Holy Spirit in the scriptures. Apparently, it is a supranatural action on the part of God but mystical

FIRST CORINTHIANS

to man (that is, a spiritual reality neither apparent to the senses nor obvious to the intelligence). The difference between those who will *not* be raised to eternal life with Christ and those who *will* is the indwelling presence of Christ's Spirit (cf. Rom. 8:1-11). The coming of Christ's Spirit to reside in us is not something we earn or merit by our perfect obedience, but it is initiated by God's Spirit because of his grace when we give him welcome by our love and faith.

Having said it is mystical to man, however, does not preclude the fact that we can understand, acknowledge in faith, and obey the directions revealed by the Holy Spirit providing the instrumentality through which God chooses to initiate his supranatural residence in people. God's action may be mystical, but the *directions* through which he promises to act are *not* mystical. The Bible clearly teaches that faithful and loving response to the commandments of God, in any dispensation of time, will be acceptable as an invitation for the Holy Spirit to take up residence within a human being (cf. Ps. 51:10-12; John 14:15-24; 15:1-11; Acts 2:38; 5:32; Rom. 8:5; Eph. 3:17; I John 3:24; 4:12, etc.). So then, the *way* God's Spirit dwells in a person is by a person's intelligent, willing, loving submission to what God says by the Holy Spirit in the revealed Word so that what he thinks, determines, and feels is under the direction of the Spirit through the Word. In other words, the instrument or vehicle or channel through which the Holy Spirit enters and resides in our bodies (or persons) is his revealed and written Word. Apart from that process he will not function residentially in us—not initially and not continually. Clearly, Paul has been teaching from the very first of this epistle that the apostolic gospel is the exclusive matrix within which these Corinthians must be living in order to be assured of the communion (residence) of God's Spirit. God's Spirit does not reside within a person outside the communion of his Word. Christ "stands at the door and knocks"—he will not force his way in to "sup" (reside) with any who are not believing and repenting (cf. Rev. 3:19-20).

The apostle turns metaphorically to the well known practice of slavery to show the emphatic subservience of the purchased one to his purchaser. It would be a familiar experience in the first century. The slave in the Greco-Roman world was chattel, purely and simply. Slaves were bought and sold as property, and masters held total sovereignty over them. Slaves gave total allegiance and obedience to their masters lest they be punished or slain without any appeal to civil courts or magistrates. The only purpose for a slave was to serve his master's will—totally. For slaves who were purchased by good and beneficent masters, this could mean protection, security, dignity and

CHAPTER 6   FIRST CORINTHIANS 6:12-20

even happiness (see the letter to Philemon). Paul preached and wrote a great deal about the good and beneficent Master, Jesus Christ. He always considered himself, and all other Christians, as having yielded both soul and body in slavery to Christ (cf. Rom. 6:15-23). Since Christ has purchased all men through his vicarious atonement (cf. Acts 20:28; Heb. 9:12; I Peter 1:18-19; Rev. 5:9), they are expected to yield, by faith, and be his slaves for righteousness. If Christ has paid our ransom, he owns us. He actually owns us twice—first by right of having created us and second by right of having redeemed us.

The person who yields himself to become a slave of Christ has no "rights" of his own. He does not belong to himself but to Christ. The only "rights" a Christian has are those granted him in the revealed will of his Master, Jesus Christ (and that is in the Bible). Any attitude or action *not* found in Christ's revealed will is *not* permissible for the Christian. See "New Life Through Accepting Jesus' Death" in *Learning From Jesus,* by Seth Wilson, pgs. 495-503, College Press.

We who have yielded to the redemption he obtained for us are his "body" here on earth—the channels through which he works. We are "instruments" of his for accomplishing righteousness in the earth. Jesus, instead of being limited to one physical body as when he was here on earth, now acts through the bodies of his people in whom he lives. You will always find in the Bible that God works through a human body in this world. The Word became flesh and dwelt among us (John 1:1-18). The Son came in a human body to offer himself as a perfect sacrifice (Heb. 10:5-10). It was in a body that man sinned; it is in a body that we sin. It was in a body that the Son of man came to earth; it was in a body that he conquered sin which had conquered us. It was in a body that he died and rose again, and now, by his Spirit, he comes to live within the body of his people. Satan always works in this world through a body also. The only way he can thwart God's purposes is to get a body surrendered to his use, available for his diabolic power and ugly purposes. This is the question of choice in a Christian's life: shall he take that which has been purchased by Christ and made an instrument of the body of Christ, and give it to some unworthy use?—that body, the means through which God's will is to be done, and yield it to the rebellious purposes of Satan? If he does, he becomes *one* with the devil. But if he is yielded to the Lord's Spirit, he is one with the Spirit of Christ. The same Spirit which enabled Jesus Christ to live day by day in a human body and never deviate from the will of God, never yield to all the tremendous temptations of the devil, will live in us and through us as our Strengthener, too. Joined to Christ, we are able to glorify God in the body. Joined to the devil, we glorify sin in our bodies.

Thus, Paul closes his exhortation (temporarily) against the seductive Gnostic sophistry that since the body is merely physical and every physical hunger (including the sexual hunger) an amoral, uncontrollable animal instinct, there is no moral guilt in sexual promiscuity. The Gnostic sophistry tried to ignore the sins of fornication, adultery and homosexuality by calling them simply physical functions like eating food. Paul replies that the human body was created for the Lord's purpose, its destiny is to be resurrected for the Lord's purpose, therefore, human bodies are members of God's personhood. To prostitute a human body for physical purposes only (especially in sexual promiscuity like animals) would be to take what belongs to God and use it for the devil. The bodies of Christian people belong to Christ even more surely by their having professed to accept Christ's redemption. Christians have been sanctified, body and soul, to glorify Christ by yielding up their bodies (and souls) in service to righteousness.

It is a fundamental doctrine of the New Testament. We cannot go to heaven if we do not yield to it. The old Gnostic sophistry is flooding the earth again today and has even washed over the gunwales of the "ship of Zion"—carnality threatens to sink the church today. Christians must insist on the sacredness of the human body and its sanctification to the will of God, no matter how unpopular the doctrine may be.

APPLICATIONS:

1. The Bible is vitally practical. It deals with the minutiae of human existence. God even expresses his will and wisdom for guidance in the matter of squabbles and grievances.
2. Christians *must* learn to settle grievances between themselves while on earth—there will be no pagan civil courts in heaven.
3. Christians are *called* to allow (suffer) wrong to be done to them rather than cause wrong to be done to another or to Christ's church.
4. One does not have to murder someone to go to hell—just be *greedy*!
5. Homosexuality is not a disease; it is not congenital; it is not mental illness—IT IS SIN!
6. The most perverse sin may be forgiven if the sinner will trust the word of Christ and be washed, sanctified and justified.
7. There is no such thing as absolute freedom—even Christian liberty is limited to God's revealed guidelines for goodness and helpfulness.
8. Any *thing, habit* or *idea* that would rule our conduct or dictate our way of thinking contrary to Christ's will is unlawful for Christians.

CHAPTER 6   FIRST CORINTHIANS 6:12-20

9. Sexual intercourse is *not* the same as or even like eating food. It is *not* merely a physical function. It is psychologically intimate and essentially moral. It is spiritual!
10. Human *bodies* were created by God as *instruments* through which human *beings* might express love and adoration for their Creator. Although the flesh will eventually die, while it lives it is to be employed only for loving God.
11. Human *beings*, if they are willing, may have the honor of sharing their human *bodies* with the *Spirit* of Almighty God.
12. The apostle Paul's teaching about the human body and its functions is as up-to-date as today's newspaper!

APPREHENSIONS:

1. What is a "grievance"?
2. Why would Christians be suing one another in court?
3. How will saints be judging the world and angels?
4. Who are the "least esteemed" by the church?
5. Could Christians actually settle disputes with one another over property outside a civil court?
6. Why does having lawsuits with one another as Christians produce defeat?
7. Would you be willing to allow yourself to be defrauded by a Christian brother before taking him to civil court?
8. Sexual misbehavior excludes people from the kingdom of God—does financial misbehavior (thievery, robbery, greed)?
9. Can the sin of homosexuality be repented of and discontinued by accepting Christ?
10. What is meant by saying that some Corinthian homosexuals were "washed, sanctified, justified"?
11. What is meant by saying this was done "in the name of the Lord Jesus"?
12. How could *all* things be lawful for a Christian?
13. What condition is meant by the term, "enslaved"?
14. Why does Paul talk about food being meant for the stomach, etc.?
15. To what extent is a person "joined" to a prostitute when having sexual intercourse with one?
16. For what purpose did God make the human body?
17. How is every sin except sexual immorality *outside* the body?
18. How does the Holy Spirit dwell in the human body?
19. What is the price paid for us?
20. Does belonging to Christ mean we have no say about what we think and do? Who does have the "say-so"?

Chapter Seven

THE PROBLEMS OF SEXUALITY AND MARRIAGE (7:1-40)

IDEAS TO INVESTIGATE:

1. Why should we accept the advice of a bachelor (Paul) on the subject of marriage?
2. Are the "unmarried" of 7:8, 25, 32, 34, those who have *never* been married?
3. What does the word "separate" mean in 7:10, 15?
4. Since Paul had no *command* from the Lord concerning the unmarried, are we still bound to obey his "opinion"? 7:25
5. Since God saw that it was not good for man to be alone (Gen. 2:18) and created a woman to be his wife, why does Paul say he who refrains from marriage will "do better"? 7:38

SECTION 1

The Purity of Marriage (7:1-9)

7 Now concerning the matters about which you wrote. It is well for a man not to touch a woman. ²But because of the temptation to immorality, each man should have his own wife and each woman her own husband. ³The husband should give to his wife her conjugal rights, and likewise the wife to her husband. ⁴For the wife does not rule over her own body, but the husband does; likewise the husband does not rule over his own body, but the wife does. ⁵Do not refuse one another except perhaps by agreement for a season, that you may devote yourselves to prayer; but then come together again, lest Satan tempt you through lack of self-control. ⁶I say this by way of concession, not of command. ⁷I wish that all were as I myself am. But each has his own special gift from God, one of one kind and one of another.

8 To the unmarried and the widows I say that it is well for them to remain single as I do. ⁹But if they cannot exercise self-control, they should marry. For it is better to marry than to be aflame with passion.

7:1a Provocation for This Discussion: Paul was not married when he wrote this epistle to the Corinthians (see 7:7-8). Many people have

CHAPTER 7　　　　　　　　　　FIRST CORINTHIANS 7:1-9

difficulty accepting advice on marriage from a bachelor. It is possible that Paul had previously been married. Some scholars think Paul implies a former marriage by his question in I Corinthians 9:5 about his right to be accompanied by a wife as other apostles did. It is doubtful that he could have been a member of the Sanhedrin (if he was) had he been unmarried. This chapter does seem to be written by someone who knew by *experience* the intimacies and problems of married life. He may have been a widower. And no one has ever glorified marriage more than the apostle Paul (cf. Eph. 5:22-23). His great tribute to Timothy's mother and grandmother shows something of the esteem with which he looked upon marriage and the home. But whether he was married or not makes no difference. He was an apostle of the Lord Jesus Christ and therefore what he teaches, even about marriage, is to be believed, trusted and obeyed.

The Christians of Corinth had previously written to Paul asking questions about sexuality and marriage. These questions would have been provoked by their constant exposure to three conflicting ideologies in respect to sexuality and marriage: (1) Jewish Christians in the Corinthian church would consider celibacy inimical to godliness. The idea of not marrying was so foreign to the Jewish mentality that the Old Testament does not even have a word for "bachelor." The godly life for the Jew meant not only marriage, but children; (2) Apparently there was already some kind of Christian asceticism or monasticism among some Christians at Corinth. They believed that the most "spiritual" people were those who were celibates. Some were teaching that those who abstained from physical marriage were the holiest of people, and if men and women insisted on marriage they should unite only in a "spiritual" marriage, a sort of Christian "brother-sister" platonic relationship. Such a marriage would not permit sexual intercourse. Paul warned Timothy that such a teaching was a "denial of the faith" and "demonic" in origin (I Tim. 4:1-5). The same apostle wrote, "Let marriage be held in honor among all, and let the marriage bed be undefiled . . ." (Heb. 13:4), and, ". . . each one of you know how to take a wife for himself in holiness and honor . . ." (I Thess. 4:4). This has been an ever recurring departure from scriptural truth. One large segment of Christendom today teaches that celibacy is the holiest state of all and that those who minister must be unmarried; (3) and finally, these Christians of Corinth were trying to practice the holiness of the gospel surrounded by the loose and wicked morals of Greco-Roman culture. Rape,

FIRST CORINTHIANS

fornication, homosexuality and other perversions were glorified in the theatre and in the cultic religions of that world. From the context of this chapter, it appears these three cultural factors provoked the Christians at Corinth to "write" to the apostle for his inspired guidance.

7:1b-2 Pressure of Desire: Paul's statement, "It is well for a man not to a touch a woman . . ." uses the Greek present middle infinitive, *haptesthai,* for the word *touch*. This word, in the middle voice, would be more accurately translated, "cling to, fasten oneself to, assimilate to oneself." In other words, Paul is not stating that men should never touch a woman at all—he was revealing (because of stressful circumstances at the time he wrote) that the wisest thing for a man to do was not "fasten" himself to a woman in marriage. Paul's command, as is clear later in the context, hinges entirely on the circumstances Christians were about to face in the Roman persecutions (7:26).

But there is an even stronger stress that might override the dreadful separation of husband and wife by martyrdom. That stress would be the drive to fulfill the human sexual urge (7:2, 5, 9, 36). God created the sexual drive in mankind, and it is good so long as it is fulfilled within biblically sanctioned marriage. So Paul writes, "But because of fornication (the word for *temptation* is not in the Greek text), each man should have his own wife and each woman her own husband." Sexual immorality (fornication) was not only practiced almost universally in first century Greco-Roman society, it was glorified in art and religion. Paul plainly states that one, (if not *the* one) primary reason for marriage is to guard against succumbing to the temptation for illicit sexual intercourse! He reemphasizes this in verses 8-9. The Greek verb *echeto,* translated "have," is in the imperative mood, and means Paul is giving a *command* here—not simply making a suggestion. Now, of course, Paul did not think relaxation from the temptation to illicit sexual intercourse was the *only* basis upon which Christian marriage is founded. He certainly emphasizes *agape* (God-like love) (see Eph. 5:22-33; Col. 3:18-19) in marriage. The Bible also indicates that human marriage is to serve the even higher spiritual goal of exemplifying to the world the commitment and intimate relationship of believers to Christ (cf. Eph. 5:22-33; Isa. 54:4-8; 62:1-5; Ezek. 16:1-34; Hosea, chapters 1-3). On the other hand, it may surprise even Christians to know that the Bible says little about a man and a woman "loving" *one another* as a *prerequisite* to marriage. The Bible says a great deal about love *within* a marriage. In the Old Testament marriages were most often *arranged* by godly parents. The young couple then married and *learned* to love one another *during* the marriage. Most of them never went through the alleged experience of "falling in love" before marriage. Love is not an accident. No one "falls" into love. True love is from the *will*—not from the emotions. True love is caring and doing good for another even when one does not *feel* like caring. A man or woman must know what love is and how to love *before* marrying or the marriage will fail. Love doesn't happen—it is not something one waits to experience—it is something done, something practiced.

The apostle's statement that "each" should have his "own" wife or husband incidentally *eliminates* polygamy as a Christian option. Paul did *not* mean that every man and woman *must* marry since he cites celibacy as the most viable choice in light of first century circumstances (7:26).

7:3-7 Practical Direction: Paul here reinforces his teaching that the pressure of sexual desire is the main reason to seek marriage. The Greek words Paul used to give directions about sexual needs in marriage are interesting. Literally, he would say, "To the wife let the husband pay the good affection due her, and likewise also the wife to the husband." The Greek word *apodidoto* ("pay") is an imperative verb and is therefore a command. The use of the word "pay" implies obligation. The word *eunoian* is a Greek word literally meaning, "well-minded" but is here used to connote (as v. 4 indicates) the conjugal duties involved in marriage. God instituted marriage as the state in which man and woman are *privileged* to fulfill sexual desires. But within that state there are also certain *duties!* When God created man he saw that it was not good for man to be alone so he created woman (see Gen. 1:27-28; 2:18-25). It is clear from Paul's instruction here that sexual intercourse within marriage is not sinful, and is not restricted to procreative purposes. Sexual intercourse, as befits a happy, godly and uninhibited marriage, is the God-ordained right of each partner in a marriage. Less than this (especially for a Christian) is to miss the mark of God's will. Marriage is God's practical way for men and women to enjoy their sexual desire in wisdom, health (both physical and psychological) and social order. Any other application of the human sexual drive results (as history verifies) in mental and physical sickness and social chaos.

In verse 4 Paul states a principle which is at variance with modern "self-assertion" hucksters. J. B. Phillips translates, "The wife has no longer full rights over her own person, but shares them with her husband. In the same way the husband shares his personal rights with his wife." In the Greek text the word used is *exousiazei*, and is literally, *authority*. That is stronger than the English translation, "full rights." It could be translated *rule*. In marriage *each* partner surrenders to be *ruled* by the other. Paul specifies this in regard to their *bodies* (Gr. *somatos*), but in other epistles he applies it to the whole realm of married life (cf. Eph. 5:21ff.; Col. 3:18-19). In marriage, both husband and wife give up exclusive rights to their own bodies (and lives), agreeing to share them fully and freely with their partner. The happiest marriages are those characterized by complete liberty, few inhibitions, and absence of any guilt complex about sexuality within the will of God. The cause of much marital trouble today is *selfishness*, not only, but certainly foremost, in the area of sexuality. The Greek word *exousiazei* is in the present tense indicating that this reciprocal surrendering of husband and wife to one another is a *continuing* and permanent relationship. The New Testament teaches that marriage was intended by God to be a permanent relationship between one man and one woman in which the two, by surrendering all personal rights to one another, become one.

Paul's teaching here should convince anyone that he was not a "Woman-hating" antagonist of marriage nor "victorian" in his attitude toward sexuality in marriage. He may have been a bachelor all his life; he definitely believed he was led by God to advise celibacy, because of the exigencies of the times, for those who could endure the single life. But he does not enjoin bachelorhood or celibacy as an absolute commandment of God.

In verse 5 Paul states one exception to the sexual responsibilities of Christian husbands and wives. But even in this one exception Paul is quick to limit sexual abstinence lest Satan tempt a man or a woman through *lack of self-control*! Once again, emphasis is placed on marriage as God's primary provision for the controlled practice of the human sexual drive. The apostle's one exception is in case one of the partners in a marriage wants to devote himself completely to prayer. But Paul warns against any lengthy abstinence even for prayer! The RSV translates the Greek word *apostereite*, "Do not *refuse* one another. . . ." The KJV translates it, "*Defraud* ye not one the other. . . ." Actually the Greek word is more emphatic than *refuse*—it is often translated, *rob, despoil, defraud, leave destitute*. The idea is that lengthy abstinence by one married partner in sexual intimacy will leave the other partner robbed, defrauded and destitute, and

CHAPTER 7　　　　　　　　FIRST CORINTHIANS 7:1-9

clearly vulnerable to Satan's temptation to illicit sexual gratification. This, too, is an apostolic command, for the Greek verb *apostereite* is in the imperative mood. There may come times when a personal time for seeking the Lord comes before the one dearest on earth (one's spouse), *but only for a limited time.* Church work cannot be used as an excuse for neglecting one's marriage. What is accomplished for the kingdom of God if one's marriage partner is tempted and lost?

The English word *concession* (RSV) in verse 6 is not a good translation of the Greek word *sungnomen.* The Greek literally means, "to think the same as." In II Maccabees 14:31 it is translated "aware." It could be translated, "with understanding." To translate the word "concession" or "permission" (KJV) implies that the rigid apostolic standard in human sexuality was celibacy but that Paul would *concede* to the less holy relationship of marriage by bending the revelation of the Holy Spirit slightly. But that cannot be correct. To Paul marriage was God-ordained. What Paul is saying here is precisely the same thing the Lord said to the Twelve in Perea (see Matt. 19:1-12). Paul was "aware" that the majority of humanity would never have the "gift" to remain celibate without being tempted to fornication. He was writing "with understanding" of that fact and so, he declared, "I wish that all were as I myself (celibate) am. But each has his own special gift from God, one of one kind and one of another—and I do not say that celibacy is an absolute command of God."

Jesus made plain the high ideal for human marriage (Matt. 19:3-9) and his disciples jumped to the hasty conclusion that every man should be celibate (Matt. 19:10-12). Jesus replied, "Not all men can receive this precept, but only those to whom it is given." He said there were a few men who had to be celibate because of circumstances beyond their control; and there were a few men who were able to remain celibate by their own choice, for the sake of the kingdom of God. But Jesus recognized that most men are not able to "receive" the condition of celibacy. Jesus made it plain that celibacy is not a matter of divine commandment but a matter of capability. Here (1:6-7) Paul says celibacy is a matter of being "gifted" (Gr. *charisma).* "*. . . But each has his own gift from God, one of one kind and one of another. . . ."* Some people have *charisma* to remain celibate and some people have *charisma* to marry. The word "special" as in the RSV, or the word "proper" as in KJV, is not in the Greek text. Celibacy is *not* a "special" gift like speaking in a foreign language, prophesying, interpreting, healing, etc. (see I Cor. ch. 12-14). It is apparently an innate ability. Regarding the matter of celibacy (Matt. 19:10-12) Matthew reports Jesus as saying, *ho dunamenos chorein choreito,* "the one with the ability to have this, let him have it!" There are some "with" the ability and some who do not have it. When God made man, he saw "that it was not good for man to dwell alone" so he made a helper "fit for him" (Gen. 2:18). Some people may be able to find completion and fulfillment without a marriage partner—but not many. Applebury states the meaning of verses 6-7 clearly: "Each one has his own gift from God; for one it may be the gift of continence; for another it may be the ability to bear patiently and lovingly the responsibilities of the home with Christian consideration for the other partner." Those who have innate ability to remain celibate in life apparently do not have the ability to deal with the responsibilities of married life. This text, incidentally, proves that the word *charisma* does not always refer to "special," miraculous gifts. There are some gifts from God (Gr. *charisma*) with which individuals are born (see Rom. 12:4-13). God gives every human being *some* charisma! In "special," miraculous gifts men exercised no decisions; these gifts came by divine intervention of the natural order; they were exercised by the operation of the Holy Spirit. But in the matter of marriage or celibacy, it is clear men are called upon to make their own choice, based upon the teachings of the apostles and their own evaluations of their innate capabilities.

7:8-9 Passion Disciplined: Paul addresses the remarks in these verses to the "unmarried males" (Greek, *agamois,* masculine, dative, plural, noun) and to the "widows" (Greek, *cherais,* feminine, dative plural, noun). It is addressed to "unmarried males" because in ancient times only men were allowed to take the initiative in choosing marriage partners. "Unmarried males" could mean either bachelors or widowers. Paul, under the direction of the Holy Spirit (see 7:40), states it would be well (Gr. *kalon*) for anyone unmarried at that time (for reasons of "the impending distress" 7:26) to remain even as he was. Paul does not say in the text that he was unmarried. The Greek text is, *kalon autois estin ean meinosin hos kago,* or "well for them it is if they remain as I also am being." We assume he was single from the context. Some think Paul had been previously married and was a widower at the writing of I Corinthians. In stating that celibacy would be *good,* Paul is not saying that marriage would be *bad.* There seem to be only two reasons Paul has for celibacy being good—because of the "impending distress" and because the celibate is able to concentrate more fully on the things of the kingdom of God than the married person is (7:25-35).

CHAPTER 7　　　　　　　　　　FIRST CORINTHIANS 7:1-9

Paul is quick, however, to *qualify* his statement that celibacy is good. Celibacy is good only if a person is able to exercise sexual self-control. The Greek phrase is: *ei de ouk enkrateuontai, gamesatosan,* or, "However, if they have no self-control, let them marry." The Greek verb *enkrateuontai* means literally, "continuing power within" since it is in the present tense. There can be no doubt that the "power within" is self-control over sexual impulses. The context demands that interpretation. The apostolic wisdom in the matter is: "It is better (Gr. *kreisson,* more profitable) to marry than to be inflamed." There is no word for "passion" in the Greek text as in the RSV translation. There is only the word *purousthai* in the Greek text which literally means, "to burn." Again, the context demands we interpret Paul to mean "burn with sexual passion." For those able to live a *constant* life of sexual sublimation, the unmarried state is good. But for those who cannot, it is more profitable to marry.

Paul wrote to the young evangelist (we presume Timothy was unmarried) that the theology which forbade marriage was a theology "departing from the faith"—in other words, *apostasy* (I Tim. 4:3). In a later section of this chapter we will be asking whether Paul's statement to Timothy means no one has the right to forbid marriage to those never *previously* married, or does it mean that no one has the right to forbid marriage to any one in an unmarried state regardless of past circumstances. But one thing is certain, Paul agrees with the rest of Biblical teaching that marriage is a godly estate.

Marriage is the only human relationship in which sexual intercourse is approved by God! The person who cannot sublimate sexual urges, fulfilling them in something higher, should get married. It should be noted that Paul advises marriage when it is first apparent that a person is not able to control sexual urges—not *after* sexual experimentation has occurred. This may seem to some that Paul is taking a rather crude view of marriage. But Paul enunciates some of the highest ideals and purposes for marriage in all the Bible (cf. Eph. 5:21ff.). What Paul says in our text here shows that God is aware of the significance and power of human sexuality. The sexual urge in mankind, if not the strongest, is certainly *one* of the *most* powerful. And that is undoubtedly God's will in order to motivate man to "be fruitful and multiply, and fill the earth" (cf. Gen. 1:28; 9:1, etc.). The Greek word *gamesatosan* is in the imperative mood in this text. That is more than a suggestion; "they should marry" is an apostolic command! It is crucial to later comments on remarriage that this *command* be remembered. Certainly, those who have once been married and later widowed or divorced would be as apt to "burn with passion" as those who have never been married. If those who once were married now burn with passion in an unmarried state, it would be better for them, too, to get married. It does not seem in keeping with God's grace to forbid divorced persons to remarry, placing them in the position of burning with passion until they engage in illicit sexual intercourse.

SECTION 2

The Permanence of Marriage (7:10-16)

10 To the married I give charge, not I but the Lord, that the wife should not separate from her husband 11 (but if she does, let her remain single or else be reconciled to her husband)—and that the husband should not divorce his wife.

12 To the rest I say, not the Lord, that if any brother has a wife who is an unbeliever, and she consents to live with him, he should not divorce her. 13 If any woman has a husband who is an unbeliever, and he consents to live with her, she should not divorce him. 14 For the unbelieving husband is consecrated through his wife, and the unbelieving wife is consecrated through her husband. Otherwise, your children would be unclean, but as it is they are holy. 15 But if the unbelieving partner desires to separate, let it be so; in such a case the brother or sister is not bound. For God has called us to peace. 16 Wife, how do you know whether you will save your husband? Husband, how do you know whether you will save your wife?

7:10-14 Command: God's commandment has always been that each human marriage is to be permanent—until death separates one member of the marriage. That has been God's will from the beginning of creation (cf. Matt. 19:8). Paul reinforces that by stating, "To the married I give *charge,* not I but the Lord. . . ." Paul uses the Greek word *parangello* which means, "a proclamation, a command or commandment . . . strictly used of commands received from a superior and transmitted to others" (see Acts 5:28; 16:24; I Thess. 4:2; I Tim. 1:5, 18; Luke 5:14; 8:56; I Tim. 6:13, 17 for usage of the word *parangello*). Paul "charges" that the wife should not divorce her husband. The RSV translates the Greek word *choristhenai* as "separate," but it is

CHAPTER 7   FIRST CORINTHIANS 7:10-16

the same Greek word used by Matthew in reporting (Matt. 19:6) Jesus' statement about "divorce." Paul is not talking here about separation without divorce. All through this context he is talking about *divorce,* the dissolution of a marriage.

Apparently in Corinth, new converts to Christ were leaving their believing partners, or unbelieving partners were leaving their believing partners, and completely dissolving the marriages by divorce. When Christians marry non-Christians, or when one unbeliever in a marriage becomes a believer and the other partner does not, there will always be difficulties. But, according to the apostle Paul, they are not insurmountable difficulties. The difficulties of such an "unequally yoked" marriage are not necessarily such as should call for divorce. The ideal situation, of course, is that both partners in a marriage be Christians. People who are contemplating marriage *can* and should choose Christian partners before. Love is *not* blind! Infatuation and emotionalism is blind. Love is not something one "falls into" but is something one wills, decides and does, and does constantly in spite of emotions or circumstances!

Marriage as an institution predates all other institutions. It was sanctioned by God before the Law of Moses or the Christian dispensation. God's will is that marriage should be permanent, no matter who is involved. When it comes right down to it, there is no essential difference between a "Christian" marriage in a church and a pagan marriage in the living room of a justice of the peace. There is no differentiate in God's will that every marriage be permanent until death. Marriage is not "a sacrament of the church" performed exclusively by and for the church. Marriage is for the maintenance of human social structure. It is an institution established by God to be practiced by the entire human race. When a man and woman sincerely agree to become husband and wife, and obey the social and civil laws for marriage in their community, they are husband and wife regardless of their religion! Marriage can only be made permanent through unreserved faith in Jesus Christ by both partners. It can never be made permanent by civil law or force. Jesus made that plain in Matthew 19:3-12. When men have "hard hearts" they will rebel against all that God has sanctified, including the permanence of marriage. The "law" is "laid down" for the lawless and disobedient (I Tim. 1:8-9) and the civil state must legislate and enforce laws which will keep sinful and wicked people from perverting marriage until they destroy social order.

FIRST CORINTHIANS

In a world where the majority of human beings are not Christians, God's ideals for marriage are seldom considered. Sometimes a Christian will compromise principle and marry a non-Christian. Sometimes, after two non-Christians are married one becomes a Christian. What is the Lord's will in such circumstances? God's will is always for the permanence of marriage. In any circumstance that would threaten to dissolve a marriage, God's will is for *reconciliation* (reunion, coming back together). While it is possible that a marriage might have to be dissolved for continued sexual unfaithfulness (see Matt. 5:32; 19:9) or because of unsolicited desertion (I Cor. 7:15) it is certainly not what God desires. He wants repentance, forgiveness and reconciliation.

Nor does the Lord desire that the conversion of one marriage partner precipitate the dissolution of a marriage. Paul says, "If any woman has a husband who is an unbeliever, and he consents to live with her, she should not divorce him." The Greek verb translated "consents" is *suneudokei* and means "willingly resolves" to *dwell* (Gr. *oikein*) with her without coercion.

There are several reasons the Lord demands permanence in marriage. We have already stated one—the need of stability in the social structure. Another reason is discussed in 7:14—the power marriage has to sanctify unbelievers. Paul's instruction to the Corinthian Christian married to an unbeliever is that the believer should "sanctify" the unbeliever through the permanence of the marriage. The unbeliever is in a "set apart" circumstance (at least that much set apart from the world) by being married to a believer. So, the marriage of an unbeliever to a believer can become a powerful tool. When a man is converted, as head of the house he should lead his family to the Lord (e.g. the Philippian jailer and Cornelius). When a wife is the Christian and the husband an unbeliever, she has to be content with a slower process. Peter says that wives should submit themselves to their husbands; the husbands will more readily be won to Christ this way than through nagging, complaining or arguing (I Peter 3:1-2). Children who have even one Christian parent are at a great advantage over children reared in non-Christian homes. So, children are "set apart" from total worldliness by just one Christian parent. God's will is that marriage with just one Christian partner be permanent wherever and whenever human beings are agreeable. Of course, Paul does not mean that any unbelieving spouse or child is "saved by association." Being married to a Christian or being born by a Christian parent does not guarantee salvation. But it does mean,

CHAPTER 7   FIRST CORINTHIANS 7:10-16

where one marriage partner is a Christian, the unbelievers in the home will undoubtedly hear the gospel or see it being lived out there more clearly and often than anywhere else!

7:15-16 Concession: "But if the unbelieving partner desires to separate (divorce) let it be so; in such a case the brother or sister is not bound." The Greek words *chorizetai* and *chorizestho* in verse 15 should be translated, "But if the unbelieving partner divorces, let him (or her) be *divorced*." There is no word in the Greek text for "desires"—that is supplied by the translators. And, as we have pointed out above, Matthew used the word *chorizetai* to describe the Lord's discussion of *divorce* (not separation). There may be cases where one partner, not at all seeking to do God's will, may dissolve the marriage (for any number of so-called "reasons") while the other partner may not be able to stop the dissolution. When the unbelieving partner in a marriage has a heart so hardened by sin he or she "puts asunder" (the meaning of the Greek word *chorizetai*) or divorces the believing partner, then the believing partner ("brother" or "sister") is not "bound." What does Paul mean by, "not bound"? At least he means the Christian brother or sister is not bound to the divorcing-unbeliever as a spouse. Most civil societies (some with more latitude than others) have laws permitting divorce. When an unbeliever sues in civil court for dissolution of a marriage from a believer, and it is granted, there is nothing legal a believer can do to maintain the bonds of that marriage. Therefore, the believer is not bound to that marriage. But the big question is: Since a believer is not bound to a marriage he or she was forced by civil law to dissolve (when the believer was unwilling to have it dissolved), may the divorced believer remarry?

Paul has already admitted the *reality* that there is a possibility of the dissolution of marriages even where one party does not want it to be so. The unbeliever who has caused divorce has sinned. He or she must become a believer, repent and be immersed in water in order to be forgiven. The question remains, however, does the New Testament absolutely and unequivocally forbid remarriage with a different partner after divorce? (see Matt. 5:31-32; 19:1-12; Mark 10:2-12; Luke 16:18; I Cor. 7:15, 39; Rom. 7:3-4). Actually, there are no absolute or unequivocal directions in this matter of remarriage. What each Christian believes or practices he does so by his inference or deductions from certain principles. It is the opinion of this writer that remarriage is not only possible for those who have violated the will of God and dissolved marriages by divorce, but that God desires remarriage in such a case for both believer and unbeliever—for both the "guilty party" and the "innocent party." The following deductions have brought this writer to his opinion:

   a. God made marriage for the whole human race.
   b. Divorce is a sin; marriage is *not* a sin.
   c. Very few men or women have the "gift" to remain sexually celibate.
   d. Paul emphatically states, more than once, that enforced sexual continence (celibacy) when a person does not have self-control is dangerous to one's salvation (I Cor. 7:2, 5, 9, 36; I Thess. 4:3-8; I Tim. 5:14, etc.).
   e. It is illogical to reason that a person who is divorced, when he or she is unwilling to be divorced, may be considered an adulterer or adulteress should they marry another partner. People cannot be *made* to be adulterers against their will! Society may gossip and stigmatize an innocent person in a divorce situation, but he cannot be an adulterer unless he has an *attitude* of promiscuity —a *heart* that is against permanence in marriage.
   f. When there is a divorce there is no longer a marriage, neither in God's eyes nor in man's eyes—THERE IS A SIN IN GOD'S EYES FOR WHICH SOMEONE MUST REPENT (preferably a repentance resulting in remarriage to the same partner). But unless there is a reconciliation of the divorced persons, the marriage is over. They are no longer married to one another.
   g. There are two circumstances preceding a divorce in which, I believe, God considers one party in the divorce innocent—sexual unfaithfulness and desertion. In both circumstances one party has to be unwilling to the dissolution of the marriage. It is, therefore, this writer's opinion that the innocent party is most certainly free to remarry—guided by his knowledge of the revealed will of God about marriage and his own conscience.

It is, further, the opinion of this writer that God desires remarriage even for the "guilty" party in divorce rather than trying to force him or her to a life of celibacy which he may not be able to endure without "burning with passion." I believe God and Christ are interested in producing the highest good in every person's life and in society in general. That is the spirit behind any Old Testament legislation or

CHAPTER 7 FIRST CORINTHIANS 7:10-16

New Testament principle (for example, "The Sabbath was made for man, not man for the sabbath").

a. For the maintenance of social order, if an unbeliever cannot be controlled from promiscuous sexual intercourse by self-control, he or she should be married according to the laws of human responsibility and to keep society from degenerating to the level of animals.
b. Paul points out in several places that while Christians are controlled by the highest principle, divine love, the non-Christian must be controlled by civil law, enforced by civil authorities (cf. I Tim. 1:8-11; Rom. 13:1-7).
c. What practical or ultimate good is going to be served by forcing those once divorced to remain celibate the rest of their lives? There really is no legislation to that effect anywhere in the Bible. There is certainly no civil law to that effect. If all Christians lived by the law of divine love, Christian husbands and wives would never divorce one another. But some "Christians" do not live on that plane—they fall—they divorce one another. Are they to be banned to a life of celibacy for the rest of their natural lives? Is that seeking their highest good? What if they do not have the "gift" of sexual self-control? Should a minister of the gospel not also seek the highest good in every *fallen* person's life?
d. Would enforced celibacy really heal the problems faced by children when divorce occurs? What if a husband is left with small children to rear? What if a wife is? Who shall support them financially? Are they better served to be reared without a father or without a mother?
e. Would enforced celibacy heal the results of divorce? Will the church be able to support both materially and psychologically, all broken homes? Should Christians leave the healing of divorce in Christian homes to the civil state?
f. Would enforced celibacy heal the problems of temptation and incontinence? (I Cor. 7:2, 5, 9, 36). Suppose we paraphrase Jesus thus, "Is it lawful to do good through the institution of marriage or to tempt to promiscuity through enforced celibacy? Marriage was made for man, not man for marriage!" *Enforced celibacy in prisons merely intensifies sexual crimes!* Christians who say those once delivered should never remarry need to look at what happens in prison among men and women separated from heterosexual marriage!

FIRST CORINTHIANS

g. In no sense of the word do I condone divorce for any cause. I do not even condone loveless marriages whether the partners remain legally and outwardly married until they die. Both of these situations are certainly less than God's ideal.

h. But, neither do I think a minister of the gospel is "partaking" of the sin of divorce by performing marriage vows (since he is authorized by the civil authorities to do so) for couples who are unbelievers; for couples where one is a believer and another an unbeliever; for couples where either one or both parties have previously been divorced. God does not approve of divorce; I do not approve of divorce. God knows that all people do not have the gift of sexual self-control without "burning"; that is revealed truth and experiential truth. God *does* approve of marriage; I approve of marriage. As a minister, I have had nothing to do with their divorce; but I can have something to do with their remarriage, and, perhaps, repentance.

i. And, of some significance, in every marriage I perform I may, in a positive way, be able to instruct and exemplify the Christian gospel—and in a negative sense I may not give anyone an opportunity to criticize the church for lack of compassion and understanding.

j. When I stand *for* marriage and the responsibilities that go with it, I am standing for law and order in the lives of unbelievers who will not be controlled by divine love but must be controlled by civil legislation.

k. Is divorce a sin for which there can be no repentance (and no forgiveness) and no restoration? If a person embezzles, is imprisoned, released and states that he is of a different attitude, is he never to be allowed to handle an employer's money again? Should a divorced person never be allowed to "handle" marriage again?

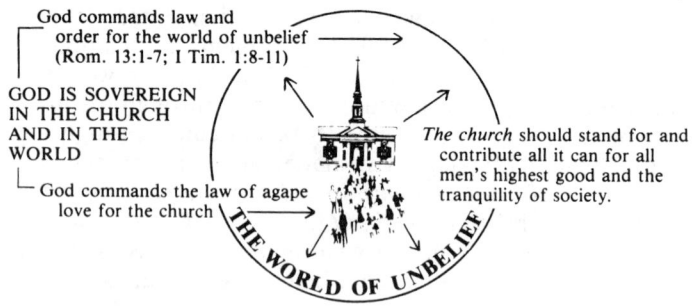

CHAPTER 7 FIRST CORINTHIANS 7:17-40

SECTION 3

The Pressures of Marriage (7:17-40)

17 Only, let every one lead the life which the Lord has assigned to him, and in which God has called him. This is my rule in all the churches. 18 Was any one at the time of his call already circumcised? Let him not seek to remove the marks of circumcision. Was any one at the time of his call uncircumcised? Let him not seek circumcision. 19 For neither circumcision counts for anything nor uncircumcision, but keeping the commandments of God. 20 Every one should remain in the state in which he was called. 21 Were you a slave when called? Never mind. But if you can gain your freedom, avail yourself of the opportunity. 22 For he who was called in the Lord as a slave is a freedman of the Lord. Likewise he who was free when called is a slave of Christ. 23 You were bought with a price; do not become slaves of men. 24 So, brethren, in whatever state each was called, there let him remain with God.

25 Now concerning the unmarried, I have no command of the Lord, but I give my opinion as one who by the Lord's mercy is trustworthy. 26 I think that in view of the present distress it is well for a person to remain as he is. 27 Are you bound to a wife? Do not seek to be free. Are you free from a wife? Do not seek marriage. 28 But if you marry, you do not sin, and if a girl marries she does not sin. Yet those who marry will have worldly troubles, and I would spare you that. 29 I mean, brethren, the appointed time has grown very short; from now on, let those who have wives live as though they had none, 30 and those who mourn as though they were not mourning, and those who rejoice as though they were not rejoicing, and those who buy as though they had no goods, 31 and those who deal with the world as though they had no dealings with it; for the form of this world is passing away.

32 I want you to be free from anxieties. The unmarried man is anxious about the affairs of the Lord, how to please the Lord; 33 but the married man is anxious about worldly affairs, how to please his wife, 34 and his interests are divided. And the unmarried woman or girl is anxious about the affairs of the Lord, how to be holy in body and spirit; but the married woman is anxious about worldly affairs, how to please her husband. 35 I

say this for your own benefit, not to lay any restraint upon you, but to promote good order and to secure your undivided devotion to the Lord.

36 If any one thinks that he is not behaving properly toward his betrothed, if his passions are strong, and it has to be, let him do as he wishes; let them marry—it is no sin. 37 But whoever is firmly established in his heart, being under no necessity but having his desire under control, and has determined this in his heart, to keep her as his betrothed, he will do well. 38 So that he who marries his betrothed does well; and he who refrains from marriage will do better.

39 A wife is bound to her husband as long as he lives. If the husband dies, she is free to be married to whom she wishes, only in the Lord. 40 But in my judgment she is happier if she remains as she is. And I think that I have the Spirit of God.

7:17-24 Discomfiture: Some, after having become Christians, were discomfited about their circumstances. Some were apparently convinced that becoming a Christian meant circumstances should change along with changes in behavior. Paul has just discussed the matter that a marriage should not be broken up just because one spouse has become a Christian and the other has not. Wanting to reinforce this principle, Paul states: "Only, let every one lead the life which the Lord has assigned to him, and in which God has called him. This is my rule in all the churches." Paul does not forbid improving one's circumstances, but he does make it a rule for the church-universal that a Christian is supposed to make the most of his circumstances, whatever they are (unless they are sinful). No violent changes in one's day-by-day circumstances are to be made just because he has become a Christian. The Christian can glorify God in most every circumstance of life. This applies to one's job, marital status, social status, or nationality. These circumstances are said by Paul to be "assigned" (Gr. *emerisen,* divided, apportioned) by the Lord. Indeed, the circumstances of our lives are regulated by the providence of God. We are citizens of a particular nation by the providence of God. We are surrounded by opportunities or lack of opportunities by the providence of God. But in whatever circumstance we find ourselves, we are to be content (cf. Phil. 4:11ff.). We are not responsible for our circumstances—but we are responsible for our attitudes and actions within those circumstances. It is often a temptation for the new Christian

CHAPTER 7   FIRST CORINTHIANS 7:17-40

to make violent changes in his circumstances or surroundings. He may want to quit his job, move from his neighborhood, break away from his social circle, and try to make a whole new set of circumstances—a whole new life for himself. But God wants the believer to be a believer in spite of and surrounded by his "assigned" circumstances. Paul states a number of analogies in order to illustrate his principle.

Strange as it may seem, some of the Jews in Corinth who had become Christians thought they should have the mark of circumcision *removed.* Jews who wanted to copy Greek ways in the Maccabean era instituted a process for removing the appearance of circumcision (see I Macc. 1:15; Josephus, *Antiquities,* 12:5:1). Others in Corinth, Christian Gentiles, thought they should submit to the rite of circumcision. The Judaizers in the earliest days of the church tried to make circumcision a dogma to be obeyed by everyone wishing to become a Christian (cf. Phil. 3:2; Acts 15:1ff.). "Circumcision" and "uncircumcision" are used frequently to symbolize Jewish and Gentile cultural habits. That may even be the case here. Paul certainly practiced many Jewish morés himself as a Christian. He did not violently renounce his Jewishness when he became a Christian. One should not divest himself of his nationality, his culture, or his physical circumstances (so long as they are not sinful) when he becomes a Christian. In whatever circumstance one is when called by the gospel to become a Christian—let him remain.

Again, if man finds himself in the circumstances of slavery when he responds to the gospel and becomes a Christian, he is not to take any violent or socially-destructive means to change his circumstances. Christianity stands for civil order. It does not condone anarchy in any form or for any reason. Jesus, under Roman rule, said: "Render to Caesar the things that are Caesar's and unto God the things that are God's." Peter wrote, "Be subject for the Lord's sake to every human institution, whether it be to the emperor as supreme, or to governors as sent by him to punish those who do wrong . . ." (I Peter 2:13-14). Read what Paul said in Romans 13:1-7; remember the examples of Daniel, Nehemiah, and Esther; see what God said to the Jewish prisoners of war in Jeremiah 29:1-8. Of course the Bible teaches by precept that all men are created equal and endowed by their Creator with certain inalienable rights. God never intended that any man should be exploited or enslaved by another. But then God never intended that any man should live in a society that worships sacred cows and monkeys while millions of people starve to death.

135

FIRST CORINTHIANS

Yet, in slavery or freedom, in poverty or plenty, every man's first responsibility is to obey the gospel. Circumstances are irrelevant to faith and love for God. Paul says "never mind" about circumstances. The Greek phrase could be translated, "It must not matter to you" what your circumstances are.

Some commentators hold that the Greek sentence (7:21b) *all' ei kai dunassai eleutheros genesthai, mallon chresai,* should be translated: "And even if you become able to be free, rather remain as you are and use it." Others hold the translation should be: "But if you become able to be free, use the opportunity and become free." Since either translation might fit the grammatical construction, we must beware of being dogmatic as to its interpretation. On the one hand, the immediate context seems to demand the meaning: "Even if a Christian slave has an opportunity to become a free man he should remain a slave and make use of that lot in life to serve God." On the other hand, the *overall context of Christian morality* would seem to demand the meaning: "And every Christian slave who has an opportunity to become a free man should avail himself of this opportunity to use in the service of Christ." Paul certainly would not advocate any Christian slave running away from his master or using violent means to obtain freedom. Paul personally sent a runaway slave (Onesimus) back to his master (Philemon). But in this case both the master and the slave were Christians and Paul exhorted such brotherhood as would practically erase the distinction between slave and master. Paul did not usurp Philemon's right to have his bondservant returned to his service. Wilbur Fields says in his commentary on *Philippians, Colossians, Philemon,* (College Press), "As Christians, we have come so far in our revulsion against slavery that Paul's attention to Philemon's legal rights as master seems to us more a violation of Onesimus' greater right to be free than a necessary preservation of Philemon's rights." The Christian should read the following on slavery (Deut. 23:15-16; Gal. 3:28; Col. 3:22—4:1; Titus 2:9-10; I Tim. 6:1-2; Eph. 6:5-9; and the entire book of Philemon). We should attempt to keep our subjective feelings about slavery at a minimum in trying to decide what Paul meant here. Paul is emphatic about the principle, "Every one should remain in the state in which he was called." He repeats it three times (7:17, 20, 24)! Verse 22 seems to reinforce this principle. But our interpretation of verse 22 will depend on our interpretation of verse 21. What Paul seems to be saying in all this is what we have said at the outset: God wants the

CHAPTER 7　　　　　　　　　　FIRST CORINTHIANS 7:17-40

believer to be a believer in spite of and surrounded by his "assigned" circumstances. Whether a Christian is a bondservant or a freeman makes no difference—let him remain there with God (7:24).

Any person who becomes a Christian while a slave is set free from the bondage of sin by Christ. This is the only freedom that really matters for eternity. And any person who becomes a Christian while a freeman is in bondage to the Lord Jesus Christ and has no spiritual rights of his own. Christians belong to Jesus as purchased slaves. He is their Master. They are to do what Christ commands; they are to serve Christ. Christians are not to surrender control of their minds or actions to anyone but Jesus. Christ is the Christian's only Master (see I Cor. 6:20). Paul is referring to the Christian's need to keep from letting some external circumstance or some threat of a fellow man usurp the right of Christ to absolute ownership.

Biblical history documents a number of examples of men and women who served God in spite of difficult circumstances. Joseph, sold in slavery, unjustly imprisoned, became second ruler in Egypt; Daniel, taken to Babylon as a prisoner of war, became third ruler in Babylon and, later, in Persia; Esther, a maiden among the exiled Jews, became queen of Persia; Mordecai, Esther's uncle, became a minister of the Persian government; Nehemiah, also of the Jewish exiles, became the king's cupbearer. It is also significant that neither John the Baptist nor Jesus insisted that people change their occupations (soldiers and tax-collectors), residences or cultural traditions (so long as they were not sinful) as a requirement for discipleship. Peter did not require Cornelius to resign his commission as an officer (centurion) in the Roman army to become a Christian; Paul did not require Sergius Paulus (Acts 13) nor the Philippian jailor (Acts 16) to change their circumstances when they became Christians.

We must not miss the fact that the main subject being discussed by Paul in this context is *marriage*. He is stating a general principle and citing various areas of application—but the main application is to marriage. If a person becomes a Christian while married to an unbeliever, the new Christian is not to seek dissolution of the marriage. The Christian is free from such a marriage *only* if the unbeliever divorces the Christian. Paul suggests that by keeping the marriage intact, the believer is able to have such sanctified influence on both unbelieving spouse and any children to the marriage there exists the best possibility of turning the whole family to Christ. Biblical examples might be cited for this principle: Joseph married an Egyptian priest's

FIRST CORINTHIANS

daughter (Gen. 41:45), retaining his strong faith and bringing up his children in the faith: Boaz married Ruth who was a Moabitess, and she became an ancestress of Christ; Rahab, a Canaanite harlot, married an Israelite (Salmon, Matt. 1:5), and became an ancestress of Christ; Esther, a Jewess, married a heathen emperor, and saved her people. Believers do not seek to reform individuals by social upheaval; they seek to reform society by converting individuals to Christ!

7:25-31 Distress: This paragraph plainly states Paul's primary purpose for advocating that it is well for the unmarried and the widows to "remain single" as he did (7:8). His primary purpose is *not* that celibacy is spiritually superior to marriage. Celibacy was enjoined in this apostolic reply to the Christians at Corinth in 56-57 A.D. *because of the stress-laden circumstances* coming upon Christians in the latter half of the first century. Persecution of Christians under Nero had already begun in 54 A.D. These persecutions continued for forty more years until they reached an intensity in 81-96 A.D. under Domitian that saw hundreds of thousands of Christians die. Simply because they were Christians, and would not worship the Roman emperor, people from all across the Roman empire were hunted down as conspirators and seditionists, enslaved and worked to death in mines and on galley-ships, starved to death by social ostracization, and slain by the thousands in gladitorial games in Roman arenas. Practically all the writers of the New Testament predicted the "fiery ordeal" that was about to come (indeed, had already begun) upon first and second century Christians. Paul predicted the Jewish persecution, the destruction of Judaism, and the consequent distress upon Christians in Hebrews chapter 10, in II Thessalonians chapter 2, and in I Tim. 4:1-5; II Tim. 4:1-8. Peter predicted it in I Peter 4:12-19. John predicted and described it in Revelation chapters 1 through 20:6 (see *Twenty-Six Lessons on Revelation,* by Paul T. Butler, pub. College Press).

Paul addresses those who had never been married in verse 25. He uses the Greek word *parthenon* (almost always translated "virgin") translated "unmarried" in the RSV. Paul says there is no specific commandment of the Lord for his emphasis on celibacy. He gives his *judgment* (Gr. *gnomen,* understanding, mind) as one by the Lord's mercy appointed as trustworthy. *Judgment* is a better translation than *opinion* (RSV), and Paul is giving a judgment which should be heeded because the *Lord* has declared him trustworthy. It is apostolic

CHAPTER 7   FIRST CORINTHIANS 7:17-40

advice—not apostolic commandment—which his Corinthian audience, especially, would well have practiced. He had wisdom and revelation about their coming "fiery ordeal" which they did not have.

The phrase "impending distress" (Gr. *enestosan anagken*) might well be translated "present distress" (as in KJV). The Greek word *enestosan* is a perfect participle—a combination of *en* and *histemi*. It could be translated "imminent," "right here," or "at hand." Paul was not talking of the end of the world. He had already cautioned the Thessalonians *not* to think of the Second Coming of Christ in connection with the impending distress coming upon first and second century Christians (II Thess. 2:1-12). Paul is suggesting unusual life-styles in view of imminently unusual circumstances much in the same way Jesus warned his disciples about their reactions to the fall of Jerusalem in 70 A.D. (Matt. 24:1-34; Luke 21:1-33; Mark 13:1-31; see *The Gospel of Luke,* by Paul T. Butler, pub. College Press). Paul's understanding in the matter of marriage was that *in view of the imminent stresses* or pressures (Gr. *anagke*) a first century Christian should remain in whatever marital state he was. If the Christian was married, he should not seek to be free; if the Christian was not married, he should not seek to be married. That was wise advice for the exegencies of those times (or any similar times afterward), but only if the Christian is able to exercise sexual self-control (7:2, 9, 36).

In verse 28 Paul reassures the Corinthians that marriage is not a sin—not even if it is done against his wise advice about the imminent distress to come upon Christians. He goes on to point out that the distress to come will, of necessity, intensify the focus of married people on things of the world and perhaps divert their priorities away from pleasing the Lord. Those who went against Paul's wisdom and married were going to have worldly (Gr. *sarki,* fleshly, physical) troubles. They would have to worry about another mouth to feed when as Christians they would be forced to starve; they would worry about seeing a beloved mate or child tortured to death in the arena. These anxieties and many others would constantly plague Christians during the great tribulation period of Roman persecution. Paul was trying to keep Christians from having to bear such burdens. The apostle reiterates that the "imminent distress" has "grown very near." The Greek participle *sunestalmenous* is a perfect tense verb combined of two words, *sun* (together) and *sustello* (draw, contract, compact, tighten). The time of distress of which he had spoken earlier was almost there.

FIRST CORINTHIANS

Paul now gives admonitions directing attitudes and behavior in anticipation of the stressful times coming upon the Corinthian Christians. First, those who were married were to make certain their first priority was serving the Lord. The married Christians would have to prepare themselves to deny the very strong temptation to compromise their faith in Christ should harm be threatened toward a spouse or child. Paul is *not* saying that in times of persecution married people should neglect domestic duties or the responsibilities of marriage. He has just admonished married Christians not to neglect conjugal responsibilities (7:3-5). He wrote to Timothy (I Tim. 5:8) that anyone who does not provide for his own family has denied the faith and is worse than a heathen. Second, Christians must have the attitude that they will not mourn the loss of earthly things. They are not even to grieve the loss of loved ones as others do who have no hope (I Thess. 4:13). Paul reported that some Christians "joyfully accepted the plundering" of their property (Heb. 10:32-34). The apostle John predicted how the pagan world would mourn the loss of material wealth at the destruction of the Roman empire (Rev. 18:9-19). Third, Christians who might have occasion to rejoice in earthly circumstances should not do so, but should remember that worldly pleasures are transitory (see II Cor. 4:16-18; I Tim. 6:6-19). Fourth, those who make purchases should not do so merely to accumulate things. Whatever is purchased is only acquired in order to be used up in serving the Lord. Only that which is done to serve Christ will last for eternity. The Greek word *katechontes* would make the phrase read, let "those who buy be as those who do not consider their purchases as their possessions." Such earthly goods as a man has are not his—they are a trust, a stewardship from the real Owner of all things. Fifth, let those who use this world, use it sparingly. So long as Christians are residing in this world they must necessarily "use" certain parts of this world. They must eat to maintain the physical body, they must clothe that body, and there are certain earthly institutions with which they must be associated, but Christians are not to use this world any more than they have to while they serve God. The Greek word *katachromenoi* means, "much use, over use, using to the utmost." Christians are to consider themselves just pilgrims or temporary residents of this world. The Christian's permanent dwelling place is not here. He is not to settle down here—not to find security here. J. B. Phillips paraphrases, ". . . indeed their every contact with the world must be as light as possible . . . ."

CHAPTER 7　　　　　　　　　　FIRST CORINTHIANS 7:17-40

The reason for these five admonitions is this world is programmed for destruction. The word *form* (RSV) in the Greek text is *schema;* it is the word from which we get the English word *schematic*. It means, "a plan, an outline, a blueprint, a design." Everything in this present existence is designed to pass away. Even the institution of marriage is designed for this world only (Matt. 22:30). Men and women should not get so attached to anything in this *cosmic* (Gr. *kosmos,* world-order) scheme of things, not even to marriage, that they cannot serve God without compromise. Not only is this world programmed to pass away—it is presently doing so. The Greek verb *paragei* ("passing away") is present tense meaning action is presently going on. This agrees with Paul's statement in II Corinthians 4:16-18 that the "outer nature" (the physical) is wasting away while the "inner nature" (spiritual) of the Christian is being renewed every day. It is the invisible, spiritual nature that is permanent—the physical is transitory.

7:32-35 Deviation: The pressures of marriage, especially in distressing times of social upheaval, might make some Christians deviate from giving first priority to the Lord's will in their lives. Paul's desire in setting forth his wisdom about celibacy is that the Corinthian Christians not yet married may keep themselves free from divided loyalties. The word translated "anxieties" is *amerimnous* in Greek and means literally, *not divided in mind*.

The unmarried man separates his mind from other things and gives it to the things of the Lord. He is under no obligation to provide sustenance, safety and security for a wife. The unmarried man may concentrate all his faculties on being acceptable to the Lord. But the married man separates his mind from the Lord's service in order to concentrate on physical things that he may acceptably fulfill his obligations to his wife—and divided he is. The Greek phrase *kai memeristai* is translated by the RSV as connected to verse 33, "and his interests are divided." The best and most ancient Greek manuscripts indicate this translation is to be preferred over the KJV which translates it, "There is difference also between a wife and a virgin" making it the beginning sentence of verse 34.

The same attitudes may be found in the unmarried woman and the virgin (note: Paul distinguishes between *the unmarried* and *the* virgin; the unmarried probably referring to widows and women whose unbelieving husbands have divorced them; the *virgin* referring to those who had not yet been married). Unmarried women separate themselves unto the Lord, dedicating both body and spirit to Christ; but

FIRST CORINTHIANS

the married woman has to concentrate on many physical things in order to fulfill her marital obligations. There is nothing necessarily sinful in fulfilling one's marital commitments. Paul even exhorted husbands and wives to do so (7:3-7). But, he warned, stressful cirstances will always tend to intensify the temptation for a Christian married person to let priorities be diverted from the spiritual and focused on the physical. Martha (probably the wife of Simon the leper, see Matt. 26:6-12; Mark 14:3) was "distracted with much serving" (Luke 10:40), while Mary, the unmarried sister, sat at the feet of Jesus and chose the "best part," (see Luke 10:38-42).

So Paul's advice to these Corinthians, is, if they were presently unmarried (whether widowed, divorced or virginal), do not seek to be married. Paul's advice was for their own benefit. He had nothing to gain from thus advising them. Neither did he intend to restrict their freedom to make their own choice by claiming any personal authority over these Corinthian Christians. The English word *restraint* is from the Greek word *brochon* which literally describes "a noose, a slip-knot, a halter, by which animals were caught and tethered." They are not to think they are *tied* to Paul's advice. But if they are wise and if they want what is well-planned or in good form (Gr. *euschemon*), and if they want to be in a position to give *unencumbered* (Gr. *aperispastows*, undistracted, undivided) devotion to the Lord, they will do as Paul advises.

Consider how dangerous it would be to marry, just for the sake of appearances, someone whose idea of loyalty to Christ is not your own! God did not create us for marriage *at any price!* Paul gives three advantages of celibacy: (a) Freedom from troubles due to distressing times; (b) relief from anxiety about the things of the world on which a "bread-winner" must necessarily concentrate; (c) freedom from distractions in order to serve the Lord more fully and intently. These three attitudes may be achieved whether married or unmarried, of course, but with much less difficulty and with more time for the Lord when not married—especially if there are times of social distress like war, persecution, economic depression, etc. Remember, God forbade the prophet Jeremiah to marry (Jer. 16:1-4) because of the distressing times in which he lived.

7:36-40 Postscript: In these verses, the apostles make a brief summary of this whole dissertation on marriage in view of imminent distress.

The RSV has done an injustice to verse 36 in its translation. First, the Greek word *parthenon* should be translated *virgin,* and *not*

CHAPTER 7   FIRST CORINTHIANS 7:17-40

betrothed. The Greek word used specifically for *betrothed* is *mnesteuo* and is found in Matt. 1:18; Luke 1:27; 2:5. Second, the Greek phrase, *ean e juperakmos,* should be translated, "if she is past the apex of her puberty" or as the KJV translates it, "if she pass the flower of her age." The Greek word *huperakmos* is a combined word; from *huper,* meaning, *beyond,* and *akme* (English, acme), meaning, *apex,* highest point of anything, full bloom of the flower.

While the RSV translation makes it appear Paul is directing this last advice toward a *young man* acting in an *unseemly manner* (Gr. *aschemonein,* again the word is a derivative of *schema,* meaning, "not according to design or plan") toward the young lady to whom he is betrothed, the better translation would have Paul advising fathers in their attitudes toward virgin daughters well past the age of puberty. Young ladies of that age might be placed in great danger of succumbing to temptation to fulfill strong sexual urges illicitly should their fathers not permit them to marry.

Marriage customs of that century forbade the young maiden to make any arrangements for marrying a man. She could not even agree to marry a man without her father's approval. It was understood in that culture that the father made all the choices of a marriage partner for his daughter and all the arrangements. If the father said she could not marry—she could not marry! Paul is directing his trustworthy advice toward Christian fathers with daughters of marriageable age, who have reached sexual maturity and, perhaps, have shown signs of sexual desire about to get out of control (see verse 37).

The RSV translates the latter half of verse 36, ". . . if *his* passions are strong . . ." but the Greek text does not have a pronoun in this phrase—it has a 3rd person, singular, present subjunctive form of the verb, "is, or, to be." The pronoun is merely *understood.* It could just as well be understood to be *her* as it could be *his.* We believe verse 36 should read, in its entirety, thus: "If any father thinks he is behaving in any unseemly manner toward his virgin daughter, if *she is in* (present tense verb) the age of sexual desire, and the man (father) thinks she ought to marry, let the father do as he wishes; the father does not sin if he gives her to marry (Gr. *gameitosan,* give in marriage) a man." This certainly fits the following verses more accurately.

The father who is firmly established in his *mind* (Gr. *kardia,* heart), is under no necessity, for his wishes in this matter are under his own authority. If the father decides in his own mind to keep his virgin daughter from marrying, he will do well. The Greek words *thelematos*

143

(will) and *exousian* (authority) should not be translated, as the RSV does, as *desire* and *control*. The RSV implies in its translation that Paul is talking about sexual desires under control, but Paul is really talking about a father's will or choice about his marriageable daughter being within his own authority and not someone else's.

Verse 38 should be translated, "So the man (father) who *gives* his virgin daughter *in marriage* (Gr. *gamizon*) does well, and the man (father) who does *not give in marriage* (Gr. *ho me gamizon*) will do better."

The apostle's final word on marriage is that Christians are to strive for God's highest ideal. That ideal is one man and one woman married until death separates them (see Matt. 19:1-9). This was God's ideal from the beginning of creation. But because man rebels against God and God's ideals, a lesser ethic must be enforced upon rebels. Laws of divorcement may be written to protect those who are divorced against their will. However, for Christians, God expects his ideal to be lovingly chosen, and practiced.

A wife is *bound* to her husband as long as he lives. The Greek verb *dedetai* (bound) is in the perfect tense and means that once bound, that binding is to continue. If the husband *dies* (Gr. *koimethe,* "sleeps"), the Christian woman is free to be married to whom she wishes, *only* (Gr. *monon*) in the Lord. Paul has already (7:10-16) discussed the hardships in a marriage where one person is a believer and the other an unbeliever. Now he insists that when a Christian woman (and it would also apply to a man) loses her spouse in death, she ought to limit her freedom to remarry to spiritual considerations. She should marry only a Christian. For a Christian to step into any relationship outside the will of God is not only to involve oneself in tragedy, and to jeopardize one's soul, but perhaps to bring sorrow into the whole Christian community and into the lives of a generation yet to be born. Christians are not to be mismated with unbelievers in any venture in life (II Cor. 6:14—7:1). In Paul's instructions to Timothy about the conduct of Christian widows (I Tim. 5:9-16) he urged the "younger widows" to marry. But Paul qualifies even that instruction with this answer to the Corinthians. It is better to remain single if marriage outside the will of God is contemplated.

To sum up, Paul answers the questions of the Corinthian Christians, who are facing "imminent distress," that it would be better for those spiritually strong who, by the grace of God, have their sexual drive under control to remain unmarried. All others should marry. They should marry "in the Lord." If a Christian's unbelieving

CHAPTER 7 FIRST CORINTHIANS 7:17-40

spouse divorces her she is "free" (to remarry) and if a Christian's spouse dies, she is "free." The married life is the norm. Celibacy is the exception, and in no way superior to marriage.

In all he wrote here to the Corinthians, Paul claims to have the approval of the Holy Spirit. The following comment on verse 40 is good:

> He wanted to assure the Corinthians that he was not speaking from human bias and prejudice. That this danger existed is proved by the number of modern Christians who have accused him of just this vice. *I think* is probably to be taken as meiosis, a figure of speech which emphasizes something by saying less than is meant. Paul believed that his advice had been given under the guidance of the Spirit of God. This does not mean that it was advice for all people in all times. Under other circumstances wise and spiritual men have differed radically from the advice given in this chapter. It does mean that his advice was best under the circumstances then existing. The one point of permanent validity must not be overlooked. The decisions of Christians in all spheres of life should be made in the light of their primary devotion to God in Christ Jesus. If Christians in all ages would make their decisions in view of that which would be most helpful for them in serving the Lord, there would be fewer mistakes to regret.
>
> *Commentary on 1 & 2 Corinthians,* pg. 126, by Fred Fisher, pub. Word Books, 1975

APPLICATIONS:

1. Biblical principles enunciated on the subject of marriage have the authority of God whether spoken by the married or the unmarried counselor.
2. Marriage is the only God-ordained relationship in which human sexual drives are to find expression and satisfaction.
3. If you want a happy marriage; do not neglect to afford your spouse all the physical satisfaction desired, along with love and the spiritual aspects of marriage.
4. The Holy Spirit of God not only approves of, but insists on, proper and regular sexual expression in marriage.
5. God's word warns that the human sexual drive is exceedingly strong.

6. God's word warns against remaining unmarried too long.
7. Anyone married to an unbeliever should go to great extremes to preserve the marriage.
8. Christians married to non-Christians will at least afford the unbelievers in that household more godliness than they would get where there are no Christians in the family at all.
9. If divorce comes in the marriages of believers or unbelievers, Christians must be involved in finding and guiding the fallen to the highest possible good for the persons and the society. This will most likely involve remarriage of divorced individuals, both believers and unbelievers.
10. In "imminently distressful" times the advice of the Holy Spirit of God, through the wisdom of the apostle Paul, is, do not marry.
11. Christians may, and must, serve God in whatever circumstances they may find themselves.
12. Christians are *not* to insist on changed circumstances in order to serve the Lord.

APPREHENSIONS:

1. What provoked Paul to write this dissertation on Christian marriage?
2. Was Paul saying in verse 1 that men should never touch women?
3. Is relaxation from the temptation to illicit sexual expression the only reason men and women should marry?
4. What spiritual symbolism is to be found in human marriage?
5. Does the Holy Spirit, through Paul, *command* sexual regularity within marriage? Why?
6. Is celibacy a miraculous gift from God? What kind of gift is it? How does one know if he has this gift or not?
7. Could the "unmarried" of verse 8 be applied to those who had been previously married and then divorced?
8. Paul emphasizes that the human sexual drive is very strong— how strong?
9. What should Christians do who are married to unbelievers? What if the unbeliever divorces the believer? May a believer ever divorce a spouse? When? Why?
10. May a believer, having divorced, or having been divorced, remarry? Under what conditions?
11. Would a minister of the gospel *sin* if he solemnized the marriage

CHAPTER 7   FIRST CORINTHIANS 7:17-40

   where one spouse has been previously divorced? Both spouses divorced? One prospective spouse is an unbeliever? Both are unbelievers?
12. Is divorce an unforgivable sin?
13. Would *enforced* celibacy produce the highest spiritual good in lives of individuals or society as a whole?
14. Should Christians really not try to change their circumstances in order to serve the Lord? What about Christian slaves?
15. Is the unmarried life preferable for anyone who wants to devote full attention to serving the Lord? For whom is it preferable?
16. Who should marry "in the Lord"?

Chapter Eight

THE PROBLEM OF CONSCIENCE
(8:1-13)

IDEAS TO INVESTIGATE:

1. Why is Paul so antagonistic to "knowledge"—is he anti-intellectual?
2. Why were Christians having a problem with foods offered to idols?
3. If eating or not eating is irrelevant, why all the fuss?
4. Is it fair to hold me responsible for someone else's weak conscience?

SECTION 1

The Principle (8:1-3)

8 Now concerning food offered to idols: we know that "all of us possess knowledge." "Knowledge" puffs up, but love builds up. ²If any one imagines that he knows something, he does not yet know as he ought to know. ³But if one loves God, one is known by him.

8:1a Provocation of Idolatry: Idolatry was a way of life. Greek cities were "full" of idols (Acts 17:16-34). In Corinth an inscription has been unearthed by archaeologists marking the location of a "meat market" in the probable vicinity of the temple of Apollo. The well of one of the shops along the south stoa has yielded a stone fragment reading, "Lucius, the butcher." In Pompeii archaeologists have found a configuration of buildings including both a chapel of the imperial cult and a counter for the selling of sacrificial meat. In the ancient world it was almost impossible to secure meat which had not been offered to an idol. Some of the pagan temples appear to have provided auxiliary "clubrooms" which offered social dining as well as the more religious cultic meals. The cultic meals, according to William Baird, were held in recognition of a host of public occasions—marriage, victory in battle, honor to a hero. The prominence of such dining customs made it difficult for the Corinthian citizen to avoid sacrificial meat. When he was invited out to dinner, it was inevitably served as the main course. If his host were a devotee of Artemis, a successful hunt would be consummated by an elaborate banquet after the animal had been sacrificed to the patron deity. Could a Christian attend such a party? If he attended should he eat the sacrificial meat?

CHAPTER 8

FIRST CORINTHIANS 8:1-3

Please study Romans, chapter 14, in connection with I Corinthians 8, 9, and 10.

Helenistic banquets were fabulous affairs. Petronius writes in *The Satricon:*

> Let's see, first off we had some roast pork garnished with loops of sausage and flanked with more sausages and some giblets done to a turn. And there were pickled beets and some wholewheat bread made without bleach. . . . Then came a course of cold tart with a mixture of some wonderful Spanish wine and hot honey. . . . Then there were chickpeas and lupins, no end of filberts, and an apple apiece. . . . The main course was a roast of bear meat. . . . It reminds me of roast boar, so I put down about a pound of it. Besides, I'd like to know, if bears eat men, why shouldn't men eat bears? To wind up, we had some soft cheese steeped in fresh wine, a snail apiece, some tripe hash, liver in pastry boats and eggs topped with more pastry and turnips and mustard and beans boiled in the pod and—but enough's enough.

Besides the Greek idols, the Roman emperors were attempting to insure allegiance by enforcing emperor worship. It was not participation in formal rituals of idol worship that bothered these Corinthians. That was strictly forbidden by apostolic command (cf. Acts 15:20, 29; I Cor. 10:14; II Cor. 6:16; Gal. 5:20; I Thess. 1:9; I Peter 4:3; I John 5:21; Rev. 9:20-21). But the worship of idols had so thoroughly saturated the culture of the first century everyone was brought directly into contact with it one way or another—even the Jews.

Practically every morsel of meat sold in public markets (I Cor. 10:25) of Greek and Roman cities had, in one way or another, been part of a sacrifice to an idol. There were public, formal worship services in pagan temples at which foods were offered; there were private, home services in honor of idols at which foods of all kinds were dedicated to the gods. So completely was this the case, the word in Hellenistic Greek "to sacrifice" had come to mean simply "to kill or to butcher." A native citizen of a Greek city like Corinth—especially if he were poor—would consider himself unfairly deprived if he were forbidden to participate in the public festivals at which idol sacrifices were served because it might be his only opportunity to eat meat for several months. These public festivals were probably held in the courts of the idol temples where tables were set up (cf.

8:10; 10:14-22) for the public. The citizen of Corinth who became a Christian would have a very difficult time trying to continue social amenities among neighbors and relatives who were not Christian. It was a tradition practiced by many pagans to take some of their sacrificial animal's carcass home with them from the ritual and serve it on their own tables to friends and relatives.

Idol worship, feasting, and the immorality that went along with it were part of the very essence of Corinthian social life and culture. It was all part of everyday living. Some Christians easily settled the issue in their own minds. They knew, "an idol is no god." Actually, some non-Christians had also decided, philosophically, that idols were not gods. The Epicureans considered the worship of idols to be nonsense. One Hellenistic writer says of the gods that they "are far away, or they have no ears, or they do not exist, or they pay not the least attention to us." The Stoics, also, abandoned polytheism for a kind of pagan monotheism or pantheism. These pagan "atheists" practiced the forms of idolatry for practical political reasons but did not believe the myths. The majority of non-Christians, however, did eat such foods as *really* offered to an idol (I Cor. 8:7). And some Christians had *not* settled in their minds that an idol was not a god. Some Christians, especially those from Jewish backgrounds, abhorred all the trappings associated with idolatry and felt as if they had sinned if they even touched such things or looked upon them.

Some idolatrous rituals pronounced holy formulas over the sacrificial animals which allegedly turned the sacrifices into the god who was to receive it. In this ritual the god himself was allegedly sacrificed and when the priests and the worshipers ate the meat of the sacrifices, the strength and glory of the god supposedly passed into the worshipers. Many pagans also believed one way to protect themselves from having demons come inside them through their mouths was to eat meat sacrificed to a *good* god (whose presence would be in the sacrificial meat) and this would put up a barrier against the evil god who might come into them through some food.

This presented a very serious problem for the infant church. It involves the most crucial elements of Christian community—love, liberty, conscience, temptation, knowledge and spiritual maturation. The apostolic resolution of the question was, and is, of immense importance. If it were a prohibition of Christianity under any circumstances to eat meat sacrificed to idols, then the Gentile convert becomes bound to a legal system as condemning as the Mosaic law

CHAPTER 8   FIRST CORINTHIANS 8:1-3

and a legalism as impossible as the Jewish rabbinical traditions. If, on the other hand, the Greek Christian was free to do as he pleased in every circumstance, he was given license to carelessly trample upon the tender scruples of a weaker brother and probably cause him to sin.

Paul suffered slanderous misrepresentation and hateful persecution as a consequence of his teaching concerning Christian liberty (see Acts 21:21-24). Although Paul was in full accord with this teaching, it was not merely his but the Holy Spirit's. And anyone who opposed it was "severed from Christ, fallen from grace" (see Gal. 5:1-12).

8:1b-2: Problem of Intellectualism: Paul is not against knowledge or use of the intellect. He "reasoned" from the Scriptures (Acts 18:4, 19). He appealed to logic and deductive processes as befitting Christians (Rom. 12:1-2). He told the Philippians to "think logically" on Christian virtues (Phil. 4:8). His warning here is against *intellectualism*. Intellectualism is the arrogant doctrine that the ultimate principle of reality is human reason. Intellectualism holds that it is possible for the human mind to discover everything man needs to know. It thus dispenses with the need for a revelation from God—eventually dispensing with the need for God at all.

Paul uses two Greek words *oida* and *ginosko* interchangeably or synonymously for *knowing* and *knowledge*. Paul does not seem to be using these two words with as much difference as most commentators allege. It is apparent from the context that he is using irony when he says we know that "all of us possess knowledge." In fact, he is probably quoting a statement from some of the Corinthians themselves. Some of them were enamored of "knowledge" (see I Cor. 1:18-31; 2:1-16; 3:18). These may have been intellectuals agreeing with the gnostic Christians who supposed that the acquisition of mystical, divine knowledge freed one from any moral qualms about participating in the expressions of pagan culture.

The trouble with intellectualism is that it *inflates* (Gr. *phusioi*) the human ego. Those who "know better" than others are always in danger of feeling superior. Knowledge which does that is not true knowledge. There is a wide distance between human knowledge and heavenly wisdom (cf. James 3:13-18). Intellectualism seeks to tear down those of inferior knowledge in order to inflate self. *Love* (Gr. *agape*) seeks to *edify* (Gr. *oikodomei,* build up) the intellectually inferior by denying self. Knowledge is necessary. It certainly is not all that is necessary in man's relationship to God and his fellow man. Just because a person has something analyzed logically, scientifically and judiciously does not mean he is prepared on that basis alone to make an ethical decision about another man's salvation or standing before God. Paul clearly admonishes Christians *not* to judge others on the basis of knowledge alone (cf. Rom. 14:14-15). Knowledge must be tempered with love. Love is the motive that will make the right use of knowledge.

The apostle challenges the intellectualistic approach to Christian brotherhood by saying, "If any one *imagines* (Gr. *dokei,* supposes, believes) that he knows something, he does not yet know as he *ought* (Gr. *dei,* is obligated, necessarily, is required) to know." Egocentric knowledge falls short of God's mark for man. There is more to ultimate truth than accumulation of knowledge for knowledge's sake. Man has a higher obligation than knowledge (I Cor. 13:1-13)—that is to *love!*

8:3 Presentation of Ideal: The object of true knowledge is not human intellectual superiority, but a participation in the divine nature (cf. II Peter 1:3-4; II Cor. 3:18; John 6:63) of God Himself. Paul puts it this way, "But if one loves God, one is known by him." The object of true knowledge is not "something" but Some One—an experiential knowledge of God and Jesus Christ, His Son (cf. John 17:3). God cannot be reduced to fact or doctrines, although he cannot be known apart from his deeds. Paul is not referring to knowing *about* God. He is talking about the knowledge of God that only comes at the point where personal commitment in faith and love is made by the whole person of man to the whole Person of God. The ultimate method of knowing is *agape* (love)—personal commitment which surrenders all of self to God. Paul's view of ultimate knowledge rests on divine revelation wherein God's knowledge of man has priority. No man can *know* God unless he first lets God know him. Man cannot even love God until he allows God to love him first (I John 4:19). As long as a man elevates himself through pride in human reason, he will not *humble* himself to be *ruled over* by God. Unless Christ takes complete possession of us we cannot know him (see John 13:6-9) because we are not letting him know us. Paul uses this same idea in Galatians 4:9—to be known by God is to know him. The point is this: when God knows us as his own, in a relationship akin to marriage (but deeper and surer), it is only then that we *know* the blessedness of being related to him. Certain aspects of the divine nature may be known factually from nature (cf. Rom. 1:19-20), but experiential, intimate and personal knowledge of God comes only to those who do his will (John 7:17). Being known by and possessed by God, enables man to see things from God's viewpoint (II Cor. 5:14-17). Only then does man begin to have proper knowledge of anything—most of all, proper knowledge about whether he may eat food sacrificed to idols or not.

Man must love God with all his mind, soul, heart and strength, and his neighbor as himself. When that decision is made we will take everything we know about God's revealed will, about the experiences of life, and about our neighbor and use it to build up the kingdom of God in people's lives. To love God is to be known by Him (I John 4:20). Love requires proper concern for a brother's lack of understanding. It is love that controls the Christian from acting according to knowledge (even when such knowledge may be correct enough in itself) when it would tempt, alienate, or otherwise cause a brother to sin who does not see the issue as clearly or as innocently as I suppose I do.

SECTION 2

The Persons (8:4-7)

4 Hence, as to the eating of food offered to idols, we know that "an idol has no real existence," and that "there is no God but one." 5 For although there may be so-called gods in heaven or on earth—as indeed there are many "gods" and many "lords"—6 yet for us there is one God, the Father, from whom are all things and for whom we exist, and one Lord, Jesus Christ, through whom are all things and through whom we exist.

7 However, not all possess this knowledge. But some, through being hitherto accustomed to idols, eat food as really offered to an idol; and their conscience, being weak, is defiled.

8:4-6 The Sure: After digressing toward the subject of true knowledge, Paul comes back to the question of eating meat sacrificed to an idol. He appeals to the validity of using empirical knowledge to establish that an idol is not a god. He uses an interesting idiom in Greek to say this. Literally it reads, *oidamen hoti ouden eidolon en kosmo,* or, "we know that no an idol in the world (is) . . ." The RSV translated it, ". . . we know that an idol has no real existence." Idols are "out of this world." They do not exist.

FIRST CORINTHIANS

Throughout chapters 8, 9, and 10 of this epistle, and in Romans chapters 14 and 15, Paul deals with the problems arising in the area of opinions because some Christians are "strong" and some are "weak." The terms "strong" and "weak" are not referring to spiritual strength or weakness—nor to morality. Both categories of brethren, if they have not love, consider themselves spiritually superior to the other. Without love, the one who "abstains" (or "the weak") will consider the other *worldly*. Without love, the one who "partakes" (or "the strong") will categorize the scrupulous as *pharisaical*. The terms "weak" and "strong" have to do with matters of opinion or individual preferences. They have to do with an individual's cultural, psychological, traditional background and experience. The translation "weak" and "strong" is unfortunate. It would be better to translate, "him who abstains" and "him who eats" as in Romans 14:3; or, better yet, "the sure" and "the suspicious" as we have done in our outline.

Since Paul classifies "the weak" (8:7) as those whose scruples cause them to *abstain* from eating meat that had been sacrificed to idols; by inference, we classify the "strong" as those who could, with good conscience, *eat* meat sacrificed to idols because they *knew* that an idol was not a god.

It should be a matter of certain knowledge to every Christian that there is only one God. He is God of the whole universe, God of all men, Creator of everything that exists, and there is one Lord, Jesus Christ, co-equal with God. It was clear to every Jew (Deut. 6:4). If there is only one God, it is clear that "an idol has no real existence." Therefore, the worship of idols is sheer folly; it is the worship of nothing.

8:7 The Suspicious: But such knowledge was not so certain in the minds of some of the Christians at Corinth. To some of the Greek-Christians the images (idols) did represent *something*. In the pagan world there were many so-called gods and lords in the heavens and on earth. So, in the mentality, opinions, or "suspicions" of the Greek-Christians these images were real beings called "gods." Paul repeats his admonition in chapter 10:19-20 that an idol has no real existence, but he warns there that eating meat sacrificed to an idol may endanger even a "sure" Christian of fellowship with demons!

The Greek phrase, *'All' ouk en pasin he gnosis,* is literally, "But not in all the knowledge." The RSV translation, *possess,* is not a good translation. No doubt, every Christian in Corinth had been

CHAPTER 8   FIRST CORINTHIANS 8:4-7

taught that there was only one God, Jehovah, and one Lord, Jesus Christ. They undoubtedly acknowledged the teaching. But what they acknowledged was not "in" them—that is, not integrated into their willingness. The knowledge that there was only one God was something about which they still had emotional reservations. Paul wrote in Romans 14:23, "But he who has doubts is condemned, if he eats, because he does not act from faith; for whatever does not proceed from faith is sin." These Greek-Christians had been taught there was only one God—they had mentally acknowledged it—but they still didn't *trust it!* In Romans 14:5, Paul writes, "Let every one be *fully convinced* in his own mind." The Greek verb there is *plerophoreistho,* meaning literally, "completely carried." It is the same verb as in Hebrews 10:22, translated, "full assurance" of faith. In other words, unless the knowledge is "carried fully" by the mind, the "weak" or "suspicious" Christian should not engage in the action.

    The question of urgency, however, is, *why* do not all Christians have full assurance that idols are nothing? Paul's answer is, "some, through being hitherto accustomed to idols, eat food as really offered to an idol; and their conscience, being weak, is defiled." The reason for their weakness is a life-time consciousness of idols as gods. RSV translates the Greek word *sunetheia* by the word *accustomed,* but it means literally, "to know with." It would be better translated, *consciousness.* The word does *not* emphasize *compulsion* to *do* right, as we think of *conscience.* It emphasizes a conscious *knowledge* of what *is* right or wrong. Paul's point is that these Greek-Christians had lived so long with idolatry in their every-day consciousness, they were simply conditioned or trained to accept the idea that an idol was really a god. People may live in an environment where what is false is so widely accepted and practiced as true, and never challenged, they grow up assuming it is true. Such attitudes become so deeply ingrained on the mind through constant exposure and the pressures of circumstance they are not easily wiped out of the mind. Jewish Christians had difficulties changing their minds about many things in the Mosaic system abrogated by the New Testament.

    The Greek phrase, *hos eidolothuton esthiousin,* is literally, "as an idol offering they eat. . . ." They felt they were still partaking in the *worship* of the idol by eating food which had been offered in the pagan sacrifices. Missionaries today have similar experiences. A belief in witchcraft or voodoo long continues to lurk in otherwise well taught Christians and they allow themselves to be bothered by it.

Plummer offers this comment: "It is the force of habits which lasts. . . . They have been so accustomed to regard an idol as a reality, as representing a god that exists, that . . . in spite of their conversion, they cannot get rid of the feeling that, by eating food which has been offered to an idol, they are taking part in the worship of heathen gods; they cannot eat from faith (Rom. 14:23)."

The meat, in itself, was neither clean or unclean. It was indifferent. But since they could not help feeling it was defiled by having been offered to idols, they went against their own judgment of what was right and thereby judged themselves. While Paul plainly classifies this as a sign of intellectual weakness, he also makes it clear in the remainder of the chapter that such weakness was entitled to forbearance and respect from Christians who were not bothered by the weakness. Foods have nothing in themselves which will bring guilt upon a person (see Mark 7:18-19; Luke 11:41). When people do something they are convinced is wrong they bring condemnation upon themselves. God is greater than our mind, and if our own mind condemns us, we will stand condemned (cf. I John 3:19-21). An uninstructed mind may condemn what is *not* wrong, or allow what *is*; but in any case, it ought to be obeyed until it is instructed.

SECTION 3

The Practice (8:8-13)

> 8 Food will not commend us to God. We are no worse off if we do not eat, and no better off if we do. 9 Only take care lest this liberty of yours somehow become a stumbling block to the weak. 10 For if any one sees you, a man of knowledge, at table in an idol's temple, might he not be encouraged, if his conscience is weak, to eat food offered to idols? 11 And so by your knowledge this weak man is destroyed, the brother for whom Christ died. 12 Thus, sinning against your brethren and wounding their conscience when it is weak, you sin against Christ. 13 Therefore, if food is a cause of my brother's falling, I will never eat meat, lest I cause my brother to fall.

8:8-9 The Sanction: Those who because of their superior knowledge eat meat sacrificed to idols without guilt are not esteemed by God any higher than those who abstain because of guilt. While

CHAPTER 8　　　　　FIRST CORINTHIANS 8:8-13

Paul is concerned here with the "strong" being careless toward the "weak," it is clear (from Romans chapter 14) the "weak" are not relieved of obligation to understand the "strong" person's liberties and, in love, allow him freedom to exercise his knowledge (cf. I Cor. 10:29). The abstainer is as responsible to love as the non-abstainer! But here in I Corinthians 8, Paul is addressing his admonition to the non-abstainers. They were apparently contemptuous of the abstainers and continuing to eat meat sacrificed to idols with the attitude that they *did not care* how their actions affected their brethren. Food, no matter what it is, is a matter of indifference. Peter had to be given a divine revelation about this matter (cf. Acts 10:9-16). Paul says, "We gain nothing by eating; we lose nothing by not eating." The issue is not eating or abstaining from any particular food. Food has nothing to do with the spiritual in man. It sustains the body only. Paul is not, of course, dealing with gluttony, or taking poisonous substances into the body which would do physical harm. He is dealing with all foods as to where purchased and what association they may have had prior to the Christian's contact with them.

The issue is: *how much do you love your brother*! The admonition is that we must be prepared to sacrifice any liberty we have concerning *things* to save a *person*. The sanction is not against food of any kind. It is against an unloving attitude.

In verse 9 Paul uses the Greek word *exousia* and it is translated, *liberty*. It is the word most commonly translated, "authority, right, power." The most common Greek word for *liberty* is *eleutheria;* also often translated, *freedom*. Paul is evidently emphasizing the *rights* the knowledgeable Christian has because of a clearer understanding. Such a one has the *right* to eat anything he pleases without guilt. But just because it is an inalienable right does not mean it cannot be willingly surrendered out of love. The Christian brother whose knowledge (cultural, experiential, or scriptural) permits him to be free of guilt in some matter of opinion, dare not practice it if it will cause another brother (who understands the practice from a different cultural or moral background) to stumble and fall in his spiritual journey. Paul uses the Greek word *proskomma* for *stumbling-block;* it means, "an obstacle against which one may dash his foot, or a hindrance over which one trips and falls." That which one Christian may do with freedom from guilt may, because of the doing, produce a serious failure in another Christian who may be encouraged to do what he considers wrong.

8:10-11 The Sin: To lead someone by your liberty to do something he believes he is not free to do, causes him to sin, to incur guilt, and destroys his union with Christ. The exercise of rights by the "strong" may destroy the fundamental moral resolve of a "weaker" brother against sinful practices so that he may be led to engage in practices *clearly prohibited* in the scriptures. Paul wrote to Roman Christians, ". . . it is wrong for anyone to make others fall by what he eats" (Rom. 14:20).

It *is* sinful to do anything that would cause anyone else to violate his own conscience. It is a sin to carelessly flaunt one's Christian liberty and undermine the moral decisiveness of another. Too many think of their *own* "rights" first. Paul said we ought to endure anything rather than put an obstacle in the way of the gospel of Christ (I Cor. 9:12). It is a sinful attitude that does *not* think *first* of pleasing one's brother for his good to edify him (Rom. 15:1-2) because our Lord did not please himself (Rom. 15:3). These principles apply to things Christians may have every right to do; things the knowledgeable Christian is certain are not at all sinful in themselves; things the Christian may do without any guilt. If, through any right we may have, a brother may be morally injured we *must suspend* that right for his salvation.

8:12-13 The Seriousness: Paul uses the Greek present participle *tuptontes* which is translated *wounding*. In present, participial, form the word means a continuous, violent, *beating*. It is the same word used to describe the beating the soldiers gave Christ (Matt. 27:30; Mark 15:19). Earlier (8:11) Paul said causing a weak brother to sin against his own conscience was to *destroy* the brother for whom Christ died. Now (8:12) he says such sin against a brother is sin against Christ. That is serious. Destroy another human being and you are actually attempting to destroy God. Paul warned the Romans "Do not, for the sake of food, destroy the work of God" (Rom. 14:20). Trample upon another human being's weaknesses and you are despising the work of God in that person's life—you are despising God! It is that serious! To have one's own way (even if that way is correct and guiltless in itself) at the expense of another person's relationship to Christ is to commit a grievous sin against the Lord.

In verse 13 Paul uses the double negative in Greek *ou me* to state emphatically that if eating meat would cause a brother to *stumble* (Gr. *skandalizei*, be scandalized, trapped, ensnared), he would *never* eat meat again. The Greek text also includes the phrase, *eis ton aiona,* which would be translated, "unto the end of the age, or world." In other words Paul is saying, "I am ready to give up any practice of my life, even if it is harmless and enjoyable and may be done with a clear conscience, *if it causes any brother to destroy his relationship with Christ.*" Only those who are willing to do the same are fit for the kingdom of God (Rom. 14:15-21).

SECTION 4

THE PROVISO

The self-denial of the "strong" brother should be allowed a proviso (i.e., a qualification). This will be amplified at more length in chapters nine and ten. Suffice it to say here, the non-abstaining brother is not obligated to give up his Christian liberty in some cases: (a) there are definite scriptural examples (as well as commands) by both Jesus and Paul (Matt. 15:1-20; Mark 7:1-13; Gal. 2:3-5; Gal. 2:11-14; 5:1-12; Col. 2:16-23) that when certain "brethren" tried to bind on them traditions and opinions as *necessary* for salvation, the Christian is *obligated* to *resist;* (b) there are people, minutely scrupulous ("nit-pickers"), who may try to use an appeal to their scruples against some area of liberty to serve their own selfish ends. This is also wrong. Christian judgment faces one of its most demanding tasks when the performance of some opinion might injure a tender conscience, while its non-performance would be surrendering to pharisaic traditionalism and harm the cause of Christian liberty. This is sometimes the case in the Christian struggle to promote liberty and Christian unity at the same time.

It would not be fitting to end comments here without suggesting some areas in modern society where the Christian love Paul is calling for may be practiced along with decisions to resist legalism:

  a. Entertainment, pastimes (movies, television, games, hobbies).
  b. Foods (Jewish *kosher* foods; Roman Catholic taboos; use of alcoholic beverages—although the Bible does not *command* total abstinence, this principle of stumbling blocks would make total abstinence the safest practice).
  c. Cultural traditions (dress and grooming; worship traditions; some economic practices; political preferences).
  d. Vocations (if a Christian works at a vocation which might cause someone to stumble, shouldn't the Christian find another vocation?)

APPLICATIONS:

1. Are there today articles or commodities or things used in or associated with ungodliness which might be neutral in themselves but injurious to a Christian's conscience? Name some.
2. Would Paul's instruction about things sacrificed to *idols* apply today in some foreign countries? Where? Why?
3. What should a Christian do in a foreign country where idols are worshiped?
4. If there are brethren in a congregation who seem to be *too* scrupulous about some things, what should the congregation do?
5. If there are brethren in a congregation who seem to be insensitive to other's scruples, what should the congregation do?
6. Would you classify yourself as "weak" or "strong"?
7. Where would you classify a Christian who thought attending movies was wrong? . . . Who thought playing cards was all right?
8. Do you think one Christian should give up *any* right he has just because another Christian *thinks* it is sinful?
9. Do you think Christian liberty is a threat to Christian unity?
10. Do you think the "weak" Christian brother is a threat to Christian unity?

APPREHENSIONS:

1. Why did some Christians *know* that an idol was not a god, and others did *not know?*
2. How pervasive was idolatry in ancient Corinth?
3. What kind of "knowledge" was Paul talking about?
4. Is it knowledge Paul objects to, or is it the misuse of knowledge?
5. How is knowledge to be used?
6. What is man's highest obligation?
7. What is the ultimate object of knowledge?
8. Who are the "strong"?
9. Who are the "weak"?
10. Why do some Christians think an idol is really a god?
11. Would a Christian who knows an idol is not a god be superior in his spirituality in the eyes of God?
12. How serious is it to do something that causes a weaker brother to feel guilty?
13. When would a strong Christian be obligated to resist the demands of a weaker brother?
14. In what areas of modern life does Paul's principle of liberty versus love apply?

Chapter Nine

THE PROBLEM OF FREEDOM
(9:1-27)

IDEAS TO INVESTIGATE:

1. Why did Paul have to write to the Corinthians about his rights?
2. How did he defend his rights?—on what basis?
3. If Paul was so defensive about his rights, why did he not use them?
4. Did Paul compromise Christian convictions to become all things to all men?
5. What does self-control have to do with freedom?

SECTION 1

Recitation of Rights (9:1-14)

9 Am I not free? Am I not an apostle? Have I not seen Jesus our Lord? Are not you my workmanship in the Lord? ²If to others I am not an apostle, at least I am to you; for you are the seal of my apostleship in the Lord.

3 This is my defense to those who would examine me. ⁴Do we not have the right to our food and drink? ⁵Do we not have the right to be accompanied by a wife, as the other apostles and the brothers of the Lord and Cephas? ⁶Or is it only Barnabas and I who have no right to refrain from working for a living? ⁷Who serves as a soldier at his own expense? Who plants a vineyard without eating any of its fruit? Who tends a flock without getting some of the milk?

8 Do I say this on human authority? Does not the law say the same? ⁹For it is written in the law of Moses, "You shall not muzzle an ox when it is treading out the grain." Is it for oxen that God is concerned? ¹⁰Does he not speak entirely for our sake? It was written for our sake, because the plowman should plow in hope and the thresher thresh in hope of a share in the crop. ¹¹If we have sown spiritual good among you, is it too much if we reap your material benefits? ¹²If others share this rightful claim upon you, do not we still more?

FIRST CORINTHIANS

Nevertheless, we have not made use of this right, but we endure anything rather than put an obstacle in the way of the gospel of Christ. 13Do you not know that those who are employed in the temple service get their food from the temple, and those who serve at the altar share in the sacrificial offerings? 14In the same way, the Lord commanded that those who proclaim the gospel should get their living by the gospel.

9:1-7 The Logic: What is freedom? Is a Christian really free? The answer to those questions depends on the meaning of the word *freedom*! Freedom is a state of *character*, not circumstances. Freedom belongs to persons and has a personal objective. Freedom is not an objective in itself. Man is not *just* free—he is free *for* some purpose. Freedom should have as its objective the production of the highest form of personality possible. Freedom should have as its purpose the production of character—good character. The "freedom" (or license) that allows self-indulgence and anarchy produces bad character because man's potential has a higher goal than self-indulgence. Freedom (the opposite of bondage and enslavement) by its very nature should exist for the purpose of removing all hindrances and restraints that would keep a person from reaching the highest potential for good of which he is capable.

This is precisely what Christian freedom is all about. God, through Christ, has set the Christian free from all hindrances and restraints that would keep him from reaching the highest possibility for which he was redeemed. God, through Christ, makes everything and everyone available for the Christian's development (I Cor. 3:21-23). It is not our surroundings or our circumstances that keep us from our highest God-ordained possibilities. Attitudes are what enslave us and hinder us. The attitudes which hinder are: (a) guilt; (b) insecurity; (c) rebellion against our Creator and his creation; (d) rejecting the truth about what is real and enduring; (e) fear of death; (f) selfishness. If these may be conquered we will be free and reaching God's potential for us no matter what our circumstances (even persecution and prison). The real issue is not physical liberation but spiritual liberation. Any man, anywhere, whether politically, socially or literally imprisoned or not, may be *spiritually free* if he trusts God's Word concerning man's true purpose and possibility.

In other words, our true freedom depends on whether we believe God's word about what he made us for and how he says we may

CHAPTER 9   FIRST CORINTHIANS 9:1-14

attain it. God made us to produce in us and for us character of the highest goodness. He made us to be "conformed to the image of his Son" (Rom. 8:29). Truth makes man free (John 8:31-32). All truth, God's truth, wherever it is, in the Bible, in creation, in other men, we are to find it, believe it and act according to it. ". . . Where the Spirit of the Lord is, there is freedom . . . And we all, with unveiled face, beholding the glory of the Lord, are being changed into his likeness from one degree of glory to another . . ." (II Cor. 3:17-18). The apostle Paul was a man free in Christ, reaching for the highest good Christ intended him to have. He explains how he *used* his freedom to reach that goal. He has said, in chapter eight, that he was not asking the Christians at Corinth to do anything that he was not doing.

Paul claimed every right allowed him by God's word. He refused to let any man, by making human rules where God never made any, take away any right by which he might reach the goal Christ intended in him. One part of Christ's goal for Paul was his world-wide apostleship. In a series of rhetorical questions, Paul sets forth the logic of his freedom and its use. His first assertion of the logic of his rights is in his question, "Am I not an apostle?" He not only had the rights of a Christian but also the special rights of one particularly commissioned by the Lord to take the gospel to the whole world (an apostle). He is not thinking here of his *authority* as an apostle, but of his right to financial *support* as one "sent" (an apostle). His second appeal to logic is in his question, "Are you not my workmanship in the Lord?" He claimed the right to support on the basis of their obligation to him as the one who brought them to Christ (see Rom. 15:26-27; Gal. 6:6). The Greek word *sphragis* is translated *seal* and means, "to authenticate, to validate." Their conversion to Christ certainly confirmed Paul's apostleship and his right to expect them to support him.

The Greek participle *anakrinousin* is present indicative, *not* subjunctive, and indicates some of the Christians were *examining* or *making judgments* about his right, not only to expect financial support for himself as he preached the gospel, but also the right to expect support for a family. Paul apparently received financial support from the church at Antioch when he was first "sent out" by that church (Acts 13:1-3); he received some support from the church at Philippi (Phil. 4:14-18). But from the beginning of his second missionary journey he chose to support himself by working at his trade as a

163

FIRST CORINTHIANS

tentmaker (Acts 15:40; 18:1-4; II Cor. 11:7; I Thess. 2:9; 4:11; II Thess. 3:8).

While the apostle used the Greek word *eleutheros,* translated *free,* in verse 1, he used the word *exousian,* translated *right,* in verses 4, 5, and 6, (see comments, 8:9 on word *liberty*). Paul lists Barnabas as one also set aside by the Lord and the church for a full-time ministry and as such, one who has the right to expect Christians to support him, and a family. Since Barnabas (see Acts 4:36; 9:26-27; 11:22-30; 13:2; 15:39) was not an apostle in the same sense as Paul, this is evidently a statement of the rights of all full-time Christian evangelists to be supported financially by other Christians. Paul's statement of the rights of an apostle, and an evangelist, to have a wife deals a death-blow to the Roman Catholic "canon-law" that popes and priests must *not* have wives. Paul substantiates the Gospel records that the apostle Peter was married and his wife journeyed with him in his evangelistic work. Our text clearly states that the "brothers of the Lord" (James, Joseph, Simon and Judas, Matt. 13:55) also had wives who accompanied them in their work. Mary, mother of Jesus was not a "perpetual virgin."

Paul's third appeal to logic is in verse 7. He uses three analogies from the common life of that time to prove his point. In II Timothy 2:1-7 Paul has similar analogies to encourage Timothy to train a company of faithful, full-time evangelists, like himself, who will be devoting all their time to teaching others. They must not get "entangled in civilian pursuits." Now, in this letter to the Corinthians, he declares that a "soldier" of Christ who has not entangled himself in civilian pursuits but has given full-time to the ministry of the Word has the right to expect to be supported financially by the "army" of the Lord, the church. Not only so, but the "soldier's" wife and family also.

9:8-12a The Law: Paul anticipates that some of the Corinthians might object that his first defense of his rights is based on human thinking. So, he asks a rhetorical question, "It is true, is it not, that as a human I am speaking these things?" He expects them to answer, "Yes!" In so doing, he is able to give impact to his introduction of the Law of Moses—the word of God—into the defense of his rights. He follows with a second rhetorical question, "The Law of Moses, does it not say the same thing?" The expected answer is, "Yes!" But Paul immediately supplies the answer, "For it is written in the law of Moses, you shall not muzzle an ox when it is

CHAPTER 9 FIRST CORINTHIANS 9:1-14

treading out the grain." Paul's quotation comes from Deuteronomy 25:4. The Israelites threshed grain by having oxen pull a stone or a "threshing sledge" with iron wheels over the grain to separate the grain from the husks. The ox was permitted to eat of the grain as he threshed. This was demanded by God in his Law to keep men from being cruel to animals. God cares about the animals in his creation. It is God's will that animals be cared for by those whom they serve. This regulation in Deuteronomy is contained in a series of laws about economic and social justice. But it is not for oxen *only* that God is concerned. Paul does not mean to say that God is not concerned for oxen—he has already established that. Surely, if God legislates that oxen serving men are to be fed by men, then men serving others in spiritual things are to be fed by those they serve. Paul applies the same Old Testament law to the support of elders who labor in preaching and teaching the Word (I Tim. 5:17-18).

The word *entirely,* in verse 10, is too strong for the context. Paul does not mean the law of Deuteronomy 25:4 was totally for man and not for oxen at all. The Greek word *pantos* might be translated here, "by all means, doubtless, at least." The teaching of Jesus (Matt. 6:25-34) explains that while God cares for birds and lilies, he will "much more" care for men who love him. Paul answers his own rhetorical question of verse 10 by stating, "It *was* written for our sake, because the plowman should plow in hope . . . of a share in the crop." The Greek word *opheilei* is translated *should,* but carries the idea of obligation or *duty*; it is sometimes translated *ought, owe,* or *bound.* The "plowman" is duty bound to "plow" in hope of sharing in the product of his labor.

The plowman's right becomes an analogy by which Paul asserts the right of a spiritual "sower" to be supported in *material* (Gr. *sarkika,* fleshly, physical) sustenance from the hands of those who have benefited from the spiritual sowing.

Almost indignantly (9:12a) Paul asks, "If you authorize others the right of sharing your material goods, shouldn't you acknowledge that we (Christian evangelists) have even greater right?" Who are the "others"? Some think they are the other apostles and other evangelists who had already been given the privilege of support by the churches (9:3-6). Some think "others" refers to the Judaizers (II Cor. chapters 3 and 4) who had taught them. In addition "others" may refer to teachers of Greek philosophy and letters. It was common practice for the peripatetic (walking-around) teachers of Greek culture and philosophy to be supported financially by the parents of their students. Whatever the case in Corinth, it is a fact of the modern world that while men and women willingly band together in cities or rural districts and pay taxes for gymnasiums, football stadiums, huge public school buildings, buses, teachers' and administrators' salaries for the secular education of their societies, some Christians often begrudge a minister of the gospel and his family a salary commensurate with the average of the membership of the church. Preachers and evangelists who are in the ministry primarily for the money are hirelings (John 10:7-18)! But that is not what Paul is discussing here. His phrase, ". . . do not we still more?" signifies the right of a faithful evangelist or preacher of the gospel to expect "even more" (or, "rather first") consideration in material support than Christians give in other areas of life.

9:12b-14 The Lord: If Paul found it necessary to be financially supported, or to marry, to reach the goal God had for his life, then he declared himself free to do so. Not only was he free to do so, he insisted the brethren acknowledge his rights. If Paul had *not* insisted that others at least acknowledge his freedom or his rights, he would have allowed the truth to be perverted and, to that extent, have forfeited his freedom by compromising with falsehood.

Now Paul might surrender his *use* of these freedoms or rights of his own to take an even better action in order to produce the highest good. But he must not surrender his *right* to such freedom for that would be surrender to spiritual slavery. Our freedom in Christ must always be defended (Gal. 5:1ff.) whether we exercise every aspect of it or not.

The very essence of freedom is choice. Freedom in its ultimate and highest sense can never be legislated or enforced. Christian freedom *is* the ultimate freedom. Christ fulfilled the law written in ordinances. Those who choose Christ are no longer limited by the law. Their goal of spiritual growth is not fettered by or limited by law. They may choose the highest spiritual goal of all—being conformed to the image of God's Son—perfection. Paul always tried to choose what he thought, guided by God's revelation, was the highest spirituality in his own life and in the life of others.

So, here, he exercises his right to surrender what he considers a lesser right (to be financially supported by the Corinthian church) in favor of a more spiritually productive right (not to put any obstacle in the way of the gospel of Christ). This was Paul's free choice for

CHAPTER 9   FIRST CORINTHIANS 9:1-14

Corinth. But apparently it was not always his choice. In a different circumstance, and with a different body of believers, he chose to accept their financial support (see Phil. 4:15-18), for their spiritual growth.

It appears the Corinthian church later accused Paul of being a false apostle because he did not take financial support (see II Cor. 12:13, 16, 17) from them. While Paul could not know ahead of time how the Corinthians would react to forfeiting his right to financial support, it must have grieved him to later be despised for an act of love he intended for their spiritual advancement. But that goes with the territory of exercising Christian freedom!

In the first covenant (the Old Testament) the Lord commanded that the priests who devoted all their life to serving in the Temple were to be sustained by sharing (Gr. *summerizontai,* a dividing-up, an apportioning) of all the offerings given by their Hebrew brethren to the Lord. Reviving this ordinance of the Lord was one of the first and most significant acts of Hezekiah in his attempt to bring repentance to the nation (see II Chron. 31:4-19).

The Lord Jesus Christ ordained the same practice for the New Testament church. The Greek word *dietaxe, ordained* or *commanded,* was used in other Greek literature to describe official *appointments* to position of authority. The Lord did not approach the matter of support for full-time Christian servants as a suggestion but as an official edict. He commanded it. The church has no choice in the matter. The individual servant of the Lord may choose to forego this right, but the church is ordered by the Lord himself to support the faithful evangelists it sets aside to full-time service in the Gospel. The laborer is worthy of his hire (Matt. 10:10; Luke 10:7; I Tim. 5:17-18).

A few commentators have used the KJV translation, ". . . they which preach the gospel should live of the gospel" to say the Lord meant "those who preach the gospel should live according to what they preach." The *context* makes it clear this is not the meaning. The RSV translation gives the correct meaning, ". . . those who proclaim the gospel should get their living by the gospel." The Greek words are even clearer; ". . . *ek tou euangeliou zen.*" The Greek preposition *ek* means "out of," or "from"; the Greek infinitive *zen* means "to live." Those who proclaim the gospel are to live out of the gospel.

FIRST CORINTHIANS

SECTION 2

Relinquishment of Rights (9:15-18)

15 But I have made no use of any of these rights, nor am I writing this to secure any such provision. For I would rather die than have any one deprive me of my ground for boasting. 16For if I preach the gospel, that gives me no ground for boasting. For necessity is laid upon me. Woe to me if I do not preach the gospel! 17For if I do this of my own will, I have a reward; but if not of my own will, I am entrusted with a commission. 18What then is my reward? Just this: that in my preaching I may make the gospel free of charge, not making full use of my right in the gospel.

9:15-16 Sacrifice: In this section the apostle begins to make a transition from the specific right of financial support he claimed, to the principle of the need for relinquishment of any right in certain circumstances. He has called upon the Corinthians to consider the *principle* (8:1-13) earlier. He illustrates the *application* of the principle in his own actions (9:1-14). He will state the purpose of the principle (9:19-27) later, but here he is proving that he has not asked the Corinthians to make a more severe sacrifice of rights than he himself had been willing to make. He uses the Greek word *kechremai,* a perfect tense verb, which indicates an action begun in the past and continuing at the present. Paul had never exercised his right to be financially supported upon the Corinthian church.

Furthermore, he denies that he has used the illustration of his own practice as some sort of subtle attempt to elicit financial support from them now. He says, ". . . nor am I writing these things in order that so it should become with me" (literal translation of the Greek). His motive in using himself as an example is pure. He says, in fact, he would rather die than have any one deprive him of the opportunity to exemplify in his own life the principle of sacrificing rights for the edification of others. And Paul never used the phrase, "I would rather die . . ." in a flippant way. He was "deadly" serious about this principle! He did *not* mean to say he *boasted* about his own sacrifices in an arrogant, self-righteous way. Paul uses the word *boasting* (Gr. *kauchema,* glorying) in the good sense, meaning, "to hold up or exalt as an example of Christian virtue" (see II Cor. 7:14-15). This translation clarifies the true meaning of the next three verses.

168

CHAPTER 9　　　　　　FIRST CORINTHIANS 9:15-18

In light of the above remarks we should paraphrase verse 16, "When I preach the gospel I have nothing to hold up or exalt as an example of Christian sacrifice—necessity lies upon me, I feel compelled to do so. I am utterly miserable and unsatisfied if I do not preach the gospel." Paul discusses his compulsion for preaching in II Corinthians 5:11-21.

The highwater mark of Christian discipleship is when a person freely chooses to give up his rights in order to remove any obstacle to the gospel of Christ being heard or seen. Giving up "rights" did not hinder Paul in his race toward the highest good God could make of his life. In fact, this discipline sharpened his self-control (cf. 9:24-27) and became beneficial in the development of godliness in him. His choice to give up the right to financial support from the Corinthians gave him opportunity to perfect his character in the area of servanthood and helpfulness. This actually helped Paul form within himself the very nature of Christ. Jesus is the perfect example of self-control and servanthood rather than rights. Having every right to expect the disciples to wash *his* feet (John 13), he washed theirs instead. One cannot be a disciple of Jesus unless he is willing to *forfeit* rights rather than let them become obstacles to the gospel. There is only one way to serve God and that is to serve mankind. If we are going to serve sinful and imperfect men, inevitably, somewhere, we will have to choose to forfeit some of our rights. Jesus did! (Phil. 2:5-11).

9:17-18 Satisfaction: What does Paul mean, "For if I do this of my own will . . ."? Did he not preach by choice? Certainly! Remember, he is speaking about the relinquishment of certain rights which were his because he *was* a full-time preacher of the gospel. Paul is trying to convince these Corinthians that there are *greater rewards* to be found in the relinquishment of rights.

We might paraphrase verses 17 and 18 thus, "If preaching is simply my way of choosing to make a living, I should be, and will be, rewarded with my living; if I could make a living another way, and I could, but I have chosen to preach anyway, then it is apparent that I consider preaching more than a way to make a living—I consider it a divine stewardship with which I have been entrusted. What reward, then, or satisfaction do I receive, if I receive no financial support? Just this: my pay is to do without pay! My joy is in making the gospel free of charge in order that no one might use the idea of my right to financial support as an obstacle to the truth of God." Paul would not allow the slightest hint of profiteering or exploitation to be found in his ministry (cf. II Cor. 2:17; 4:2).

FIRST CORINTHIANS

Great satisfaction comes from giving up rights when others may be served for the sake of Christ. Paul refused to lose the satisfaction he received in such service by *insisting* on a few rights or liberties. He would rather die than be robbed of the great enjoyment he received in sacrificing for others. "It is more blessed to give than to receive" (Acts 20:38). Satisfaction and contentment is part of a godly character. God has given us the freedom to choose to renounce certain freedoms or rights he has given us in order to have this contentment. This satisfaction which Paul enjoyed is somewhat like the satisfaction a mother or father gets when giving up one of their "rights" to help a precious child. It is the satisfaction a teacher gets when he surrenders one of his "rights" to help a student reach his highest potential. It is the satisfaction a craftsman gets when he gives up his "right" to sleep and to food in order to produce the finest work of which his hands are capable. Paul was no masochist. He did not give up financial support because he loved to suffer. He sought no self-righteous merit (cf. Phil. 3:1-16). His aim was to glorify Christ and present no obstacle whatsoever to the salvation of any man. If Paul had been persuaded that *refusing* the financial support might become an obstacle, he would not have refused it. Could refusal ever become a problem? Apparently the Corinthians made it a hindrance to accepting Paul's apostleship (cf. II Cor. 11:7-11; 12:11-18; II Thess. 1:9; 3:8). And even in modern times, some self-supporting preachers and missionaries have found it an obstacle to their ministries.

The comments of Fred Fisher, *Commentary on 1 & 2 Corinthians,* pg. 146, pub. Word, are pertinent here:

> Paul would have rebelled against the modern practice of paying preachers a salary as if they were mercenaries selling their services. He would have insisted, I think, that churches should support their ministers. There may not seem to be much difference between giving a minister so much support and paying him the same amount in salary. The money is the same. But the principle is not. "Salary" implies payment for services received. "Support" implies that the church enables the minister to be free from worldly concerns so that he may carry on his ministry. His "reward" should not be earthly, but heavenly. The problem is that the misuse of the word "salary" may lead both the church and the minister to take a worldly view of the ministry.

CHAPTER 9　　　　　　　　FIRST CORINTHIANS 9:19-27

Though the modern preacher has a right to expect the church to support his ministry with financial remuneration, he should be willing to relinquish that right should it become an obstacle to the proclamation of the gospel. Furthermore, no Christian preacher should consider financial support his source of satisfaction in the ministry. His satisfaction ("boasting") should be found in servanthood.

SECTION 3

Reasons For Relinquishment (9:19-27)

19 For though I am free from all men, I have made myself a slave to all, that I might win the more. 20 To the Jews I became as a Jew, in order to win Jews; to those under the law I became as one under the law—though not being myself under the law—that I might win those under the law. 21 To those outside the law I became as one outside the law—not being without law toward God but under the law of Christ—that I might win those outside the law. 22 To the weak I became weak, that I might win the weak. I have become all things to all men, that I might by all means save some. 23 I do it all for the sake of the gospel, that I may share in its blessings.

24 Do you not know that in a race all the runners compete, but only one receives the prize? So run that you may obtain it. 25 Every athlete exercises self-control in all things. They do it to receive a perishable wreath, but we an imperishable. 26 Well, I do not run aimlessly, I do not box as one beating the air; 27 but I pommel my body and subdue it, lest after preaching to others I myself should be disqualified.

9:19-22 To Save Some: It is important that Paul lists the salvation of others as his first reason for willingness to relinquish rights. This is the priority he is trying to establish in the consciences of the Corinthians.

When Paul says he is free from all men, he means he is free from being bound by any man's scruples (see I Cor. 10:23, 29, 30; Rom. 14:1-4). He does *not* mean that he has no moral obligation to be his "brother's keeper." All men have that liability. And this is exactly the point to be made in this passage. Though free from the scruples of all men, Paul will gladly relinquish this freedom and submit to their scruples in order to win them to Christ. He does more than merely acknowledge other men's right to have and to practice scruples different than his, he declares his practice is to enslave (Gr. *edoulosa,* aorist tense, "enslaved at some point in the past") himself to other men's scruples in order to save them. The Greek word translated *win* is *kerdeso* and often translated *gain* (as in money or business profit); it is used metaphorically in the scriptures to describe winning someone to the gospel. When we win someone to Christ, we not only gain them for Jesus, we gain a brother (see Matt. 18:15) and are ourselves profited. This is Paul's motivation for sacrificing any right to "gain a brother."

Paul was a Jew. He was reared in the strictest sect of the Jewish culture—the Pharisees (see Phil. 3:4-6). We would suppose he preferred to practice, whenever possible, Jewish cultural habits. He undoubtedly preferred *kosher* food as much as Peter (cf. Acts 10:14); he carried with him the Jewish abhorrence of images and idols (see Acts 17); he went customarily to Jewish synagogues to worship and preach; he practiced Jewish purifications (Acts 21:26) in order to conciliate his Jewish brethren; he defended himself against the charges that he had profaned the Jewish temple (Acts 24:5-21); and reminded Agrippa that he had always lived among the Jews according to the strictest sect of the Pharisees (Acts 26:2-8). When he was among the Jews, Paul honored their Jewish scruples and lived as they did, ate what they ate, abstained from that which they considered unclean, observed their days and seasons. However, when any Jewish brother demanded that Paul keep the law of Moses as a necessity for salvation or membership in the kingdom of God (the church), he vehemently and immediately denounced it as apostasy (cf. Galatians, Romans and Hebrews). He would have Timothy to become circumcised in order not to offend his Jewish brethren (Acts 16:1-4), and on the other hand, he would refuse to yield to the Judaizers who insisted he compel Titus to be circumcised (Gal. 2:3) in order to keep the law of Moses. All this he did in order to bring as many Jews as he could into the saving grace of Christ.

And it was the amazing grace of Christ that could make this Pharisee of the Pharisees, Paul, equally at ease involving himself in Gentile culture ("those outside the law"). He was truthful and firm, but never rude and insulting toward Gentiles for their belief in idols (cf. Acts 19:37). He was so thoroughly familiar with their philosophies, arts, and politics he could communicate the gospel to them in their

CHAPTER 9   FIRST CORINTHIANS 9:19-27

frame-of-reference (Acts 17:22-33; 16:35-39). He fellowshiped with Gentile Christians as his brethren and defended their gospel liberties even against the "pillars of the church" (Gal. 2:1-21). He could eat with unbelievers and even partake of meat sacrificed to idols without wounding his own conscience (I Cor. 10:27-30). Paul could be knowledgeable, courteous and friendly toward unbelievers, and could freely fellowship with Gentile Christian brethren in an atmosphere of perfect equality. But he would never use his liberty as license for immorality (see I Peter 2:16; Gal. 5:13; I Cor. 8:9). Paul considered himself under law to Christ (Rom. 6:12-23). The "law" of Christ is the law of love (Rom. 12:10; II Cor. 5:14; I Tim. 1:5; John 13:34-35; 15:12-17; Gal. 5:14; Col. 3:14-15; James 2:8; Matt. 22:39-40). Love is more compelling and constraining than any law (I Cor. 13:1-13; I John 3:14-24; 4:7-12; 4:13-21). Only under the compulsion of Christ's love is there power to relinquish one's rights for the salvation of another. Only in the constraint of Christ's love is there power to keep the commandments of God's *new* covenant in daily living. Every condescension Paul-the-Jew made to Gentile culture he did so in order to win every Gentile he could to Christ. But he would never participate in any cultural usage, Gentile or Jewish, which compromised the new covenant of faith in Christ.

To the overscrupulous (Jew or Gentile) Paul became scrupulous. He would observe any man's scruples so long as that man did not attempt to bind them on others as *necessary* to covenant relationship with Christ. Every Christian has the same obligation toward all men (cf. I Cor. 8:7; Rom. 15:1; I Thess. 5:14; I Cor. 13:4-7; Acts 20:35, I Cor. 10:33).

In the latter half of verse 22, the verb *gegona* is perfect tense and means, "I *became,* and am *becoming,* all things to all men." It is something he had practiced ever since becoming a Christian and would continue to practice. His statement here does *not* mean he became a two-faced hypocrite. It does *not* mean he compromised any doctrinal or ethical truth. It simply means he tried to project himself into each individual's circumstances as much as possible in order to win them to Christ. It means he made every attempt possible to *understand* the thinking, feelings and actions of others. It means he had an honest interest in people as persons and not just as numerical-conversions. Someone once described teaching, medicine, and the ministry as "the three patronizing professions." But when we "patronize" people we make no effort to understand them—no effort to find some point of personal contact. Paul did *not* patronize people. He made every effort to understand them and live with them within their own cultural, educational and social milieu. The Living Bible paraphrases I Corinthians 9:22: "Whatever a person is like, I try to find common ground with him so that he will let me tell him about Christ and let Christ save him." One of the greatest hindrances to the spread of the Gospel throughout the world is that people of all races and cultures simply do not try to understand one another in matters not clearly commanded in the New Testament. Even Christian people are unwilling to forfeit their rights in order to make such understanding possible. Until Restoration Movement people are willing to sacrifice some of their overly-cherished Anglo-Saxon traditions and customs in order to "understand where others are coming from" we will never accomplish the great ideal for which the Movement began—Christian unity!

9:23-27 To Save Self: The Greek phrase (verse 23), *panta de poio dia to euaggelion hina sugkoinonos autou genomai,* should be translated "All these things I do because of the gospel in order that I may become a joint partaker of it." One commentator insists, "The suggestion that this (verse) means, 'lest I lose my share in salvation' (ICC), misses Paul's meaning. The context indicates that he was concerned with the salvation of others, but that he had no doubt about his own." In the first place, the Greek preposition *dia* denotes "cause or reason." In the second place the Greek verb *genomai* is in the subjunctive mood and indicates Paul was *hoping* to become a joint partaker. In the third place the *context* (9:23-27) *does* suggest Paul feared he would lose his share in the gospel if he did not run so as to obtain it.

Even the word *prize* (verse 24) reinforces the idea that Paul was concerned with the possibility of forfeiting his share in the gospel. The Greek word *brabeion* is translated *prize* and is related to the Greek word *brabeuo* which means "to decide, arbitrate, rule, umpire, award, referee." The *brabeion* was the *prize* awarded by the referees or "rulers" of the Greek games to an athlete who won his race or other contest (see Phil. 3:14; Col. 3:15). The Corinthian brethren would understand immediately the figure of the Greek games as an analogy of the Christian life. Since the time of Alexander the Great, athletic games had been popular throughout the Greek world. The most famous, of course, were the Olympic Games held at Olympia (located in the Peloponnesus). The first games in recorded history were held in 776 B.C. The Roman emperor Nero drove a *quadriga*

CHAPTER 9 FIRST CORINTHIANS 9:19-27

(a chariot pulled by four horses) in the races in 66 A.D. (about 10 years after Paul wrote this letter). Nero was thrown from his chariot and nearly crushed to death; restored to his chariot he continued the contest for a while, but gave up before the end of the course. The *brabeus* (judge or referee), however, knew an emperor from an athlete and awarded Nero the crown of victory. Overcome with happiness when the crowd applauded him, he announced that thereafter not only Athens and Sparta but all Greece should be exempt from any tribute to Rome. The Greek cities accommodated him by running the Olympian, Pythian, Nemean, and Isthmian games in one year; he responded by taking part in all of them. The Isthmian games were second in popularity only to the Olypmics, and were held every third year. Paul must have been an avid sports fan, for he used athletic contests often to illustrate his messages (cf. Phil. 3:14; Gal. 5:7; II Tim. 2:5; 4:7-8; Heb. 12:1).

The Greek word *agonizomenos* is translated *athlete* in verse 25. Its literal meaning is "one who struggles, one who contends, one who agonizes." Our English word *agony* comes from this word. Jesus' struggle in the Garden of Gethsemane is called *agonia* (Luke 22:44). Jude writes that Christians are to "contend earnestly" (Gr. *epagonizesthai*) for the faith once for all delivered to the saints (Jude 3). Right relationship with God is a *struggle*—make no mistake about that! It involves agony and pressure. Christians are contenders, combatants, strugglers.

Every "agonizer" (athlete) must exercise self-control in all things in order to compete as a winner. Paul uses the Greek word *egkrateuetai* translated *temperate* in the KJV, but *self-control* in the RSV. It literally means, "within-strength," or "inner-strength." Self-control is the fruit of the Spirit of God in the Christian (Gal. 5:23). Self-control is what the Christian must "make every effort to" add to his life as a supplement to faith, knowledge, virtue, etc. (II Peter 1:6). Athletes in the Greek games had to endure, according to Horace, the regimen of obedience, sparse diet, and severe training for ten months before he was qualified to enter the actual game. Modern athletes spend weeks and months disciplining their minds and bodies in rigorous training and competition. Some modern professional golfers have been known to practice swinging their clubs until their hands are blistered and bleeding. These all submit to self-discipline in order to win a perishable trophy. Should not Christians, then, be willing and able to exercise self-control for the imperishable crown of eternal life? Should not Christians be willing and able to relinquish a few "rights" or "freedoms" in order to win the game of life?

For Paul there was no *uncertainty* in his regimen of self-discipline. He did not run his race of life *aimlessly* (Gr. *adelos,* unevident, unclear, uncertain). He did not consider the Christian struggle a session in "shadow-boxing" or quixotic jousting with windmills. For him the Christian life was a contest to win, a war in which there was no substitute for victory (Eph. 6:10-23). It was a trial that demanded *severe* self-discipline.

In verse 27 the Greek word *hupopiazo* is translated *pommel* and means literally, "to give a black eye by striking the face." Figuratively Paul is saying, "I beat my body black and blue . . ." to keep it under control. It is inconceivable that Paul is saying he practiced literal flagellation (whipping) of his own flesh. He clearly taught that *literal* severity to the body was of no real spiritual value (Col. 2:18, 23; I Tim. 4:1-3; 4:8; Rom. 13:14). Withdrawal into a monastery and daily scourging of the flesh does not solve the problem of worldly-mindedness. It may, in fact, intensify it by pride in self-righteousness. The other Greek word in verse 27, *doulagogo,* translated *subdue,* is literally, *lead as a slave.* This clarifies Paul's practice of self-control. He, Paul, that is, his *mind,* controlled by the Spirit of Christ, led his *body* as a slave. He articulated this with precision in Romans 6:12-23; 8:5-11; 12:1-8.

Athletes set goals. Their goal is always to win! They must be willing to give up any "freedom" which might be a hindrance to reaching that goal. The Christian's goal is to be transformed in character into the image of Christ. Christians need to see the goal *clearly.* One of the most distressing things about modern man is the obvious aimlessness and distortion in setting this as a goal. If any Christian is not willing to give up whatever is necessary for him and others to attain the highest potential God has for them, that Christian will, at the end of the race, find himself rejected. *Adokimos* is the Greek word translated *disqualified.* It is a word from the ancient alchemist (who was both a pharmacologist and a metallurgist) and his practice of testing metals and *casting aside* those which were spurious.

This is not the final word of the New Testament on Christian freedom. But it is perhaps the clearest and most persuasive presentation to be found. Only the teachings and examples of the Living Word, Jesus Christ, are more compelling.

The man who has surrendered to evil and rebellion against God has imprisoned his "self" behind walls of fear, alienation, hate,

CHAPTER 9 FIRST CORINTHIANS 9:19-27

falsehood and impotence. Man was not made for that kind of character. He cannot be free with that nature controlling him. Those characteristics severely limit any potentiality he may have for growth into the image of Christ. The man who is good only because there is a law standing in his way to being bad is not free either. The only man who is truly free, is the man who is good because he wants to be good for Jesus' sake. It is Jesus Christ who makes us free men by making us new creatures through regeneration. His Spirit is born in us and we are changed into His image from one degree of glory to another as we surrender to his new commandment (compulsion) of love.

APPLICATIONS:

1. Are you *free* in Christ? Free to do what? Do you really *feel* free or do you feel bound? Is freedom ever free of all responsibility?
2. Do you believe all Christians are obligated to give financial support to the ministers of the gospel?
3. How much financial support do you think they should have?
4. What do you think would be the result if all present-day preachers and missionaries decided to find employment away from their ministries in order to support themselves? Would the church survive? grow?
5. Have you ever relinquished any conscientious right belonging to you as a Christian for the sake of a "weaker" brother?
6. Would you rather die than cause a weaker brother to stumble?
7. How far would you go in accommodating yourself to a foreign culture in order to save lost sinners? How far should you go?
8. Could you give up celebrating Thanksgiving if it offended someone? Could you drink a glass of wine with your meal if the culture where you ministered expected it? Could you give up the use of a musical instrument in worship if it offended someone?
9. How much self-control do you exercise in order to be faithful to Christ? In what things or areas? Are you satisfied with your self-control?

APPREHENSIONS:

1. What is freedom?
2. What has the word of God to do with the Christian's freedom?

FIRST CORINTHIANS

3. Should the Christian guard his freedom in Christ? How?
4. What does the Bible say about financial support for ministers of the gospel?
5. Did Paul's decision not to ask the Corinthian church for financial support have any bad effects? What?
6. Is preaching the gospel more than a way to make a living? What is it?
7. What rights would Paul have to relinquish to make his ministry effective among the Jews? among the Gentiles? did he?
8. When Paul said he became "all things to all men" did he mean he could participate in anything anyone else did? What did he mean? Would you?
9. Was Paul afraid there was a possibility that he might lose his share in salvation? Is the Christian life a serious matter? How serious?
10. What is self-control? How does a Christian control self?

Chapter Ten

THE PROBLEM OF PRESUMPTUOUSNESS (10:1-33)

IDEAS TO INVESTIGATE:

1. Why would Paul bring up the failure of the Israelites right here?
2. Why are idolatry and immorality usually coincidental?
3. When is "the end of the ages"?
4. Are all temptations common to all men?
5. In what way is the "cup" which we bless a "participation" in the blood of Christ?
6. Was it possible for the Corinthians to be "partners" with demons?
7. Are *all* things really lawful for a Christian?

SECTION 1

Illustration (10:1-5)

10 I want you to know, brethren, that our fathers were all under the cloud, and all passed through the sea. ²and all were baptized into Moses in the cloud and in the sea, ³and all ate the same supernatural food ⁴and all drank the same supernatural drink. For they drank from the supernatural Rock which followed them, and the Rock was Christ. ⁵Nevertheless with most of them God was not pleased; for they were overthrown in the wilderness.

10:1-4 Privileges: The Corinthians are given a short review in Israelite presumptuousness. The descendants of Jacob ("Israel") were delivered from Egyptian bondage under the privilege of great, supernatural works. They were *immersed* (Gr. *ebaptisanto*) or surrounded by *water* in the cloud and the sea to protect them from the Egyptians. God gave them miraculous guidance in the unknown wilderness by a cloud and a pillar of fire. He sustained them by supernatural food and drink (cf. Exod. 13:1—17:16). God chose them for a messianic destiny. Since the Messiah was in their loins, God gave them the privileges of the Messiah's supernatural sustenance. It was the Anointed One of the Father who actually gave them the miraculous water in the wilderness. Jesus later made it plain that it was not Moses who gave them the bread from heaven, but God himself (John 6:32-33), and man's life is perpetuated not by physical bread but by the supernatural bread—the Word of God, even Jesus.

The ancient Israelites presumed these initial privileges meant God would surely continue to give them security without any need for an exercise of faith and holiness of life on their part. Hebrews 3:7-19 tells us why they became overconfident and presumptuous—pride and the deceitfulness of sin. Later Jews were so smug as to believe that as long as they had the Temple in their midst, God would not punish them for blatant sin (Jer. 7:4-11).

The Greek word *pneumatikon* is usually translated *spiritual*, but is correctly translated here *supernatural* (see comments on I Cor. 2:14-16). The emphasis of the context is the supernatural sustenance the Israelites were privileged to enjoy. The food and water they consumed was real and physical enough, but its origin was supernatural. The supernatural Spirit of God and Christ was with the Israelites through their journey to the promised land (see Isa. 59:21; 63:11-13). But God's Spirit was with them there in an even more important way. He provided the Israelites with *spiritual* bread and drink through Moses' teachings about the Messiah (see Deut. 8:3; 18:15). That "supernatural" Rock (the Christ) "followed" them in deed and word wherever they went in the wilderness. They were being sustained physically and spiritually by every word that proceeded out of the mouth of God (through Moses).

10:5 Perfidy: This is the point Paul wishes to illustrate. Divine privileges obligated the recipients to respond in holiness and love. The Israelites were privileged, by God's grace, to receive supernatural and spiritual fellowship with the Creator above and beyond all other people. But they were unwilling to exercise self-control, holiness and love for their Benefactor. They "sat down to eat and drink and rose up to dance."

Those who are Christians (including apostles) have privileges and liberties beyond anything the Israelites ever enjoyed. Most of the Israelites (all of responsible age except Joshua and Caleb) God destroyed in the wilderness. They never went into the promised land! They failed because they used the freedom from bondage God gave them for occasion to indulge their own fleshly desires. They would not control themselves and sacrifice the flesh for the greater messianic goal set before them in the teaching of Moses.

CHAPTER 10   FIRST CORINTHIANS 10:6-13

The Christians at Corinth had been baptized into Christ, set free, protected and sustained. They had heard Paul and other Christian teachers emphasize their freedom in Christ. They had been taught, and now believed, that an idol was nothing. They had been taught that all of God's creation was good and "everything belonged to them" (I Cor. 3:21-22). Paul evidently felt the Corinthians (especially the "strong" brethren) were dangerously close to becoming as presumptuous as the fleshly-minded Israelites were after their release from bondage.

There is a *risk* in freedom. When people are made free they are, by the nature of freedom itself, made vulnerable to options. Free people are autonomous (self-ruled) and may no longer be controlled by outside force. The only thing forced by freedom is *responsibility*. There is always the risk with freedom that people will "use their freedom as a pretext for evil" (I Peter 2:16). While there is risk in freedom, the alternative, trying to produce righteousness and morality by force of law, is unacceptable. Righteousness cannot be wrought by force; it can only be produced in a matrix of freedom to choose motivated through the compulsion of faith and love.

Of course, *God* must *reveal* to man precisely what kind of thinking and acting constitutes righteousness, goodness and morality. God has, by the redemptive work of Christ, made right thinking and acting possible. But God cannot, and will not, make man's choice for him. That is the *risk* God takes when he sets us free in Christ. The risk itself is *not* bad. Man could never *grow* into the potential for which he was created if the freedom to choose was not there. When man becomes proud and presumptuous, disaster is certain. That is when man rejects God's *revelation* (which is all wise and all powerful) directing him to true righteousness and goodness.

Often God reveals to man what righteousness is by revealing and warning against unrighteousness. That is what the apostle Paul does in this dissertation. He warned that overconfidence (which is really a lack of faith in God) makes man vulnerable to the temptations of *immorality, idolatry* and *insensitiveness.*

SECTION 2

Immorality (10:6-13)

6 Now these things are warnings for us, not to desire evil as they did. 7 Do not be idolaters as some of them were; as it is

written, "The people sat down to eat and drink and rose up to dance." 8 We must not indulge in immorality as some of them did, and twenty-three thousand fell in a single day. 9 We must not put the Lord to the test, as some of them did and were destroyed by serpents; 10 nor grumble, as some of them did and were destroyed by the Destroyer. 11 Now these things happened to them as a warning, but they were written down for our instruction, upon whom the end of the ages has come. 12 Therefore let any one who thinks that he stands take heed lest he fall. 13 No temptation has overtaken you that is not common to man. God is faithful, and he will not let you be tempted beyond your strength, but with the temptation will also provide the way of escape, that you may be able to endure it.

10:6 Imperative Instruction: The actual, historical experiences and divine judgments upon Israel in the wilderness *became* (Gr. *egenethesan,* aorist verb) warnings for us, not to *ardently desire* (Gr. *epithemetas*) evil as they did. The word *warning* is *tupos* in Greek. It is the word from which we get the English word *type.* A "type" is "the *imprint* left when a die or other instrument is struck." John's gospel uses the word *tupos* when reporting Thomas' statement that he would not believe in the resurrection of Jesus unless he saw the "print" of the nail in Jesus' hand. Paul is saying that God recorded the history of Israel's forfeiture of its privileges and its fall in the wilderness to *strike* an indelible *tupos* (imprint or image) of the consequences of presumptuousness and overconfidence. The lesson is *historical*—not mythological, or allegorical, or theoretical.

Israel's divine judgment in the wilderness is separated from us by more than three thousand years. Israel's circumstances, technologically and culturally, differed from ours today like light and darkness. Our privileges, both spiritual and physical, surpass theirs. However, human nature and the human predicament are exactly the same. Man still cannot come to virtue and goodness without the grace of his Creator. Man still is tempted to be presumptuous, overconfident and independent of his Creator. So, man still refusing to learn from history, dooms himself to repeat it.

10:7 Idolatry: Idolatry is *immoral.* "Moral" means, "that which is right" and "immoral" means, "that which is wrong." It is wrong and immoral to worship other gods. The *first* commandment of the Decalogue is, "Thou shalt have no other gods before me" (Exod.

CHAPTER 10　　　　　　FIRST CORINTHIANS 10:6-13

20:3; 20:23; Deut. 5:7). No object, thing, creature, human being, angel or spirit (except the Holy Spirit of God) is to be revered, worshiped, adored, exalted, prayed to, trusted in, or looked to for eternal life. To do so is idolatry. That which a man trusts and serves or puts first or gives the essence of his life to is his god. Jesus stated an unequivocal truth: "No man can serve two masters." No man can obey contradictory orders from two masters. No man can continue that way; sooner or later a man's motives and goals force him to choose which master he wishes to please. Then he will despise the other for interfering. The issue is: Man is so created that he takes on the nature of that which he worships (see Hosea 9:10; Ps. 115:3-8; Rom. 1:18-32).

10:8 Illicit Intercourse: The Greek word *porneuomen* is translated *immorality* (RSV) and *fornication* (KJV) and is the word from which we get the English word *pornography*. It probably refers to illicit sexual intercourse. The Israelites apparently indulged in fornication and adultery as they worshiped the golden calf (see Exod. 32 and Deut. 9); Paul may be referring to their fornication at the time of Balaam and Balak (see Num. 24-25).

We have already learned from this letter (ch. 5-7) that all forms of illicit sex were commonplace in Corinth, and that the Christians had a difficult time overcoming what was so socially acceptable by their heathen contemporaries. The seven churches of Asia Minor were also beset with this temptation to sexual perversion (cf. Rev. 2:14-15; 2:20-23). The Roman empire is characterized or symbolized in the early centuries (100-500 A.D.) as "the great harlot" (Rev. ch. 17-18). The Gnostic cult within the first and second century church taught that since all matter or all that is physical is evil, and all that is mental or spiritual is holy, so long as you did not think evil you should never be concerned about misusing your body. One could only sin with the mind, according to the Gnostics, not with the body. Gnostics said as long as you know or think what is right you are righteous no matter what you do with your body. Ancient Gnosticism has crept into the twentieth century Christian church under the guise called "situation ethics." Situation ethics says whenever a person does the most loving thing in any situation he has acted morally. Classic illustrations of this principle have pictured sailors, having been deprived of sexual release for months at sea, being "loved" by prostitutes because they have "done a good thing" in satisfying the sailor's sublimated sexual urges when he has come ashore on liberty. Some Christians have rationalized illicit sexual relations with persons other than their spouses by declaring they are "helping" their illicit partners find "love and tenderness" and relief from "frustration" for the first time in their lives.

Sexual intercourse with a person outside the bonds of matrimony, or with a person other than one's singular spouse, is immoral in any circumstance. It is immoral because God has declared it to be so in his Word. No amount of human reasoning or feeling can change or temper that divine edict!

10:9 Incredulity: Unbelief is immoral. Paul warns, "Do not put the Lord to the *test.*" The Greek word translated test is *ekpeiradzomen,* which is literally, *overtest,* or, *test beyond what is acceptable.* God does want us to put the promises he has revealed to us in his Word to the test. At least as far as reason and propriety will allow. He does want us to test his Word to confirm its historicity and accuracy.

But to keep asking God to prove himself and his promises *beyond* the Word is to put him to the test! The Israelites did this when they asked for more proof than the Lord had already given of his presence among them (cf. Exod. 17:7; Deut. 6:16; Num. 21:4-6; Heb. 3:7-19).

This same unbelief appears to have been a problem with the Corinthians. It is demonstrated by their clamoring for the continuance of miraculous gifts which were given exclusively to create belief and were to "pass away" (see I Cor. ch. 12-14). At the same time the Corinthians shunned the gifts designed to edify and which were to abide. When the evidence is sufficient, demanding more from the Lord is to "put him to the test" and is immoral. Jesus warned the Jewish rulers who kept asking him for more "signs" that they were committing the *unpardonable sin.*

The Israelites in the wilderness had every opportunity and privilege God could offer to create faith and commitment in their hearts. But they asked for more. The Corinthians had every opportunity and privilege Christ could offer to give them liberty and freedom. They seemed to be demanding more. Paul warns them they are putting the Lord to the test. The New Testament is Christ's final and complete "Bill of Rights" for the church. Any Christian who presumes to demand more is putting the Lord to the test.

10:10 Ingratitude: Christians are not to *grumble.* The Greek word is *egongusan* (Eng. *gong*) and is an onomatopoeic word, i.e., a word which represents the significance by the sound of the word, like the English word *murmur.* In the papyri the word is used of the impudent complaining of a gang of workmen. The word is almost always used

CHAPTER 10　　　　　　　　　FIRST CORINTHIANS 10:6-13

with the connotation of private or nearly inarticulate *complaining.* The Israelites were inveterate complainers (Num. 14:1-3; 14:27; 16:41; 17:5, 10; 20:2-13; see also Matt. 20:11; Luke 5:30; John 6:41, 43; 6:61; 7:32; Acts 6:1; Phil. 2:14; I Peter 4:9). It often appears that those most blessed and privileged are the most presumptuous and complaining. *Ingratitude* is the mother of all manner of wickedness (see Rom. 1:21ff.). Moses warned the Israelites against ungrateful presumption (Deut. 8:11-20). Paul is here warning all Christians about presuming upon the Lord's grace by complaining. Grumbling is immoral!

10:11-13 Indolence: Paul repeats his use of the Greek word *tupos,* type or imprint, in reference to God's historical dealings with the presumptuous Israelites. The RSV translates *tupos* with the word *warning* because the Christian age was the ultimate purpose for God's dealing with Israel as he did. The judgments and redemptions God worked upon Israel were recorded ultimately for the Bride of Christ—the New Testament church. Paul says they were *written* (Gr. *egraphe,* Eng. graph, engraved, graphically) for our *instruction* (Gr. *nouthesian,* combined word from *nous,* mind, and *tithemi,* to put; literally, a putting in mind). Our *instruction* is to be more than teaching, it is indoctrination—we are to have it put into our minds so that it becomes a part of our mentality or way of thinking.

The next phrase is, in Greek, *eis hous ta tele ton aionon katenteken,* or in English, *upon whom the end of the ages has come.* It is an extremely significant phrase because it is so decisive in stating apostolic eschatology in one declaration! It *clearly* declares the Christian age as the goal of all past ages. The Greek word *katenteken* is a perfect tense verb and may be translated, "has *come down* in the past with a continuing result." The decisive word in the whole phrase, however, is the Greek word *tele,* translated, *end.* It is the word from which we get the English prefix, *tele,* or *telo,* meaning, end, perfect, final, complete. The Greek word *teleios* means "having reached its end, finished, completed, perfected or final. The Christian age, begun on the Day of Pentecost (Acts 2:17ff.), is the *final* age. There will be *no more* ages or eras or dispensations. The only great event in the framework of time yet to come is the *end of time,* at which point Jesus will come again visibly to deliver the faithful living and dead to glory and to judge and deliver the unfaithful living and dead to Hell. The church age *is* the kingdom age. There is *no* kingdom dispensation yet to come. Paul's use of the perfect tense verb *katenteken* and his use of the noun *tele* settles the issue of Christian eschatology once for all. All the previous dispensations or ages of history were pointing toward the Christian age as their goal. The coming of the Christian age means that the goal has been reached, that the last phase of redemption has begun. So Paul is urging the Corinthians that self-discipline is now imperative. God has no other plan of redemption than the one in the New Testament. God has no other revelation than that written down in the New Testament. God has no other time or age in which he will work with mankind than this age. "Behold, now (in the Christian age) is the acceptable time; behold, now is the day (or age) of salvation" (II Cor. 6:1-2). To wait for or hold out to others any hope of another time-frame (or dispensation) after this age in which God will offer salvation to any group of people is presumptuous. This phrase has behind it inspired, apostolic authority. It is in complete harmony with all the rest of the Bible in teaching that the Christian age (the church age) is the last age of time. There is no millennium (in the sense of a latter dispensation) yet to come. If there is any millennium at all in the framework of time, we are now in it.

Paul's purpose in making his unequivocal statement about the Christian dispensation being the last of God's dispensations in time is to *prove* his argument about the necessity for Christian resistance to temptation in this earthly phase of life. There is no other probationary or proving phase of life. We are becoming what we shall be. *Therefore,* let any one who thinks that he stands take heed lest he fall. Let anyone who thinks *privilege* secures his standing before God, take heed lest he be indolent toward the *responsibilities* involved. To be indolent is to be lazy, to deliberately avoid responsibility or exertion; indolence is slothfulness. The Corinthians were prone to be slothful in exercising Christian charity and brotherhood toward "weaker brethren." They were arrogant in their liberty supposing such privileges secured their spiritual superiority. They presumed they "stood" while the weaker had "fallen."

Some Corinthians had clearly rationalized their arrogant disregard for "weaker" brethren by claiming they were participating in things they just could not quit. They probably argued that their old habit of eating at the feasts honoring idols was just too ingrained to be given up. They plead, our temptation is unique—no one knows how strong this temptation is. Besides, they knew an idol was no god so they were free to participate. Let the "weaker" brother look out for himself. He should get rid of his scruples and grow up to our level

CHAPTER 10   FIRST CORINTHIANS 10:6-13

of spirituality, they probably argued. Paul's answer was that *any* temptation may be resisted; *any* test endured.

The Greek word *eilephen,* translated *overtaken you,* is third person, singular, perfect tense, indicative mood, active voice. It means Paul is indicating these Corinthians had *already* been taken in the temptation of presumptuous arrogance and it was *continuing* in their lives. The apostolic revelation is that *every* temptation is *common* to mankind. The Greek phrase *ei me anthropinos* is translated "that is not common to man." *Anthropinos* literally means "is human." Now the devil may use different tools or agents in different cultural milieu or in different historical times, but his temptations to rebel against God generally fall into three or four general categories ("the lust of the flesh, the lust of the eyes, and the pride of life," I John 2:16). Jesus was tempted in the wilderness (Matt. 4:1-11; Luke 4:1-13) essentially in these three categories; Eve and Adam were tempted in the Garden of Eden in these three categories (Gen. 3:1-7). The Corinthians could not excuse their weaknesses by claiming their temptations were unique. No man can!

On the positive side, every human being who wishes may have the help of God for every temptation he faces. God will not permit any man to be tempted beyond the availability of help. Notice that the Bible does *not* promise any man (especially Christians) that they will have *no* temptation. As a matter of fact, temptation is one of God's ways of disciplining his children. God does not want his children to do evil, nor does he push them in that direction (James 1:13-15). But he does want them to develop spiritual maturity and strength and this can only be done as his children wrestle with and conquer temptation (see Heb. 10:32-39; 12:1-17; James 1:2-11; II Cor. 1:3-11; 12:1-10). Jesus, fully human as he was fully divine, proved in the flesh that all temptation is common to mankind and that every temptation may be overcome if human beings will avail themselves, by total faith, of the help of God. Jesus never used his divinity nor his miraculous power to extricate himself from a temptation. He always relied on the word of God in total commitment to God's faithfulness (see Matt. 4:1-11, et al.).

With every temptation God allows he makes available an attendant way of escape. The Greek text has the definite article *ten* before the noun *ekbasin.* In other words, Paul says, ". . . with *the* temptation will also provide *the* way of escape." It is not *a* way of escape, but *the* way of escape. Every temptation has its own way of escape. The temptation and the way of escape come in pairs. God sees to it that one does not occur without the other. No man can plead "not guilty" by saying the way of escape was not made available because Paul says God sends with every temptation the escape *that you may be able to endure.* If a Christian sins it is not because he did not have the way to escape it; it is because he did not *avail* himself of the way of escape. Sin cannot overpower a person unless the person allows it. God expects all men to *resist* temptation (Prov. 1:10; 4:14; Rom. 6:13; Eph. 6:13; II Peter 3:17). God encourages all men to seek his help (Heb. 2:18; II Peter 2:9; Heb. 4:14-16, etc.). Great men of faith have resisted (Abraham, Gen. 14:23; Joseph, Gen. 39:1-9; Job, Job 2:9-10; the Rechabites, Jer. 35:5-6; Daniel, Dan. 1:8; Christ, Matt. 4:1-11; Luke 4:1-13; Peter, Acts 8:20). Spiritual indolence is inexcusable!

SECTION 3

Indulgence (10:14-22)

14 Therefore, my beloved, shun the worship of idols. 15 I speak as to sensible men; judge for yourselves what I say. 16 The cup of blessing which we bless, is it not a participation in the blood of Christ? The bread which we break, is it not a participation in the body of Christ? 17 Because there is one bread, we who are many are one body, for we all partake of the one bread. 18 Consider the people of Israel; are not those who eat the sacrifices partners in the altar? 19 What do I imply then? That food offered to idols is anything, or that an idol is anything? 20 No, I imply that what pagans sacrifice they offer to demons and not to God. I do not want you to be partners with demons. 21 You cannot drink the cup of the Lord and the cup of demons. You cannot partake of the table of the Lord and the table of demons. 22 Shall we provoke the Lord to jealousy? Are we stronger than he?

10:14-18 Gregariousness: Paul is not teaching a lesson on Christian communion or the Lord's Supper here. He is using Christian communion as an *analogy* or an illustration of the principle of *fellowship.* It should be logically apparent to any thinking individual that the congeniality of dining and drinking with someone indicates the diners are like-minded, agreed in aims and purposes. This was certainly

CHAPTER 10   FIRST CORINTHIANS 10:14-22

true in ancient cultures more than in modern American culture. People do not participate, continually, at meal-tables with their enemies; at least they are not that congenial with enemies by their own free choice. For example, when Christians eat and drink with Christ at his Supper they are testifying to all they are in "fellowship" with Christ. They demonstrate they have freely chosen to *participate* in what he is, in what he is for and against, and in what his aims and purposes are. As Paul will show, the Corinthians, by attending the pagan feasts dedicated to idols were testifying to all they were in "fellowship" with that for which the idol stood.

This passage in no way teaches the idea that the emblems of the Lord's Supper become the actual body and blood of Jesus Christ. Neither does it teach that should we miss participation in the emblems due to circumstances beyond our control we lose contact with the blood of Christ. The death of Christ becomes efficacious to us through obedient faith, to be sure, but a person might have perfect attendance at the Lord's Supper and still lose contact with the blood of Christ *if* he is trusting in the ritual to make him meritoriously fit for salvation. The Pharisees never missed a tithe, never missed a fast, never missed a regulated time of prayer, but they were trusting in their own self-righteousness for approval before God rather than in God's mercy. The real issue here is not the *observance* of the Lord's Supper, *per se,* but that of *divided loyalty.* A man cannot *participate* with Christ and *participate* (or indulge) with the devil at the same time. A man cannot serve two masters. A man cannot serve God and mammon.

Another illustration is presented. The priests of the old covenant gave testimony to the fellowship they had with God when they participated in the ritual of offerings upon the altar of God. They did not partake, literally, of the altar—the altar itself was emblematic of the spiritual fellowship they had by faith. This meaning must be applied to all physical acts of New Testament Christianity. There is nothing supernatural or miraculous in the water in which a believer is immersed. The participation the believer has with the efficacious death of Christ is by faith. Immersion in water, in obedience to the command of Christ, symbolizes that faith. Refusal to be immersed, since that is the express act commanded in the New Testament for demonstrating initial faith, would symbolize unbelief. Partaking of immersion in water and the Lord's Supper testifies to, demonstrates and symbolizes the spiritual (unseen) reality of the believer's oneness with Christ. But the things themselves have no efficacy because *things* are amoral. Persons are moral. The efficaciousness of Christ's death is appropriated through the exercise of a person's faith. Proof that the altar *itself* contained no efficacy in which priests participated is clearly established by the prophets of the Old Testament who denounce the unbelieving priesthood of their day as enemies of God all the while they are performing the rituals at the altar.

10:19-22 Guilt: The preceding principle is exactly what Paul says he is trying to communicate to the Corinthians. Is the food, *per se,* offered to idols anything? No! Are the wooden or stone or metal images, in themselves, anything? No! A person is not defiled by touching an image or a piece of food sacrificed to an image. The issue is that what those pagans deliberately, willingly, and with personal, moral choice sacrifice to images is really (by their own understanding and choice) sacrifice to demons. These pagans know that the stone image is not a god in itself, but they are worshiping the personal being (an evil being) which it represents.

These "strong" Christians at Corinth had lost sight (from their misunderstanding of Christian liberty) of the fact that deliberately joining in the festivities and meals around the altar to an idol indicated they were willing to participate in the worship of the evil being represented by the image. They may have been "strong" enough not to have thought of their actions this way, but everyone else (including Christians more sensitively scrupulous) saw in it Christians willing to join in the worship of demons.

An idol or image may be only a piece of wood or stone, but it is a ready tool for the devil and his demons by which to deceive and seduce men into unbelief. We repeat—things are amoral. But evil persons may use things to corrupt and condemn men. Although Christians may understand that a thing is neither right nor wrong in itself, when they participate in the wrong use of an object, they become partners with the evil person who is using that object to destroy goodness. This is not guilt by association, but guilt by participation. Can we buy, sell, attend, defend things and places devoted to sin and destruction of mind and body without sharing in the devil's work?

All a person has to do to become a partner of the devil and his work is to refuse to become a partner with Christ and his work! Some people think they may be neutral, not an enemy of Christ, yet not a friend of the devil—so they think. Wrong! Jesus said (Matt. 12:30-31) "He that is not with me is against me; he that gathereth not with me, scattereth." Paul says it, "You cannot drink the cup of the Lord and the cup of demons." To refuse to surrender to the Lordship of

Jesus is not neutrality—it is the enthronement of self. The person who rejects Jesus as king, makes himself king. To worship man is idolatry and, actually, "demonolatry" (see Rom. 1:22-25). Rejection of Christ is immoral because it is a rejection of absolute truth. To refuse to participate in the work of Christ is to join in the work of the demons of hell. There is no middle ground!

SECTION 4

Insensitiveness (10:23-30)

23 "All things are lawful," but not all things are helpful. "All things are lawful," but not all things build up. 24Let no one seek his own good, but the good of his neighbor. 25Eat whatever is sold in the meat market without raising any question on the ground of conscience. 26For "the earth is the Lord's, and everything in it." 27If one of the unbelievers invites you to dinner and you are disposed to go eat whatever is set before you without raising any question on the ground of conscience. 28(But if some one says to you, "This has been offered in sacrifice," then out of consideration for the man who informed you, and for conscience' sake—29I mean his conscience, not yours—do not eat it.) For why should my liberty be determined by another man's scruples? 30If I partake with thankfulness, why am I denounced because of that for which I give thanks?

10:23-24 Carelessness: As mentioned earlier, with Christian liberty there is risk. There is always an ever present danger that the Christian will become selfishly concerned foremost about his liberty and unconcerned about the scruples of his brother. Thus Paul repeats the fundamental principle of Christian liberty, "All things are lawful . . ." qualifying it with, "but not all things are helpful." The Greek word *sumpherei* is translated, *helpful,* but means literally, *brought together.* It is often translated by the English word *expedient,* and is more accurately understood by the word *advantageous,* or, *profitable.* Paul goes on to say, "All things are lawful, but not all things build up." The Greek word *oikodomei* is a word from the construction trades, *oikos,* house, and, *demo,* to build. One might even translate the phrase, ". . . not all things are *constructive.*"

FIRST CORINTHIANS

The liberty of the Christian is not for the sake of self-indulgence. Christ set men free to reach their highest potential. Their highest potential is in the service of others—to be helpful, to build people up to do constructive things for others, so they may be reborn in the image of Christ. "He who would be greatest among you must be the slave of all" (Mark 10:44).

Actually, Paul is not saying a Christian is free to do anything he wishes, participate in every human behavior, partake of any object on earth, or even think anything he wishes to think. Christian freedom is limited by the revealed (Biblical) word of God. When Paul says, "All things are lawful" the immediate context must be remembered. The context is the specific discussion of *eating meat sacrificed to idols*. Paul declared Christ had set all Christians free from the legal restrictions of the Mosaic law concerning foods. If the law of Moses had not been superceded, no Christian could eat meat which had been butchered by a pagan lest he be ceremonially unclean. But the Mosaic restrictions no longer applied. Such *food* was not contaminated. Paul is saying "All foods formerly prohibited by the Mosaic law are lawful" (see I Tim. 4:1-5). He was not saying, "All actions are lawful." But while all foods were lawful, the Christian might sin partaking even of lawful food if he should wound the conscience of a weaker brother by doing so.

Life can never be at a standstill. If it is not growing or developing toward the higher—if it is not being constructive—it is declining toward the lower. What is not used for growth will become atrophied and eventually destroy and be destroyed. Christian freedom that is careless and unconcerned about helpfulness and growth, inevitably contributes to destruction. Paul expressed this principle graphically in Romans 14:19 "Let us then pursue what makes for peace and mutual upbuilding" or in Romans 15:2, "let each of us please his neighbor for his good, to edify him." And now to the Corinthians, the shocking words, so diametrically opposed to modern, worldly "me-ism," "Let no one seek his own good, but the good of his neighbor." The Christian is not simply to help his neighbor if the opportunity to do so happens to present itself. The Christian is to *seek* good for his neighbor. The Greek verb *zeteito* is present, imperfect, active, meaning the Christian is to go on and on and on *seeking* good for his neighbor. That is the Christian's job! It may be of significance that Paul does not limit his exhortation to the Christian here to seek the good

CHAPTER 10　　　　　　FIRST CORINTHIANS 10:23-30

of a "brother." He literally wrote, "No one the thing of himself let him go on and on seeking, but the thing of the other." The word *other* is the Greek word *heterou* which denotes generic distinction or difference in character. It is translated *neighbor*. Christians are to put to practice the limits of love on Christian liberty toward all men.

10:25-27 Complication: With the issue of Christian liberty and scrupulousness, comes the temptation upon the stronger to implicate the weaker in behavior contrary to the weaker one's conscience. Paul states the principle by which the Christian conducts himself properly and then he illustrates it with an hypothetical situation. First, "Eat whatever is sold in the meat market without raising any question on the ground of conscience—for the earth is the Lord's, and everything in it." The Greek word *makello* translated *meat market* is found nowhere else in the New Testament. It is probably a word coined by the Greeks from the Latin word *macellum* which meant "a bench or stall for marketing merchandise, especially, meats; it came to designate a slaughterhouse" and since warfare usually turned a town into a "slaughterhouse" or a "shambles" that is how the word came to be translated *shambles* in archaic English. A drawing of archaeological discoveries in the ancient city of Pompeii shows both the slaughter-house and the meat-shop next to the chapel of Caesar. This confirms the suggestions of our text that there was a very close connection between the meat-market and pagan idolatry. It would have been very difficult for any one, even a Christian, to buy meat in such a market without being immediately associated with worshiping at the temple of the idol.

So, writes Paul, the helpful or constructive (edifying) thing for a Christian to do, should any plate of meat be set before him, would be to refrain from questioning whether the meat came from the pagan "meat-market" or not. The Greek clause, *meden anakrinontes* (translated, *discerned* in I Cor. 2:14-15), translated here *do not question,* means literally, *do not carry on an investigation.* It is a legal term. Paul is not, of course, forbidding all questioning of right and wrong. He is not discussing the conscience of the eater at all—but the conscience of the server. The instruction is that the guest is not to implicate the conscience of the host by asking questions about the meat set before them.

Out of pure worldly arrogance, a strong, more sophisticated person may be tempted to implicate a weaker (more scrupulous) person just to elevate his own image of "wisdom" or "sophistication" by exposing the scruples of the more conscientious person. Paul says this is not fitting Christian conduct. It is not right for a strong Christian to exploit the scruples of a weaker brother or a pagan intending to display his own "knowledge" or "freedom" by agitating for such a comparison.

It is significant that Paul is setting forth proper ethical behavior of the Christian toward the unbeliever. There may be some Christians who think unbelievers do not deserve to be treated ethically. It is also interesting there is an assumption that the Christian would wait to be invited by the unbeliever to his home and would not push himself into the pagan's fellowship uninvited. He says, *kai thelete poreuesthai,* "and if you wish to go. . . ." He does not command them to go, or even encourage them to go—but to go if they *wished.* And if they accept the invitation, Christian helpfulness, Christian purpose to edify, yes, Christian love, requires that no complicating implications be raised. To do so would be immoral!

Christians will not try to destroy weaker, even unbelieving, persons by irritating or ventilating consciences, without positive instruction in what is right and wrong so that edification will result. Conscience is a functioning characteristic—not a diagnosing or circumscribing characteristic. The conscience functions on the basis of what the mind diagnoses as right and wrong. The conscience does not tell a person *what* is right and wrong, its function is to *judge* the heart for having *done* either the right or the wrong. *Information* as to *what* is right and wrong comes from revelation—from the word of God, the Bible. For the Christian to go into a home and begin to fuss and cross-examine an unbeliever as to how abominable it is to serve meat purchased in an idol-market, is to proceed to destroy the unbeliever. No Christian is to use his "knowledge" or his "liberty" to destroy another.

10:28-30 Callousness: The questions arise, "What if a Christian conscientiously believes it is not wrong for him to eat meat from the pagan meat-markets and there is an unbeliever present who believes it is wrong for the Christian to do so?" "And, what if the unbeliever says to the Christian, 'This has been offered in sacrifice'?" Is the Christian to reply, callously, "If my eating offends you or bothers you, that is your problem, not mine. I know it is not wrong so I am going to eat it!"? Paul says an emphatic, No! The Christian must sacrifice his liberty of conscience to the scruples of even an unbeliever.

CHAPTER 10 FIRST CORINTHIANS 10:23-33

Out of consideration for the possible salvation of the unbeliever, and even for the sake of the unbeliever's over-scrupulousness, the Christian is not to eat.

With all the freedom in Christ and with the liberated conscience of the believer comes the danger of callousness on the part of the person who knows an idol is not a god. It is often true that the non-Christian has a much stricter opinion of the proper behavior of a Christian than a fellow-Christian has. So the Christian must be willing to sacrifice his "rights" even when the unbeliever is excessively scrupulous. If a Christian is insensitive and disregards the scruples of an unbelieving friend, he almost inevitably damages his influence for Christ with that friend.

The final sentence of verse 29, "For why should my liberty be determined by another man's scruples?" is *not* a cry of rebellion on the part of the "stronger" brother. Verses 29b and 30 are rhetorical questions from the apostle Paul, in anticipation of the answer in verses 31, 32, and 33. The Greek expression, *hinati gar he eleutheria mou krinetai* . . . , is stronger than the most English translations present it. It might be translated, "To what end or purpose is my liberty to be determined by another man's scruples?" J. B. Phillips has it correctly translated in *The New Testament In Modern English,* "Now why should my freedom to eat be at the mercy of someone else's conscience? Or why should any evil be said of me when I have eaten meat with thankfulness, and have thanked God for it? *Because,* whatever you do, eating or drinking or anything else, everything should be done to bring glory to God." Why should the strong Christian brother be willing to make such sacrifices as to surrender his freedom to someone else's conscience? Or, conversely, if what the strong Christian eats is something for which he is able to thank God, and he is slandered for it, why is it proper that evil has been spoken of him? *Because,* any action that violates another man's conscience does not bring glory to God; and that includes even an action for which a strong Christian may give thanks to God.

10:31-33 Conclusion: Paul is ready to move on to another "problem that is plaguing the saints" but before he does he wants to sum up what he has said about Christian liberty. The Greek verb *poieite* (English, *do*) is used twice in verse 31. In that Greek form it may be either present indicative or present imperative. It appears Paul uses it both ways in this verse. It might be paraphrased, "So, whether you eat or drink, or whatever you are continuing to do, I command you to do all to the glory of God." The application of the actions of a Christian is as wide as the total sphere of the Christian's movement in society. The actions of a Christian will have influence on everyone who sees him, hears him, or makes contact with him in any other way (see Rom. 14:7-9). And this is particularly true of the influence a Christian may have on unbelievers. In the Christian, the unbelieving world is seeing an attempt to live out in the flesh the personality or character of God and Christ. God is glorified when Christians live according to the principles of self-sacrifice and love enunciated by Paul in these chapters (8, 9, 10).

Strange as it may seem, there are Christians who, while being careful not to offend an unbeliever, are careless about offending a brother in Christ. That is somewhat like the behavior of certain persons toward their immediate family members—showing deference and politeness to strangers while being rude and insensitive toward father, mother, brothers and sisters. So, Paul makes a point of saying, "Give no offense to Jews or to Greeks or to the *church* (Gr. *ekklesia,* congregation) of God."

Paul never compromised on matters that were essential to one's belief in Jesus. He never compromised on matters of moral behavior clearly delineated in the scriptures. He would not even compromise on a matter of indifference (circumcision) when the Jews insisted that it was a matter of covenant relationship to Christ. So, those areas are *not* in the scope of his statement, ". . . just as I try to please all men in everything I do. . . ." He did accommodate himself to the scruples of others in matters that were opinions and not essential to covenant terms with Christ. Paul did not curry the favor of men. His primary goal in life was to please God (Gal. 1:10; I Thess. 2:5-6). A better translation of the Greek word *aresko* would be "seems proper." Paul is saying, ". . . just as I try to behave as seems proper toward all men in everything I do, not seeking my own advantage, but that of many, that they may be saved." Paul would do anything, short of apostasy and immorality, to save a man. He would sacrifice any of his privileges or "rights" to win men to Christ. He imitated Christ. He commands (Gr. *ginesthe,* imperative mood, *Be!*) all Christians to be imitators of him as he is of Christ. Verse 1 of chapter 11 should be considered the closing statement of the discussion of chapter 10. May God grant us the power and the motivation to do everything possible to win men to Christ!

CHAPTER 10   FIRST CORINTHIANS 10:23-33

APPLICATIONS:

1. God gave great privileges to the Israelites he did not give to others—they defaulted. *What about Christian's privileges?*
2. Since the Old Testament events are warnings to us, should we not study them more frequently?
3. What responsibilities are incurred by the privileges of freedom?
4. What "idols" are you tempted to worship?
5. Unbelief is immorality.
6. We must make constant, deliberate and overt expressions of thankfulness, because ingratitude is the most heinous of all sins.
7. Do not be lead astray—the church age is the last age there will be.
8. God makes a way to avoid every temptation to sin known to man. The question is, Do we believe God?
9. Taking the Lord's Supper is more than participating in a ritual. It is a weekly oath or testimony by the Christian that he is likeminded and of the same purpose as Christ.
10. To be insensitive to another person's moral reservations or scruples is a sin for the Christian.
11. To implicate another person with guilt by questioning or belittling another person's scruples is wrong.
12. Every Christian who desires to glorify God must agree that his liberty is to be determined by the scruples of others!
13. The Christian must be willing to give up anything, or to do anything short of apostasy and immorality to win men to Christ.

APPREHENSIONS:

1. Why does Paul give a short review of Israelite history?
2. What kind of privileges did God give Israel in the wilderness?
3. What kind of responsibilities are demanded as a response to such privileges?
4. What is the risk of freedom?
5. How were the experiences of the Israelites *types* of all human experiences toward God?
6. Why is idolatry almost always associated with illicit sexual behavior?
7. What is "putting the Lord to the test"? Do Christians today do that? How?
8. Why are Christians warned against "grumbling"?

9. When did the "end of the ages" come? Why is it significant that we understand this? Why do so many people today insist the "end of the ages" is yet to come?
10. Are there any temptations unique to just you?
11. Are there any temptations for which there are no escapes? Why, then, do men fall into temptations?
12. Can a Christian eat food sacrificed to an idol without participating in the worship of demons?
13. Are *all* things lawful to a Christian? What does Paul mean by his statement?
14. How careful must the Christian be about criticizing and ridiculing another person's scruples?
15. Should a Christian condescend to behaving according to a weaker brother's more rigid scruples?
16. What is the purpose in allowing another person's scruples determine one's liberty?
17. Should we do anything, short of apostasy and immorality, to win others to Christ? Give up anything which is merely a matter of opinion?

Chapter Eleven

THE PROBLEM OF DISORDERLY WORSHIP
(11:1-34)

IDEAS TO INVESTIGATE:

1. Why would order in worship be a problem to Christians?
2. What do head-coverings have to do with proper worship?
3. Is it really degrading for a man to have long hair?
4. Must there be factions in the church in order to find out who the genuine believers are?
5. Does eating meals in the church building profane the Lord's house?
6. What is eating the Lord's Supper in an "unworthy" manner?
7. What is eating and drinking "without discerning the body"?

SECTION 1

Opening Words (11:1-2)

11 Be imitators of me, as I am of Christ. ²I commend you because you remember me in everything and maintain the traditions even as I have delivered them to you.

11:1-2 Commendation: Clearly, the first verse of the eleventh chapter should be the closing verse of the tenth chapter. It belongs to that context. Paul changes the subject to disorder in worship in 11:2. He commends the Corinthians for "remembering" to consult him about their problems, and for "maintaining" the apostolic teachings ("traditions") he had taught them. Paul is using the word *traditions* to mean Holy-Spirit-inspired-doctrines—not human traditions. He distinguished clearly between the two. In Galatians 1:14 and Colossians 2:8 he speaks of *human* traditions. In I Corinthians 11:2 and II Thessalonians 2:15; 3:6, he refers to apostolic "traditions" which were *delivered* and *taught* by the apostles and *received* by the Christians as the word of God (see I Thess. 2:13). This is precisely why Paul could address this church, with all its faults and difficulties, as "brethren," and "saints." They may seem grossly immature, but they knew where to turn for the truth! The *only source*

FIRST CORINTHIANS

for solution for the problems that plague the saints is the apostolic word ("traditions").

SECTION 2

Order, a Requirement for Godly Worship (11:3-16)

3 But I want you to understand that the head of every man is Christ, the head of a woman is her husband, and the head of Christ is God. 4 Any man who prays or prophesies with his head covered dishonors his head, 5 but any woman who prays or prophesies with her head unveiled dishonors her head—it is the same as if her head were shaven. 6 For if a woman will not veil herself, then she should cut off her hair; but if it is disgraceful for a woman to be shorn or shaven, let her wear a veil. 7 For a man ought not to cover his head, since he is the image and glory of God; but woman is the glory of man. 8 (For man was not made from woman, but woman from man. 9 Neither was man created for woman, but woman for man.) 10 That is why a woman ought to have a veil on her head, because of the angels. 11 (Nevertheless, in the Lord woman is not independent of man nor man of woman; 12 for as woman was made from man, so man is now born of woman. And all things are from God.) 13 Judge for yourselves is it proper for a woman to pray to God with her head uncovered? 14 Does not nature itself teach you that for a man to wear long hair is degrading to him, 15 but if a woman has long hair, it is her pride? For her hair is given to her for a covering. 16 If any one is disposed to be contentious, we recognize no other practice, nor do the churches of God.

11:3 The Issue: The eleventh chapter of this letter very evidently deals with problems reported to the apostle Paul about public worship in the Corinthian congregational assemblies. Actually, chapters 12, 13 and 14 also deal with the problem of disorderly worship. But, since these chapters treat problems distinctly different than those of chapter 11, we will treat them separately.

The Hebrew word *shakhah* is the most usual word translated *worship* in the Old Testament. It means, literally, "to bow down, to prostrate oneself." The Greek word in the New Testament most often translated *worship* is the word *proskuneo* and also means, "to bow down, to prostrate oneself, and to do obeisance." The English word *worship* is a contraction of the early English word *worthship*. The old English *worthship* gives us an exact idea of what our modern word *worship* means. The one to whom we give *worship* must be *worthy* of absolute homage, honor, reverence and obedience.

Worship is essentially an attitude instead of an act! First, the performance of certain rituals of worship without the proper attitude is condemned by the Scriptures as "an abomination before God." On the other hand, a false emotion that discounts as irrelevant clear commands about definite acts of worship betrays a disobedient attitude and makes a mockery of worship.

Attitude in worship is the fundamental issue Paul deals with in chapter eleven. It is the issue of obedience to the revealed will of God as spoken and written by the apostles. The problem has manifested itself by two symptomatic actions in the public worship of the Corinthians; they are (1) the man-woman relationship; (2) the Christian-brother relationship.

In worship the outward man is bound up in the inward man. Worship is an outward act or acts springing from, and under the control of, inward attitudes and impulses of love and obedience. It is said, "To worship God is to make Him the supreme object of our esteem and delight, both in public, private and secret." It is apparent from chapters eleven through fourteen, the primary problem of the worship of the Corinthian church was that it was directed toward themselves. They were so interested in calling attention to themselves and to their supposed superiorities over others, they were not making God the supreme object of their esteem. The key verse to this huge context of four chapters (11-14) is probably, "For by one Spirit we were all baptized into one body—Jews or Greeks, slaves or free—and all were made to drink of one Spirit" (12:13).

While it is true regarding salvation and grace that men and women are of equal worth to God, it is also true that God has ordered certain hierarchies of authority within this world and his kingdom so long as it is in the world. In the church there are elders, evangelists and deacons to lead and shepherd the congregation. In the home the husband is the authoritative head. Evidently some of the Corinthian women misunderstood the teaching, "In Christ there is neither male nor female . . ." (Gal. 3:28). Some of them had cast off the cultural modes of ancient dress which particularly stressed and emphasized their *femininity,* hence their subordination to their husbands. While the primary focus of the apostle's discussion is on woman's subordination to man, the issue is not simply a wife's obedience to her husband's loving authority. It is much broader than that and covers attitudes of all women and men—married or unmarried. The broader issue is that women (and men too) must *not rebel* against the *divine order* of femininity and masculinity!

Paul discusses the divine order by declaring that the head of every male person (Greek *andros* instead of *anthropos*) is Christ. No man should wear a sign of subordination to other men when he prays (or worships). There is only one mediator between man and God, himself man, Jesus Christ (I Tim. 2:5). In the same *divine order*, the head of a female person is a male person. This does not deny that Christ is the head of the woman also, nor does it mean that a female person is inferior or of less importance than the male. Paul is reinforcing God's order as it was ordained from the beginning (Gen. 2:18) when the woman was created as a *helper* for man. The divine order of masculinity and femininity involves differing functions which require hierarchies of authority. Man functions as leader, protecter, provider; woman functions as mother, helper, supporter. This in no way means one is superior and the other inferior. It does not mean that the male person makes all the decisions arbitrarily and without consulting the wisdom of the female person. But Paul's teaching (in harmony with the rest of scripture) does mean that the husband is the final authority and the leader in the home.

11:4-12 The Illustration: Lenski says the general custom among Greeks was that slaves should cover their heads while free men went bareheaded. If a man wore a covering over his head in Paul's day it signified he was acknowledging final loyalty to a human being. It is wrong for a man to dishonor his masculinity in any way. God made man masculine. God made man to lead and be the final authority in the human order. On the other hand, the general custom among Greeks was that women, who desired the honor and protection femininity afforded them, wore veils in the public presence of men. Some of the Corinthian Christian women were apparently praying and attending public worship without being veiled. They were declaring their rejection of the divine order of human hierarchy by casting aside the first century symbols of this divine order.

In Paul's day the veil worn by women probably covered the whole head with openings for the eyes and reached clear down to the feet. No respectable woman would go without a veil in public for if she did she would be in danger of being misjudged. The woman's veil in those days was an important part of feminine dignity and gave her security and protection. Sir William Ramsay explains: "In Oriental lands the veil is the power and honor and dignity of the woman. With the veil on her head she can go anywhere in security and profound respect. She is not seen and therefore not subject to male familiarities and crudities. It is a mark of thoroughly bad manners to become familiar with a veiled woman in the street. She is alone. The rest of the people around are non-existent to her, as she is to them. She is supreme in the crowd. . . . But without the veil the woman is a thing of nought, whom anyone may insult. . . . A woman's authority and dignity vanish along with the all-covering veil that she discards."

The veil was the woman's badge of honor and respect. It showed that she had a definite place as a person in God's order. Woman was not created to be simply a "thing" or an "object" to be exploited by any and all men. She is to be honored, protected, cherished, loved, served, and led by her husband because she is a female.

Any man who prayed or prophesied with his head covered dishonored Christ ("his head"). A man worshiping in those days with his head covered symbolized he acknowledged some other human authority before Christ. The male Christian who worshiped with uncovered head signified he was accountable only to Christ. But the woman who prayed or prophesied with her head unveiled dishonored her husband ("her head"). She would dishonor her husband unveiled just as if she had her head shaved. Shaving of the head in ancient times (as even now in most cultures) was a sign of disgraceful and shameful conduct. At the end of World War II, those French women who had fraternized with Nazi soldiers were caught and their heads were shaved in public. Any woman in the civilized world of the apostle Paul, Greek, Roman, Jew or Syrian, would have felt terribly ashamed to have had her head shaved. Since that was the case, says Paul, the women of Corinth should have covered their heads in public —especially in the worship services of the church. For the Christian woman of Corinth to go with her head uncovered was to act the part of a shamed woman whether she was one or not. And that, in turn, brought shame upon her husband, and upon the church.

In verses 7 through 9 Paul gives us clear scriptural proof of the divinely ordained human hierarchy. Woman was made from man, not man from woman. Man was made *first* and then the woman was made from his body (see Gen. 2:21-22). *Man* is *first* in the divine *order.*

FIRST CORINTHIANS

Furthermore, woman was made *for* man, not man for woman (see Gen. 2:18). *Man* is *first* in divine *purpose*. Both the origin of woman and the reason for her being is found in man. There is no room for human speculations or rationalizations when we have both the creation account and the apostolic reiteration. No matter how much political and philosophical rhetoric and no matter how practical and appropriate it may sound when some activists demand that females have, not only the right, but the obligation to reject the customary, biblically-taught, function of femininity, and step into the world of maleness and function as any man, it is clearly not the revealed will of God!

The Greek text of verse 10 reads, *dia touto opheilei he gune exousian exein epi tes kephales dia tous angelous.* Translated, literally, "On account of this, she ought, the woman, authority, to be having, upon the head, on account of the angels." The New American Standard Version translates this sentence, "Therefore the woman ought to have a symbol of authority on her head, because of the angels." The NASV has supplied the words, "*a symbol of*" since they are not in the Greek text. The New International Version *supplies* the same words. The Revised Standard Version supplies, "*a veil*" where there are no words in the Greek text. These versions are supplying words to give the sentence the *usual* interpretation.

>   This interpretation is the usual one, but some commentators have differed. They have taken "authority" as referring to the woman's authority over her own natural head. There is justification for this interpretation in the Greek words (i.e., authority upon). This combination of words is found three times in the book of Revelation with the meaning "have control of" (11:6, "over the waters"; 14:18, "over fire"; 20:6; "over such," meaning the saints). In each case the combination of authority plus the preposition (Greek, *epi*) is the same. If this translation is taken, it is possible that the expression means that the woman should maintain control over her head so that it would not expose her to indignity. The woman's veil then became her willing subjection to her husband, her refusal to expose herself to others. However, the ultimate significance of the two interpretations is the same. Willing subjection to her husband's authority was a recognition of that authority, and this is the meaning of the clause. Even so, it would seem that the usual interpretation has the best claim to validity (Fred Fisher, *op. cit.,* p. 177).

CHAPTER 11   FIRST CORINTHIANS 11:3-16

We are not so sure the words "a symbol of" or "a veil" should be supplied here. We *are* sure the woman (and the man) should acknowledge that she "is to be having authority upon the head." There are women today who have all the symbols (hats, dresses, cosmetics) of womanhood but verbally and vehemently declare their rejection of the subordination of femaleness to maleness in the divine order of creation. It is more than a mere *sign* of authority the woman is to put on. She is to be mentally, emotionally and physically subordinate to the man. This does *not* degrade the woman! In subordinating herself to man she is actually taking her God-ordained place. She is filling the place of *honor* God created for her. Strange as it may seem to modern female activists, the woman's place of dignity is in her femininity. By God's word it is the woman's *right* to have the protection, dignity and honor that she alone can have in femininity. If she forfeits her femininity, she forfeits her rights! That is diametrically opposite to much modern feminist philosophy.

The reference, "on account of the angels . . ." simply reinforces the idea that all God's creatures have their place. The angels who left their assigned place in the created order of God forfeited their rights, dishonored God and themselves, and were cast into the abyss (cf. II Peter 2:4; Jude 6).

Just because woman's divinely ordered place is in subordination to man does not mean that man can exist independently of woman. For as the woman was made *out of the man* (Gr. *ek tou andros*), now the man is born *through woman* (Gr. *dia tes gunaikos*). Men and women are equally dependent upon one another—*but* each in their own God-ordered place!

11:13-16 The Indictment: The woman must not arrogate to herself the man's place (pray with her head uncovered in cultures where it is a shameless usurpation of maleness to do so). The man is not to arrogantly defy God and take the woman's place (wear long hair in cultures where it is not masculine to do so). Rebels and fanatics defy God's created order; Christians obey it. It *is* unnatural and rebellious for men to wear their hair long like women. Nature itself shows that man, being short-haired, is intended by the God of nature to be unveiled; woman, being long-haired, is intended by the same God to be veiled. Generally speaking, in the more refined and advanced civilizations, men have always worn their hair short and women have worn theirs long. Plummer writes in the International Critical Commentary on I Corinthians, "At this period, civilized men, whether Jews, Greeks, or Romans, wore their hair short" (p. 235).

FIRST CORINTHIANS

"The long hair of the Greek fop or of the English cavalier was accepted by the people as an indication of effeminate and luxurious living. Suitable for women; it is unsuitable for men." (*The Expositor's Greek New Testament,* I Cor. 11:14). "Homer's warriors, it is true, wore long hair, a fashion retained at Sparta, but the Athenian youth cropped his head at eighteen, and it was a mark of foppery or effeminacy except for the aristocratic knights to let the hair afterwards grow long. This feeling prevailed in ancient times as it does in modern times." (*Expositor's Greek New Testament,* I Cor. 11:14).

According to Philip Vollmer's *Modern Student's Life of Christ,* archaeologists object to the conventional pictures of Christ with long hair because they are not true to history. A German painter, L. Fahremkrog, says Christ certainly never wore a beard and his hair was beyond doubt closely cut. For this we have historical, archaeological proofs. The oldest representations, going back to the first Christian centuries, and found chiefly in the catacombs of Rome, all picture Christ without a beard. All the pictures of Christ down to the beginning of the fourth century at least, and even later, are like this. The further fact that Christ must have, in his day, worn short hair can be proved by the scripture. Among the Jews none but the Nazarites wore long hair. Christ was indeed a Nazarene, but not a Nazarite. Then, like the rest of the Jews, he wore his hair short. Further evidence is furnished by Paul here in I Corinthians 11:14, where he expressly declares that it is a *dishonor* for a man to wear his hair without having it cut, something that no apostle would have said had his Master worn it thus. One thing Jesus did not do was dress in such a bizarre way as to attract undue attention to himself. He was so much a conformist in his appearance, apparently, the soldiers had to ask which one he was when they went to arrest him in the Garden of Gethsemane!

Some have tried to equivocate over this passage about the prohibition of long hair on a man. They ask, "How long is long?" or, "How long should a *woman's* hair be?" The point of this discussion is that the man is *not* to have what the woman is to have. Actually, the expression "long hair" in 11:14-15 is from the Greek word *komao* which means "let the hair grow." The idea of length is not one of relativity here. It is not how long some woman's hair is in proportion to how short some man's hair is. Every man or woman with respect to their hair falls into one of two categories. Their hair is either *natural length* or it is not natural length. We either let our hair grow or we do not let it grow. We either cut it or we do

CHAPTER 11   FIRST CORINTHIANS 11:3-16

not cut it. Paul's instruction might be translated, "If a man let his hair grow, it is a shame unto him. But if a woman let her hair grow, it is a glory to her: for her hair is given her for a covering." The Greek word translated "nature" is *phusis* and could be translated, "instinctively." *Instinctively,* creation expects men to have short hair and women long hair. It is disgraceful in a man to be like a woman, and in a woman to be like a man.

God expects those who trust him to keep the distinctions between maleness and femaleness, both outwardly and inwardly, clear and unequivocal. Deliberate effeminacy in men and masculinity in women has always been an abomination to God. Israelite men were not to wear women's clothing, nor were women to wear men's clothing (Deut. 22:5). Homosexual behavior was a sin punishable by death in the Old Testament (Lev. 18:22; 20:13; Deut. 23:17-18). Effeminacy is prohibited in the New Testament (I Cor. 6:9-10) along with homosexuality by either male or female (Rom. 1:24-27).

Many of the heathen poets and philosophers of the Greek and Roman civilizations considered long hair in men a mark of effeminacy. Livy, Roman poet and historian, spoke strongly against the effeminacy of his age. Juvenal, disgusted by the sexual excesses and perversions of his day, spoke loathingly of the dandies whose manners, perfumes, and desire make them indistinguishable from women; and by the women who think that emancipation means that they should be indistinguishable from men.

In Zephaniah 1:8 God said that he would "punish the officials and the king's sons and all who array themselves in foreign attire." It has been thoroughly documented that the world-wide mania for long hair on men and hierarchical equality of women with men is fundamentally a *rebellion* against the divinely created and revealed order of God for the human race. When God's people, by their modes of dress, indicate they are more in harmony with the "foreign" (heathen) culture than they are with God's standards, it is time to apply the teachings of the apostle here in this eleventh chapter.

Notice the words used by the apostle in this context: "dishonors," "disgraceful," "improper," "is it proper?" and "degrading." For women (or men) to rebel against the place God has decreed for femininity or masculinity is serious sin. One cannot give acceptable worship to God in such rebellion. We repeat, the place *God* has ordered for femininity and masculinity is the basis of Paul's instruction here. Man praying with his head covered, dishonors his masculinity which is from God; woman praying with her head uncovered, dishonors her femininity which is from God. Man's dignity, or place, is to *lead* in society, to *protect* the weaker sex (female), to *provide* for the basic unit of society (the family) and to *discipline*. Woman's dignity is to be a *mother,* to be a *helper* in many things (see Prov. 31); to give sexual intimacy to her husband (see I Cor. 7), to help *rear* children (Eph. 6:1-4)—in essence, woman's dignity is to be feminine!

The apostle is *not* here advocating a dictatorship of the husband over the wife. In fact, as some see it, the husband as dictator and tyrant, and the wife as some non-thinking, non-speaking, non-human slave is not taught in the Bible at all. Many women—married women, too—in the Bible made decisions, spoke as individuals, and made crucial contributions to history. What the Bible does teach is that man has certain functions and woman has certain functions—neither is to replace the other. There are things women are not supposed to do and things men are not supposed to do (see Luke 8:1-3; Acts 9:36; 18:24-28; 21:19; Rom. 1:1-16; I Tim. 2:12-14; 5:9-16; Titus 2:3-5).

In verse 16 Paul makes the matter of subverting masculinity and femininity as God has revealed it, a matter of *disobedience* to apostolic practice and that is disobedience to God. Paul does *not* mean by verse 16, "If anyone objects or wants to argue against what I have said, just forget about it because I didn't mean it anyway." Paul *is* saying that "if any man, after this clear statement from me, is disposed to dispute the divine order of masculinity and femininity, and appears to be contentious, we simply say that we (the apostles) disapprove of the disordering of the places of male and female, and so do the churches of God." With any person who would dispute Paul's instruction here, argument is useless. Authority is the only solution to the controversy. Apostolic authority is unquestionable. And no man is justified, except on clearly scriptural grounds to reject the accepted and practiced customs of the local congregation of believers, (see I Cor. ch. 8-10).

SECTION 2

Oneness, a Requirement for Godly Worship (11:17-34)

17 But in the following instructions I do not commend you, because when you come together it is not for the better but for the worse. ¹⁸For, in the first place, when you assemble as a

CHAPTER 11 FIRST CORINTHIANS 11:17-34

church, I hear that there are divisions among you; and I partly believe it, [19] for there must be factions among you in order that those who are genuine among you may be recognized. [20] When you meet together, it is not the Lord's supper that you eat. [21] For in eating, each one goes ahead with his own meal, and one is hungry and another is drunk. [22] What! Do you not have houses to eat and drink in? Or do you despise the church of God and humiliate those who have nothing? What shall I say to you? Shall I commend you in this? No, I will not.

23 For I received from the Lord what I also delivered to you, that the Lord Jesus on the night when he was betrayed took bread, [24] and when he had given thanks, he broke it, and said, "This is my body which is for you. Do this in remembrance of me." [25] In the same way also the cup, after supper, saying, "This cup is the new covenant in my blood. Do this, as often as you drink it, in remembrance of me." [26] For as often as you eat this bread and drink the cup, you proclaim the Lord's death until he comes.

27 Whoever, therefore, eats the bread or drinks the cup of the Lord in an unworthy manner will be guilty of profaning the body and blood of the Lord. [28] Let a man examine himself, and so eat of the bread and drink of the cup. [29] For any one who eats and drinks without discerning the body eats and drinks judgment upon himself. [30] That is why many of you are weak and ill, and some have died. [31] But if we judged ourselves truly, we should not be judged. [32] But when we are judged by the Lord, we are chastened so that we may not be condemned along with the world.

33 So then, my brethren, when you come together to eat, wait for one another—[34] if any one is hungry, let him eat at home—lest you come together to be condemned. About the other things I will give directions when I come.

11:17-19 Cliques Stated: The church at Corinth was especially troubled by problems of worship. This was in part due to the variety of religious backgrounds among its members. The Jews in the Corinthian church would be accustomed to the simple, subdued, but dignified services of the synagogue. The synagogue would have been male-oriented. The women would have kept silent. Scriptures would be read, a scholarly dissertation of the scriptures would be given, prayers said, and, as the worshipers departed, offerings would be placed in the alms boxes. Most of the Gentiles in the Corinthian church, however, would be accustomed to the idolatrous services associated with Dionysus, god of intoxication and revelry—wild orgiastic feasts where food and wine were consumed in great quantities. The cult of Mithras, which was so popular with the Roman troops, initiated its converts in the *taurobolium*—a pit in the ground over which a bull was slaughtered. As the blood poured over him, the new devotee eagerly let it immerse his eyes, nose, and tongue. This makes it clear there would be difficulty in the Corinthian church about how the worship services should be conducted.

A serious problem had arisen about the observance of the Lord's Supper. Paul was very distressed over the reports of their conduct. Apparently there were *cliques* (small, exclusive groups) forming according to social and economic levels and separating from one another. It is clear that the worship service of first century Gentile churches was preceded by a communal meal (a fellowship supper). Paul says in this very chapter that the worship service in Corinth observed such a meal before worship (11:20-22). By having this "fellowship supper" they may have thought they were making progress in their Christian commitment. But Paul says they were coming together not for the better but for the worse! They would have been better off not even to have come together to behave as they were.

Division is abhored by the Lord whether it is over church leaders, over opinions, or over social and economic status. Paul does not say here (v. 18-19) that *divisions* (Gr. *schismata*) and *factions* (Gr. *haireseis,* or heresies) are necessary in the church in order to prove who belongs to God. He certainly would not advocate that Christians should form denominations and sects and cliques so the world would be able to find the true God. Jesus prayed just the opposite (see John 17:1ff.). He is pointing out, however, that when people form cliques within the church, those who refuse to join them and refuse to approve of them, are themselves recognized as genuine in their faith. A Christian who is a genuine brother to all Christians will not only refuse to join cliques and factions, but he will resist them with loving admonition.

11:20-22 Communal Supper: William Barclay in his commentary writes about the communal meal in the first century church:

> The ancient world was in many ways a much more social world than ours. It was the regular custom for groups of people to meet together for common meals. There was, in particular, a

CHAPTER 1   FIRST CORINTHIANS 11:17-34

certain kind of feast called an *eranos* in Greek language, to which each participant brought his own share of the food, and in which all the contributions were pooled to make a common feast. The early church had such a custom; they had a feast called the Agape or Love Feast. To it all the Christians came, bringing what they could, and when the resources of all were pooled, they sat down to a common meal. It was a lovely custom; and it is to our loss that the custom vanished.

This meal probably grew out of the fact that when Jesus first instituted the Lord's Supper it was in connection with the Passover meal he and his disciples had just eaten. It was a way of producing and nourishing real Christian *fellowship* (Gr. *koinonia,* sharing, participating). It offered the well-to-do a regular opportunity to share their material blessings with the poor. After this meal, all the Christians would partake of the bread and wine of the Lord's Supper, to memorialize his atoning death for the sins of all men.

But in the church at Corinth things had gone sadly wrong with the "Love" feast (and as a consequence, it had defiled their act of partaking of the Lord's Supper). Paul treats this problem with one of the angriest outbursts in the whole epistle. He begins with sarcasm, "When you meet together, it is not the Lord's Supper that you eat." William Barclay again:

> In this church there were rich and poor; there were those who could bring much of the finest of foods to the Love Feast and there were slaves and poor who could bring little or nothing. For many a poor slave the Love Feast must have been the only decent meal in the whole week. . . . The rich did not share their food but ate in little exclusive groups by themselves, hurrying through it in case they had to share. The meal or gathering at which the social differences between members of the church should have been obliterated only succeeded in aggravating these same differences.

Some in the Corinthian church began to eat before the others arrived, gorging themselves, consuming most of the provisions, and letting the others go hungry. The "drunken" are the wealthy who had the leisure to come early. They fed themselves full, and drank until they became inebriated. How shameful! The "hungry" were the slaves, common laborers, foundry workers, tired dock hands, and sick and disabled who were poverty stricken. Most of these would

FIRST CORINTHIANS

of necessity arrive late for the communal meal in the evening because they had to work until the sun set; these needed the most and received the least. It is scandalous to become drunken at the worship service; it is even worse to be "drunk" with a false sense of superiority and an indifference to the needs of the brethren.

What started as a "love" feast turned out to be an orgy of squabbling, hurt feelings and even drunkenness. This, of course, destroyed all possibilty of properly commemorating the Lord's sacrifice in the Lord's Supper. Paul insists that this prostitution of Christian fellowship destroys the true meaning and purpose of the Lord's Supper. They go through the ritual of the Lord's Supper all right, but it does not glorify Christ. They have hardly turned away from showing their contempt for Christ in their factious gluttony before they are pretending to join their snubbed brethren in "communing with the Lord."

Paul is not prohibiting Christians from having "fellowship suppers" in the "church-building" in verse 22. In the first place, so far as we know historically and archaeologically, there were no buildings built specifically as church-buildings before 200 A.D. The Christians at Corinth were meeting in people's private homes (see I Cor. 16:19). Furthermore, it is clear that what Paul condemned was the manner in which they were conducting themselves, not the place of the supper. Paul's suggestion is that if they are going to continue with their insensitive arrogance and gluttony to humiliate their brethren, they should stop the "love feast" and eat in their own homes. The place had nothing to do with their despising the church of God—it was their carnality.

Once again we behold actions so carnal and shameful in Christians we wonder how Paul could call them "brethren." But with only a little soul-searching we all should acknowledge we are "ignorant" and "obstinate" brethren—in differing areas of behavior.

11:23-26 Covenant Shared: This parenthetical section—a review from Paul concerning the establishment of the Lord's Supper—serves as a reminder of the spiritual purpose of the Lord's Supper. Paul had not been an eyewitness to the initial institution of the Supper. But that did not matter since the Lord Himself revealed to Paul the historical and spiritual details of it—and Paul had taught that to these Christians at Corinth.

In this text the apostle is emphasizing covenant, not ritual. Some would make the ritual the Christian's covenant. The Lord's Supper is *not* our covenant—it commemorates our covenant. Isaiah predicted at least twice that God would make the Servant (the Messiah) *himself* our covenant (42:6 and 49:8). Isaiah's statement 42:6, "I have given you as a covenant to the people, a light to the nations," is *unquestionably* messianic (see Isa. 42:1-4 and Matt. 12:18-21) in its context. Jesus Christ, himself, is our covenant. When we observe the Lord's Supper we are *remembering* that through faith we have appropriated *him* (Jesus) as our covenant. Of course, observance of the Supper is an *act* of faith on our part, but neither our faith nor the ritual is our covenant. It is through faith that we have been made *partakers of the divine nature* (see II Peter 1:3-4). Jesus, himself, dying and atoning for our sins and rising from the dead to supply the new creation of his Spirit within us, *is* our covenant. How does one *partake of a person* as a covenant? Through assimilating his *word* (his Spirit, his will). We "eat his flesh and drink his blood" by believing and obeying his word (see John 6:63). It would be of *no* profit to us even if we could engage in some ritual where we ate the actual, literal, physical flesh and blood of Jesus. It is his will, his personality, his mind, and his actions he wants us to assimilate (to partake of, to have *koinonia* with).

Our communion (participation) is in his person, his nature, and must not be confined merely to rituals. Participation in the life of Christ may involve observance of clearly revealed ceremonies or actions specified by Christ or the apostles, but the ceremonies are not the covenant. A covenant is an oath. God's oath in the new dispensation was the Messiah himself (see Heb. 6:17, where it should be translated, ". . . he interposed *himself* with an oath"; see II Cor. 1:20, where *Jesus* is said to be God's oath of confirmation to all his promises). A covenant is a reconciliation. "God was in Christ, reconciling the world unto himself" (II Cor. 5:19). The ceremony of the Lord's Supper is the weekly reminder that we share in a Divine Person—not a system of rituals.

"Do this in remembrance of me," involves *more* than remembering the crucifixion scene. It involves remembering that ". . . one died, therefore all died." It involves remembering that "from now on . . . we regard no one from a human point of view . . ." (see II Cor. 5:14-21). It involves remembering that we *participate* in the very life of Jesus Christ, or that he controls, directs, orders our lives. When Jesus died, *we* died—if we accept his death for us. I no longer direct me—Jesus does.

Had this been the case in Corinth, the brethren would not have arrogantly and greedily disregarded their brethren. They would have waited at the "love feast" for the poor, lower-class, late-comers and would have "counted them better than themselves" for this is the *mind of Christ* in which Christians are to participate (see Phil. 2:3-8). This is the life we are to have in us, being lived out through us. This is being in covenant with Jesus. The Corinthians were faithfully gathering to observe the ritual, but they were not partaking of the covenant!

Twice in this context the Greek adverb, *hosakis,* "as often as" is used to qualify the imperative verb, *poieite,* "Do." There really is *no* distinct, categorical commandment from the Lord or the apostles as to when the Lord's Supper *must* be commemorated. No particular day is commanded and no commandment is made as to frequency. Since no explicit directive is given in the New Testament, our next best guide about time and frequency of observance would be some precedent set by the apostolic (first century) church. We would certainly be on safer ground by seeking apostolic precedent than by trying to guess about the matter some twenty centuries removed from the beginning of the church.

From Acts 20:7 and I Corinthians 16:2 we observe that the first century church met every first day of every week to do two things: "break bread" (Acts 20:7) and "put something aside" (take up an offering) (I Cor. 16:2). Even if we assume the phrase "break bread" in Acts 20:7 refers to the "love feast," we are still compelled to acknowledge (from our text here in I Cor. 11:23-26) that the "love feast" was followed by the observance of the Lord's Supper. However, we may just as well assume the phrase "break bread" refers specifically to the Lord's Supper rather than the "love feast." Whatever the case may be, we must admit the church at Troas, in the first century, observed the Lord's Supper at least *every* first day of the week.

Since the church at Troas was undoubtedly established and taught by the apostle Paul, we must assume they met *every first day of the week* to break bread in accordance with apostolic instruction. Alexander Campbell wrote in *The Christian System,* pp. 274-275:

> The Apostles taught the churches to do all the Lord commanded. Whatever, then, the churches did by the appointment or concurrence of the apostles, they did by the commandment of Jesus Christ. Whatever acts of religious worship the apostles

CHAPTER 11   FIRST CORINTHIANS 11:17-34

taught and sanctioned in one Christian congregation, they taught and sanctioned in all Christian congregations because all are under the same government of the same king. But the church in Troas met upon the first day of the week for religious purposes.

Among the acts of worship, or the institutions of the Lord, to which the disciples attended in these meetings, the breaking of the loaf was so conspicuous and important, that the churches are said to meet on the first day of the week for this purpose. We are expressly told that the disciples at Troas met for this purpose; and what one church did by the authority of the Lord, as a part of his instituted worship, they all did.

Many of the early church "fathers" (Christian leaders of the church in the second century) testify in their writings that the Lord's Supper was observed on *every* first day of the week. Justin Martyr, who wrote about 140 A.D., says:

> And on the day called Sunday, all who live in cities or in the country gather together to one place . . . when our prayer is ended, bread and wine and water are brought and the president in like manner offers prayers and thanksgiving, according to his ability, and the people assent, saying amen; and there is a distribution to each, and a participation of that over which thanks have been given, and to those who are absent a portion is sent by the deacons.

In the compilation of writings called "The Teaching of The Twelve," written about 120 A.D. Christians were exhorted to gather *every* Lord's Day to break bread and give thanks. The Ante-Nicene fathers confirm this practice of observing the Lord's Supper every Sunday.

So, while we have no categorical command from the Lord about the frequency of its observance, we surely have clear apostolic precedent for observing it every first day of the week.

There may be a number of reasons we have no distinct and dogmatic order about the frequency of observing the Lord's Supper. First, if the Lord has to spell out in minute detail every spiritual action we are to take, he leaves no room for spiritual growth and character-building. It is in accepting the responsibility for discovering some truths, rather than in having them spelled out in detail, that we come to spiritual maturity. Perhaps that is why the Lord left the matter of frequency merely implied in the New Testament. Further, knowing the tendency of man to be legalistic, the Lord undoubtedly decided not to legislate the Supper's frequency. He would not want men to use a command about frequency of observance to attack, condemn and destroy ignorant and immature babes in Christ. Jesus would want this very significant and intimate act of worship to be done from love not from legalism. And if the Lord places in his word a veiled hint (or precedent) about its frequency, love will find it!

Observance of the Lord's Supper is not merely a remembrance of the past redemptive deeds of Christ—it is also a *telling-forth* (Gr. *katangellete,* a proclamation, a declaration) of the future redemptive deed of Christ in his Second Coming. The Christian, by observing the Lord's Supper every week, is declaring to the world around him that he believes the death of Jesus Christ to be efficacious for the forgiveness of sin and participation in the Spirit of God by grace. In observing the Lord's Supper the Christian is telling the world there is salvation in no other name under heaven than that of Jesus Christ. This testimony will go on, and on, and on, and on, in the world, as often as it is done, until Christ returns. The Lord's Supper is also a declaration to the world that Christians believe Christ is alive, risen from the dead, ascended to the right hand of God the Father, there making intercession on behalf of those who love him. It is a proclamation that Christians believe Jesus Christ to be living and communing in the Spirit with the church every time the Supper is observed (see Matt. 18:20). If this be the case, let us not argue about frequency of observance. Let us rather rejoice that we have apostolic precedent for observance at least every first day of the week when the church gathers for corporate worship. Consider the possibilities of intensifying the Christian proclamation with more frequent observance. Why not observe the Lord's Supper on other corporate gatherings of a congregation? Why not on Wednesday night at "midweek" service? Why not at ladies' meetings, men's meetings, youth meetings? The spiritual oneness, and moral constancy that would permeate a congregation meeting early every morning of every week, before scattering to different places of employment, would soon result in an evangelistic harvest.

11:27-29 Criticism of Self: A primary purpose of the Lord's Supper is, on the basis of Christ's loving atonement, to stimulate the participant into an examination of himself and his relationship to the *whole body* of Christ. This was what Jesus used it for on the very night he

CHAPTER 11   FIRST CORINTHIANS 11:17-34

instituted it. There, he challenged the apostles to examine their own hearts about betraying him. And each one did, asking, "Lord, is it I?" All the disciples, at that first Communion, were prodded into thinking of themselves in relation to Jesus and to one another. The Greek word *dokimazeto* is translated *examine himself.* It is the same Greek word used in II Corinthians 13:5 where the KJV translates the word, "prove." To examine is to test or prove. It means, literally, we are to put ourselves on trial.

But what is eating the Lord's Supper "in an unworthy manner"? The Greek word from which we get the English word *unworthy* is *anaxios. Axios* is the Greek word from which we get axiom, axiology, and axiomatic. The word in both Greek and English means, "value, proper, good, right, and worth." It is, therefore, possible to observe the Eucharist in an improper way. To do so makes a person guilty (Gr. *enochos,* liable to judgment of law) of the body and blood of the Lord (guilty as if the participant had crucified the Lord). Paul clearly says, "For any one who eats and drinks *without discerning* the body eats and drinks judgment upon himself."

To "discern the body" during observance of the Lord's Supper is not to be confined simply to a mental image of the crucifixion. To "discern the body" in this *context* refers specifically to *brotherhood.* It means to refresh one's memory about Jesus dying for *all* believers, rich or poor, famous or unknown, strong or weak. It means Christians, prompted by the Lord's Supper, are to discern the "body" in its membership, in its *koinonia* (fellowship). Too often, we focus too much on ourselves, even at the Lord's Supper. It *is* in keeping with the intent of Paul's discussion of the Supper here to have the burdens and needs of other members of the church upon our minds and hearts as we observe it. The less we think of ourselves during the Supper, the more likely we are to observe it as Paul wanted the Corinthians to observe it. The one way to drink it in an unworthy manner is to isolate oneself from the rest of the body in attitude and action. No man is unworthy in and of himself to partake. The Supper should be observed by sinners who are repenting. Sin should not keep us away from the Communion—it should drive us to it so we may get the right attitude. But the person who, like some of these Corinthians were doing, observes the Lord's Supper and is insensitive toward any other member of the body, drinks judgment upon himself.

The Lord's Supper was ordained by Christ to prompt people to love him and his body, the church. *It* is a "love" feast. It must be observed in unity. No one should dare observe it if he is not in harmony with his brethren. To observe the Lord's Supper and at the same time be slandering a brother, or disregarding a brother's needs, or agitating division within the body, is to profane and make a mockery of it. Such would be to blaspheme the very life he hypocritically professes to be sharing—the Life of Jesus!

11:30-34 Consequences of Such a Sham: Having the wrong attitude and still trying to play the role of a worshiper of God can have dire consequences. A separatist, schismatic attitude about the body of Christ while trying to pretend oneness and unity causes spiritual *sickness*, and, eventually, spiritual *death*. This is precisely the reason for so much spiritual sickness among Christians today. Too many Christians are "going through the motions" as they gather about the Lord's Table, but they haven't really surrendered to the mind and will of Jesus Christ as he revealed it "once for all" in the Scriptures. Too many, even Christians, want to judge the scriptures by their feelings and selfish desires rather than judging their feelings by the scriptures. This is the very point Paul is making here in Corinthians. He reminds these Christians at Corinth they must not judge their fellow church members by their feelings, but by the objective work of Christ documented in the New Testament. That is, all sinners are equally lost; all believers are equally redeemed. All Christians are equally members of Christ's body, the church. There may be different places of service within the kingdom of God, but every citizen is a servant. There is only one Master, and he is Jesus. Of course, there are specific hierarchical orders God has ordained within human society (even in the church), but still, there are no kings, only servants.

Paul told the Corinthians their spiritual sickness (Gr. *arrostoi,* feebleness) was directly due (Gr. *dia touto,* on account of this, therefore) to their profanation of the Lord's Supper by misdiscerning the body. The Bible speaks of spiritual sickness often (see Isa. 1:5; 33:24; Hosea 5:13; Ps. 30:2; Isa. 53:5; Jer. 6:14; 8:11; etc.). Spiritual sickness, and eventually, death, results from at least two causes: (a) improper ingestion of spiritual food—either not enough or the wrong food (see John 6:35-65 and Luke 12:1; Heb. 5:11-14; I Cor. 3:1-4, etc.); (b) exposure to the infectiousness of sin (Eph. 5:3-14; II Peter 3:17). Sin, if not treated by the spiritual healing of faith in Christ, invades our minds and infects them much like viral micro-organisms that cause physical illness and death. Sin, allowed to incubate, grows and develops and when it is "fullgrown" brings death (James 1:14-15).

CHAPTER 11 FIRST CORINTHIANS 11:17-34

Unworthy observance of the Lord's Supper brings condemnation to the whole body of Christians (11:34) when worship is profaned by play-acting. It is contagious. Hypocrisy and division will soon infect an entire congregation so that swift, radical, spiritual-surgery is sometimes called for (cf. I Cor. 5:1-13; Rom. 16:17-18; II Thess. 3:6-15; Titus 3:10).

The only worthy way to observe the Lord's Supper is to discern the body. Thus, from now on regard no one from a human point of view, but be consistently controlled by the love of Christ. At the Lord's Table concentrate on the fact that because one has died for all—all must die to self and live no longer for self but for him who for your sake died and was raised (see II Cor. 5:14-17; Gal. 2:20). Concentrate on viewing every Christian, every member of Christ's church, as an equal member of the body, a new creature in Christ. If all who meet at his Table will do this, every week, the church will be healthy and alive. Churches may *appear* to be alive and be dead (Rev. 3:1). Churches may *appear* to be healthy and be sick (Rev. 3:15-17). The Lord wants the church to be healthy at the very core of its being. This will be true only when the church partakes of the Lord's Supper in a worthy manner.

APPLICATIONS:

1. Have you ever *thought* about what worship is? Is it all feeling? Do you worship when you attend church services?
2. Should women wear head coverings today when they go to church? Do you? Why do Jewish men wear head coverings in the synagogue?
3. What about women cutting their hair in modern society? Shouldn't they let it grow to its full, natural length?
4. As a woman, do you believe you should be subordinate to a husband? As a man, do you believe you should rule over your wife?
5. If you were asked to make a decision about whether young men should wear long hair or not, what would you decide? Why? How long is long?
6. Would you compromise Paul's teaching here on hierarchy or order within the earthly kingdom of God should it become a matter of contention?

FIRST CORINTHIANS

7. What would you answer a member of a denominational church who said I Corinthians 11:18-19 teaches there *should be* denominations in Christianity?
8. Is it forbidden to have meals and eat in the church building?
9. Do you think of yourself as being locked into a covenant with God? What is the basis of your covenant? What are its terms?
10. How often do you think we should observe the Lord's Supper? Would you object to or appreciate observing it more than once a week?
11. Have you ever thought of your partaking of the Lord's Supper as a proclamation by you? To whom do you make your proclamation?
12. Do you ever feel like you are unworthy to take the Lord's Supper? When? If you had committed a terrible sin on Saturday, should you partake on Sunday?
13. Have you ever partaken of the Supper without having "discerned the body"?
14. What do you think is necessary for a congregation to be partaking of the Lord's Supper in a worthy manner?

APPREHENSIONS:

1. What is the apostolic "tradition"? Why should we obey apostolic tradition if Jesus condemned the traditions of the Pharisees? (See Matt. 15:1-20.)
2. What is worship?
3. Why is Paul discussing such insignificant things as veils on women and long hair on men in connection with worship? What is the fundamental issue he is discussing?
4. What is the proper order of heirarchy in the home? Where is the man's position? What is the woman's role?
5. Why does a man dishonor God by covering his head as he worships?
6. Why is the Bible so explicit about the feminine and masculine roles?
7. What does Paul mean when he says, "we recognize no other practice, nor do the churches of God"?
8. Why did Paul say, ". . . there must be factions among you *in order that* those who are genuine among you may be *recognized*"?
9. What specific faction is Paul talking about in this context?

CHAPTER 11   FIRST CORINTHIANS 11:17-34

10. Were Christians actually getting drunk just before the worship service?
11. How often are we to observe the Lord's Supper?
12. Is the ritual of the Supper our covenant?
13. What were these Corinthians doing that Paul accused them of partaking of the Supper in an "unworthy manner"?
14. What is "discerning the body"?

Chapter Twelve

THE PROBLEM OF MAINTAINING UNITY IN THE MIDST OF DIVERSITY
(Miraculous Gifts)
(12:1-31)

IDEAS TO INVESTIGATE:

1. Why couldn't a person without Christ's Spirit in him utter the words, "Jesus is Lord"?
2. Why does Paul say God "inspired" the various workings of the Spirit?
3. How are we all "baptized" by one Spirit into the body of Christ?
4. Why did God adjust the human body to give greater honor to the inferior part?
5. If Christians are to "earnestly desire the higher gifts," what are they?

SECTION 1

Sovereign of Diversity (12:1-3)

12 Now concerning spiritual gifts, brethren, I do not want you to be uninformed. ²You know that when you were heathen, you were led astray to dumb idols, however you may have been moved. ³Therefore I want you to understand that no one speaking by the Spirit of God ever says "Jesus be cursed!" and no one can say "Jesus is Lord" except by the Holy Spirit.

12:1 Purpose of Chapter: Although the chapter begins, "Now concerning spiritual gifts . . ." its main purpose is not to discuss the nature of miraculous gifts. Nor is its primary purpose the discussion of the place or purpose of miraculous gifts. If their purpose is mentioned in this chapter at all it is only because their purpose may have some bearing on the main problem. The main topic is the *correction of faulty attitudes* these Christians had toward miraculous gifts. This chapter (and the two chapters following) is as relevant as today's church affairs. Christians are still, today, expressing attitudes toward *alleged* miraculous gifts that disrupt the unity of Christ's church.

CHAPTER 12   FIRST CORINTHIANS 12:1-3

Actually, the word "gifts" is not even in the first verse. The Greek text has only the word *pneumatikon* which should be translated, "spiritual things, or matters." Translators have supplied the word "gifts" in this first verse. It might very well have been translated, "Now concerning the spiritual attitude you have toward spiritual gifts," since that is clearly the main point of this whole chapter.

A brief consideration of the purpose of miraculous gifts will help us understand this chapter. The *primary* purpose of miraculous gifts was *evidential*. Miraculous gifts were to confirm the deity of Jesus and to validate the message of the apostles as that of the Holy Spirit. Miracles were not granted to transform, convert or indicate the worker of such miracles had reached a higher phase of sanctification. In the infancy of the Church, when congregations everywhere were compelled to depend upon the oral instruction of the apostles and other evangelists, God saw fit to confirm the heavenly origin of their message with miracles (see Heb. 2:3-4; II Cor. 12:12; John 3:2; 10:37-38; 14:11; Acts 1:8; I Cor. 14:22, etc.). When the Church was still a child, it spake as a child (dependent upon confirmation of its message by the Father); but when the Church became a grown, integrated man, it put away childish things. When the body of Christ was fully formed and permanently established (incorporating both Jew and Gentile) with elders, deacons and evangelists, and when the Truth was fully revealed and propositionalized in the New Covenant scriptures, then the miraculous support by which it was sustained in its infancy was no longer needed and, therefore, passed away. This was according to the pre-ordained plan of God (see I Cor. 13:8-13). Most certainly, the miraculous gifts of the Holy Spirit were not given to the primitive church to be used as toys for amusement and entertainment. The possession of a miraculous gift was *not* a signal from God that the possessor was to be elevated in importance above any other Christian brother, gifted or non-gifted. For expanded treatment of the purpose of miraculous gifts and their cessation see Special Studies at the end of this chapter.

There must have been wholesale discrimination and division going on in the Corinthian church over possession and non-possession of miraculous gifts from the Holy Spirit. Those few who had been given these gifts felt they were spiritually superior to those who had not received miraculous gifts. The "gifted" were even discriminating among themselves as to which "gifts" were more important and which ones were of very little value. Some of the "gifted" were even declaring that those without miraculous gifts to exercise could not prove

FIRST CORINTHIANS

they had the Holy Spirit dwelling in them! Paul's response to these egotistical Corinthians is certainly relevant for the twentieth century.

In verse 2 Paul reminds the Corinthians how they were led astray to dumb idols by pagan priests who pretended to have miraculous gifts and divine revelations from "the gods." Archaeologists have found in the ancient city of Pompeii in the ruins of a pagan temple, a secret stair by which the priest mounted to the back of the statue of Isis; the head of the statue shows the *tube* which went from the back of the head to the parted lips. Through this tube the priest concealed behind the statue spoke the "answers" of Isis. These pagan priests usually tried to prove that only they had the "spirits of the gods" in them by ecstatic trances, pseudo communication with the "gods" by uttering unintelligible mutterings; by pretended "prophecies"; and by attempting to communicate with the dead. These pagan priests often contradicted themselves and represented the "gods" as cursing what they had once blessed. Heathen priests also promoted hatred, revenge, envy and immorality as part of the religion of the "gods."

The Corinthian Christians were having difficulty determining whether pagan priests possessed the Spirit of God and spoke divine revelations or not. And, further, they were being confused by the self-appointed "spiritual elite" within the church as to whether the non-gifted Christian had the Holy Spirit or not. Paul sets out to clear up the confusion. He takes three chapters (12-13-14) to do so. He begins by stating that "no one speaking by the Spirit of God ever says, Jesus be cursed." All heathen religions would say that of Jesus. But the Holy Spirit would *never* contradict himself, and curse the Son of God. The Corinthians may know assuredly that no pagan priest speaks by the inspiration of the Holy Spirit!

Contrariwise, any person who says Jesus is Lord, and exhibits a life surrendered to the lordship of Jesus, does so in partnership with the Holy Spirit. Any person agreeing to be ruled by Christ *has* the Holy Spirit. One does not have to receive the miraculous gifts of the Spirit to have him within them. It is only through the instrumentality of the Holy Spirit that any person is able to confess Jesus as Lord. The lordship of Jesus is revealed by the Father through the Holy Spirit (see Matt. 11:25-30; 16:17; John 14:1—16:33; Romans 8:1-17; I John 4:1-6), and the Holy Spirit *documents* the lordship of Jesus through the written word. The lordship of Jesus is not something which men may discover for themselves—it is something which God, in his grace, revealed to the world.

CHAPTER 12 FIRST CORINTHIANS 12:1-3

The primary purpose for miraculous gifts of the Spirit was to give the infant church an infallible guide by which to determine whether a preacher or teacher was speaking under the auspices of God and his Spirit or not. Before the New Testament scriptures were completed, and God's revelation to man was finalized, these miraculous powers were necessary. The spiritual gifts enabled the Corinthians to recognize pretenders in their day; the truth of the Bible enables the church to do the same today.

Part of the difficulty we have in understanding the problem in Corinth over miraculous gifts of the Spirit is due to the fact that such phenomena no longer exist. The pseudo "miraculous gifts" of modern Christendom are, at best, psycho-somatic, but for the most part, hoaxes. The gifts Paul discusses were unquestionably miraculous and unique. They were also transitory (see I Cor. 13:8-13). John Chrysostom (345-407 A.D.) wrote that Paul's discussion of miraculous gifts was obscure, even to the church of his day, because of the fact that such phenomena no longer took place.

So, the proper attitude toward miraculous gifts of the Holy Spirit is to acknowledge that the real test of the Spirit's presence is the total commitment of life to the lordship of Jesus. A person might have been given the power to do miracles and not have had the sanctifying presence of the Holy Spirit within. Judas Iscariot was empowered to work miracles right along with the rest of the apostles (see Matt. 10:1-8) and it is clear that he did not have the Holy Spirit in his heart for he was a thief from the beginning (John 12:6). It is apparent that some of these Corinthian Christians, while having power to do miracles, were dangerously close (if not at the point) to rejecting the lordship of Christ and doing despite unto the Holy Spirit by their proud and arrogant misuse of the "gifts."

Paul wants these "saints" to know that now that they are Christians they must allow Christ to exercise total lordship in their lives. They must speak and act according to the Spirit of Christ whose revelation for life comes through the apostolic word. If they have enthroned Christ as the Lord of their hearts, they are not going to envy another's "gift." They will be glad for every service that glorifies Christ. They are not going to call another Christian inferior because he has no *miraculous* gift.

There are no more miraculous gifts exercised in the church. They are no longer needed. They served their purpose. But there are *functional* "gifts" within the church today. *Every* Christian has some functional gift (see Special Study: *Gifts and Miracles*). So the principles of Paul's correction about attitudes toward "gifts" applies to the church for all time. Wrong attitudes, or worldly-mindedness, toward the gifts or abilities or circumstances with which God has blessed every Christian will lead to the same consequence in the church today as it did two thousand years ago—division and eventual destruction. There is great diversity and individuality in the gifts of God's grace—but there must be *unity* in Christian's minds and hearts!

SECTION 2

Source of Diversity (12:4-11)

4 Now there are varieties of gifts, but the same Spirit; 5and there are varieties of service, but the same Lord; 6and there are varieties of working, but it is the same God who inspires them all in every one. 7To each is given the manifestation of the Spirit for the common good. 8To one is given through the Spirit the utterance of wisdom, and to another the utterance of knowledge according to the same Spirit, 9to another faith by the same Spirit, to another gifts of healing by the one Spirit, 10to another the working of miracles, to another prophecy, to another the ability to distinguish between spirits, to another the interpretation of tongues. 11All these are inspired by one and the same Spirit, who apportions to each one individually as he wills.

12:4-7 Provenance: The word *inspires* in verse 6 is a translation of the Greek word *energon* which actually means, "energizing, working, or operating." Paul emphasizes over and over that it was the "same God" or "same Spirit" who *energized* or *operated* the miraculous gifts through those who were given them. These special gifts all came from God and were, therefore, to be used to *edify* (build up) the church, not to divide and destroy its oneness. These gifts all had their source in the power of One Divine Person, so, there was *one purpose* (God's) for their use. If it was the same God who was the Source of all the gifts, then they were all given for the *common good* (Gr. *sumpheron,* literally, "together-profiting"). They were not given to promote the superiority of those possessing them—they were to serve every member, one way or another, in the body of Christ. No gift of God to man, whether miraculous or non-miraculous, is ever given to

CHAPTER 12   FIRST CORINTHIANS 12:4-11

be used selfishly for the promotion of human pride or superiority. Gifts are given for service. It may not have been Paul's intention to teach the doctrine of the Trinity, but the oneness of the threefold personage of the Godhead is certainly delineated when he states, "... the same Spirit ... the same Lord ... the same God."

12:8-10 Particularity: In verse 4 the apostle indicated there were *varieties* of gifts given to the Corinthians. The Greek word translated *varieties* is *diaireseis* and means literally, "to take apart," or, "in many parts," hence, "differences" or "distinctions." The Corinthian church probably had a full complement of all the gifts God intended the first century church to have. Verse 4 also contains three significant Greek words explaining the purpose of the variety. The Greek word translated *gifts* is *charismaton;* literally, "things of grace." The Greek word translated *service* is *diakonion;* literally, "deaconries." The Greek word translated *working* is *energematon;* literally, "operatings." God purposely gave great variety of miraculous gifts in order that the whole church might have a miraculously sustained ministry, so necessary for the extremely crucial infant years (approximately 30-100 A.D.) of its existence. The emphasis is definitely on variety for the purpose of service and ministry.

Nine supernatural gifts are listed. Each had a particular function to perform in sustaining and maturing the church. When we read that these gifts were supernatural we must not forget the trials, temptations, doubts and fears those first century Christians endured. The New Testament (Acts, Hebrews, I Peter, Galatians, Thessalonians, Revelation) documents for us a fearsome record of their sufferings. They needed divine demonstrations to nourish courage, faith and endurance. Christians of that century did not have Bibles of their very own. Precious and few were the manuscripts or copies and those were circulated from one church to another. The infant church also needed direct, divine guidance in discerning the truth from all the deceptive falsehoods of paganism and the Judaizers.

The "gifts" as Paul lists them are:

a. "the utterance of wisdom" (Gr. *logos sophias*); probably supernatural power to reveal Christian *principles* of thought and behavior; revealed applications of gospel facts.

b. "the utterance of knowledge" (Gr. *logos gnoseos*); probably supernatural guidance in knowing the *facts* of the gospel so they might confirm "prophecies"; the importance of this is evident from I Corinthians chapter 15.

c. "faith" (Gr. *pistis*); probably the faith to "move mountains" (I Cor. 13:2; Matt. 17:20) or do miraculous works; J. W. McGarvey said that no amount of personal faith ever enabled one to perform a miracle to whom such power had not been given. We must be careful to distinguish between the use of "faith" in connection with spiritual gifts and the personal faith that saves. Jesus gave Judas "faith" to perform miracles (Matt. 10:1-8) but Judas did not, evidently, possess faith of his own in Christ sufficient to acknowledge him as his savior.

d. "healings" (Gr. *iamaton*); undoubtedly supernatural power was given to certain individuals to cure illnesses and diseases; perhaps some could heal certain diseases and others different diseases; it is not stated that anyone had power to heal all diseases.

e. "the working of miracles" (G. *energemata dunameon*, operations of powers); probably has to do with miracles other than healings; perhaps supernatural power to bring the judgment of God upon persons opposing God (Ananias and Sapphira, Elymas) or powers over nature and things.

f. "prophecy" (Gr. *propheteia*); probably supernatural endowment to proclaim (and predict when necessary) and preach the gospel inerrantly, and directly without having been eyewitnesses as the apostles were; the word "prophecy" may be used for non-miraculous preaching (see Rom. 12:6).

g. "ability to distinguish between spirits" (Gr. *diakriseis pneumaton*); literally, "critiquing of spirits"; probably supernatural endowment of the ability to judge between true and false teachers and doctrines with immediacy. In the infant church (without a proliferation of written scriptures) there was no objective test available to determine correct teaching versus false so supernaturally endowed gifts to make such distinctions were necessary. Now, with the Bible complete, in thousands of human languages, the supernatural gifts are no longer necessary. Doctrine and teachers are to be measured according to the written apostolic word (see I John 4:1-6; II Thess. 3:6-15; II Tim. 3:16-17).

h. "various kinds of tongues" (Gr. *gene glosson*); probably supernatural endowment to speak in a human (foreign) language unknown, except by miraculous endowment, to the speaker

CHAPTER 12 FIRST CORINTHIANS 12:4-11

and often unknown to the listeners requiring an interpreter. These "tongues" (languages) were human languages. They were not totally "unknown" (as the KJV implies) (see Acts 2:8ff.) (see comments on I Cor. 14:1ff.).

i. "interpretation of tongues" (Gr. *hermenia glosson*). The word *hermenia* is the word from which we get the English word *hermeneutics*, "the science of interpretation and explanation." When a Christian, under supernatural power of God's Spirit, spoke in a language foreign to himself and his hearers, it required someone supernaturally endowed with the gift of understanding the unknown language to *translate* the *message* in the language known to the hearers. The main purpose of the phenomena of speaking in a language unknown to the speaker was the manifestation of a miracle (see I Cor. 14:22). At the same time, however, getting the message of the "unknown" tongue to the audience was so important, Paul's instruction to the Corinthian church was, "if there is no one to interpret, let each of them (tongues speakers) keep silent in the church." Those with the gift of foreign-language-speaking could control their utterings. (See John 1:41-42 for two examples of the Greek word *hermenia* being used to mean "translate.")

12:11-Partitioning: Miraculous gifts were apportioned according to the sovereign *will* and *choice* of the Holy Spirit. It was *not the desire of the recipient* that determines the gift. Modern, pseudo, charismatic gifts are allegedly given on the basis of the recipient's faith and desire. The Bible clearly documents the fact that supernatural endowments of the Holy Spirit of God were given exclusively according to God's purpose. Paul makes it plain in three of his other epistles (Rom. 12:6; Eph. 4:7; Heb. 2:4) that all "gifts," supernatural and natural, are distributed entirely according to the purpose of God.

In his parable Jesus taught that all "talents" and "pounds" were distributed according to the "owner's" will. Servants all received different measures and were responsible only for the measure they had received—not for what another had received. There is no room for pride or jealousy when we acknowledge the truth that everything we have is from the "same God" and "according to his omniscient will."

The RSV is not as accurate as it could be in verse 11 had it been a more literal translation. The Greek text reads: *panta de tauta energei to en kai to auto pneuma, diairoun idia hekasto kathos bouletai.* A more literal translation would read: *And all these things the same Spirit operates, distributing separately to each one as he purposes.*

Christians, of all people, must recognize and admit that human beings have *absolutely nothing at all* (miraculous gifts, functional gifts, material gifts) unless received from God, to be used as he purposes in his revealed will, the Bible. He is the source of all we have so that no man might boast in the presence of God (cf. I Cor. 1:30).

Section 3

Sagaciousness of Diversity (12:12-26)

12 For just as the body is one and has many members, and all the members of the body, though many, are one body, so it is with Christ. 13 For by one Spirit we were all baptized into one body—Jews or Greeks, slaves or free—and all were made to drink of one Spirit.

14 For the body does not consist of one member but of many. 15 If the foot should say, "Because I am not a hand, I do not belong to the body," that would not make it any less a part of the body. 16 And if the ear should say, "Because I am not an eye, I do not belong to the body," that would not make it any less a part of the body. 17 If the whole body were an eye, where would be the hearing? If the whole body were an ear, where would be the sense of smell? 18 But as it is, God arranged the organs in the body, each one of them, as he chose. 19 If all were a single organ, where would the body be? 20 As it is, there are many parts, yet one body. 21 The eye cannot say to the hand, "I have no need for you," nor again the head to the feet, "I have no need of you." 22 On the contrary, the parts of the body which seem to be weaker are indispensable, 23 and those parts of the body which we think less honorable we invest with the greater honor, and our unpresentable parts are treated with greater modesty, 24 which our more presentable parts do not require. But God has so composed the body, giving the greater honor to the inferior part, 25 that there may be no discord in the body, but that the members may have the same care for one another. 26 If one member suffers, all suffer together; if one member is honored, all rejoice together.

CHAPTER 12　　　　　　　FIRST CORINTHIANS 12:12-26

12:12-13 The Organism: The "body" of Christ (the church) is an *organism,* not an organization (see Special Study, "Is the Church An Organization or an Organism?"). On the Day of Pentecost (Acts 2:1ff.) when the apostles began to carry out the command of their Lord, the resurrected Christ in heaven was united, as the Head, to the spiritual body (the church) being formed on earth in order that the work of redemption, attained by Christ in his physical body, might be practiced and proclaimed and increased in Christians (the body) until he comes. Of course, the church (Christians) can never add a word, a thought, or a deed to the finished work of Christ's vicarious death and the Holy Spirit's revelation of the New Testament scriptures. Jesus completed all that forever. But the Lord in that human body was not ending something, he was beginning a great program which he himself, in the limitations of a human body could never complete (the task of world-wide proclamation of redemption, see Col. 1:24-27). When Jesus was here in his physical body there was no part of human life that his *holy* nature did not penetrate with the redemptive purpose of God; his incarnation was an invasion of holiness on all fronts and in every aspect of human need. He penetrated every level of life with righteousness: social, political, ecclesiastical, moral, educational and familial. That is the work his body (the church) is commissioned now to do.

The definition of *organism* is: "Any highly complex thing or structure with parts so integrated that their relation to one another is governed by their relation to the whole." An organism is something living where the whole exists for the parts, and each part for the whole and for all other parts. That is precisely what Paul is saying to the Corinthians in these verses about the church. Plummer says: "The Church is neither a dead mass of similar particles, like a heap of sand, nor a living swarm of antagonistic individuals, like a cage of wild beasts; it has the unity of a living organism, in which no two parts are exactly alike, but all discharge different functions for the good of the whole. All men are not equal, and no individual can be independent of the rest; everywhere there is subordination and dependence."

Paul is saying that every individual has some function to discharge, and all must work (see Eph. 4:15-16) together for the common good. The all-important operation of an organism is unity in loving service. The Church is an organic body of which all the parts are moved by a spirit of common interest and mutual affection.

FIRST CORINTHIANS

Christ's "body" (the church) *is* one. Any member contributing to the destruction of this oneness, either by refusing to function (as it has been gifted) or by hindering another member from using its gifts (through jealousy or pride), is in danger of being cut off (see Matt. 5:29-30; John 15:1-11). The *oneness* of mind, love and purpose in his disciples was what Jesus prayed for on the night before his death (John 17:1ff.). He knew the world would never believe God sent him if his disciples could not function as many different members in one whole, living, organism. Just as a human body must have all its "members" (parts) functioning properly in order for one body to be whole and serving its purpose, so it is with "Christ," says the apostle. Paul is using "Christ" in verse 12 as a metonymy for the church. All members in a physical body cannot have the same function, but the fulfillment of the body's purpose demands that each member function according to its part. The body cannot be whole and cannot reach its fullest potential when one of its members does not function properly.

Paul wrote verse 13 in Greek thus: *dai gar en heni pneumati hemeis pantes eis hen soma ebaptisthemen . . . ,* literally, "for indeed by one Spirit we all into one body were immersed. . . ." The emphasis is, of course, on the *oneness* of the instrumentality of the Corinthian's immersion (see Acts 18:8). The Greek preposition *en* used with the dative case *pneumati* should be translated causally (see examples of *en* translated causally at Luke 24:49; II Thess. 2:13; I Peter 1:2) when the context demands it. The Corinthians were not initially immersed *in* the Spirit but *by* the revealed will and command of the Spirit. Their initial immersion was in water in obedience to apostolic preaching. *Some* of the Corinthians later received the miraculous gifts of the Spirit. But the possession of miraculous gifts did not *necessitate* the "immersion of the Holy Spirit." The immersion (baptism) of the Holy Spirit was administered only by direct endowment of Christ (see Matt. 3:11-12; Luke 24:48-49; John 1:33; 20:22-23; Acts 2:1-21; 10:44—11:18). Miraculous gifts of the Spirit were incidentally imparted to those (the apostles and Cornelius' family) who received the "immersion (baptism) of the Spirit." All other Christians, except the foregoing, who received supernatural endowments, received them by the laying on of the hands of an apostle. Therefore, when Paul says *en heni pneumati,* "by one Spirit," he is indicating that all the Corinthians, Jews or Greeks, slaves or free, were immersed in water in obedience to the revealed will of the *same* Spirit of God. His argument is that since they were all obedient to the will of the same Spirit,

CHAPTER 12 FIRST CORINTHIANS 12:12-26

they are all members of the same body. Any person immersed in water in obedience to the revealed will of the Holy Spirit as preached and written by the apostles is a member of Christ's body and equally important. Such a person is then personally responsible to the Head (Christ) of the body to use with humility and gratitude any and all endowments (gifts) he may have for the edification and increase of the whole "body of Christ." All who have been immersed into Christ's body by the *instrumentality* of the Holy Spirit were made to drink of one and the same Spirit of God (see John 7:37-39; Isa. 44:3; 55:1; 58:11; John 4:10, 13; 6:35; Rev. 21:6; 22:17). All Christians of all ages *drink* of the Holy Spirit without receiving the "baptism of the Holy Spirit." The New Testament plainly teaches that drinking of the Holy Spirit is the same as "partaking of the Holy Spirit" (Heb. 6:4) or the same as "partaking of the divine nature" (II Peter 1:4) or the same as having the abiding, indwelling presence of the Holy Spirit (John 14:23; I John 2:24; 3:24, etc.).

12:14-20 The Organs: Paul uses the human body, the physical body, to illustrate the wisdom of diversity. Every organism or body consists of more than one member or organ. And no *one* member or organ can supply every need the whole body must have to function as a whole; proper functioning in order to bring about the common good of the whole body requires the contribution of what each member has. Picture what a human body would look like, and how it might function, if it were all ear or all eye! Not only would it be a monstrous looking thing, it would be a malfunctioning thing, perhaps even a dying thing. God made unity, but not uniformity; he did not reduce all human beings down to sameness. Every member cannot have the same function, and, while it may *appear* that some members have more important functions than others, it is not so.

Because one member of the church in Corinth did not have the popular miraculous gift of speaking in a foreign tongue (or had no miraculous gift at all) he was not to be considered unimportant or unnecessary. If the Corinthian church had received only the miraculous gift of "tongues" what a useless body it would have been!

Furthermore, since God arranged the organs in that body (the Corinthian church) as *he* chose, for Christians to rearrange the priorities and functions of the members was rebellion against God. Whatever gifts God gives (miraculous or non-miraculous) he gives not to please men but to fulfill his redemptive purposes for the world. God certainly did not create diversity of functions in the members

233

of the human body to *destroy* the body. Neither did Christ's Spirit give diversity of miraculous and non-miraculous gifts to *destroy* his church. A body has to have many members to function properly. All members cannot have the same function. But the fulfillment of the body's purpose must have each member functioning according to its part. The body cannot do without one of its members. The Corinthian church was dividing and destroying itself over the use and abuse of the different miraculous gifts, thinking some were important and some were not needed.

12:21-26 The Operation: The very fact of diversity should preclude the possibility of discord. Diversity is given by God in order that the members may care for one another. What one lacks another supplies. Where one cannot function, another functions. This text teaches that Christians ought to: (a) realize they need each other; (b) respect each other; (c) sympathize with one another.

In the human body God has *adjusted* (Gr. *sunekerasen,* literally, "blended" or "mingled together") all the organs and parts of the body in such a way that no organ can be considered inferior or useless or not needed. Those parts of the human body which seem to be weaker we find to be indispensable. One need only to lose the use of an arm, an eye, or even a finger to learn how indispensable each member is. Those parts of the human body we think are *less honorable* (Gr. *atimotera*), such as the sexual organs, God invests with greater honor. The sexual organs which some think dishonorable and uncomely have the function of procreation. Thus greater honor is given to those members of the body which men tend to think of as inferior.

These same principles are true in Christ's spiritual body, the church. Some, in the church at Corinth, were categorizing the miraculous gifts in degrees of greater importance, lesser importance and no importance. In chapter 14 we shall learn that the one gift they thought "superior" was tongues and the "inferior" gift was prophecy. God revealed through Paul that the divine categorization of gifts was exactly *opposite* from that of men. It is true in the body of Christ today (universally, or locally). Every member has at least one non-miraculous gift. That gift comes by the grace of the same God to all. The body as a whole cannot get along without that gift. Some gifts are not as flamboyant as others. But the non-flamboyant may be more important. The less sensational gifts are certainly not to be considered "inferior"; they may, in fact, be superior!

CHAPTER 12   FIRST CORINTHIANS 12:27-31

There can be no such thing as isolation in the church. In the body there is no question of relative importance. If any limb or organ ceases to function the whole body is thrown out of order. This is even more true in the spiritual body (the church). When church members begin to think about their own superiority over one another, the possibility of the church functioning properly is destroyed. If any one member of the body suffers abuse, misuse or nonuse, all the other members together suffer some malfunction or loss. If any one member of the body seems to have a more honored (Gr. *doxazetai,* glorified) function or gift, the whole body should rejoice together that this member is making his God-given contribution to the common good of the whole body, realizing that from God's perspective his *glorious* function is of no more significance than someone else's *non-glorious* function. It is not easy for human beings to have the divine perspective. It requires faith! It requires setting the human mind on the things of the Spirit (Rom. 8:5-17)! It requires the control of the love of Christ over our thoughts until we no longer regard anyone from a human point of view (II Cor. 5:14-21). Men tend to want to categorize, make themselves superior and others inferior, and lord it over one another—but it shall *not* be *so* among Christians! (Matt. 20:20-28). The devil will always make the divine perspective concerning gifts, talents, abilities and functions to be impractical and unfair. So the Christian must surrender his evaluations and priorities totally to the direction of the Spirit of God in his word, the Bible. The Christian's only option is to perceive and classify gifts as the Bible does.

SECTION 3

Singleness in Diversity (12:27-31)

27 Now you are the body of Christ and individually members of it. 28 And God has appointed in the church first apostles, second prophets, third teachers, then workers of miracles, then healers, helpers, administrators, speakers in various kinds of tongues. 29 Are all apostles? Are all prophets? Are all teachers? Do all work miracles? 30 Do all possess gifts of healing? Do all speak with tongues? Do all interpret? 31 But earnestly desire the higher gifts.

And I will show you a still more excellent way.

FIRST CORINTHIANS

12:27-30 The Reality: Paul says, "Now you *are* the body of Christ and individually members of it." Whether men like it or not, understand it or not, God has *appointed* (Gr. *etheto,* placed, set, deposited, constituted, ordained) in the church first apostles, second prophets, third teachers, etc.

The way in which God created the human body and how it is to function is a fact that has to be accepted. The same holds true in the spiritual body of Christ, the church. The appointments and gifts God gives to the various members of the church are to be accepted. God ordained the varieties of functions in the church to produce singleness (unity) of purpose and practice. There *is* one body. But there is still individuality. And the oneness of the body is sustained only when there is surrender of the members to Christ's revealed will concerning variety and individuality. We dare not try to fit all members of the body into one mold of functioning. Sameness is not necessary—in fact, it is unhealthy. Sameness in miraculous gifts would never have produced a strong, growing body of Christ in the first century. Sameness in non-miraculous functioning will not produce spiritual increase and development. It is not sameness of function which produces unity in the body. Unity comes by obedience to the Head!

12:31 The Route: Singleness in diversity is attainable! There is a *way* for a multi-talented church in any cultural, social, economic, educational and political circumstance to be one body of Christ. That *way* is agape-love!

Paul has not yet discussed the idea that some supernatural gifts were "greater" than others. He went to great lengths (12:1-31) to demonstrate that each *member* (gifted or not) is as important to the body as any other. But, in chapter 14, he categorizes the usefulness of miraculous gifts, declaring that the gifts which edified and gave a steadying influence on the whole congregation (such as prophecy) were the "greater" gifts. The Corinthians apparently had a mania for the more spectacular, exhibitionist gifts such as "speaking in tongues." In chapter 14, Paul reprimands that atitude. He may be rebuking it here in 12:31.

> . . . in I Cor. 12:31 perhaps we should read a mild rebuke. It could just as accurately be translated, "But you are zealously seeking the greater gifts." In the second person plural of the present tense, indicative and imperative forms (in Greek) look alike. The context and line of thought must indicate which it

is. In view of the overall teaching of I Cor. 12-14, rebuking pride in some gifts, and expressing the same divine source for all different gifts, and teaching "to each is given the manifestation of the Spirit *for the common good*" (I Cor. 12:7 RSV), is it not more likely that Paul is disapproving of their desire for the greater gifts?

It seems clear that in these chapters he is teaching against both selfish pride in some gifts as greater and failure to use the gifts for others.

Learning From Jesus, by Seth Wilson, pub. College Press Publishing Company, pp. 471-472.

Paul's main concern was that the whole church be edified (see I Cor. 14:18, 19, 26). All supernatural gifts were to be practiced solely to that end. And some gifts were more apt to produce edification of the body than others.

Prompted by the Spirit of Christ the apostle declares "there is yet a more excellent way I will show you" to produce unity in the body. That, of course, is the way of *agape-love.* Paul elucidates on the superiority of love over supernatural gifts in chapter 13. *Agape-love* is a virtue every Christian must have. To have a supernatural gift and not have agape-love makes the supernatural gift less than useless. Supernatural gifts were temporary. They were endowed by God for a specific time and place in the infancy of the Church. They were destined to become obsolete and vanish. Not so with agape-love. The completed New Testament scriptures and Christians practicing agape-love is all the church now, in its manhood, needs. Love is far superior to miraculous gifts. Love is able to overcome, to produce, and to sustain where miraculous gifts alone never could. Love alone will produce oneness in the body of Christ whether there is ever a miraculous gift or not. Supernatural gifts alone will not produce oneness. Indeed, gifts alone will produce pride, jealousy and division.

The doctrine Paul introduces here (and amplifies in chapter 13) applies at all times, in every circumstance, for the body of Christ. It matters not in a congregation how erudite the preacher, how rich and influential the members, oneness is the consequence of agape-love. *The body of Christ must have oneness!* It is not his body if it doesn't!

FIRST CORINTHIANS

APPLICATIONS:
1. Have you ever thought about the fact that you would never have been able to call Jesus "Lord" without the work of the Holy Spirit?
2. Does that help you know that *you have* the Holy Spirit?
3. What is your attitude toward the "gifts" of God? (both miraculous and non-miraculous)?
4. Do you think the church has a responsibility to inform Christians as to the attitude Christ wants concerning "gifts"? What about your church?
5. Although you cannot expect a miraculous gift today, you still have many non-miraculous gifts from God—are you functioning as an integral part of the body of Christ with your gifts?
6. Would you serve the church more if you were more talented or "gifted"?
7. Have you been immersed into the body of Christ by the revealed will of the one Spirit of God?
8. What does it do for your understanding of the functioning of the church in the world today to think of it in comparison to the human body?
9. Try to think of as many non-miraculous "gifts" as you can to which God may give "the greater honor" today! Make a list. (Compare Rom. 12:1ff.)
10. Does the whole church where you attend suffer when one member is not functioning according to his "gift"? Does the whole church rejoice when one is honored? Which is easier for the church to do?

APPREHENSIONS:
1. Why is one's attitude toward a gift (miraculous or non-miraculous) more important than the gift itself?
2. Are those claiming today to have miraculous gifts of the Holy Spirit (and claiming Jesus as "Lord") while rejecting other apostolic doctrines, really letting Jesus be Lord?
3. Why, when the New Testament is so plain to say that miraculous gifts are distributed according to the will of God, do so many clamor for miraculous gifts today as if such gifts are available because they desire them?
4. Would it help the unity of the church if Christians were reminded more often that they have absolutely nothing except it has been

given them by God? Are we guilty sometimes of thinking, "I worked hard for that and I deserve it"?
5. Is the church actually the "body of Christ" in the world today? Why is it a body? What is the difference between an organism and an organization?
6. How does man mix himself up about the significance of certain parts of the "body" (both physical and spiritual bodies)?
7. What would happen to the body if there were no diversity in its members?
8. Why is it unhealthy to try to fit all Christians into one emotional, cultural, functional mold and do away with individuality?
9. Why must we see the functioning of the members of the church through the perspective of God?
10. Is there a way to have unity through diversity? What is that way?

Special Study
GIFTS, MIRACLES
(Heb. 2:3-4)
Introduction

I. DEFINITION OF MIRACLE

   A. "An event occurring in the natural world, observed by the senses, produced by divine power, without any adequate human or natural cause, the purpose of which is to reveal the will of God and do good to man" (McCartney, in *Twelve Great Questions About Christ*).

      1. Hume once argued: there is more evidence for regularity in nature than for irregularity; therefore, regularity and not irregularity must be the truth of the matter.

      2. Certainly there is more evidence for the regular occurrence of nature than for any supernatural occurrence. If there weren't we could not talk of miracles.

      3. The argument of miracle rests on the regularity of nature generally.

      4. Only if all the historical evidence available to man could show there is no being outside nature who can in any way alter it can there be an argument against the possibility of miracles. This the evidence does not do—indeed cannot do!

   B. In our text four different words are used:

      1. *semeiois* = signs
      2. *terasin* = wonders
      3. *dunamesin* = powerful deeds
      4. *merismois* = distributions (of the Holy Spirit)
      5. Milligan (Hebrews) says these words classify miracles as:
         a. to their design (signs)
         b. to their nature (wonders)
         c. to their origin (supernatural power)
         d. to their Christian aspect (distributions of the Holy Spirit)

II. THE FACT OF MIRACLES RESTS ON THE HISTORICITY OF OUR NEW TESTAMENT TEXT

   A. Were these writers eyewitnesses?
   B. Are they credible?

SPECIAL STUDY: GIFTS, MIRACLES

  C. Are the documents authentic?
  D. This is another subject—but it is the fundamental subject.

III. PURPOSE OF MIRACLES

  A. As our text points out, the primary purpose of miracles was to "bear witness" that the message from Jesus and that Jesus Himself was from God. John 10:25, 37, 38; 15:10-11; Matt. 9:1-8

  The miracles do not prove Jesus to be the Son of God—many men worked miracles—but they prove Him to be a truthful messenger, and this truthful messenger says that He is God. Christ may have wrought miracles and not have been God; but He could not have wrought miracles and said that He was God without being God.

  B. To demonstrate the mercifulness of God in the case of individual men. Miracles illustrate and explain the teaching of Jesus on the love and mercy of God.

  C. To demonstrate God's wrath upon sin and rebellious sinners Matt. 21:18-19 (cursed fig tree), Acts 13:11 (blinding of Elymas) Acts 5:5-10 (Ananias and Sapphira). Bible miracles taught not only God's love and goodness but also His power and authority, and sometimes His righteous and fearful judgments.

  D. Miracles of the Bible demonstrate clearly that miracles were never intended to be universal:

  1. In extent: for they were always limited to few and special cases. Never have they been used to relieve suffering or prolong life here for all of God's people universally.

      a. Some received no miraculous deliverance here (Heb. 11:35-40)
      b. John the Immerser, greatest born of women, worked no miracles, nor was he delivered miraculously (Matt. 11:7-11; John 10:41).
      c. Jesus could have healed all or raised all from dead but He didn't.
      d. Paul healed many, but did not heal Trophimus and Timothy (II Tim. 4:20; I Tim. 5:23).

  2. In result: All who were delivered from sickness had at other times to suffer again and die. All who were raised

FIRST CORINTHIANS

from the dead had to die again. Peter was delivered twice, but not a third time. (God was no less compassionate and Peter no less believing.)

IV. PASSING OF MIRACLES (AS SUCH)

A. It would take some convincing to persuade me that God does not work providentially in history today. I believe He answers when we pray (sometimes yes, sometimes no, sometimes without acting at all).

1. I teach Life of Christ, Old Testament Prophets and Revelation. You cannot study and teach those books and believe them for 20 years without believing God is active in the affairs of men and nations.
2. I do not deny that God could reinstitute an age of miracles such as we read about in the Old Testament and New Testament if it suited His purpose.
3. It is just that I believe He will not because He has no further need of such miracles and signs. Here is why I believe that:

B. "When that which is perfect is come, that which is in part shall be done away . . ." I Cor. 13:10.

1. The reason for the election of the Jews in Christ (Eph. 1) was for "a plan in the *fulness of time,* to unite all things in him . . ." (not for heaven, but for earth). Thus the plan was to unite both Jew and Gentile, slave and free, man and woman, into one body, the church. This is why the spiritual miraculous gifts were given in Ephesians 4:11f., for this ministry of unifying. These miraculous gifts were to last until the *teleios* "man" was formed (Eph. 4:13).
2. The identical context, outline, illustrations, and terminology in I Corinthians 12—14 leads us to conclude that such is also the meaning of *teleios* there . . . to perfect both Jew and Gentile in the one body.
3. It is unquestionably apparent that the problem in both Ephesians and Corinthians was the immaturity and schismatic tendencies of the early church. In light of the frequent association of love with perfection (maturity)—and in light of the fact that the entire epistle of I Corinthians

SPECIAL STUDY: GIFTS, MIRACLES

deals with the grand theme of divine love in the context of the childish immaturity of so many Christians at Corinth, it seems best to define "the perfect" in terms of the ultimate goal, aim, and end which Paul seeks to accomplish which is growth and maturity in Christ.

4. Paul's description of the carnal immaturity of Christians at Corinth serves to underscore his emphasis on the ultimate goal which he sets for them in chapter 13. Chapter 13 must be read in the context of the whole book and may not be interpreted apart from his charge in 14:1—"Make love your . . ." and in 14:20 "Do not be children in your thinking; in malice be babes, but in thinking be perfect."

5. When the "perfect" comes, says Paul, the tongues, etc. would cease. These miraculous gifts were not proofs of spiritual maturity. Paul does not say that these will cease when Jesus comes again, nor when the Corinthians get to heaven. Rather that in time, during their life on earth, the miraculous demonstrations will cease.

6. I do not think "perfect" means just the completed canon of New Testament books; it also has to do with a "perfected" church.

   a. The canon's formation was by uninspired men (so far as we know). I believe every book in the New Testament is inspired and apostolic. But what if another scroll of antiquity is found with the same credentials as the books we now have? We would not have a "perfect—complete" New Testament!

   b. The "perfect law of liberty" was already at work when James wrote of it in James 1:25. This perfect law was in action before the completion of our 27 books of the New Testament were formed into a New Testament. One could look into this law then and be blessed in obedience to it. It was the perfect law of freedom because it accomplished what the incomplete Law of Moses could not do. It is significant in this context that James also speaks of the children of God as being perfect and complete in the church (James 1:4-5).

C. The end for which miracles were wrought, to attest to the veracity of Christ and His claims, to bring the church to

FIRST CORINTHIANS

maturity, and to bring about faith through which we may partake of the divine nature (II Peter 1:3-4)—this is the ultimate goal of God's work with us. MIRACLES CAN NEVER BE AN ACCEPTABLE SUBSTITUTE FOR THIS INDWELLING (I Tim. 1:5; II Peter 1:3-11; I John 1:5-8; 3:1-6; I Cor. 12:31—14:1; II Cor. 3:18). (See *A Study of the Work of the Holy Spirit in Christians,* by Seth Wilson, mimeo, Ozark Bible College bookstore.)

1. Miracles are signs or works of the Holy Spirit, not the Holy Spirit Himself. They are the effects of which he is the cause. Miracles have been found where the personal indwelling of the Holy Spirit did not occur. (Matt. 10; Luke 10; apostles and 70 disciples worked miracles months before Jesus said the Holy Spirit had not come yet (John 7:38). King Saul on his way to murder God's anointed was made to prophesy by the Spirit of God (I Sam. 19:18-24). Balaam's ass (Num. 22:25-30). Cornelius (Acts 10:44-48).

2. It is evident that some men whom Christ called "workers of iniquity" claimed to have worked many miracles in His name. If they speak that boldly to His face, at judgment, does it not appear that they will be sincerely convinced that they have actually wrought such mighty works by His power here?

3. It does not appear that miraculous demonstrations are necessary effects whenever or wherever the Holy Spirit dwells in men. I Corinthians 12:3, the man who honestly says Jesus is Lord manifests he has the Holy Spirit. I Corinthians 12:29-30 shows that not all in the New Testament church had the gifts of miraculous works.

4. The word of God has the power to regenerate and to sanctify through faith which allows the Spirit of God to dwell in us (Eph. 3:16-19; I Tim. 1:5; Gal. 5:22-25; II Peter 1:3-4; II Cor. 3:18).

5. Miraculous deeds did not guarantee a spiritual church. The Corinthian church "came behind in no gift" and was enriched "in all utterance and in all knowledge" (I Cor. 1:5-7); yet that church was notorious for errors in doctrine and evils in practice.

SPECIAL STUDY: GIFTS, MIRACLES

6. Are such wonders and signs always caused exclusively by the Holy Spirit? May some of the experiences and utterances be caused by the workings of the subconscious mind, by something like hypnotic influences? (See *The Psychology of Speaking in Tongues,* by John P. Kildahl, Harper & Row.) Scriptures warn of the possibility (at least in the first century) of "lying wonders" (Matt. 24:24; 7:22; II Thess. 2:9; I John 4:1-6; Rev. 13:14; 16:14; 19:20). Even the Old Testament warned against false prophets with signs (Deut. 13:1-5; 18:22; Isa. 8:20).
7. Isolated wonders do not necessarily prove a divine revelation from God. Bible miracles were part of a coherent combination of many miracles and messages to which they were significantly related. The extent and quality of Bible miracles and revelations is different from the many alleged miracles and prophecies of today or centuries since apostles. Philip's miracles and those of Simon Magus were different. Even Pharaoh could see (or should have) the difference between Moses' miracles and those of his magicians (Gal. 1:6-9). Even a gospel by angels, if different than Paul's would be condemned.
8. I John 4:6 says it is not the Holy Spirit if men show they do not hear (heed and keep) the words of the apostles. James 3:13-18 shows that the Spirit of God does not cause men to be jealous and factious—divisive. WHEN THERE ARE SO MANY DENOMINATIONAL FACTIONS, ALLEGING TO HAVE THESE MIRACULOUS SIGNS AND WONDERS, YET STRIVING TO MAINTAIN THEIR DENOMINATIONAL DIFFERENCES EVEN IN THE FACE OF PLAIN SCRIPTURAL TEACHINGS, WHAT ARE WE TO CONCLUDE ABOUT THEIR CLAIMS?

V. FUNCTIONAL GIFTS (Rom. 12:1-13)

A. I believe all men and women have gifts from their Creator.
1. All may not have the same gifts or latent potentialities.
2. Some may have many more potentialities than others.
3. BUT THEY ARE ALL NEEDED AS FUNCTIONS IN THE BODY OF CHRIST. This is the important point:

No gifts, capacities, talents, abilities (all given by the grace of God) are more important FUNCTIONALLY, than others.
   4. The whole context here indicates Paul is talking *not* about miraculous gifts given by God for the same purposes as those of I Corinthians 12-14; but of functional gifts, one of which at least every member of the body has (". . . I bid every one among you . . .").
B. I like the way Carl Ketcherside explains it in *Mission Messenger* Vol. 36, No. 10, Oct. 1974, "Functioning Gifts."
   1. Any gift freely bestowed by God is a gift of the Spirit, regardless of how it is communicated to the recipient. That is why I object to designating any period of time a charismatic age. There is no such thing as a charismatic age, for the simple reason that there is no non-charismatic age. There has never been a time when the will of God was not enhanced and promoted by gifts of grace. A gift is not charismatic because of its nature, method of reception, or effect, but because of its origin. It is charismatic because it is a gift of *charis,* grace.
   2. The man who has the enviable gift of understanding and relieving the needy is "charismatic" as surely as one who has the gift of prophecy. The one who can give cheerfully and freely as his contribution to the work of the saints is "charismatic." In view of this, I am not turned on by such expressions as "The Spirit is working again in our time." The Spirit has never ceased working.
   3. The gifts of God are varied. Paul wrote to a congregation which came behind in no gift and told them that the ability to restrain sexual passion, making marriage unnecessary was a *charisma* of God. But he also implied that the gift of sexual need which could be gratified in marriage was a *charisma.* "I would that everybody lived as I do; but each of us has his own special gift from God—one in one direction and one in another" (I Cor. 7:7). It is quite evident that Paul's gift was in a different direction than that of the majority.
C. Ephesians 4:7 "But grace was given to each of us according to the measure of Christ's gift."

SPECIAL STUDY: GIFTS, MIRACLES

1. Do not the parables teach that men are *given* (how else, but by the grace of God) "talents" and "pounds" according to different measures, and each one is expected to *use* them (none are non-functional) and be rewarded according, not to what he does not have, but according to how he uses what he does have?
2. Now if we will follow the leading of the Spirit in His revealed will and make sure instead of worrying about "having the Spirit" that the "Spirit has all of us," we will "use" our *praxin* (function, or action) *charismata* gifts for the benefit of the one body.

    Actually, if we simply let ourselves be "transformed" by "the renewing of our minds . . ." (Rom. 12:1-2) we will use our gifts of grace for the upbuilding of the body in love.

    Even unconverted men and women have *charismatic gifts! functional gifts*—whatever they have in potentialities they have by the grace of God but they are not allowing the Spirit to use them for the upbuilding of Christ's body.

D. Does all this mean that the special *super*natural gifts should also be continued by the Holy Spirit in the church today? No.
  1. They were for special needs. The functional gifts will always be needed.
  2. I do not need to see a miracle performed by anyone else, nor have one performed upon me, to produce faith in the revealed Word of God.
  3. The original envoys of Jesus who gave the message were thoroughly accredited and their message was confirmed by miracles, wonders and signs. There is no sense in having miracles to confirm miracles, and once truth is confirmed it never needs to be confirmed again.
  4. The spectacular, *super* natural, signs and wonders were to cease (there is no doubt about that), but the functional gifts through which every member of the body may *love* man and God will abide!
  5. AFTER ALL, THE GRACE OF GOD HAS GIVEN EACH OF US GIFTS FOR FUNCTIONING IN THE

CHURCH AND WE USE THEM ACCORDING TO THE MEASURE OF OUR FAITH.

The miraculous, supernatural gifts could be given and made to function regardless of the measure of the faith of the person.

Special Study

PAUL'S POWER TO GIVE CHARISMATIC POWER
(Acts 19)

A. There is much ambiguous, scripturally-imprecise and confusing exegesis of Acts 19:1-7 being done today.
  1. "Have you received the Holy Ghost since you believed? The apostle Paul asked this very important question of twelve saved disciples of Christ, at Ephesus. Acts 19:2 . . . Later . . . when they prayed together, 'The Holy Ghost came on them; and they spake with tongues and prophesied.' This should have been expected since in all four gospels we are told that Jesus will baptize with the Holy Ghost." From—*The Baptism in The Holy Spirit According to God's Word,* a tract by the Full Gospel Assembly, 3688 Lee Rd., Shaker Heights, Ohio, 44120.
     a. Note: The writer *omitted* the statement of the Scripture that "Paul laid their hands on them. . . ." and *inserted* something that is not even in the text, "Later . . . when they prayed"!
     b. The same tract says, "Must I speak in Tongues? Yes, this is important! . . . To refuse tongues is to refuse to yield yourself completely to God . . ." and further on, "It is very important to pray in tongues! Practice this new language of the Spirit until it becomes as natural as breathing." Why does it need *practice* to become natural if it is supernatural?
     c. The tract also states, "To manifest God's love for our fellow man we must have supernatural power."
  2. From another interesting but ambiguous and self-contradictory book *A Handbook on Holy Spirit Baptism,* by Don Bashan, pub. Gateway Outreach, p. 16, "At times baptism in the Holy Spirit may come immediately following conversion, like in Acts 10. . . . Most Christians today receive the baptism in the Holy Spirit only after instructions and specific prayer. . . ." Cornelius was not "converted" until baptism in water.
     a. From the same book, p. 100, "How can I receive the baptism in the Holy Spirit. . . . By no means should anyone who is not a believing Christian pray for baptism in the Holy Spirit. . . ." Cornelius received it before he was a Christian.

FIRST CORINTHIANS

   b. Page 104 tells how one knows he has received the baptism of the Holy Spirit. "At this point you may actually *feel* the presence of the Holy Spirit, physically. His presence may come as a warmth enveloping you, or as a silent powerful Presence enfolding you. You may experience a tingling sensation or a gentle vibration as if touched by an electric current. But even if you feel nothing, rest quietly in the confidence that the Holy Spirit is now coming upon you in power and is about to furnish you with a new language of prayer and praise to God."
3. Why all this confusion? Because of poor hermeneutics. People let their hermeneutics be influenced by their emotions and/or psychological needs.
   a. Many people want to lump everything said and/or promised concerning the ministry of the Holy Spirit into one category—the supernatural baptism of the Holy Spirit.
   b. This brief study proposes to show that there are definite, scriptural differences and distinctions:
      (1) all ministries and works of the Holy Spirit are not alike in degree or manifestation.
      (2) specifically, the power of the apostle Paul was not power to baptize anyone in the Holy Spirit, nor even power to become an agent through whom Christ would baptize anyone in the Holy Spirit,
      (3) specifically, to show that Paul and the other apostles could impart only the charismatic gifts of the Holy Spirit by the laying on of their hands, and that that power ceased when the apostles died.
B. Paul did not give the "Baptism" of the Holy Spirit in Acts 19 because there are only two instances of the Baptism of the Holy Spirit in the Scriptures.
   1. Acts 2, the Day of Pentecost
      a. Nothing could be clearer than the fact that it was the Apostles and the Apostles only, who received Holy Spirit baptism on the Day of Pentecost.
         (1) It was not some psychical or emotional experience for the purpose of converting those who received it—they did not need to be converted.

PAUL'S POWER TO GIVE CHARISMATIC POWER

    (2) It was an outward manifestation, a special miracle for a Divine purpose.
        (a) It was something that could be seen and heard (not felt).
        (b) There were immediate effects; they spoke with foreign languages; they spoke as the Spirit gave them utterance.
        (c) Only the apostles spoke in other tongues; and very obviously, they spoke in the different native languages represented by that audience.
        (d) They gave utterance only to the words which the Spirit placed upon their tongues. They themselves did not comprehend the scope of their utterances: Peter did not comprehend that the "promise was to all who were afar off."
    (3) Holy Spirit baptism was not for the purpose of converting anyone.
        (a) Holy Spirit baptism was to be conferred by Christ as a promise to be fulfilled.
        (b) Water baptism was a command to be obeyed by all who wished forgiveness and salvation.
        THIS IS THE FUNDAMENTAL DISTINCTION BETWEEN THE BAPTISM OF THE GREAT COMMISSION AND HOLY SPIRIT BAPTISM. THE FORMER WAS A COMMAND TO BE OBEYED: THE LATTER WAS A PROMISE TO BE FULFILLED DIRECTLY FROM HEAVEN. The former to be administered by any evangelizer; the latter was administered only by Christ.
    (4) Holy Spirit baptism was a special miracle for
        (a) clothing the apostles with divine authority, power and infallibility; and for incorporating the Jews (Gentiles in Acts 10-11) into the Body of Christ.
        (b) With their authority and infallibility guaranteed and perpetuated in their writings, there was no longer any necessity for special authority or infallibility.
        (c) Hence, we find no evidence in the New Testament that the apostles ever conferred their authority upon any other man or group of men. THEY HAD NO

FIRST CORINTHIANS

SUCCESSORS. THEY COULD NOT *BAPTIZE* ANYONE WITH THE HOLY SPIRIT. ONLY CHRIST COULD DO THAT.

2. Acts 10-11, Cornelius
   a. Nothing could be clearer than that even the Jewish apostles had difficulty accepting their own Old Testament prophets that Gentiles were to become members of the Messiah's kingdom.
      (1) They persisted in preaching the Gospel to the Jews only for several years following the day of Pentecost.
      (2) Finally, a series of divine interventions became necessary to break down this wall of prejudice and bring about the admission of the Gentiles.
      (3) God did it in such a way as to leave no doubt in the minds of the Jews . . . by Holy Spirit Baptism. There are no Holy Spirit baptisms between Acts 2 and the one of Cornelius!
   b. What happened in connection with the conversion of Cornelius does not happen with any other conversion in the book of Acts,
      (1) and even this did not cause the conversion nor was it a result of the conversion . . . it came directly and arbitrarily from Heaven.
      (2) It certainly was not to give Cornelius faith.
      (3) It was not to purify his heart.
      (4) Nor was it to make Cornelius and his household Christians . . . they became Christians the same way all other persons became Christians in New Testament times, by repenting, believing and being immersed in water (Acts 10:47-48).
      (5) That text substantiates beyond any possibility of doubt that the Holy Spirit baptism was a promise to be fulfilled directly from Heaven, whereas Christian baptism was a command to be obeyed by believers; and that the baptism permanently incorporated into the structure of the Church was *not* Holy Spirit baptism, but baptism in water!
      (6) The Holy Spirit baptism of Cornelius' household demonstrated once for all that the blessings of the New Covenant were for Gentiles as well as Jews AND ON THE SAME TERMS!

PAUL'S POWER TO GIVE CHARISMATIC POWER

The *only* instances of Holy Spirit Baptism recorded in the New Testament (Acts 2, 10-11) had no connection with conversion regeneration or sanctification of the saints. It was not conferred for the purpose of giving faith to the non-believer or purifying the sinful heart; nor is there any evidence that it was bestowed in answer to prayer. It is not connected in any direct way with the remission of sins.

It was conferred upon the apostles as representative of the Jews at Pentecost and upon Cornelius as representative of the Gentiles to signify God's acceptance of both Jew and Gentile into the kingdom of Christ on the same terms. Those are the only two instances of which we have any scripture record of the baptism of the Holy Spirit (we may safely assume it was given to the apostle Paul as one born out of due season).

The Baptism of the Holy Spirit ceased when its ultimate end was accomplished. No person has any justification from the Scripture for asking for, expecting, or claiming Holy Spirit baptism today!

C. Paul did give the charismatic power of the Holy Spirit to some Christians.
   1. The greatest measure of Spirit-power ever bestowed upon human beings was, as we have looked at, the OVERWHELMING MEASURE (or, the Baptism).
   2. The charismatic power of the Spirit is inferior to the overwhelming.
   3. This is not my attempt to impose limitations upon the operation of God's Spirit.
      a. It is not a question of power, but of fact.
      b. *How* The Spirit manifests Himself and the channels through which He exerts His powers are clearly indicated by Scripture.
      c. Any other point of reference as to how He functions (human reason, emotion, alleged miracle) cannot be depended upon.
   4. The charismatic power was:
      a. conferred upon some Christians
      b. in the apostolic age,
      c. inferior to the Baptism of the Spirit,
      d. conferred not by the Lord from Heaven, but by the laying on of the hands of the apostles.
      e. primarily for evidential purposes, to confirm their message,

FIRST CORINTHIANS

    f. commonly designated "gifts" and listed by Paul in I Corinthians 12.
5. There are some cases of the conferring of the evidential power of the Spirit preliminary to Paul's giving of it in Acts 19 which will help in over-all understanding of it.
    a. The first case of miracles performed by anyone other than an apostle is described in Acts 8.
        (1) Philip the evangelist, 8:6-8
            (a) Philip given this power when the apostles laid hands on him, Acts 6:1-6
            (b) He went down to the city of Samaria and proclaimed unto them Christ, Acts 8:5.
            (c) Simon the converted sorcerer continued with Philip; Simon was a baptized Christian, but did not have the power to do miracles; he wanted to buy the power.
        (2) It was not until the apostles from Jerusalem went down to Samaria and laid their hands on the people whom Philip had converted that they received the charismatic powers of the Holy Spirit, Acts 8:17.
            (a) Simon still did not have the power of the Holy Spirit the others had and sought to buy it.
            (b) If the baptismal power or even the charismatic power of the Holy Spirit belongs to all Christians and can be gotten by prayer only, why didn't the Samaritan Christians have it? Why couldn't Philip, who did have it, pass it on to these Christians?
            (c) If it is so imperative for every Christian to have, why didn't Simon have it? He recognized that it came *only* by the laying on of the hands of the apostles!

OF COURSE THE POWER OF THE HOLY SPIRIT WAS NOT FROM THE APOSTLES, PER SE . . . . IT DID NOT ORIGINATE WITH THEM . . . . THEY WERE THE SPIRIT'S INSTRUMENTS.

    b. The case of Timothy
        (1) Some think that the "laying on of the hands of the eldership" (I Tim. 4:14) imparted to Timothy the charismatic gift of the Holy Spirit.

PAUL'S POWER TO GIVE CHARISMATIC POWER

- (2) We know that the laying on of hands was done by persons *other* than the apostles for purposes *other* than the conferring of charismatic gifts of the Holy Spirit (Acts 13:2; James 5:14, etc.).
- (3) Paul explicitly states in II Timothy 1:6 that Timothy did not receive his speical gift of the Holy Spirit at the hands of the elders, BUT BY THE LAYING ON OF PAUL'S HANDS!
- (4) Timothy laid hands on some (I Tim. 5:22) but no mention is made that he conferred the charismatic power of the Holy Spirit in so doing.

c. There is *no evidence whatever in the New Testament* that the early Christians who were not apostles, had the power themselves to confer these extraordinary charismatic gifts of the Holy Spirit on others.
- (1) It is clear that the impartation of the charismatic power of the Holy Spirit *required the personal presence of an apostle.*
- (2) However much the apostle Paul may have desired to impart some charisma to his brethren at Rome, he could not do so without visiting them personally (Rom. 1:11-12).

Paul could not even confer these miraculous gifts by telling the Christians at Rome to "lay their hands on his inspired epistle" which they received from him and could touch! Paul could not even pray for them from a distance and confer charismatic power.

6. Paul in Acts 19
   a. We do not know why Paul asked them whether they had received the Holy Spirit.
   - (1) Actually the original Greek text omits the word *given*. 19:2 KJV ASV
   - (2) This may indicate they did not know the Holy Spirit *existed*.
   - (3) Regardless of their lack of knowledge, Paul knew immediately they had not been baptized in the name (authority) of Jesus Christ. If they had been baptized in water according to the Great Commission, they would have known the Holy Spirit existed.
   b. Paul's question as to whether they had received the Spirit

when they believed, does not say whether he referred to the miraculous or the indwelling of the Spirit.
- (1) However, we do know that when he saw something was wrong with their water baptism he baptized them.
- (2) HE THEN LAID HIS HANDS ON THEM AND CONFERRED THE HOLY SPIRIT IN A MIRACULOUS WAY!

c. We cannot receive the charismatic power of the Spirit today as did those in Acts 19.
- (1) If we could, it would mean that everyone who was actually baptized into Christ and saved, should have the apostle's hands laid on them that they might receive the Spirit.
- (2) If that is so, we cannot be Christians today because there are no apostles to lay hands on us and confer the Spirit in this way.
- (3) It would mean that if one were really a Christian, he would speak with tongues or languages and prophesy by inspiration of the Spirit.

d. Why did Paul confer the miraculous Spirit-charisma on these men? To prove that God approved of Paul's baptizing them again in the name of Jesus instead of allowing them to continue in John the Baptist's baptism. That was the purpose of Pentecost Holy Spirit miracles—to supercede John the Baptist's baptism.

D. The Purpose of the Charismatic Power of the Holy Spirit was *Evidential*.
1. Its primary and almost sole purpose was to confirm the Word that was preached by apostles, evangelists and other selected Christians.
2. It may have had a secondary purpose to establish the saints in their most holy faith—BUT ONLY TO CONFIRM THE WORD BEING PREACHED TO THE SAINTS . . . . IT WAS ONLY AS THE SAINTS OBEYED THE WORD PREACHED THAT THEY WERE EDIFIED . . . THE CHARISMATIC GIFTS SIMPLY CONFIRMED THE PREACHED WORD AS AUTHORITATIVE!
3. Consider these scriptures: Mark 16:20; Rom. 1:11; Heb. 2:3-4; I Cor. 2:1-5; Rom. 15:18-19.

PAUL'S POWER TO GIVE CHARISMATIC POWER

4. In the infancy of the Church, when the local congregations everywhere were compelled to depend upon the oral instruction of the apostles and their co-laborers for guidance in faith and practice, God graciously confirmed the Word by signs and miracles in those selected to preach.

5. A child just learning to walk often has to rely upon its parents for the additional strength and guidance that it needs. So the Church. When the Church was still a child, she spake as a child, she felt as a child, she thought as a child; but when the Church became a grown integrated man, she put away childish things (I Cor. 13:11; Eph. 4:13-16). When the body of Christ was fully formed (both Jew and Gentile incorporated) and permanently established (with her elders, deacons and evangelists); when Truth was fully revealed and embodied in the New Testament THEN THE SUPERNATURAL SUPPORT BY WHICH SHE WAS SUSTAINED THROUGHOUT THE PERIOD OF HER INFANCY, THE CHARISMATIC MEASURE OF THE HOLY SPIRIT WAS NO LONGER NEEDED, AND PASSED AWAY!

6. Most certainly, the special charismatic measure of the Holy Spirit was not given to the primitive Church as toys with which they were to amuse themselves in the presence of a cynical world. They did not need it to motivate them to go everywhere to preach the word; once the Word of Christ's death and resurrection was validated by preachers who proved their message by gifts, those who accepted went everywhere preaching it. Even the apostles did not have the power to use their gifts of healing whenever they had any sick person.

    (1) Why would Paul leave his friend and traveling companion sick, having the power to heal him (II Tim. 4:20)?

    (2) Why could not Paul, or some other Christian with charismatic power, remove Paul's thorn in the flesh? (II Cor. 12:7ff.).

    (3) *The Handbook on Holy Spirit Baptism,* p. 22 says, "Just as there are reasons why people do not respond to the gospel message, so there are many reasons why people do not respond miraculously when a prayer for healing is offered." Page 24, "If those who insist the age of miracles has ended had lived in Jesus' day, the age of miracles might never have begun."

FIRST CORINTHIANS

Answer: The miracle of charismatic power in its working did not depend upon faith or expectation. Jesus worked miracles on people who could not have believed in Him, on people who did not believe in Him, and so did the apostles.

E. Duration of the Charismatic Measure of the Holy Spirit
1. The conclusion from the foregoing studies is that since no one but the apostles had the power to impart the charismatic measure of the Spirit; and this they did only by the laying on of their hands personally, IT FOLLOWS THAT WHEN THE APOSTLES CLOSED THEIR EARTHLY LABORS AND WENT TO THEIR ETERNAL REWARD, THE POWER TO IMPART THE EVIDENTIAL MEASURE OF THE SPIRIT CEASED.
2. What the apostles conferred was NOT the baptism of the Holy Spirit. Only Jesus from heaven, directly, conferred that measure of the Spirit and that in only two recorded instances.
3. When all those Christians died who had received this measure (charismatic) at the hands of an apostle, (the Christians scripturally unable to pass it on) the charismatic manifestations of the Holy Spirit naturally ceased to be wrought. THIS IS MADE VERY CLEAR IN THE NEW TESTAMENT.

Conclusion

The Holy Spirit

by Don DeWelt, College Press Publishing Company

5. What shall we say has happened to certain persons of our day who claim to have been baptized in the Holy Spirit?

We shall not at all doubt their sincerity, nor shall we say nothing of import has happened to them. We shall be forced to say by our study of the subject that their experience is *not* the baptism in the Holy Spirit as we find it described in the book of Acts.

What has happened to such persons is self-induced. Please do not forget that Mormons (Latter Day Saints), claim the very same experiences of speaking in tongues. Christian Scientists also claim supernatural healings. Mohammedans claim supernatural aid in their

PAUL'S POWER TO GIVE CHARISMATIC POWER

conquests for Allah. The simple fact that something strange happened to certain persons does not mean God has visited them.

We must never make the tragic mistake of believing in an experience, or in the testimony of an experience, and then attempting to support such experience with the Bible.

We cannot offer a logical explanation for every experience—it is not necessary that we do so—all we need is a knowledge of the Word of truth concerning the experience.

What has happened to a number of our brethren in the past few months might be explained in a number of ways—the important fact is, "Does the Word of God support it?"

From my study I cannot see Biblical support for present-day claims to the baptism in the Holy Spirit.

The Eternal Spirit, Vol. 2

by C. C. Crawford, College Press Publishing Company

Friend, you need not pray for Christ to come down from Heaven to save you; you need not pray for someone to come back from the dead to save you. You have the Word, the Word of faith, which is being preached in every community in the land, the Word that Christ died for your sins, that He was buried, and that He was raised up the third day (I Cor. 15:1-5), and that God's gift of salvation may be your possession on the conditions of your belief in Christ, repentance toward Christ, confession of Christ, and baptism into Christ. Miraculous manifestations, ecstasies, trances, visions, powers and endowments are not necessary at all to your personal salvation. You have the Word of the living God,—the Gospel which is the power of God unto salvation. You are fully capable of hearing, accepting and obeying that Gospel any time you desire and will to do so; and if you refuse or neglect to do so, you are utterly without excuse. If you will hear neither Moses nor the Prophets, neither Christ nor the Apostles, you would not be persuaded even if one should rise from the dead (Luke 16:31).

Special Study

IS THE CHURCH AN ORGANIZATION OR AN ORGANISM?

I. Definition of terms:

Webster's New Collegiate Dictionary

Organism: "Any highly complex thing or structure with parts so integrated that their relation to one another is governed by their relation to the whole."

Organization: "An organism; any vitally or systematically organic whole; an association or society" with emphasis upon system and structure.

Thomas M. Lindsay, D.D., Principal of the Glasgow College of the United Free Church of Scotland in *The Church and The Ministry in the Early Centuries,* page 8.

"Organism, where the whole exists for the parts, and each part for the whole and for all the other parts."

"I devoutly believe that there is a Visible Catholic (universal) Church of Christ consisting of all those throughout the world who visibly worship the same God and Father, profess their faith in the same Saviour, and are taught by the same Holy Spirit; but I do not see any Scriptural or even primitive warrant for insisting that catholicity (universality) *must* find visible expression in a uniformity of organization . . ." page viii of Preface.

". . . (the church is a self-governing society) where the individual rights and responsibilities of the members would blend harmoniously with the common good of all."

"The individual believer is never lost in the society, and he is never alone and separate. The bond of union is not an external framework impressed from without, but a sense of fellowship springing from within. The believer's union to Christ, which is the deepest of all personal things, always involves something social. The call comes to him singly, but seldom solitarily," page 7.

A. H. Newman in *A Manual of Church History,* Vol. I.

"When applied to Christians the word (ekklesia) means in the New Testament: (1) The entire community of the redeemed,

IS THE CHURCH AN ORGANIZATION OR AN ORGANISM?

considered as an organism held together by belief in a common Lord and by participation in a common life and salvation, and in common aims and interests."

International Standard Bible Encyclopedia, Vol. 1, p. 652, article on "Church"

"And the unity of which Paul writes and for which he strove is a unity that finds visible expression. Not, it is true, in any uniformity of outward polity, but through the manifestation of a common faith in acts of mutual love (Eph. 4:3-13; II Cor. 9)."

". . . if each believer is vitally joined to Christ, all believers must stand in a living relation to one another. In Paul's favorite figure, Christians are members one of another because they are members in particular of the body of Christ (Rom. 12:5; I Cor. 12:27)."

Baker's Dictionary of Theology, article on "Church" p. 123.

". . . the one church of God is not an institutional but a supernatural entity which is in process of growth towards the world to come. . . . All its members are in Christ and are knit together by a supernatural kinship."

What is the Scriptural definition of the church in relationship to "Organism" or "Organization"?

Read: I Corinthians, chapter 12, in its entirety
Ephesians, chapter 4, in its entirety
Romans 14:1 — 15:13 (the church functioning as an organism)

Thus the conclusion:

Although divinely appointed offices are provided for the visible church, the church on earth is essentially an *organism* and *not* a systematic, structuralized *organization,* as organization is commonly thought of today. The church is a living, vital organism wherein its members are so integrated and controlled by the Head, even Christ, that their relation to one another is governed by their relation to the Head and to the whole body. The church as an entity exists for the individual member and the individual member exists and functions for the edification of the whole and other members.

FIRST CORINTHIANS

Some pertinent comments on I Corinthians 12:12-31 from the *International Critical Commentary on I Corinthians* by Plummer and Robertson:

". . . though the gifts of God's Spirit may be many and various, yet those who are endowed with them constitute one *organic* whole."

"The ultimate aim of the Christian is the well-being of the whole body, of which the controlling power is Christ, who is at once the Head and the Body, for every Christian is a member of Him."

"The Church is neither a dead mass of similar particles, like a heap of sand, nor a living swarm of antagonistic individuals, like a cage of wild beasts; it has the unity of a living organism, in which no two parts are exactly alike, but all discharge different functions for the good of the whole. All men are not equal, and no individual can be independent of the rest; everywhere there is subordination and dependence."

". . . every individual has some function to discharge, and all must work together for the common good. This is the all-important point—unity in loving service. The Church is an organic body of which all the parts are moved by a spirit of common interest and mutual affection."

"God made unity, but not uniformity; He did not level all down to monotonous similarity . . . every member cannot have the same function, and therefore there must be higher and lower gifts. But pride and discontent are quite out of place, for they are not only the outcome of selfishness, but also rebellion against God's will . . . it was not our fellow-men who placed us in an inferior position, but God; and He did it, not to please us or our fellows, but in accordance with His will, which must be right . . . there is no such thing as independence in an organism . . . all parts are not equal, yet no one part can isolate itself."

II. Discussion of Unity as it is related to the Nature of the Church, Organism or Organization.

    A. The hue and cry in contemporary Protestantism is unity, visible unity at almost any cost.

        1. Mostly liberals are pushing this movement.

        2. Some evangelicals and their denominations are clamoring for visible unity.

IS THE CHURCH AN ORGANIZATION OR AN ORGANISM?

   B. Even among the Restoration brotherhood

      1. Some of the Disciples of Christ leaders and churches are planning on "restructuring" the brotherhood in preparation for merger with other denominations to form a visible, unified church.

   C. The emphasis in this movement for unity is placed almost exclusively upon Organization, Structuralism, Federation.

      1. Hardly, if ever, is oneness by spiritual brotherhood stressed.

      2. Oneness of doctrine and faith is *deemphasized*.

      3. Contemporary theologians now pressuring for structural unity interpret the nature of the church as an Organization —but is it?

III. What motives are behind the ecumenical thrust for an organizational church?

   A. Ecumenists feel that a united church under one organization would be able to affect the larger affairs of human history and to control events here and now such as banning of atomic tests, elimination of racial segregation and many other problems.

      But will the means such a "world-church" uses to accomplish these be political pressure or regeneration of men's hearts?

   B. Ecumenists feel that a pagan world would be more impressed and more likely converted by a "world-church" organization.

      But what is the true missionary situation today? The missionaries under national federations such as the N.C.C. are decreasing proportionately while the missionaries sent independently are increasing!

   C. Ecumenists feel that one consolidated church would impress a religious stamp upon the culture of the world whereas now education, arts, professions, politics are being dominated by secularism.

      1. But this secularism is not due to lack of organization, but simply because the church in every community has become too secularized—Sunday social clubs, having lost their vital message of salvation.

FIRST CORINTHIANS

   2. We need not *reorganization,* but *regeneration!*
D. Ecumenists either fear or envy, or both, as they behold the visibly united Roman Catholic Church. Ecumenists believe that the influence of Catholicism (felt in government, labor, industry, communications, education, etc.) is due to visible organizational unity.
   1. But Catholicism's basis for organizing is for political warfare and influence—union of church and state.
   2. Separation of church and state is a basic tenant of Protestantism (and the Bible, we might add).
E. Ecumenists believe that the particularly visible unity for which our Lord prayed can only be realized within the framework of one ecclesiastical structure.
   1. The Lord *did* pray for visible unity! John 17:21
   2. The nature of that unity must be defined.
      a. Would federal union of churches fulfill the will of God for visible unity?
      b. Or is unity to be a spiritual, doctrinal harmony revealed authoritatively and exclusively in the New Testament?

IV. What of the Ecumenical Movement? Can the Church obtain unity through Organization or has she unity now Organically? What would the believer be called upon to promote or surrender in ecumenicism? CAN AN EVANGELICAL BELIEVER OR CHURCH UNITE WITH THE ECUMENICAL MOVEMENT AND NOT SURRENDER THE "FAITH ONCE FOR ALL DELIVERED"?
A. Christianity is the only true revealed religion; it is not of human origin. The Christian *must,* therefore, compare religious movements and philosophies with what God's revelation says.
B. What Christ will the ecumenical movement hold to?
   1. The Christ of the modernist—human only.
   2. The Christ of the existentialist—a mere subjective ideal.
   3. The Christ of the syncretist—a conglomeration of all the Christs.
   4. Or the Christ revealed in the Scriptures, human and divine,

IS THE CHURCH AN ORGANIZATION OR AN ORGANISM?

the Son of the living God, in whom only is salvation and immortality.
   5. The question cannot be avoided, the church cannot live in a vacuum, if she is to preach a vital message of hope and life to a dying world.
C. What will be studied by ecumenical preachers and taught by them?
   1. Will it be the social gospel of the liberal?
   2. Will it be neo-orthodoxy (agnosticism using scriptural terminology)?
   3. Will it be atheism or communism?
   4. Will it be the Bible as the supernaturally revealed Word of God?
D. How inclusive will the ecumenical "world-church" be?
   1. C. C. Morrison writes, "What in a united church shall we do with our differences? There can be only one answer. They must be welcomed and embraced as essential to the fulfillment of the Christian life."
   2. To Mr. Morrison, diversities of belief and faith are a spiritual asset . . . NO NEED FOR A UNIFYING FAITH AS LONG AS WE HAVE A UNIFYING ORGANIZATION.
   3. But in this wide inclusiveness what divergencies will be tolerated?
      a. Denial of the blood atonement by substitution?
      b. Denial of the humanity and divinity of Christ?
      c. Denial of the indwelling of the supernatural Holy Spirit?
      d. Denial of Heaven and Hell and the immortality of the soul? THE VERY SUBSTANCE OF CHRISTIANITY WILL BE LOST IF TRUTH BE SACRIFICED TO OBTAIN ORGANIZATIONAL UNION!
E. What of the ecumenical concept of the church?
   1. In its hysteria for organization will it demand membership in the external society in order to obtain salvation, fellowship and toleration?
   2. If so, God stands helpless until the church is properly functionalized . . . the heathen await salvation until it can be organized!

3. Will not a centrally controlled church also mean centrally controlled clergy, laity, journalism, finances, etc., etc.?
4. Will not this also bring about a bureaucracy similar to federal governments—more and more bureaus, offices, secretaries, building up of empires, funds.

V. The Authority of Scripture is essential to the life and unity of the Organism (the Body of Christ—the Church).
   A. The proper function of the Body of Christ as an organism is dependent upon the authority of Scripture.
      1. For it is in Scripture *alone* that the mind of Christ is expressed.
      2. For an organism to live and function it must receive instructions from and obey its head—Christ is the head of the church.
   B. The major cause for division and sectarianism in Christianity is the rejection of the authority and veracity of apostolic teaching.
      There is a real lack of Biblically authoritative preaching in the pulpits of the churches today.
   C. The ecumenical/organizational thrust is an outcome of the rejection of the authority of Scripture.
      The ecumenists want to replace Scriptural authority with organizational authority.
   D. The history of man testifies to man's own realization of his estrangement from God.
      1. Neither by his own wisdom (I Cor. 1-2) nor by nature (Rom. 1) has man been able to find reconciliation or restored fellowship with God.
      2. A revelation from God Himself unto estranged man was needed.
      3. Christianity makes exclusive claim to be the only revealed religion and to have absolute claim upon the souls of men.
      4. All that is needful for the salvation of man and the maintenance of the Body of Christ has been revealed.

IS THE CHURCH AN ORGANIZATION OR AN ORGANISM?

    5. The repository of that revelation is in the Bible.
       a. IN THE BIBLE WE HAVE OBJECTIVE TRUTH.
       b. And because it is *REVEALED TRUTH,* the written Word possesses authority to command belief from all men.

E. The leading theological emphasis (control) within the ecumenical organization is the *authority of experience.*
    1. Most of the leaders of ecumenism are either neo-orthodox/existential or liberal.
    2. All religious authority for faith, life and action is, for them found by experience and subjectivity.
       a. Religious truth and faith is based on how the individual feels about it—the Bible is only true if the man feels it is true!
    3. But, WHOSE EXPERIENCE IS VALID?
       a. Shall we take a survey of the membership of the church to determine the authoritative message of God; or will the subjective judgments of church councils, religious leaders and professional theologians be accepted—
       b. OR SHALL WE GIVE THE CHURCH OVER TO COMPLETE ANARCHY AND CHAOS BY LETTING EVERY MAN DECIDE FOR HIMSELF WHAT IS TRUE AND RIGHT SIMPLY ACCORDING TO HIS FEELINGS?

F. If the church is to exist as a living, vital, compassionate, feeling organism—each member so integrated with the other yet functioning as a whole it must:
    1. Have one mind (the mind of Christ, its head).
    2. Partake of one food (the Bread of Life, John 6).
    3. Speak the same thing (one objective message of truth, Gal. 1:8-9).
    4. Have each member working its own "due measure" (Eph. 4).
    5. This oneness is not to be found in organizational structure—ONLY WHEN EACH MEMBER SURRENDERS

HIMSELF TO THE MIND OF CHRIST AS AUTHORITATIVE IN ALL MATTERS OF FAITH AND ACTION ... AND AGREEING THAT THE MIND OF CHRIST IS FOUND IN OBJECTIVE REVELATION (THE SCRIPTURES)—Only then, will the church be a vital organism functioning for the salvation of mankind.

VI. Is Structural Organization the only way to the visible Unity for which Christ prayed in John 17:21—or may the church as an Organism attain it?
- A. It is true that Christ's prayer (John 17:21) demands visible unity of believers.
   1. How else could the world behold and believe? It cannot behold the invisible.
   2. But notice also that the Lord defined the unity he desired with the clause, "... as thou, Father, art in me, and I in thee."
- B. The same oneness that exists in the Godhead organism forms the pattern of unity for the organism which is the church.
- C. One in DOCTRINE.
   1. Father, Son and Holy Spirit taught the same doctrine.
   2. John 7:16; 8:26-28; 12:49
   3. Those who advocate structural unity in organization abhor the idea of oneness of doctrine.
      a. They say doctrinal unity is impossible.
      b. They fear that doctrinal emphasis will offend and destroy unity.
      c. If doctrinal unity was essential between Father and Son, how can the church composed of fallible men exist without it?
   4. Organizational union without organic unity in doctrine will NEVER impress the world.
- D. One in PURPOSE.
   1. There was mutual agreement in carrying on the work of redemption between the Father and Son (cf. John 5:19-29; 6:38-40; 17:4).

IS THE CHURCH AN ORGANIZATION OR AN ORGANISM?

    2. The church must echo that agreement of purpose by proclaiming the same agreement in message (salvation).

       The rapid growth of the first century church can be ascribed to the unity of its message of redemption.

    3. The Organizational union in ecumenism today has multiple purposes.

       a. Social gospelizing (improving living standards).
       b. Political influence and pressure.
       c. Enlarging the structure of church union.

E. One in LOVE.

    1. There can be no doubt that Father and Son were one in love (cf. John 10:17).

    2. The pagan world stood amazed at the demonstrations of love in the lives of Christians in the early centuries.

       a. The church was of one heart and of one soul.
       b. Each member felt what the other members felt; for what affected one affected all.

    3. Generally speaking the ecumenical movement stresses economic necessity and ecclesiastical pressure as its cohesives.

       A union which must be held together by the cold, lifeless and unfeeling necessities of economics and ecclesiasticism HAS NO RESEMBLANCE TO A UNITY ENGENDERED BY LOVE . . . WHERE EACH MEMBER IS OF ONE HEART AND SOUL!

F. Now the question: How may the ecumenists argue for organizational unity from Christ's prayer in John 17:21? Does the Godhead form a corporate unity that can be seen?

    1. In the Old Testament dispensation it was necessary to have physical representations of spiritual truths (sacrifices, tabernacle, priests, etc.).

       a. The Israelites even demanded a physical king whom they could see. They were not content with the rule of the king of Heaven in their hearts.
       b. It is still true of men today who are not content with the church as an Organism and the rule of Christ in their hearts, but must have an outward, structural world-church organization.

FIRST CORINTHIANS

   2. The New Testament dispensation is on a much higher spiritual plane.
      Its worship is more spiritual than visible and ritualistic.
   3. When we understand the higher plane of New Testament revelation.
      We will see more than organization in John 17:21.
   G. The first century *does* refelct *somewhat of* the unity for which Christ prayed.
      1. Unity of doctrine, faith, life and purpose
      2. But even the early church never reached the fulfillment of His prayer.
      3. Paul's epistle (Gal., Col., I & II Cor.) shows how he withstood the infiltration of false doctrine lest it divide the church.
      4. In Ephesians Paul stresses the fact that knowledge of Christ and speaking the truth in love is one of the great necessities to unity.
   H. Under no condition can the Lord's prayer, John 17:21, be interpreted as a prayer for:
      1. "one over-all organization under central control," or
      2. "a single comprehensive organization of the churches.

VII. Life and Unity is *in* Christ.

   A. The Church receives not only her origin and position but her continuing life in Christ.
      1. Cf. John 15:1-5
      2. External connection with a visible organization does not save.
         a. Men must be internally connected with Christ Himself.
         b. A man might be entirely destitute of spiritual life and still be connected to a visible organization.
   B. The ground of unity among believers is their spiritual union with Christ.
      1. By surrender to Him in faith and obedience to His commands we are united to Him.

IS THE CHURCH AN ORGANIZATION OR AN ORGANISM?

      2. Out of this union of each individual believer springs the organic unity that unites all in a fellowship whether separated by time, space, language or race.

  C. Hindrance to unity does not consist in the lack of one external organization to which people can cleave, but to the absence of internal connection with Christ.

      1. The building of world-church organizations means nothing in the sight of God if the churches are not IN Christ.

      2. Search as much as you like—YOU WILL FIND NO DRIVING COMPULSION BY CHRISTIANS OF THE FIRST CENTURY TO ESTABLISH A WORLD-CHURCH ORGANIZATION WITH ECCLESIASTICAL HEADS AND COMMITTEES AND COUNCILS!

      3. Winning ecclesiastical battles for amalgamation and merger means nothing in the sight of God if churches are not *IN CHRIST.*

         a. To be IN Christ means a vital relationsip to Christ as the Head—obedience to the Head.

VIII. To Be of One Mind (One Faith) is Necessary to the Life of the Church As An Organism.

  A. Rom. 15:1-7; I Cor. 1:10; Phil. 1:27; Eph. 4:4-6; John 14:1-11

  B. The ecumenical movement does not subscribe to the proposition of ONE FAITH as defined in Scripture.

      1. The World Council of Churches has openly declared war on the idea of ONE FAITH as being divisive, bigoted, prejudicial and intolerant.

  C. But the first cause of division in the early church was heresy (those who divided over the ONE faith) rather than schismatism (those dividing over non-essentials).

      1. Heretics are different than schismatics—heretics seldom desire to leave the church but prefer to remain and control the church to proclaim their false doctrines:

      2. THE APOSTLES DID NOT BROADEN THE DEFINITION OF FAITH SO THAT ALL SHADES OF BELIEF COULD LIVE COMFORTABLY WITHIN THE CHURCH.

- a. They were pointedly restricted and confined to the ONE faith that revealed through the apostles (Gal. 1:6-9; Jude 3).
- b. They absolutely refused to accept peace at the cost of revealed truth.
3. If we say that all modes of faith have equal standing (as the W.C.C. does) WE WILL SOON BE SAYING THAT NO FAITH IS NECESSARY.

  A faith that is not contended for has little value in the sight of men and will soon be the death of the organism of the Body of Christ.

D. The ecumenists continually insist that all Christians may be united by having ONE *subjective* faith.
  1. BUT WITHOUT ONENESS OF OBJECTIVE FAITH THERE CAN BE NO SUBJECTIVE FAITH!
  2. Diverse gospels produce diverse subjective faiths and beliefs.
  3. Destroy the essence of Christianity (the ONE revealed, objective faith) and you destroy the organism which results from that objective faith!
  4. The system of doctrine contained in the Bible (especially New Testament) is itself AN ORGANISM—destroy one vital doctrine and terrible sickness and weakness will result.
  5. The church is responsible to God as "the pillar and ground of the truth."
     - a. A world organization without a clearly defined Biblical doctrine (objective faith) is a violation of that trust.
     - b. HOW CAN ORGANIZATIONAL VISIBILITY BE CONSIDERED MORE IMPORTANT THAN VISIBILITY OF UNITED TRUTH?

E. Genuine and permanent unity simply cannot exist without agreement on essential teachings of Christ.
  1. Stifling controversy over basic doctrines and minimizing differences may hasten the organization of a world-wide church, BUT WILL THE END RESULT BE A CHRISTIAN CHURCH?

IS THE CHURCH AN ORGANIZATION OR AN ORGANISM?

    2. Unity of faith cannot be accomplished in a generation—especially in a generation that is scripturally illiterate.
        a. Paul says it takes "diligence" (hard work) to have unity—patient, courageous *work*.
        b. It takes teaching—"speaking the truth in love . . . *growing up.* . . ."

IX. The Church is An Organism Because it is A Universal Church.
    A. The existence of the church is not dependent upon visible organization.
    B. The church is not a matter of sight but of faith.
        1. If the essence of the church were her visibility, then there would be no need of faith to realize her existence in far distant places—unseen.
        2. If one organization were essential to unity then faith in the essential oneness of the church would be a delusion.
    C. The concept of universal organism appears in various figures of speech.
        1. The Body—church in Corinth was not in organizational union with the church in Jerusalem or Rome yet she is spoken of as the body of Christ.
        2. Bride—pluralities of brides do not exist in the sight of the Bridegroom.
        3. Temple—the Temple is one (cf. Eph. 2:21-22).
    D. Although organizational union is not essential to universal unity—that universal, spiritual unity must be of necessity manifested visibly.
        1. Recognizing and submitting to the absolute Headship of Christ is an outward and visible manifestation of spiritual unity.
        2. Observance of divinely instituted ordinances is a visible manifestation of spiritual unity. (cf. Acts 2:42)
        3. Holiness, Sanctification, Separation from the world is a necessary and distinctly visible manifestation of unity.
            a. WITHOUT HOLINESS THE CHURCH CAN NEVER EXPECT TO ACHIEVE UNITY UPON EARTH (James 4:1).

b. Unjustified division finds root in the evil lust of the human heart.
c. Let us seek first a holy church and unity will be added to her.
4. Discipline is an outward manifestation of unity.
   a. There can be no unity if the church tolerates immorality and heresy.
   b. EVEN THOSE OF EVANGELICAL FAITH OFTEN EXPRESS THE FEAR THAT THE EXERCISE OF DISCIPLINE WILL DRIVE PEOPLE AWAY FROM THE CHURCH.
      (1) History reveals just the opposite to be true.
      (2) Note the effect of discipline in Acts 5.
      (3) The world beholds other societies exercising discipline over its membership while the church, checked by cowardice or false tolerance, fails to remove even the most flagrant violators of her laws. NO WONDER THE WORLD SCORNS THE CHURCH!

Conclusion

I. The Body of Christ

   A. The body (the church) receives life from the Head.
      1. Members of the body have union together *not* through external organization but by virtue of their spiritual union with Him.

         Structural organization is not stressed in the New Testament.
      2. Compare these scriptural references.
         Rom. 12:5; I Cor. 12:12-31; Col. 1:18; 2:19; Eph. 1:22-23; 4:1-16; 5:23-32
      3. These scriptures plainly teach that the body of Christ exists as an organic whole.
      4. An overall organization was non-existent in the 1st century church.
         a. Because individual or groups of churches had separate organizations does not imply that the church was divided or fragmented.

IS THE CHURCH AN ORGANIZATION OR AN ORGANISM?

      b. The fundamental idea of the above scriptures is that the Church is an organism.

  B. The term body focuses special attention to the Head.

    1. The focal point of interest of the human body is the head.

    2. Col. 1:18 . . . Man is not the head of the church nor even the center of the universe—man is the body and exists to give glory to the Head.

      a. The primary reason for the creation of the Church was for the glory of God focused on the Lord Jesus Christ.

  C. The body receives life from the Head.

    He is the Vine, we the branches. . . . He is the Bread of Life.

  D. The concept of the body is essentially spiritual.

    The visible church contains dead members who do not belong to the living organism . . . tares and bad fish are in the visible church but not the invisible (Matt. 13).

II. The Analogy of the Human Body (I Cor. 12)

  A. The body consists of many different members united in one organic whole, each necessary for the perfection and good of the whole and animated by one life principle, controlled by the head.

  B. A body consists of many parts but there is in it an essential unity (the church).

    1. Every member is important to the body.

    2. The diversity of gifts contributes to the glory and usefulness of the body.

    3. The analogy of the term body implies a far more intimate relationship between believers than members of an external ecclesiastical organization can ever attain!

      a. WHEN ONE MEMBER SUFFERS, ALL MEMBERS SUFFER.

      b. WHEN ONE MEMBER REJOICES, ALL REJOICE.

      c. There is no cold, detached unconcern for suffering, but HEARTFELT CONCERN.

      d. There is no envy over another's honor or joy.

FIRST CORINTHIANS

4. Even the Head is closely associated with the suffering and rejoicing of the body (Matt. 25).
   NO HUMAN ORGANIZATION CAN MATCH THE ONENESS AND CLOSE RELATIONSHIP THAT EXISTS WITHIN THE BODY OF CHRIST!!

C. The scriptures stress that increase of the Body depends upon closer union with Christ (John 15).
   1. The ecumenists stress structural organization for increase of the body.
      a. But mere organization cannot convert the human soul and give it victory over Satan.
      b. THE GREAT AND PRIMARY EFFORT SHOULD BE TO INCORPORATE THE MEMBERSHIP OF THE CHURCH INTO CLOSER UNION WITH CHRIST!! TEACH, TEACH, TEACH.
      c. Mere incorporation into external mergers for the sake of structural union is not fulfilling Christ's prayer in John 17!!

III. What Does All This Mean Practically?

A. It means that mergers into structural world-church organizations are contrary to the revealed will of God in the New Testament for unity of believers.

B. It means that "brotherhood" organizations, officers, offices, agencies, societies, secretaries are not necessary to the unity for which Christ prayed.

C. It means that the truth (the One objective faith) cannot be compromised for the sake of superficial tranquility.

D. It means that the Church in some instances has failed to rise to the challenge of perfecting the unity of believers and perfecting the church as an *organism*.

   The Lord is not as impressed with our attendance craze and promotional madness as He is with patient, loving, diligent "feeding of the flock . . . the growing up together by a steady diet of the *meat of the gospel*. . . ."
   WHY MUST THE SUCCESS OF PREACHERS OR CHURCHES BE MEASURED SOLELY BY ATTENDANCE FIGURES, DRIVES, CONTESTS AND SUPERSTRUCTURE OF ORGANIZATION?

IS THE CHURCH AN ORGANIZATION OR AN ORGANISM?

    2. Let us never let the fires of evangelism be extinguished . . . God forbid!

        a. But LET US STRIVE TO REACH THE ORGANIC UNITY EXPRESSED IN I Corinthians 12 and we will HAVE SPONTANEOUS EVANGELISM IN ALL THE MEMBERSHIP!

        b. When we *truly become a body,* an organism, then will the world believe!

  E. The distinguishing mark of the Church is holiness, sanctification.

    NOT ATTENDANCE, NOT NEW BUILDINGS, NOT EVEN ADDITIONS—BUT UNWORLDLINESS!!

  F. The distinguishing mark of the church is "speaking truth in love. . . ."

    1. NOT ORGANIZATION, NOT SOCIAL AFFAIRS, NOT POWER, NOT PRESTIGE (Rev. 2-3)

    2. WHY ARE WE GOING OVERBOARD FOR ATTENDANCE AND LETTING "BABES IN CHRIST" AND OTHER MEMBERS OF THE BODY BECOME SPIRITUAL ILLITERATES, INACTIVE AND DEAD BY NEGLECT THROUGH FAILURE TO RECOGNIZE THAT THE CHURCH IS AN ORGANISM . . . NOT AN ORGANIZATION!

Chapter Thirteen

THE PROBLEM OF MAINTAINING LOVE
IN THE MIDST OF DIVERSITY
(Miraculous Gifts)
(13:1-13)

IDEAS TO INVESTIGATE:

1. Why does Paul assume some of the Corinthians might not have love?
2. What is love? Who has authority to define love?
3. Why would the miraculous gifts "pass away"?
4. To whom does the analogy of childhood and manhood apply?
5. Why is love greater than faith and hope?

SECTION 1

Giftedness Without Love (13:1-3)

13 If I speak in the tongues of men and of angels, but have not love, I am a noisy gong or a clanging cymbal. ²And if I have prophetic powers, and understand all mysteries and all knowledge, and if I have all faith, so as to remove mountains, but have not love, I am nothing. ³If I give away all I have, and if I deliver my body to be burned, but have not love, I gain nothing.

13:1 Is Heedless: Verse 31b of chapter 12 should be verse 1 of chapter 13. There the Greek word *huperbole* (English *hyperbole*) is translated "more excellent." Literally, the Greek word means "a throwing beyond—a surpassing." Paul is going to show (in chapter 13) a way to unity in diversity that *surpasses* all other ways, and that way is agape-love. There are four words in the Greek language for love—*storge,* affection (e.g. familial love); *phileo,* friendship (e.g. fraternal); *eros,* passion, desire (e.g. sexual love); and *agape,* self-sacrificing, caring (God-like love). Only *phileo* and *agape* appear in the New Testament. Paul uses only *agape* in this chapter.

Agape-love is not only commanded, but motivated by God and Christ. "We love, because he first loved us . . ." (I John 4:19; see also I John 4:10). God created man with an intellect, a will and emotions. Man has the ability or faculties to love. God demonstrated love in Christ and commands us to love, *but he will not force us to love.*

Love is the only thing man really has to give. Agape-love is a deliberate choice of the will. It is the absorption of every part of our being (intellect, will and emotions) in an obsession to care. It is definitely not physical or circumstantial. It is love which deliberately, by an act of will, chooses its object, and through all circumstances or in spite of them, goes on loving continually. C. S. Lewis, in *The Four Loves,* says it is a love that enables man "to love what is not naturally lovable; lepers, criminals, enemies, morons, the sulky, the superior and the sneering." It is a love that demands complete self-denial. It is always used when the will is involved. It is the word Jesus used when he commanded, "Thou shalt love thine enemy. . . ." Agape-love is the one thing that is completely indestructible; while other things pass away, love lasts. It is not dependent on anything outside itself; it is not affected by the worthiness or unworthiness of the one to be loved. If this love really grips our whole being, our Christian experience will be utterly revolutionized.

Professor Donald Nash, in the Kentucky Christian College bulletin's *Word Pictures,* has written this definition of Love:

> Almost every Christian with a cursory knowledge of the Bible is cognizant of the fact that there are two Greek words for love in the New Testament, but few know their basic connotations. Valuable insights can be gained by delineating between them.
>
> *Agape* is a love called out by a realization of the value of the object loved. It is not an emotion or passion, since it can be and is commanded in the scriptures. It has been defined as intelligent good will toward all men. Christianity took the word from pagan uses and enlarged, ennobled and inspired it. Because it is used of the love God had for the world in Christ it has something of the idea of sacrificial devotion to others in which self is forgotten.
>
> *Phileo* is a love called out by an appreciation or pleasure in the object loved. This is an emotion. It suggests friendship and affection. It cannot be commanded and is not in the scriptures since it is spontaneous. It needs intercommunication between the lover and the object loved. It suggests love between two people with common interests.

FIRST CORINTHIANS

So, I am as a Christian to love all men with *agape* love, for I realize the intrinsic soul's value of everyone as God's creation. I should be willing to make sacrifices of personal desires and interests for all. But I am not commanded to love everyone *phileo,* since this is impossible. It comes from a common bond of fellowship.

For this reason Jesus is said to love the whole world *agape.* He recognized the worth of all and died for all (John 3:16). But he loves only Christians *phileo* (John 16:27), since only between Christians and the Father is the mutual bond of a common interest in righteousness, the common bond of prayer, and same spirit of friendship.

Sometimes it is said that *agape* is divine love and *phileo* human love; that *agape* is the higher love and *phileo* the lower. This is not exactly the case. God loves both ways, so one could not be human and the other divine. *Phileo* is actually the love of close, intimate relationship, and so Peter sought for Jesus to affirm this in him (John 21:15-19). I love the world *agape,* but my family and close friends *phileo.*

Agape is the higher, divine love only in the sense it calls for the type of sacrifice Christ manifested on the cross. It can only be truly produced in us by surrender to Christ and the indwelling of the Holy Spirit (Gal. 5:22). It is demonstrated in those great virtues so beautifully and powerfully portrayed by Paul in I Cor. 13, which only the true Christian possesses in the Biblical sense.

The Corinthians were gauging holiness by possession of miraculous gifts (especially by possession of the more spectacular gifts such as speaking in languages), and not by the love expressed in practical living. No matter what gifts (miraculous or non-miraculous) a Christian has, the fruit of the Spirit lived out in his life—i.e., his spiritual character—is the real yardstick by which to measure his holiness. There is a direct relationship between one's sanctification and the love he expresses. There is *no* relation whatsoever between sanctification and the possession of miraculous or non-miraculous gifts. The proof is in these Corinthians! They had all the miraculous gifts available (1:7), but still they ended up as the most carnal church described in the New Testament. Gifts serve their purpose only when they are governed by agape-love.

It is character, not charisma that counts. It is goodness, not giftedness that really matters. God supplies gifts, talents, blessings to all

CHAPTER 13   FIRST CORINTHIANS 13:1-3

men and women (even to pagan unbelievers), but God has so made his creatures that they may *give* or *withhold* their love. Giftedness without love shrivels character and thwarts God's will for the possessor of such giftedness. God gives gifts to men for the building of character through the expression of love. But in the ultimate analysis, men are free to love God or despise him, and, in this sense, therefore, responsible for their own character. When time ends and Jesus comes again, men will go right on being in character what they have chosen to be, as John wrote in Revelation, "Let the evildoer still do evil . . . and the righteous still do right . . ." (Rev. 22:10-11).

Even if a Christian had supernatural power to talk in the language of angels, predict the future, know and understand everything there is to know, have miraculous power to remove all obstacles, give away all his earthly goods and become a martyr, but did *not* have agape-love, what would he be? He would be only a *noise* (Gr. *chalkos echon e kumbalon alalazon,* brass sounding or cymbal tinkling). Eloquence, erudition and oratory may command admiration, but only love really communicates to the heart. Men with miraculous gifts but without love will embitter the lives of other people because without love there is the inevitable self-centeredness which produces exploitation, cruelty, envy, hatred, and fighting. Love is the tie that binds all other virtues of the human personality together in harmony and stability. The loveless person is a spiritually unbalanced person. The church at Ephesus (about 100 A.D.) was a shocking picture of busyness, patience, discernment, toil, endurance, but absolutely *without* the one thing that matters—agape love, (Rev. 2:2-4). Regardless of everything else the Ephesian church was, she was without the power to meet the "soon to come to pass" waves of persecution, tribulation, false teaching and carnality of the pagan Roman empire (100-300 A.D.).

13:.2 Is Hollow: The Greek word *kumbalon,* cymbal, means, literally, "hollow." Giftedness without love is vain and empty. There really is no value in having any gift without having love. Without love life is lost! He that selfishly saves himself (love only himself) will *lose* his life for life has being only as it emanates agape-love (cf. Matt. 10:39; 16:25; Mark 8:35; Luke 9:24). The man without agape-love is *nothing* (Gr. *outhen,* nil, not anything). He is lost!

13:3 Is Hellish: Man without agape-love is of *no profit* (Gr. *opheloumai,* no gain, profitless, useless). He is like saltless salt, fit only for the dung-heap. Without love a person does not gather with Christ but joins the devil in scattering (see Matt. 12:30). That is what these Corinthians, possessed of miraculous gifts without love, were doing. Someone has analyzed I Corinthians 13:1-3 as follows: "Thought, purpose, logic, industriousness, but without the radiance of love. Isn't that an accurate description of Satan?" Even the demons believed, and shuddered (James 2:19). They were "gifted" but they had no love.

What makes love so great? All gifts, sacrifices and services are hypocrisy without it (Matt. 6:1-18). Motivation is important. God is not interested in empty works of merit. He is evidently not impressed with our gifts as much as with the way we use them. Love is the one thing all men understand. Love may be communicated without language. Love never fails to glorify God. Love never fails to improve the character, both of the lover and the loved. Agape-love does not have to wait upon a feeling to be activated.

SECTION 2

Giftlessness With Love (13:4-7)

4 Love is patient and kind; love is not jealous or boastful; ⁵it is not arrogant or rude. Love does not insist on its own way; it is not irritable or resentful; ⁶it does not rejoice at wrong, but rejoices in the right. ⁷Love bears all things, believes all things, hopes all things, endures all things.

13:4-6 Rejects: In these verses are listed the perversities of character with which love has nothing to do. Only agape-love has the power to restrain from doing what is wrong, hurtful and destructive (see II Cor. 5:14); (a) Love is not *impatient*. Love suffers and waits. Love refuses to give way to anger and vindictiveness. Love waits, hoping for repentance. Love is not resentful when treated unjustly. Love is David with Saul—Christ with the Pharisees. Love never gives up, never dies—it goes on and on; (b) Love is not *unkind*. Some patiently endure wrong out of sheer obstinancy, but to be kind to the person who has done the wrong is the victory of agape-love. Barclay says, "There is so much Christianity which is good but unkind." The Greek word translated "kind" is *chresteuetai* which means literally, "serviceable, good, useable." In other words, kindness means action, service, giving. The greatest good a Christian can ever do this side of heaven is to be *kind* to people (see Luke 10:29-37). William Penn said: "I expect to pass through life but once. If therefore

CHAPTER 13   FIRST CORINTHIANS 13:4-7

there is any kindness I can show or any good thing I can do to any fellow being let me do it now and not defer or neglect it, for I shall not pass this way again." (c) Love is not *jealous*. Only agape-love can see all the inequalities of life and remain content with its own place. Paul had learned contentment in whatever state he found himself (Phil. 4:11-13). Where there is no love, there will inevitably be envy, jealousy and hatred. Absence of agape-love left Cain open to envy and produced the first murder in human history. In its baser form, jealousy not only desires what others have, but being unable to attain it, begrudges the good others have. It does not even care so much that it does not have these things as it wishes others had not gotten them. Agape-love rejoices when others have good fortune. (d) Love is not *boastful*. The Greek word here is *perpereutai* and is used only in this one place in the New Testament. In classical Greek it means, "wind-bag" or "braggart" and Moffatt has translated it, "*does not make a parade of itself.*" Love does not "show off." Love is quiet, unassuming, and humble. When love does anything it does not do it for praise or the applause of others. Love is not conceited. (e) Love is not *arrogant*. The Greek word for arrogant is *phusioutai,* "puffed-up." Love is not contemptuous of others. Love is not the Pharisee who thanks God he is not like publicans (Luke 18:9-14). Love is not obsessed with self-importance. Give a man a little earthly authority or position and one soon sees whether he has love or arrogance. (f) Love is not *rude*. The Greek words are *ouk aschemonei,* meaning literally, "does not act unbecomingly, or, without graciousness." There is the type of Christian who thinks real loyalty to the Bible means one must act bluntly, candidly, without tact and charm, almost brutally. There may be candidness there, but there is no winsomeness. Love is courteous, tactful, polite, and respectful without compromising truth. Love applies the "Golden Rule." Love makes it possible to be right without being rude. (g) Love *never insists on its own way*. The Greek reads: *ou zetei ta heautes*; love is willing to sacrifice its own interests for that of others. Love does not demand its own rights (even though it may have some) above those of others. Barclay writes: "In the last analysis, there are in this world only two kinds of people—those who are continually thinking of their rights and those who are continually thinking of their duties . . . those insisting on their privileges and those who are remembering their responsibilities. . . ." There can never be true love where there is the "Me first" attitude. (h) Love is not *irritable,* (Gr. *paroxunetai,* from which we get the English word *paroxysm,* which means, "a fit, an attack, a convulsion of emotion"). The Greek word means, literally, "hyper-sharp, or, intense sharpening." The word *easily* in some versions, is not in the Greek text. Barclay translates, "Love never flies into a temper fit." Having a paroxysm of exasperation is an indication of the absence of agape-love. The Jewish rabbis made four classifications of people dealing with provocation: (1) those easily provoked but hard to pacify—their loss is cancelled by their gain; (2) those hard to provoke but hard to pacify—their gain is cancelled by their loss; (3) those easily provoked and easily pacified—they are evil; (4) those hard to provoke and easily pacified—they are righteous. But agape-love is never bad-tempered. Love must be angry with sin, but never irritable with the sinner. Greatness is not in position, but in disposition! (i) Love is not *resentful.* The Greek phrase is, *ou logizetai to kakon,* literally, "does not keep books or an account-ledger of evil." Love will always keep a record of the many kindnesses it receives, but never a record of wrongs done to it. Love does not nurse grudges; it makes a concerted effort to forget all wrongs done to it. (j) Love does *not rejoice at wrong.* The Greek word translated *wrong* is *adikia* and means, *injustice.* Moffatt translates, "Love is never glad when others go wrong; love is gladdened by goodness." Love does not delight in exposing the weaknesses and sins of other people. Love will agonize over the sin and condemn the sin, but will always yearn to cover and protect the person who has fallen. Some people get a certain malicious pleasure in hearing about someone else's fall or trouble. Love does not do that. Love wants the truth. Love is brave enough to face the truth. Love has nothing to conceal and so is glad when the truth prevails. But love always uses the truth to build up, never to destroy.

13:7 Reverse: Love respects and urges men to do that which is positive good. Love cherishes the righteousness that can only be done when agape-love of God is working through believers. (a) Love cherishes the *bearing of all things.* The Greek word is *stegei.* It means primarily, "to protect, or preserve by covering—to keep off something that threatens," thus it came to mean "to endure." Love would rather protect than attack. Love gets under the load of life and bears it to the limit. We must learn to bear offences done to us if we ever expect to be able to forgive. C.S. Lewis writes, "To love at all is to be vulnerable. Love anything, and your heart will certainly be wrung and possibly be broken. If you want to make sure of keeping it intact, you must give your heart to no one, not even to an

CHAPTER 13 — FIRST CORINTHIANS 13:4-7

animal. Wrap it carefully round with hobbies and little luxuries; avoid all entanglements; lock it up safe in the casket or coffin of your selfishness. But in that casket—safe, dark, motionless, airless—it will change. It will not be broken; it will become unbreakable, impenetrable, irredeemable. The alternative to tragedy, or at least to the risk of tragedy, is damnation. the only place outside Heaven where you can be perfectly safe from all the dangers and perturbations of love is Hell.'' We must bear one anothers burdens if we wish to fulfill Christ's law of love (Gal. 6:1-5). We must bear the distasteful task of attempting to restore wandering brethren (James 5:19-20). (b) Love wants to *believe all things.* Agape-love is not blind gullibility. It does not follow every kind of doctrine. Love speaks the truth (see Eph. 4:11-16). Love is discriminating and rejoices only in the truth. But love is not innately suspicious. Love strives to ascribe the best motives to others in their actions. Love looks for the best in everyone and everything. Love takes people at their word and always hopes in their trustworthiness, as long as it can, and then mourns over those who stumble and fall. (c) Love tries to find *hope in all things.* When love is disappointed in someone in whom it "believed" love will yet hope for better things. Love never despairs completely of anyone. Jesus never considered any man hopeless—he tried to the very end to reclaim Judas Iscariot. Hope does not, of course, try to persuade itself that a thief is honest or that the criminal is innocent, but it knows God is not willing that any man should perish. So love always hopes for repentance. (d) Love *endures all things.* The Greek word is *hupomenei,* literally, "remaining under." This does not mean passive resignation, but the kind of spirit which conquers its setbacks, trials and circumstances by faith in God. It is the kind of "dogged constancy" which "hangs-in" in spite of hardships and obstacles. It is the enduring love shown by the patriarch Job, who said, "I know that my Redeemer lives, and at last he will stand upon the earth." It is the overcoming endurance of the apostle Paul who said, "For the sake of Christ, then, I am content with weaknesses, insults, hardships, persecutions and calamities; for when I am weak, then I am strong'' (II Cor. 12:10).

The Christians at Corinth were "eager for manifestations of the Spirit" (I Cor. 14:12) but they did not have agape-love. Paul admonished them to "strive to excel in building up the church" (I Cor. 14:12), but their passion for the spectacular miraculous gifts, to satisfy their egomania, was dividing and tearing down the church.

In his attempt to stop this self-destruction, Paul inserts this parenthetical treatise on love and states emphatically that Christians would be much better off to have love whether they *ever* had a miraculous gift or not. He proves, in fact, that while Christians may get along without any miraculous gifts at all (13:8-13), they can never get along without agape-love. Love will more than make up for any lack of giftedness anyone may ever have, miraculous or otherwise. John the Baptist had no miraculous gifts, but he had love. The women who ministered to Jesus had no miraculous gifts such as the apostles had, but they had love. Dorcas had no miraculous gifts, but she had love. Love *surpasses* all other ways of edifying, or building the church. It surpasses all "gifts" of teaching, preaching, liberality, ruling, organizing, mercifulness, or whatever. Love is the supreme way. No Christian who really loves is inferior.

SECTION 3

Giftedness is Temporary, Love is Eternal (13:8-13)

8 Love never ends; as for prophecies, they will pass away; as for tongues, they will cease; as for knowledge, it will pass away. 9For our knowledge is imperfect and our prophecy is imperfect; 10but when the perfect comes, the imperfect will pass away. 11When I was a child, I spoke like a child, I thought like a child, I reasoned like a child; when I became a man, I gave up childish ways. 12For now we see in a mirror dimly, but then face to face. Now I know in part; then I shall understand fully, even as I have been fully understood. 13So faith, hope, love abide, these three; but the greatest of these is love.

13:8-9 The Passing: The text clearly states that these miraculous gifts would stop. They would fulfill their purpose and cease to exist. The question is; *when* were these gifts to stop? Again, this text clearly says the gifts were "imperfect" (Gr. *merous,* "in part"). Verse 11 of this chapter states the gifts were for an "infant" church (Gr. *nepios,* lit. "without the power of speech"—see Matt. 21:16; 11:25; Rom. 2:20; I Cor. 3:1; Heb. 5:13). If we are to believe the Bible, miraculous gifts were never intended to be universal or perpetuated beyond the lifetime of the apostles. Miraculous gifts were never given to all believers. They were never to heal all believers, edify or deliver all

CHAPTER 13   FIRST CORINTHIANS 13:8-13

believers. There are clear indications that Christians could be endowed with miraculous gifts only through the laying on of the hands of the apostles (see Acts 8:14-24).

The "infant" church had difficulty in two areas: (1) in believing that Jews and Gentiles were acceptable to God on the same terms (faith, repentance and immersion in water for the forgiveness of sins), without the Law of Moses. Judaizers constantly harassed the church insisting their message of circumcision and the Law was the true way to salvation. So the message of the gospel had to be confirmed by miracles before the church could ever be fully weaned from the infantilism of the Law to the manhood of the gospel (see Gal. 3:23—4:7; Eph. 4:11-16; Heb. 5:11—6:12). When the church finally shed its immaturity (and when God destroyed the threat of Judaism by destroying Jerusalem and the Jewish nation at the hands of the Romans in 70 A.D.) miracles were no longer needed; (2) distinguishing between true apostolic doctrine and false doctrine. Once the apostolic teaching was put on record (written in our New Testament books) and verified by miraculous manifestations, there was no longer any need for these miracles. Miracles evidently passed away as the generation of believers upon whom the apostles had laid their hands passed away, for there is no divine sanction for perpetuating miracles beyond the hands of the apostles.

Paul uses the Greek word *katargethesontai* to declare the gifts of prophecy and knowledge will be *abolished*. The Greek word literally means, "reduced to inactivity." When he says tongues will *cease* he uses the Greek word *pausontai,* meaning "to stop, to make an end." They are strong, unequivocal words, predicting the cessation of miraculous gifts.

13:10-12 The Perfect: The miraculous gifts were partial ("imperfect") and temporary ("will pass away"). When the *perfect thing* (Gr. *teleion*) came, the *partial thing* (Gr. *to ek merous*) was *abolished* (Gr. *katargethesetai*). The Greek word *teleion* is a noun in the *neuter* gender. It should not, therefore, be translated to mean, "when Christ comes again." The word *teleion* is *not* referring, either grammatically or contextually, to a person, but to some thing. The word *teleion* means, "that which has reached its goal; that which has matured or come to its fulfillment." It does not mean that which is sinless.

The *perfect thing* in this context is referring to the *mature* church; the church which no longer needs miraculous confirmation of the apostolic message. The perfected, matured church will have had enough miraculous confirmations and guidance to acknowledge that the Judaizers, Gnostics, Nicolaitans, and other abberant religious teachings are false. The perfected, matured church will know that Gentiles or Jews do not need to keep the Law of Moses to be members of Christ's body. The church in its manhood will be able to eat and digest the strong "meat" of the final, complete, New Testament scriptures. The mature church will realize that agape-love is the surpassing way to sanctification and evangelism—and that possession of miraculous gifts is not the way.

When spiritual maturity came, from the completed, integrated church, from the completed apostolic revelation, from perfected, Christ-like love, the church *reasoned* or *reckoned* (Gr. *elogizomen*), or thought, like a *man* (Gr. *gegona aner*), *abolishing the things of the infant* (Gr. *katergeka ta tou nepiou*). As long as the church was spiritually immature, it *spoke like an infant* (Gr. *elaloun hos nepios*), it *thought like an infant* (Gr. *ephronoun hos nepios*), and it *reasoned like an infant* (Gr. *elogizomen hos nepios*). As long as the church was infantile, unable to distinguish between true and false without miraculous guidance, it was not seeing the whole picture of redemption and sanctification. Paul says in verse 12, the infant church was then seeing only a reflection (Gr. *esoptrou,* in a mirror) and that, dimly. The Greek word *ainigmati* is translated "darkly" in the KJV and "dimly" in the RSV, but it is the word from which the English word *enigma* comes. *Enigma* means, "puzzling, perplexing, questionably, or obscurely." As long as the infant church was eager for miraculous manifestations of the Spirit in preference to agape-love, the aim of the completed New Testament scriptures, they could never see themselves or circumstances as they really were.

Paul is saying that as soon as the completed apostolic revelation had been written down, the church would see the *whole scheme* of redemption and sanctification—it would no longer be enigmatic—and the church would grow and mature through agape-love, and the temporary, partial manifestations of the Spirit would cease to exist for the church. When the faith was once for all delivered to the saints (Jude 3) the church could distinguish true from false, good from evil, by the completed apostolic word (I John 4:1-6). God granted to the church in his word *all* things that pertain to life and godliness (II Peter 1:2-4). God has given in the completed scriptures everything the church needs to make the man of God *complete*, thoroughly furnished (equipped) for *every* good work (II Tim. 3:16-17). The

CHAPTER 13   FIRST CORINTHIANS 13:8-13

church in its mature manhood, without miraculous gifts of its infancy, may now look in the perfect law, the law of liberty, and persevere (James 1:22-25). The church may now see the whole picture of redemption and sanctification—in the New Testament scriptures it lacks nothing that pertains to life and godliness. The *aim* of the apostolic message and ministry is not miraculous manifestations of the Spirit, but *love* that issues from a pure heart and a good conscience and sincere faith (I Tim. 1:5).

13:13 The Perpetual: Love will never *fall* (Gr. *piptei*), it will endure forever. Love never falls to the ground—there is nothing temporary about love. Love never loses its strength—it is inexhaustible. Love never leaves its place—it is unassuming and immovable.

Faith possesses the past by giving us a conviction of things not seen. Hope claims the future, and looks beyond to the glory not yet realized. But love is the *goal* God has for us. And faith and hope are the *means* to that end. Paul does not mean that love will outlast faith and hope. He does not mean that faith and hope will someday cease. Faith and hope and love will all go on as long as our relationship to Christ lasts—for eternity. We will trust, put our hope in, and love God in heaven, forever. But love is the *greatest*. Faith and hope serve to develop godliness, but *love is* godliness, for, "God is love" (I John 4:16).

Our "possessions" and "gifts" we leave behind us. Only godliness abides. At the gates of death we will lay down forever the various weapons and tools which God, in his marvelous grace, has put into our hands for this earthly pilgrimage. All our gifts and every other capacity designed for this temporary earthly existence we shall resign. But we will carry through the pearly gates the moral and spiritual character which the Holy Spirit, through the conflicts and testings of life, has developed within us through the word. Faith, hope and love abide—but the greatest is love. *Make love your aim* (I Cor. 14:1).

APPLICATIONS:

1. If God said he would grant *you* one wish, either the supernatural power to predict the future, or the trials and tribulations that would help you love your enemies like David or Jesus—which would you wish?
2. What do you think this chapter has to say to those today who insist the church, and Christians, need to have miraculous gifts of tongues, healing, prophecy, etc.?

FIRST CORINTHIANS

3. Do you really believe that just plain, old, Christian love is the most important thing for Christ's church today, or ever?
4. Do you think the church has it?
5. How do you think the church, or Christians, may get it?
6. Do you know people who believe that Christian love accepts all things—true and false, right and wrong?
7. Where do you think you might improve your agape-love-life?
8. Do you think the church today is more mature (less childlike) than the church of the first century? How?
9. Is love the most important virtue you wish to cultivate in your Christian experience?
10. May agape-love be cultivated? In what way?

APPREHENSIONS:

1. What is agape-love? How is it different from other aspects of love?
2. Why are all Christian gifts and Christian actions hollow without love?
3. May a Christian do an act of love without feeling like it?
4. What is kindness?
5. What does courtesy have to do with Christian love?
6. Why were miraculous gifts destined to pass away?
7. When did miraculous gifts pass away?
8. What is the "perfect" that was to come?
9. When did the church see "in a mirror, dimly"?
10. When did the church see "face to face"?

Special Study

LOVE IS A MANY-SPLENDORED THING*

LOVE is a many-splendored thing. So says a popular song title. But no popular song can really plumb the depths of love's splendor.

But what is love? Love is not self-defining. This is the supreme fallacy of situation ethics, which says "do the most loving thing in every situation." We must go to the Word of God for precept and example. And I Corinthians 13 is not the only Biblical definition of love.

Some will say, "Love is concern," but how do you explain the many hungry people whom Jesus did not feed; the many lame He did not heal? Must a concerned love always be manifested according to our concept of concern?

Some will say, "Love is giving," but how do you explain Jesus' rebuke of Judas when he suggested that the precious ointment Mary had poured upon Jesus could have been sold and given to the poor? Must a giving love always be manifested in the way the world thinks?

Some will say, "Love is speaking pleasantly," but how do you explain the words Jesus spoke to the Pharisees, and sometimes to His disciples, which were harsh, demanding, and rebuking? Must love always be communicated in such a manner as to please the hearer?

Love is many-faceted. There is more to love than often meets the spiritual eye. I hope to present you three oft-unseen facets of the brilliance of God-like love, *agape* love. Love is discerning, demanding, deliberate.

Love is discerning—Love is discerning (discriminating; critical; judgmental; penetrating). In reality love is truth-oriented; truth-focused; truth-centered; love is something done but always in a *truth* frame-of-reference. *Agape* love makes every attempt to see things, issues, and persons as they are in reality for a purpose—a good purpose. *Agape* love could never reject truth in favor of falsehood—it could never be satisfied with only half-truth about issues or persons. "Little children, let us not love in word or speech but in deed and in truth" (I John 3:18).

> The Christian loves truth (Ephesians 4:15; 2 Thessalonians 2:10), but he never cruelly or unsympathetically uses the truth in order to hurt. . . . The Christian is never false to the truth, but he always remembers that love and truth must go hand in hand . . . Christian love does not shut its eyes to the faults of others. Love is not blind. It will use rebuke and discipline when these

---

* A sermon from Hebrews 12:5-11, delivered at Ozark Bible College Chapel.

are needed. The love which shuts its eyes to all faults, and which evades the unpleasantness of all discipline, is not real at all, for in the end it does nothing but harm to the loved one (Barclay, Wm., *More New Testament Words,* Harper & Row, p. 22).

"Love . . . does not rejoice in wrong, but rejoices in the right . . ." (I Corinthians 13:6). Would Jesus have shown love to Judas by concealing from Judas the truth about himself? Would Paul have shown love to all the churches to whom he wrote the epistles had he concealed from them the truth about themselves? In that penetrating, piercing confrontation between Jesus and the Jews, Jesus seemed almost astounded that they would seek to kill Him because He told them the truth about themselves (John 8:39-47). He did it because He loved them.

Paul wrote the Christians in Galatia, "Am I therefore become your enemy, because I tell you the truth?" (Gal. 4:16). When God's Word pierces our facade of sham and discerns us as we are and deals with us realistically—it is an expression of God's love.

In relationships love is person-oriented; it deals with persons discerning, judging, estimating what they ought to be and can be with the help of God and Christian brethren. A person who, by experience and wisdom, knows something that would benefit me and keeps it from me does not love me. If I do not share with my children some truth that will help them, I do not love them.

There are some of you here this morning living in the joy of being better than you were because your teachers have dealt with you on the basis of their judgment of what you could become! It seemed distasteful to you at first—you disliked us and accused us of putting you down—but now you know we judged that you could be better than you were and we insisted on it. Love demands that those who have the advantage of experience and leadership relate to others on the basis of building up—not leaving others to go backward . . . or even to remain where they are!

In remedies, love is always seeking that which is practical—helpful. That which is the most helpful in a situation, may not always be the most glorious or win the most applause. But love seeks the long-range remedy. Love is never satisfied with superficialities or stopgap measures. (Read Heb. 12:11, 12.)

In an old book given to me by Seth Wilson, I found some ageless principles stated as well as I have ever seen them stated. One of those principles is:

SPECIAL STUDY: LOVE IS A MANY-SPLENDORED THING

> ... If the moral powers (of man) are not employed on right objects and directed to a right end, there is not only perversion but deterioration. The more inactive they are the more they deteriorate. If, therefore, we would do the highest good to men we must seek, not only to perfect their powers, but to perfect the moral powers by directing them rightly. Our object must be to produce a change not merely in the condition, but in the state of men; and not merely in their intellectual state involving acquisitions and capacity, but in their moral state which involves, or rather which is, character (Hopkins, Mark, *The Law of Love and Love As a Law,* 1881, p. 199).

Loving, doing the highest good to men, means discernment!
Love is demanding—Love restrains.

Our love to God is shown in the keeping of His commandments (Exodus 20:6; 1 John 5:3; 2 John 6). Love is more than a mere affection or sentiment; it is something that manifests itself, not only in obedience to known divine commands, but also in protecting and defense of them, and a seeking to know more and more of the will of God in order to express love for God in further obedience (compare Deuteronomy 10:12). Those who love God will hate evil and all forms of worldliness, as expressed in the avoidance of the lust of the eyes, the lust of the flesh, and the pride of life (Psalm 97:10; 1 John 2:15-17). Whatever there may be in his surroundings that would draw the soul away from God and righteousness, that the child of God will avoid (*International Standard Bible Encyclopedia,* Vol. 3, p. 1933, article, "Love").

Love does not indulge. Dr. James Dobson, in his book, *Dare To Discipline,* says,

> Perhaps the most common parental error during the past twenty-five years has been related to the wide-spread belief that "love is enough" in raising children ... the greatest social disaster of this century is the belief that abundant love makes discipline unnecessary.

A New York psychologist, Peter Blos, is quoted in *Time,* November 29, 1971:

... Parents should set limits, affirm their personal values, deny the "calmor for grown-up status," and refuse to be intimidated by charges of authoritarianism.

Permissiveness, or indulgence, is no sign of love! Permissiveness can be the most unloving thing one person ever does to another! Jesus would not indulge Peter and the other disciples even in some actions that appeared correct (e.g., when they would forbid Him from going to Jerusalem and be killed, etc.). He would not indulge the rich young ruler to keep the riches which were strangling his loyalties.

Love refuses. It sometimes has to say "No!"

> When we understand what *agape* means, it amply meets the objection that a society based on this love would be a paradise for criminals, and that it means simply letting the evildoer have his own way. If we seek nothing but a man's highest good, we may well have to do the hardest thing to him—for the good of his immortal soul. . . . In other words, *agape* means treating men as God treats them—and that does not mean allowing them unchecked to do as they like (Barclay, *More New Testament Words,* p. 16).

Curtis Dickinson, in the *Christian Standard*, January 25, 1958, "Love's Constraining Power," wrote,

> It is easy to camouflage weakness and conformity under the disguise of love. . . . It is just because God loves you that He cannot overlook you. . . . It is precisely because we love our children that we cannot let them escape punishment. How ridiculous, if we said of a child, "I love her so much that no matter what she does I will consider it all right."

God said "No" to the perfect man in Eden, because He loved Adam! God said "No" to one of the greatest saints of all. Three times God said "No" to Paul, because God loved Paul! For a good mental and moral exercise why don't you personally run through your mind all the great men of the Old Testament to whom God said "No!" Now list mentally all the churches and people to whom the apostles wrote letters stating many emphatic "No's!" Add them all together!

Those whom the Holy Spirit has made overseers in the Lord's church are bound by their love for the Lord, for His church, and for

SPECIAL STUDY: LOVE IS A MANY-SPLENDORED THING

its people, sometimes to say "No!" It is not something in which they take selfish, prideful pleasure—it is something for which they feel an obligation, and consider a privilege, because it gives them an opportunity to love for real!

Love reiterates and reinforces. Love does not give up with the first discernment or demand. Love repeats and repeats and repeats (read *The Hound of Heaven,* by Francis Thompson). Love hounds, stalks, trails. The immature tend to classify discerning, demanding love as nagging or harping, or nit-picking. Does the discerning, demanding love of God give us cause to accuse Him of nagging or harping? Were the Old Testament prophets nit-picking when they repeated and repeated God's message?

Continued reminders to you students to keep your dormitory room clean and orderly, continued reminders to pay your accounts, continued reminders to dress modestly, continued reminders to drive like a Christian, continued reminders to conduct your man-woman relationship with decorum—these are not nagging, nit-picking—these are fundamental issues of life and Christian witness . . . and the reminders are reiterations of love! It never ceases to amaze me that athletes and choir members, can so graciously accept all the repetition of practices and dress-alike uniformity; and then get all upset and accuse their deans of nagging and nit-picking when they reiterate and reinforce moral and spiritual values.

Love is deliberate—*It is real. Agape* love is sincere, genuine. J. B. Phillips translated Romans 12:9, "Let us have no imitation Christian love. Let us have a genuine break with evil and real devotion to good." *Agape* love will not stand for sham, superficiality, or unstable emotionalism. (Note: I said emotional*ism*. Love is part emotion but not all emotion.) *Agape* love is not the silly, selfish sentimentalism so often portrayed by the world.

> This *agape*, this Christian love, is not merely an emotional experience which comes to us unbidden and unsought; it is a *deliberate* principle of the mind, and a deliberate conquest and achievement of the will. It is in fact the power to love the unlovable, to love people whom we do not like (Barclay).

Agape has to do with the *mind*: it is not simply an emotion which sweeps over us at intervals when we are in the right mood. It is a principle by which we deliberately live, every day, no matter what mood we're in or how we feel. It is a conquest, a victory, an achievement. No one ever naturally loved his enemies. *Agape* love demands the whole man; mind, will, and heart. There may be some of you students I know more intimately than others. But it does not mean that my *agape* love for any of you is any more or less than the other. *Agape* love does not depend upon circumstances! It is a real love! Many is the time we have been tempted to love some of you only according to how we feel, or by emotions alone, but that is not real love!

Love is reliable. It is decisive, dependable, firm, stable, consistent. Dennis Vath wrote in *Christian Standard,* November 5, 1966:

> Jesus loved consistently. True *agape* love is consistent. It does not always compliment. It is not always manifested in a pat on the back, for this is not always in our best interests. *Agape* love does not always agree. Scripture tells us that the one God loves is the one He chastens. *Agape* on the human level does not allow itself to be dominated or abused, because it is not in a person's best interests to allow him to take advantage of anyone.

One mark of love often overlooked is that characteristic of being able to make a decision, a consistent decision, a stabilizing decision and then to stand firm in that decision. Could you honestly say you believed the leadership of this college loved you if it could not make a decision, consistently, and stand firm?

Love is risky. *Agape* love will never let a man be selfishly-safe. *Agape* love insists upon self-sacrifice. Eugene Nida writes in *God's Word in Man's Language*:

> The Conob Indians of northern Guatemala . . . describes love as "my soul dies." A man who loves God according to the Conob idiom would say, "My soul dies for God." This not only describes the powerful emotion felt by the one who loves, but it should imply a related truth—namely, that in true love there is no room for self. . . . True love is of all emotions the most unselfish, for it does not look out for self but for others. False love seeks to possess; true love seeks to be possessed. False love leads to cancerous jealousy; true love leads to a life-giving ministry.

The person who will not risk being hurt or thought badly of—the person who is afraid to do what is best for another because he is afraid

SPECIAL STUDY: LOVE IS A MANY-SPLENDORED THING

of that person's displeasure with him—that person does not know how to love! Beloved, it may seem to you that we deliberately set out at times to court your displeasure with us! We do! Because we want to love you with a real love, we are not primarily concerned with what you feel toward us at first. Because we know that almost always you will someday understand the love behind our counsel and love us in return! Any parent who so fears to risk his child's temporary displeasure that he fails to enforce some genuine, loving restraint, is not worthy to be a parent. And this applies in the family of God!

Conclusion—Love is a many-splendored thing. Love is like a many-faceted jewel; there are many sides to it and they all reflect the glory of God. I have tried in these moments to catch your spiritual eye with three of the more brilliant facets of this superb gem. I would invite you to take up the Word of God and make your own study of the nature of God, finding still other facets and reflections as you hold it in your gaze.

Our love for you is an attempt to reproduce in you this splendored thing. We are going to love you discerningly, demandingly, deliberately, We are going to love you with our mind and our will as well as our emotions. You may not be pleased with us always, but we are not going to let our love be directed by that. C. S. Lewis writes in *The Four Loves*:

> To love at all is to be vulnerable. Love anything and your heart will certainly be wrung and possibly broken. If you want to make sure of keeping it intact, you must give your heart to no one. . . . Wrap it carefully round with hobbies and little luxuries; avoid all entanglements; lock it up safe in the casket of your selfishness. But in that casket—safe, dark, motionless, airless—it will change. It will not be broken; it will become unbreakable, impenetrable, irredeemable.

To you, my beloved brother or sister, I am vulnerable. I cannot lock myself up. Break my heart if you will, I will still love you discerningly, demandingly, deliberately. To appropriate a phrase from Isaiah, "Behold, I have graven you on the palms of my hands; your walls are continually before me."

Special Study

THE CHRISTIAN SYNDROME
(John 15:1-17)

If ye keep my commandments, ye shall abide in my life; even as I have kept my Father's commandments, and abide in his love. These things have I spoken unto you, that my joy might remain in you, and that your joy might be full (John 15:10, 11).

The word "syndrome" is a technical word used in the field of psychology, applied to a group of symptoms or signs that occur together and characterize a mental or physical state. The word "syndrome" is from two Greek words *syn* and *dramein* and literally means "run together." There are three fundamental elements (symptoms) which "run together" and form the joyful Christian syndrome. If any of these elements is missing, the syndromatic cycle is broken and the Christian life is unstable. Interestingly enough, all three elements in the Christian syndrome were present in man's experience in the Garden of Eden before man sinned. And the thrust of the redemptive plan of God through Christ is to restabilize man in this cycle of joy.

Liberty—Before a person can have joy, he must be free. The real hindrances to true freedom are not rules and regulations, but guilt, fear, and selfishness. The man who is free of guilt, fear, and himself is a truly liberated man no matter what his circumstances. Guilt, fear, and selfishness are the elements the devil uses to keep men in bondage (compare Heb. 2:5-18; John 8:31-36). Psychiatrists tell us that guilt and fear and selfishness are probably the most mentally and spiritually enslaving, unbalancing elements affecting men.

The real and only cure for this bondage—the only way to be set free—is simple, complete, unreserved faith in the substitutionary, atoning death of Christ. There is no way in this world or the next for man to punish himself enough, or do enough good works, or sacrifice enough to get rid of his guilt, fear, and selfishness. There is no way for man to psyche himself into good and positive feelings each day to get rid of his bondage. The only way for man to be absolutely certain he is not guilty is to believe God. God has said in His Word that Jesus Christ died your death for you. He suffered your guilt for you.

Many Christians today bring themselves into bondage by refusing to accept God's offer of liberty, gratis. They insist on atoning for their own guilt or trying to earn their own righteousness by competing, even in the Christian ministry, for success according to a

SPECIAL STUDY: THE CHRISTIAN SYNDROME

carnal or worldly standard. Before the Christian life-style or ministry can ever become a joy the Christian must be freed of the guilt that comes from a sense of failing to meet worldly standards of success.

God's standard is faithfulness. We are going to be surprised when we get to heaven—Jesus says so in Matthew 25:31-46. God does not count success as the world does. He keeps a different set of statistics from those of worldly-minded, success-oriented, guilt-ridden men.

God has punished my guilt in Jesus Christ. His Word says it. I believe it. That settles it. I'm free. I don't have to earn my own absolution or succeed as the world measures success. I don't have to get rid of my own guilt—I couldn't if I tried! When Christ died, the guilty me died.

Love—Because God has objectively, judicially, and propositionally freed me, I love Him. Loving Him is not something I can produce without an adequate cause. "We love because he first loved us" (I John 4:19). Jesus commanded His disciples to love others as He had loved them. Perfect love has its origin in the divine Lover. Our love is a rebound—a reaction—a response.

God motivates love in us. Love in us is the motivating factor in the syndrome. This is where the system of situation ethics falls into a fundamental fallacy. It makes love the standard rather than the motivation of Christian conduct.

> Love can never of itself be a standard to determine what is right or wrong. I might love my country with all my heart but that love itself does not tell me how to express my feelings for my country. There must be laws to tell me what taxes to pay as my share in government and what rights and privileges my neighbor and I have in relation to each other. Without such laws it is obvious that anarchy would prevail (Donald A. Nash, "Situation Ethics or Social Ethics," *Christian Standard,* March 8, 1969).

Love moves me to want to do something. Love demands and insists that I seek an acceptable expression of the urge to do. Just doing will not satisfy love—doing what is pleasing is the only acceptable expression of love. Who is to say what is pleasing and edifying? Ultimately God alone can say!

Law—This is where law becomes a necessity in the syndrome of joy. Law defines love. Even before man sinned, God defined how Adam was to love his Creator. God gave Adam the command that he should not eat of the tree of knowledge of good and evil. God also gave Adam

FIRST CORINTHIANS

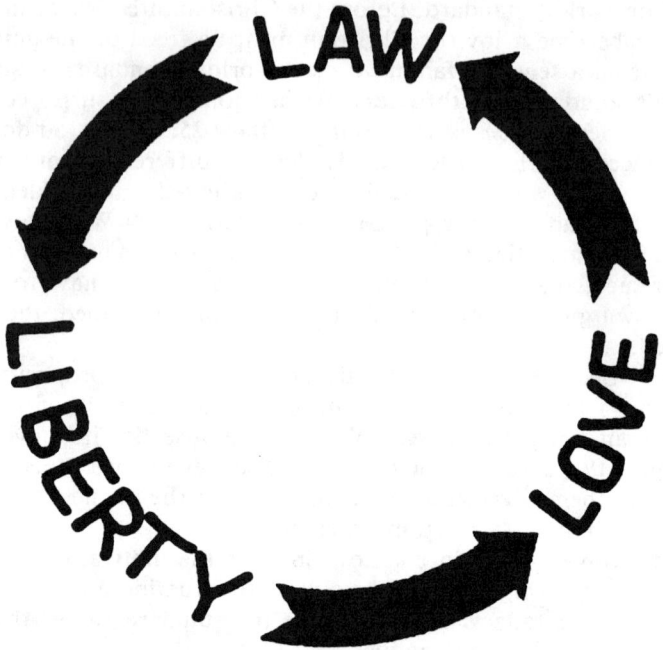

the command to till the Garden of Eden. As long as Adam believed God and remained free of the bondage of selfishness, guilt, and fear, Adam loved God. But Adam's love did not of itself tell him *how* to love God. God told Adam how, by giving Adam commandments.

We do not even know how to love our fellowman properly without the divine commandments of God. Love does not indulge—it edifies. But who knows what is edifying for his fellowman? Who even knows what is edifying for himself? God, the master psychologist, knows. He made man. In Him man subsists (lives) and consists (holds together). Without Him, man comes apart.

Once for all, keeping the commandments of God is not legalism! Nor is the keeping of the rules and regulations of man necessarily legalism. Legalism is an attitude. If the laws are made, or kept, with the intent that in so doing one is justified before God in the keeping—this is legalism. If, on the other hand, the commandments are made in love and kept from a motivation of love—this is where true liberty is found!

SPECIAL STUDY: THE CHRISTIAN SYNDROME

If commandments are given from a motivation of love they will be given only to assist the one obeying to reach the fullest potential for which he was created. If commandments are obeyed from a motivation of love they will become a way, a method, a tool both pleasing and profitable (certainly, not grievous) to reach toward that highest potential for which the obeyer was created.

This is truly liberating, maturing, perfecting. Now whether we make laws or keep laws in love depends on whether we are truly liberated in the grace of God.

The syndrome of Christian joy—liberty, love, law—one follows the other and they all run together in a never ending cycle.

Chapter Fourteen

THE PROBLEM OF EDIFICATION IN THE MIDST OF DIVERSITY
(14:1-40)

IDEAS TO INVESTIGATE:

1. Who is supposed to "earnestly desire the spiritual gifts"? Are we, today, to desire them?
2. In what way were the Corinthians apparently using "speaking in tongues" so that the tongues were unedifying?
3. What is the significance of the Old Testament prophecy from Isaiah in this context?
4. Why did Paul state, ". . . and the spirits of prophets are subject to prophets"?
5. Is it really "shameful" for a woman to speak in church?

SECTION 1

Preaching by Prophecy (14:1-12)

14 Make love your aim, and earnestly deisire the spiritual gifts, especially that you may prophesy. ²For one who speaks in a tongue speaks not to men but to God; for no one understands him, but he utters mysteries in the Spirit. ³On the other hand, he who prophesies speaks to men for their upbuilding and encouragement and consolation. ⁴He who speaks in a tongue edifies himself, but he who prophecies edifies the church. ⁵Now I want you all to speak in tongues, but even more to prophesy. He who prophesies is greater than he who speaks in tongues, unless some one interprets, so that the church may be edified.

6 Now, brethren, if I come to you speaking in tongues, how shall I benefit you unless I bring you some revelation or knowledge or prophecy or teaching? ⁷If even lifeless instruments, such as the flute or the harp, do not give distinct notes, how will any one know what is played? ⁸And if the bugle gives an indistinct sound, who will get ready for battle? ⁹So with

CHAPTER 14 FIRST CORINTHIANS 14:1-12

yourselves; if you in a tongue utter speech that is not intelligible, how will any one know what is said? For you will be speaking into the air. 10There are doubtless many different languages in the world, and none is without meaning; 11but if I do not know the meaning of the language, I shall be a foreigner to the speaker and the speaker a foreigner to me. 12So with yourselves; since you are eager for manifestations of the Spirit, strive to excel in building up the church.

14:1-5 Prophecy is Understandable: It will be profitable at the start of this chapter to reiterate the fundamental principles of Biblical hermeneutics. (1) The true interpretation is what the *author* intended to say; (2) The Bible is written in *human* language. If human language is to mean anything at all it must (granting differences in structure) *mean the same thing to all* human beings; (3) Each passage must be understood in the light of its *historical* background, its *grammatical* structure, and *parallel words* or passages; (4) Each word, paragraph, chapter, is to be understood according to its *context*; (5) And each passage is to be interpreted in the light of the *whole scheme of redemption* (the entire Bible). Remember, Paul *expected* the Corinthians to understand him and God expects *all* human beings to *understand* the Bible alike.

The teaching of this chapter was initially given to *promote unity* among Christians, in the first century, in Corinth. Unity could only result when all the Christians at Corinth understood and obeyed the will of God as expressed in this teaching. Understanding and obeying the will of God revealed in the scriptures is *still* the only basis for Christian unity. Let us exert every mental and spiritual effort possible to understand and obey the will of God in this chapter.

Miraculous gifts served their purpose (integration of cultural differences among believers and verification of apostolic doctrine) and ceased. But that does not mean the *generic* principles taught in chapter fourteen (which is, all things done to edify, and done decently, in order) are irrelevant to the believers today. God's principles are always true and never change. The *administration,* or application, of those principles may, due to time or culture, serve their purpose and cease. This was the case with miraculous gifts. Both miraculous gifts and love come from God. Paul expected the Corinthian church to practice both in the will of God. Chapter fourteen gives some practical way that love controls the use a person makes of his gifts.

FIRST CORINTHIANS

The Greek word *prophetes,* prophecy, is literally, "forth-speaking." In this context it must mean more than just predicting the future, since all *teaching* in the first century church did not involve the necessity of predicting the future. The word *propheteian* in Romans 12:6 may not include the miraculous element at all since it is listed with the "functional" (Gr. *praxin*) gifts; it probably means simply, preaching. There was a "school of the prophets" in the Old Testament (also called "sons of the prophets" II Kings 2:3, 5, 7, 15; 4:1, 38). Prophets with the miraculous power to predict, did not have to go to school to learn how to predict! Evidently the title "prophet" could be applied to a person learning to "prophesy" in the sense of preaching.

Yet, in the context of I Corinthians, chapter 12-14, "prophecy" is clearly to be understood as a miraculous gift. Here it is more than merely preaching or teaching by natural faculties. Whether it was teaching and preaching, or predicting, or both, it was under the inerrant direction of the Holy Spirit in order to deliver to the first century church an infallible message from God.

The Greek text of 14:1, like the Greek of 12:1, says, *zeloute de ta pneumatika, mallon de hina propheteuete,* literally, "be zealous for the spiritual things, and rather, in order that you may prophesy." Once again, as in 12:1, the word "gifts" (Gr. *charismata*) is omitted. The most spiritual thing to want is the desire to edify others—that is done by teaching.

The apostle warns that speaking in a *tongue* (Gr. *glosse,* language) usually resulted in utterance of a non-understandable mystery. The Greek word *musterion,* mystery, means, "that which is unrevealed," not that which is unknowable; it would be knowable if revealed, or interpreted. The word "unknown" (supplied in KJV) is not in any Greek text, and should not have been supplied since it is *not* stated anywhere in the New Testament that first century "tongues" were non-human, unknowable utterances. Of course, God knows all human languages, dialects, phonics or "tongues," (see Rev. 5:9; 7:9; 9:11; 10:11; 11:9; 13:7; 14:6; 16:16; 17:15 where "tongue," *glosson,* is used clearly to mean, human languages). When one of the Corinthian Christians spoke with "other tongues" (Gr. *heterais glossais,* Acts 2:4; and *heteroglossois,* I Cor. 14:21) he did not speak to his fellow Christians because he was speaking in a *foreign language,* but he did speak to God since God understands all languages. When a Christian in the Corinthian church spoke in a language they never learned, they did so from the supernatural gift God gave them. When

CHAPTER 14   FIRST CORINTHIANS 14:1-12

there was no interpreter present, they exercised that gift only for God's benefit (since it had not been translated, it was understood by no one else—not even the speaker). God gave the speaker words and information directly from heaven in a language the speaker had not studied or spoken natively. When there was no translator present, speaking in language foreign to the speaker resulted, for the speaker, in a purely *subjective* experience. Thus, the gift of tongues was experiential only for the speaker—and that only in a limited sense if he does not have the gift of interpretation. Paul is pointing, in this context, to the *superiority* of the gift of prophecy over the gift of tongues. Thus to speak only for personal experience is to abuse the gift.

Contrary to the very limited, often self-centered, profitableness of "tongues," the gift of prophecy, since spoken in the vernacular of the audience, speaks to all for edification, encouragement and consolation. Prophecy did not need a translator; it could be understood by all.

Paul was willing that tongues be practiced by all the Corinthian Christians as he would qualify their use in 14:6ff. However, the Greek word *thelo* (14:5) translated "I would," "I wish," or "I want" is a present active indicative verb and is better translated, "I am willing." He was "willing" that tongues be spoken *only* if interpreted; but he was "more" (Gr. *mallon,* "rather") willing that the gift of prophecy be exercised. The one who prophesied was *greater* than the one who spoke in an untranslated language, because prophecy edified everyone. If the untranslated language was translated, then the church was edified. And, we note, the words "some one" in the RSV are not in the Greek text. The one who speaks in the untranslated language is to interpret (Gr. *ektos ei me diermaneun,* "except unless *he* interprets"). The moment language was translated and understood by the whole church it became, in essence, a prophecy (a revelation, a teaching). What, then, was the need for speaking in foreign languages? As we shall see in another section, this gift was primarily and exclusively to be used as a *sign* for unbelievers and the spiritually immature.

14:6-12 Prophecy is Upbuilding: To read this section, one might think Paul's main subject is tongues—but it is the superiority of prophecy. In these verses the apostle illustrates and explains further the inferiority of tongues to prophecy. Some Bible students forget the main issue here and assume the emphasis is on tongues.

FIRST CORINTHIANS

Paul could have spoken to the Corinthians, by the power of the Holy Spirit, in a multitude of foreign languages (see I Cor. 14:18). Evidently, he did not have the power to translate these "tongues." Even though he could speak in more tongues than any of them, he would have benefited no one except himself, subjectively, and God, unless the tongues could have been translated into a revelation or knowledge or prophecy or teaching.

Imagine a Japanese Army bugle call being blown by an American soldier at an American Army camp! The call would be an *enigma* (remember, Paul used this word *enigma* in 13:12 to characterize these miraculous gifts). Musical instruments which do not give distinct, recognizable *notes* (Gr. *phthongois*) and bugles which do not give recognizable *calls* (Gr. *phonen,* phonetics) are not only useless, they are confusing. Paul uses the Greek word *diastolen,* distinct, to characterize the function of musical instruments. It is the word from which we get the English word *stole,* and means literally, "a vestment worn by someone to distinguish them from others." He uses the word *adelon* to characterize misuse of a bugle and the word means, "Indistinct, not obvious, uncertain." Musical instruments and, especially bugles, are intended to communicate messages. If they do not they are useless and confusing.

In verse 9 the suggestion is that those with the gift of "tongues" not speak in the public assembly unless they may specifically speak *a clear word* (Gr. *eusemon logon,* literally, "a word that well-signifies"). Foreign languages without interpretation are not clear signals—they are undistinguishable sounds.

In 14:10 Paul says there are multitudinous "kinds" (Gr. *gene, geneses,* families) of *phonetics* (Gr. *phonon*) in the *world* (Gr. *kosmos*) and not one without *meaning* (Gr. *aphonon,* literally, "without its own phonetics"). Yet, if one of these "phonetics" is sounded or spoken and *not* translated, and a listener does not happen to know the language being spoken miraculously, he would be a *foreigner* (Gr. *barbaros,* barbarian) and the speaker would be a *foreigner* (Gr. *barbaros*). Paul is using the term *barbaros* literally, and not figuratively. Those who do not understand one another's human language are foreigners to one another. It is clear that Paul is speaking of *actual* human languages when he says "tongues" and *not* of the modern phenomena called *glossolalia* (a word not found in that form in the New Testament at all). The modern, alleged, "speaking in tongues" has been thoroughly analyzed by linguistics and philologists and their conclusions repudiate it as being any form of language at all (see *The Psychology of Speaking In Tongues,* by John P. Kildahl, pub. Harper and Row, 1972). Dr. Kildahl also documents cases where actual human language, spoken in an audience where the language was not understood except by the speaker, received a so-called miraculous interpretation and it was not at all what the speaker said. Modern glossolalia is pseudo-miraculous!

Paul repeats, in 14:12, the overriding, central principle of these three chapters (I Corinthians 12-13-14) again. That principle is, strive to *excel* (Gr. *perisseuete,* abound, fully) in building up the church. So the teaching thus far is that teaching by revelation ("prophecy") builds up the church, while miraculous speaking in foreign tongues which are not translated or interpreted does not build up the church.

SECTION 2

Proving by Tongues (14:13-25)

13 Therefore, he who speaks in a tongue should pray for the power to interpret. 14 For if I pray in a tongue, my spirit prays but my mind is unfruitful. 15 What am I to do? I will pray with the spirit and I will pray with the mind also; I will sing with the spirit and I will sing with the mind also. 16 Otherwise, if you bless with the spirit, how can any one in the position of an outsider say the "Amen" to your thanksgiving when he does not know what you are saying? 17 For you may give thanks well enough, but the other man is not edified. 18 I thank God that I speak in tongues more than you all; 19 nevertheless, in church I would rather speak five words with my mind, in order to instruct others, than ten thousand words in a tongue.

20 Brethren, do not be children in your thinking; be babes in evil, but in thinking be mature. 21 In the law it is written, "By men of strange tongues and by the lips of foreigners will I speak to this people, and even then they will not listen to me, says the Lord." 22 Thus, tongues are a sign not for believers but for unbelievers, while prophecy is not for unbelievers but for believers. 23 If, therefore, the whole church assembles and all speak in tongues, and outsiders or unbelievers enter, will they not say that you are mad? 24 But if all prophesy, and an unbeliever or outsider enters, he is convicted by all, he is called to account

by all, ²⁵the secrets of his heart are disclosed; and so, falling on his face, he will worship God and declare that God is really among you.

14:13-19 Intelligibility Abdicated: Those Corinthian Christians who clamored for the gift of tongues because it was spectacular were abdicating the only means of building Christ's church—intelligible communication. The Greek word here for "tongues" is *glossa*; the Greek word for "speaking" is *lalon*. Modern charismatics have combined the two words into one, *glossolalia,* to denote modern, alleged, "tongues-speaking." But, we repeat, the word glossolalia is not found in the New Testament. There is a distinct difference, literally, between the Greek New Testament words *ho lalon glosse* and the modern word *glossolalia,* and there is also a difference in the connotations implied. Needless to say, then, there is a distinct difference between what was practiced in the first century and today.

In the Greek translation of the Old Testament (the Septuagint, or LXX), the word *glossa* is used for (a) the human *organ* known as the tongue, and; (b) the language of a known people, but *never* for some ecstatic, esoteric babble. The same is true of the New Testament. In Acts 2:8, when Peter and the other apostles spoke in *other glossa,* men from all over the world heard in their own *dialect* (the Greek word *dialekto* is used in Acts 2:8).

The Greek word *gene* refers to a "family" or genre (genealogy) of *glossa,* (see 14:10). This indicates that the tongues being spoken by the Corinthians were clearly distinguishable one from another and, were not unknowable, but one family or genre of human language or another.

The Greek word *hermeneuo* (14:5, 13, 26, 27, etc.) is not used in the Bible to mean the interpretation of an unknowable language into a known language. The word *hermeneuo* always means to translate words from one knowable language into another knowable language (cf. John 1:38, 42; 9:7; see also Ezra 4:7) so that there may be an understanding; (see also Matt. 1:23; Mark 5:41; 15:22, 34; Acts 9:36; 13:8; Heb. 7:2; II Peter 1:20). When *hermeneuo* is translated, "translate," we see clearly that Paul is talking about *knowable* languages being translated into other knowable languages, and not about "unknown" and unknowable gibberish. Paul warns, "Therefore, he who speaks in a tongue should pray for the power to translate."

CHAPTER 14 FIRST CORINTHIANS 14:13-25

Reasons the modern phenomenon called *glossolalia* is *not* the miraculous speaking in "tongues" of the first century church:

  a. Scriptural reasons cited above.
  b. Today's phenomenon is not received by the laying on of the hands of an apostle.
  c. Ecstatic, esoteric glossolalia similar to Christian glossolalia has been practiced, and is being practiced, by pagans in ancient and modern times (Hittites, Phoenicians, Egyptians, Greeks, East Africans, Islamics, American Indians, Caribbean voodoo practitioners, and many others).
  d. Ecstatic gibberish has been practiced by a multitude of different religious groups who have *fundamental doctrinal abberations* when compared with the Bible (Roman Catholics, Mormons, Jews, cultists of all varieties). The Spirit of God would not *contradict* his apostolic word, nor would he give credence by miraculous manifestations to these *apostate* religious groups.
  e. Writings of the early church "fathers" (immediately after the first century) indicate Biblical "tongues" were not manifested in their time (Irenaeus, Origen, Chrysostom, Augustine of Hippo; see Kildahl, op. cit., pp. 14-15).
  f. In the history of modern, so-called, tongues there are no scientifically confirmed recordings of anyone speaking in a foreign language which he had never learned (Kildahl, p. 39).
  g. Dr. Kildahl, in order to investigate "interpretations" played a taped example of tongues-speech privately for several different "interpreters." In no instance was there any similarity in the several "interpretations" (Kildahl, p. 63).
  h. Kildahl writes of a man raised in Africa, of missionary parents, who decided to test the "interpretation of tongues." He attended a tongues-speaking meeting where he was a complete stranger. At the appropriate moment, he rose and spoke the Lord's Prayer in the African dialect he had learned in his youth. When he sat down, an "interpreter of tongues" at once offered the meaning of what he had said. He interpreted it as a message about the imminent second coming of Christ (Kildahl, p. 63).
  i. Personal friends of mine, of the so-called charismatic persuasion, and books in my personal library from charismatic practitioners,

FIRST CORINTHIANS

offer instruction on how one may *learn,* by *human* means, the act of tongues-speaking. How does one learn that which is miraculous?

j. Much modern, so-called, tongues-speaking is allegedly *not* under conscious control of the person who allegedly speaks and yet this very chapter (I Cor. 14) says *it must be* (I Cor. 14:26-33), so that they can determine who is to speak and when they are to speak.

k. According to one former member of a tongues-speaking denomination, 85% of modern, so-called tongues-speaking is done in the public assemblies, by women. Yet, Paul directs (14:33-36) that women should be silent in the public assemblies.

Paul explains that even the bona fide speaking in tongues by miraculous gift is unfruitful as far as intelligent communication is concerned, unless there is a translator present. When a Corinthian Christian prayed in a foreign language he did not know, his spirit might receive some emotional, subjective, excitation, but there would be nothing by which his *mental,* spiritual growth (edification) could proceed. Speaking in a tongue without a translator did not bring the mind into play, and anything said would bear no edifying fruit to the congregation. The same principle is true of all singing in congregational worship. Singing is a means of instructing the congregation unto edification (see Eph. 5:19). If the singing is unintelligible, for any reason, it is foolish to say, "Amen," because no instruction or edification has taken place. *Edification cannot take place without instruction*!

Although Paul was probably writing about singing done in Corinth by Christians with the miraculous gift of tongues—and therefore, singing in a foreign language—a great amount of today's so-called religious music is neither Christian nor intelligible. In some cases, the words of today's songs, when distinguishable, are actually anti-scriptural. The twentieth century church needs to restore the New Testament teaching about music. Too many "Christian musicians" have succumbed to the "performer mentality," and, at the same time, many congregations have adopted the "audience-mentality" toward music. The New Testament concept of music in the worship assembly gives no credence to the modern mania for "the beat," "performance-mentality," and unintelligible, imprecise, vague generalizations. The desire to "show-off" as a "performer" is precisely the attitude that was destroying the Corinthian congregation. It is the issue to which

CHAPTER 14   FIRST CORINTHIANS 14:13-25

the apostle Paul addresses as much as half of this epistle! It is still relevant!

Speaking, praying or singing in a foreign language (tongue) had to be translated and made understandable if done at all in the worship services, otherwise the "outsider" could not be edified. The Greek word *idiotes* (14:16, 23, 24) (from which the English word *idiot* comes) meant someone excluded, for one reason or another, from any specific group of people, e.g. the civilian as opposed to the soldier, the uneducated man as opposed to the scholar, the private citizen as opposed to the public official. Paul is clearly using the word *idiotes* to denominate those in attendance at Christian worship services at Corinth who were unskilled in foreign languages, and had no miraculous way of translating the tongues. They could neither speak in foreign languages or translate. Thus they were the same as foreigners or "outsiders." Some commentators classify the "outsider" as one who is neither an "unbeliever" or a Christian, but a proselyte or a catechumen (learner). But the "outsider" is expected to be able to say "Amen" to any translated speech in a foreign tongue (14:16). Thus, it would appear, the "outsider" is a Christian, not ignorant, but outside the select group of Christians in the Corinthian congregation who had received special, miraculous gifts.

Any use of gifts that did not produce understanding for the whole congregation, might serve some selfish purpose for the gifted person but others are not edified. It would appear Paul disapproved of "private" use of speaking in tongues for the Corinthians. Such "private" use was selfish, childish, and, if indiscriminately used, produced the aura of insanity and foolishness. Speaking miraculously in a foreign language must communicate to the *minds* (Gr. *nous,* mind) of all present in the assembly, including the speaker, both the ungifted and the unbeliever. The tongues were to be translated into the languages of those present in the service.

The apostle had the miraculous gift of tongues in greater capacity than all the Corinthians together, but his counsel was (and his counsel would be apostolic doctrine) that five words spoken in a language all hearers could understand with their minds were worth more than ten thousand words unintelligible to the hearers, although spoken by direct miracle from God. The Greek word *katecheso* is translated "instruct" and is the word from which we get the English word *catechism*; it generally means "instruction in the fundamentals of a subject." God gave the infant church gifts for the sole purpose of instruction and edification (Eph. 4:11-16).

14:20-25 Immaturity Accentuated: Not only did the obsession for the spectacular gift of tongues-speaking (untranslated) show these Corinthians would abdicate intelligent communication, it also accentuated their spiritual immaturity (see I Cor. 3:1ff.). To speak in a language without translating, only for the speaker's glory, and to elevate egotism over "line upon line, precept upon precept" processes of instruction is not only immature, it is a sign of unbelief.

So Paul starts this paragraph with an admonition for the Corinthian Christians to "grow up"! They were not to have a child's "show-off" mentality. He *did* want them to be "infant-like" (Gr. *nepiazete*) in evil, but he wanted them at the same time, to be "mature" (Gr. *teleioi,* perfected, complete, matured, reach the goal) in *phresin,* mentality.

It is interesting that Paul quotes from the prophet Isaiah (14:21) and calls it "the law." He is emphasizing that prophecy in the Old Testament was just as authoritative as the law of Moses. But the significance of Isaiah's prophecy here is the context from which this prophecy came. Isaiah 28:11-12 comes from the prophet's reproach of his Hebrew contemporaries (750-700 B.C.) who *kept asking* for miraculous signs that Jehovah was going to deal with them in judgment as the prophets kept insisting he was. They were "unbelievers." The covenant people would not (except for a small remnant) accept the "line upon line, precept upon precept" teaching of the prophets. They scoffed at that kind of instruction as fit for babies. And they were angry that the prophets inferred they were babies. They considered themselves sophisticated and mature. God said, however, "You are wrong; line upon line, precept upon precept is not for babies, but for the mature. The spectacular is for babies, and I am going to show you something spectacular since that is the only way some of you will believe. I am going to deliver you into captivity and you will hear foreign languages. Your hearing foreign language will be evidence that the teachings of the prophets were for spiritual maturation." Isaiah was talking to "inside unbelievers" when he wrote to the Jews and that is precisely why Paul quotes Isaiah here. Isaiah was talking about spiritual maturity as opposed to childish "unbelief," and that is the very purpose Paul had in quoting it here to these childish, unbelieving Corinthian Christians.

There were two kinds of people in the Corinthian church. There were the believers who welcomed "line upon line" teaching. They believed the messages of the "prophets" and did not need continual miracles to remain steadfast in the faith. Then there were the "unbelievers" who had to have miracles at every public worship or they did not think they could maintain their faith. God was displeased even with the Old Dispensation people who put him to the test beyond what they should have (see I Cor. 10:9 and Exod. 17:7). Jesus called the Jews who kept on asking for miraculous signs, "an evil and adulterous generation" (see Matt. 12:39; 16:4). So, "tongues" were a *sign* for the immature, the "unbelievers," even the "unbelievers" within the membership of the church, as well as for unbelievers outside the membership. "Tongues" served as signs that there was a divine presence, that the one, true God was speaking to the world through the apostle's doctrine and the messengers of Christ's church.

But, if the whole church did nothing but speak in tongues, that would be as far as outsiders and unbelievers would get. *They would not be instructed*—only amazed. And, if the whole church did nothing but speak in tongues the outsider and unbeliever would probably say the tongues-speakers were all "out of their minds" (Gr. *mainesthe,* insane, out of control mentally). The outsiders and unbelievers would not be caused to worship God if the whole assembly spoke in tongues. Not even the miraculous really *converts* unbelievers without extensive, logical, direct, communication of the teachings of God. "Prophecy" makes believers out of unbelievers and edifies immature believers. Tongues were merely to signal the divine presence; "prophecy" (teaching) was for "outsiders" and "unbelievers" to convict them and cause them to humbly worship God and acknowledge God's presence in the church. The Corinthian church needed a lot less of the tongues (and these were miraculous tongues), and a lot more of the prophecy.

SECTION 3

Pefecting With Decorum and Decency (14:26-40)

26 What then, brethren? When you come together, each one has a hymn, a lesson, a revelation, a tongue, or an interpretation. Let all things be done for edification. 27 If any speak in a tongue, let there be only two or at most three, and each in turn; and let one interpret. 28 But if there is no one to interpret,

let each of them keep silence in church and speak to himself and to God. ²⁹Let two or three prophets speak, and let the others weigh what is said. ³⁰If a revelation is made to another sitting by, let the first be silent. ³¹For you can all prophesy one by one, so that all may learn and all be encouraged; ³²and the spirits of prophets are subjects to prophets. ³³For God is not a God of confusion but of peace.

As in all the churches of the saints, ³⁴the women should keep silence in the churches. For they are not permitted to speak, but should be subordinate, as even the law says. ³⁵If there is anything they desire to know, let them ask their husbands at home. For it is shameful for a woman to speak in church. ³⁶What! Did the word of God originate with you, or are you the only ones it has reached?

37 If any one thinks that he is a prophet, or spiritual, he should acknowledge that what I am writing to you is a command of the Lord. ³⁸If any one does not recognize this, he is not recognized. ³⁹So, my brethren, earnestly desire to prophesy, and do not forbid speaking in tongues; ⁴⁰but all things should be done decently and in order.

14:26-33a Decorum: If the Corinthian church (or any church in any age) was to ever reach maturity, or perfection (reach the goal God had for it), it would have to bring order out of the confusion caused by the childish attitudes and practices with miraculous gifts. Paul sets forth specific "rules" of conduct to be followed for this problem of the Corinthian church of the first century. These are not, specifically, rules for the church today since miraculous gifts no longer exist. However, the principle teaching, that *all* things should be done decently and in order in the church, still applies. Therefore, there is much for us to learn from this section.

The idiomatic phrase, "What then, brethren?" is much like the modern phrase in English, "How about it, then, folks?" Paul is saying, "This, then, is the way it is to be when you meet in your Christian assemblies." He recognized that there would be a multitude of people with gifts all at the same gathering. He also realized that a person with a miraculous gift could hardly be asked *never* to use it. After all, God would not give any gift, miraculous or non-miraculous, and forbid its use. God would certainly want it to be used. But the controlling principle for use of all gifts was, "Let *all* things be done for edification." These are the apostolic rules:

CHAPTER 14   FIRST CORINTHIANS 14:26-40

1. If any are to speak miraculously, in a foreign language, there must be only two, or at most three, *and each in turn* (Gr. *kai ana meros,* the word *meros,* means, to divide up, to allot, to distribute). One at a time!
2. Those with the gift of "tongues" were permitted to speak *only* if they knew there was a *translator* (Gr. *hermeneuto*) present. If there was no translator present, they were to keep silent! Any so-called "private" exercise would be misuse.
3. If any prophesied, only two or three were to prophesy. And, they were told, prophesying would be each in turn—*one at a time,* (14:30-31).
4. Those with the gift of "prophecy" were to exercise their gift only when there were "others" present to *discern* (Gr. *diakrinetosan,* the word from which the English words, critique, criticize, critic, meaning, "to judge, to discriminate, to decide"). The "discerners" had the miraculous power to *decide* (not interpret) whether a prophet spoke from God or not.
5. Evidently, no one prophet had all the truth to proclaim. One by one they were to teach at each corporate assembly of the church. And *all,* even those who taught, were to do some learning at one time or another (14:31).
6. All gifts were to be kept under these controls, for the spirits of the prophets are subject to the prophets (and so were the spirits of the language-speakers). Every apostolic command here by Paul presupposes that these gifts could be, and were to be, exercised under their *control.* Paul would not have insisted on the gifts being exercised by only two or three, and one at a time, had they not been controllable. No tongues-speaker, or prophet, was to jump up and begin to exercise a gift when another was doing so. No one was to claim he could not help himself—that it was the Holy Spirit forcing him to exercise his gift. *These gifts were not exercised spontaneously!*

    God would never produce disorder and confusion! God brings order out of chaos. God does not produce fragmentation—he creates wholeness. The Greek word *akatastasia,* translated, *confusion,* means, "instability, anarchy, revolution," and from it we get the English words, *catastasis, catastrophe,* and *catatonia.*

FIRST CORINTHIANS

The church today, though not possessing miraculous gifts, will do well to learn a lesson from the fundamental principle Paul teaches here. The principle is decorum, orderliness. Worship does not, in fact should not, have to be *spontaneous,* to be worship! Of course, worship must come from the heart. And, simply following a regimen of worship ceremonies does not insure that worship is being done. But neither does spontaneity! Paul is saying to these Corinthians (and to all Christians) that God is not pleased with any worship service that is disorderly and confusing. The worship of God must be intelligent, instructive, maturing, and orderly (according to a design, with regularity). If spontaneity must suffer, then let it suffer. This is true of "youth sessions" as much, or more, than "adult sessions." How can Christians learn to "order" their lives if they are taught that the worship of God is some exercise in spontaneity, impulsiveness, and confusion?

14:33b-40 Decency: Is it indecent for a woman to speak in church? The instruction concerning women in the public assembly, in this context, must have involved the misuse of miraculous gifts. We really do not know what the problem was, specifically, but it was probably one of the following situations:

a. either some women had miraculous gifts and were using them publicly which, in that culture especially, was an indecent usurpation of male leadership in the public assemblies; the dignity of man and woman is preserved only if the place God has ordained for each is maintained (see our comments in I Cor. 11:1ff.).

b. or, some women, who did not have miraculous gifts, were prodding and agitating their husbands or others who did have gifts to use them contrary to the apostolic guidelines; this also was indecent behavior for women.

c. or, some women who did not have miraculous gifts were insisting they were going to teach in the public assemblies without gifts.

The *point* is, even had there been women in the Corinthian church with miraculous gifts, they were not to exercise them in the public assemblies. This certainly is *not* the case with most of the so-called "charismatic" assemblies in modern times.

The apostle reiterates a teaching he has made in other places in the New Testament. He says, ". . . women should be subordinate, as even the law says." The Greek same word *hupotassesthosan* (be subject, subordinate) is used in Ephesians 5:21ff. and in Colossians 3:18.

CHAPTER 14   FIRST CORINTHIANS 14:26-40

The woman was created by God *subordinate* to her husband. Male chauvinism has nothing to do with it—it is divinely ordained.

Paul anticipated there would be those who would not agree with his teaching about women in the public assembly, but he reminded them that the word of God did not originate with them, nor did it come to them alone. Actually, Paul says, "Did the word of God *go forth from you* . . . or are you the only people who have and know the word of God?" The Greek word is *exelthen,* "go forth." In other words, the word of God is not subject to the whims of the Corinthians—the Corinthians are to be subject to the word of God.

Furthermore, Paul speaks the word of God. Any member of the Corinthian church who would disobey the apostle's instructions about the use and misuse of miraculous gifts in this letter is not possessed of God's truth, nor is he spiritually-minded. This warning is as relevant for the church today as it was for the first century church.

When all is said and done, it comes down to this: "Earnestly desire to prophesy," because that is what converts and edifies. "But do not forbid anyone who has the miraculous gift of speaking in a foreign language to do so" for God had a purpose for the exercise of all the miraculous gifts. "But let *all* things be done decently and in order." The word *decently* is a translation of the Greek word *euschemonos,* and means literally, "well-schematized," or, "with good schematics." Any worship of God that does not follow God's schematic (plan, blueprint, order, arrangement) is *not decent!* The words *in order* are translated from the Greek words, *kata taxin*; the word *taxin* is related to the Greek word *tagma,* and both are used to signify "to arrange something in order, especially in a military order." It would not, therefore, be altogether unscriptural to say that the worship of God in the church's corporate assemblies, should be *regimented*!

We believe the apostolic doctrine concerning miraculous gifts is clearly set forth in these three chapters (I Cor. 12-13-14). We believe all Christians, using accepted hermeneutical rules, should understand this teaching alike. But we also acknowledge that as long as some accept what they believe they have experienced in the place of understanding what Paul teaches here, there will continue to be division among Christians, just as there was nearly two thousand years ago, when Paul wrote to the brethren at Corinth.

A quotation from Seth Wilson, Dean Emeritus of Ozark Bible College, is in order here. Dean Wilson has spent nearly fifty years researching this subject and counseling individuals and congregations who are "plagued by this problem."

FIRST CORINTHIANS

The tongues-speaker (modern-day) who says, "You cannot understand or give any true judgment about a gift from God which you have not experienced and do not believe in," is saying, in effect, that it is not subject to critical examination in the light of Scripture. An error which grows out of this is the belief that one cannot understand the Bible unless he has been "baptized in the Holy Spirit." To say that only the believer in the tongues experience is qualified to comment on it begs the question, supposes that it is always from God, and puts the subjective (inward and personal feeling) above the Scripture as a source of truth. This takes the attitude that tongues speaking is something that is beyond the realm of reasonable evidence or factual investigation.

—*from an unpublished essay on the Holy Spirit by Seth Wilson*

APPLICATIONS:

1. The attitude of the Corinthians toward miraculous gifts shows conclusively that possession of miraculous powers, *per se,* does not produce holiness or Christian maturity.
2. It is possible to have a miraculous gift and be carnally-minded.
3. Teaching the word of God (in Corinth, by "prophecy" since there was as yet no completed New Testament scripture) in understandable human language is to be preferred above every other exercise in the church.
4. Edification, maturation, is the goal of everything God does through members of the body of Christ.
5. God wants Christians to be mature in their thinking and reasoning.
6. Self-glorification is childish and forbidden in Christians.
7. God demands order and planning in the corporate assembly of the Church—and in private worship, too, we might add.
8. No personal experience, miraculous or non-miraculous, can be a substitute for obedience to the apostolic word.
9. A thorough study of this chapter (using proper hermeneutical principles) shows conclusively that modern, pseudo-miraculous gifts, do not fit the apostolic revelation concerning miraculous gifts.

CHAPTER 14   FIRST CORINTHIANS 14:26-40

APPREHENSIONS:

1. Is the word "gifts" in 14:1? What does its absence probably indicate?
2. Why did Paul emphasize seeking the gift of prophecy?
3. Does it not seem in 14:4 Paul is rebuking (mildly) some of the Corinthians for seeking to "edify" only themselves by using the gift of tongues without interpretation? Why would we reach that conclusion?
4. Why would using a miraculous gift only for oneself be wrong?
5. How do we know Paul is talking about human languages, knowable languages, when he says "tongues"? (14:10)
6. Why were the gifts given to the Corinthians? (12:7; 14:5; 14:12; 14:19; 14:26)
7. Did the possession of a miraculous gift mean the possessor's own abilities to think and reason were suspended in the exercise of the gift? (14:13-19)
8. Are Christians supposed to think? Like mature adults? (14:20)
9. Why does Paul quote from Isaiah 28:11-12 in this discussion of "tongues"?
10. Who is the "outsider"? Who is the "unbeliever" in Corinth?
11. Which was better for the outsider and unbeliever to experience in the congregation at Corinth—"tongues" or "prophecy"? Why?
12. Did Paul give "rules" for the use of miraculous gifts? Name the rules!
13. Why did Paul address the subject of women speaking in the church here? What does he say about it in chapter 11?
14. What is the Greek word which is translated "decency"?
15. Is Paul's emphatic statement about the church's need to follow planned, regimented worship relevant for the church today? How? or why?

Chapter Fifteen

THE PROBLEM OF THE RESURRECTION (15:1-58)

IDEAS TO INVESTIGATE:

1. In accordance with what "scripture" did Christ die and arise from the dead?
2. When did the resurrected Christ appear to five hundred brethren at once?
3. Is it the death of Christ, or the resurrection of Christ, that takes away sin?
4. Are there different "orders" of being resurrected from the dead?
5. What is "being baptized on behalf of the dead"?
6. What kind of body will believers have after the resurrection?

SECTION 1

Its Historicity (15:1-11)

15 Now I would remind you brethren, in what terms I preached to you the gospel, which you received, in which also you stand, ²by which also you are saved, if you hold it fast—unless you believed in vain.

3 For I delivered to you as of first importance what I also received, that Christ died for our sins in accordance with the scriptures, ⁴that he was buried, that he was raised on the third day in accordance with the scriptures, ⁵and that he appeared to Cephas, then to the twelve. ⁶Then he appeared to more than five hundred brethren at one time, most of whom are still alive, though some have fallen asleep. ⁷Then he appeared to James, then to all the apostles. ⁸Last of all, as to one untimely born, he appeared also to me. ⁹For I am the least of the apostles, unfit to be called an apostle, because I persecuted the church of God. ¹⁰But by the grace of God I am what I am, and his grace toward me was not in vain. On the contrary, I worked harder than any of them, though it was not I, but the grace of God which is with me. ¹¹Whether then it was I or they, so we preach and so you believed.

15:1-2 Existentialism: This chapter clearly shows that some of the Corinthians were dealing with the gospel existentially. Some of them

CHAPTER 15   FIRST CORINTHIANS 15:1-11

had gotten the idea (perhaps from some Gnostics) that the source of the gospel was in *their* feelings, opinions and decisions. Paul warned them in 14:36, "Did the word of God originate with you, or are you the only ones it has reached?" They were looking upon the gospel *not* as a *revelation* of the truth they had *received* (15:1-2), *not* as something that had *objectivity* in itself outside of them, but as something they could invent or decide to suit their own carnal desires. There were some who were teaching (see comments 15:33) there was no resurrection of the dead (15:12) and that Christianity was for this world only, just like other religions.

Existentialism is a philosophical revolt against objectivity. It is rooted in introspection, subjectivism, and focuses entirely on the experiential. It determines the worth of knowledge not in relation to objective fact and revealed truth, but according to the value determined by the autonomous (self-ruled) consciousness of the individual human being. In other words, everything is valuable only in relation to what each individual feels or decides about it. And the individual's decision is based on that individual's feelings. Feelings are the only criteria for decision. Existentialism is the ultimate relativism. Each individual is his or her own "absolute." One individual must never let another individual decide for him, nor must he use another individual's feelings for his choice. Truth, for the existentialist, "becomes" at any given moment whatever he decides it is to him. It is in this self-sovereign determination of truth that the individual allegedly finds his existence. Existentialism is a philosophy as old as man. Centuries before Christ, Greek philosophers were expounding forms of existentialism. It is also as common as "Main Street, America." It is the philosophy of the masses, whether they know it or not, and is expressed in such phrases as, "Whatever turns you on!" or "Everybody ought to do their own thing," or "I know what I feel, regardless of what the Bible says." The existential theologian usually approaches Christianity with an "orthodox" vocabulary, but his terms have meanings different than what would be expected. Since, for the existentialist, nothing can be true unless he has personally felt it, experienced it, and decided it, he says: (a) God could not be God and be human, so God is "wholly other" and, therefore, a divine-incarnation could not have actually occurred. Since the supernatural cannot be incarnated, wherever the Gospels say Jesus did something miraculous, we must understand it as a Christian accommodation of pagan mythology; (b) there is Christian resurrection, but this is merely

FIRST CORINTHIANS

a subjective resurrection of the Jesus-faith in my feelings, and only when I decide it has happened; (c) Heaven is something I feel in my personal Christian experience; it is not an objective place.

It will be apparent as we study this chapter that the Corinthians had been taught a somewhat existential approach to the resurrection of the dead. Paul wants them to understand clearly that the Gospel was something which he *delivered* to them; they did not have it within themselves. The origin of the Gospel had nothing to do with their feelings or autonomous decisions. While they would be responsible to decide for themselves what to *do* about the logical, spiritual and moral demands of the Gospel, their decisions would not determine whether the events had happened or not. The gospel is a fact whether men decide it is, or not. The gospel originated in a Person (Christ) and in deeds he did which were prophesied long before in "the scriptures." There are *clues* all the way through this epistle to substantiate the proposition that the Corinthians were taking an existential approach to the gospel: (1) their decision to follow certain teachers based on their own feelings, chapter 1; (2) their toying with the idea that the doctrine of the "cross" was foolishness; (3) their inability to accept the idea of "revelation" in human words, chapter 2; (4) their constant infatuation with the spectacular, ego-inflating miraculous gifts, chapters 12-14; (5) their humanistic skepticism concerning the nature of a resurrected body, chapter 15:35ff.

Paul is going to remind them (in chapter 15) of the "gospel which he gospelized" (Gr. *euangelion ho euengelisamen humin*) to them. He is going to remind them "with what word" (Gr. *tini logo*), or "in what form," or "in what terms" he had preached the gospel to them. They had *received* the gospel on the terms (or, "in the form") of its *historicity*. But now they were doubting. Now they were approaching it existentially, subjectively. Their steadfastness in the faith, indeed, their salvation, is conditioned upon their holding fast (Gr. *ei katechete,* if you hold fast) the gospel in the precise terms it was preached to them. Those terms were its *empirical historicity.* Paul reflects that the Corinthians might have believed his initial message of the gospel to them in a haphazard way. The Greek word *eike* is translated "in vain"; it does not mean "without cause" but "without due consideration, rashly, superficially." Did the Corinthians first believe the gospel by some shallow enthusiasm or through some passing fancy for a new thing? Did they not give serious thought when they embraced the gospel? There are people today whose allegiance to Christ has been made without regard to "the terms" or the

CHAPTER 15 — FIRST CORINTHIANS 15:1-11

form of the gospel. One's emotional attachment to Jesus must be preceded by and controlled by a constant reception of the gospel, mentally, in both its form and its substance. A hasty experiential and existential attachment to Jesus is vulnerable to the vacillation of feelings and circumstances. Such an attachment cannot produce steadfastness nor can it save. It is important to take note of the word "if" in 15:2. Salvation is free—but salvation is conditioned upon man's holding to the gospel in its apostolic form. The Greek word *katechete* means, "to have and to hold as in marriage," "to be affected by, subjected to, to seize, to possess." Man's response to the free gift of salvation demands more than a superficial fancy or whim. It is a life and death commitment; an eternal allegiance.

15:3-4 Empirical: Paul delivered to the Corinthians the *fundamental essence* (Gr. *protois,* "first things") of the gospel. That fundamental essence is the death, burial and resurrection of Jesus Christ. He wants the Corinthians to remember he preached, and they believed, that the resurrection of Jesus Christ was a matter of empirical history. At Corinth Paul "persuaded" and "taught" the gospel a year and a half (Acts 18:1-11). His proof of the gospel was empirical, logical, and historical. This is where the gospel begins. This is its basis. The death, burial and resurrection of Jesus Christ happened whether men wish it had or not, whether men decide it has or not. Christ arose whether men love it or despise it, and nothing can ever erase it from history. Men may accept or reject its moral imperatives, but they cannot "feel" it or "decide" it out of existence. In the same way, men "deliberately ignore the fact" of a world-wide flood (II Peter 3:3-7), but they cannot ignore the fossil evidence out of existence.

Our faith in Jesus Christ rests solely on the historicity of his resurrection, for if that is not an empirical fact, everything else he claimed, and is claimed for him, is open to suspicion of deliberate fraud or ignorant mythology. And, whether he rose from the dead or not rests solely upon the authenticity, credibility, and accuracy of the texts of the Bible. The gospel is not true because it works; *it works because it is true!*

Simon Greenleaf (1783-1853), one of the greatest legal minds in U.S. history, former head of the Harvard Law School, set forth the following rules of evidence in his book, *The Testimony of The Evangelists,* pub. Baker Book House, pp. 1-54:

1. The foundation of Christianity is based on facts. These facts are testified to as having occurred within the personal knowledge

of the Gospel writers. Christianity, then, rests upon the credibility of these witnesses.

2. A proposition of fact is proved, when its truth is established by competent and satisfactory evidence beyond reasonable doubt.
3. In the absence of circumstances which generate suspicion, every witness is to be presumed to be credible, until the contrary is shown . . . The burden of impeaching his credibility lies upon the objector.
4. All witnesses are entitled to the benefit of the axiom that men ordinarily speak the truth (are honest) when they have no prevailing motive or inducement to the contrary.
5. The ability of a witness to speak the truth depends on the opportunities he has had for observing the facts, the accuracy of his powers of observing and the trustworthiness of his memory. The authors of the Gospels can be granted at least the abilities of most human witnesses until the contrary is shown.
6. There must be enough disparity in the number and consistency of the witnesses to show there is no room for collusion, yet enough agreement to show they were independent recorders of the same events.
7. The testimony of the witnesses must conform in general with the experiences of others concerning similar circumstances or subject matter.

The four Gospels are accurate records. Any honest researcher should declare their compliance with the accepted "rules of evidence" unimpeachable. As authentic, competent, credible works of history, the four Gospels are impeccable.

Paul's reference to Christ's death, burial and resurrection, "in accordance with the scriptures" is significant. He means that the fundamental facts of the gospel, the death, burial and resurrection of Jesus Christ, were predicted in the Old Testament scriptures. That is a presentation of evidence which can be tested scientifically, or legally, at any time, by anyone who is honest enough to forego personal presuppositions. Prophecies made centuries before their fulfillment, the fulfillment of which is documented in minute detail, and in which factors of their fulfillment is beyond the power of human planning or manipulation, are sufficient evidence to prove the proposition that Jesus is the Christ, or no proposition can ever be proved! Blaise

CHAPTER 15　　　　　　　　　FIRST CORINTHIANS 15:1-11

Pascal, one of the greatest scientific minds of all time, wrote these meaningful words: "The greatest of the proofs of Jesus Christ are the prophecies. They are also what God has most provided for, for the event which has fulfilled them is a miracle of God." The betrayal and trial of Jesus of Nazareth is predicted in Isaiah 53:7; Zech. 11:12-13; 13:7. His death is predicted in Isa. 53:4-9; Zech. 12:10; Ps. 22:16). Even his dying words were foretold (Ps. 22:1ff.; 31:5). His burial in a rich man's tomb was predicted (Isa. 53:9). His resurrection was predicted (see Isa. 53:10-12; Ps. 16:10-11; Acts 2:25-32; 13:33-35). There are over 300 prophecies concerning the Messiah, including the exact village of his birth, the exact year of his birth, the miraculous nature of his brith, all the main events of his life and ministry. If these were not fulfilled in Jesus of Nazareth, in whom were they fulfilled?—Alexander the Great? Julius Caesar? Winston Churchill? Most of these prophecies about the Messiah were not fulfilled by the friends of Jesus, nor even by Jesus himself, but by his enemies or disinterested parties! There was no collusion between Jesus and his friends to fulfill these prophecies. The Old Testament canon of scripture was already set and well known by the Jews hundreds of years before Jesus was born and for any man to have changed them or altered them to fit the life of Jesus, after the fact, would have required so many things out of the ordinary in the way of favorable circumstances, miracles would have been demanded. To fulfill these prophecies without supernatural ability to anticipate human behavior and natural circumstances would be impossible! The apostle Peter declares that the fulfillment of prophecy is a surer proof of the deity of Christ and the infallibility of the scriptures than what he had witnessed with his own eyes! (cf. II Peter 1:16-19). This may be why Paul introduced prophetic evidence of Jesus' resurrection before introducing the evidence of eyewitnesses! Jesus expected prophetic evidence to take precedence over what people saw with their eyes (see Luke 24:25ff.)!

15:5-11 Eyewitnessed: Paul appeals to eyewitnessed testimony to establish the fact of the resurrection of Christ. "To establish the historicity of the facts of Christianity, nothing more is demanded than is readily conceded to every branch of human science. Christianity does not profess to convince the perverse and headstrong, to bring irresistible evidence, to vanquish every question. All it professes is to propose such evidence as may satisfy the disciplined, teachable, honest, serious searcher." Simon Greenleaf, *op. cit.*, p. 2.

FIRST CORINTHIANS

The question, therefore, before the Corinthians was, could they believe the testimony of the eyewitnesses named by the apostle Paul: (1) were those people Paul named competent witnesses—were they capable of having seen Jesus crucified, buried, and risen from the dead? were they in a position to have known the facts? were they so credulous they would have believed anything? Their records (the Gospels) candidly portray one another as incredulous, "of little faith," "unbelieving," even skeptical; (2) were the eyewitnesses people who would lie? were they honest or dishonest? did they have anything to gain by lying about the events they said they witnessed? did they have anything to gain by fabricating the events recorded in the Gospels? The gospel, in the form they proclaimed it, brought them no power, no riches, no accolades from the mighty—only persecution, slander, poverty and death—yet they went to their death insisting on its historicity; (3) were the eyewitnesses so few as to give reasonable doubt to their testimony? There were the women, the eleven apostles in a group, ten apostles in a group, Peter and James individually, over five hundred brethren at one time, and the guards at the tomb and their superiors (Matt. 28:11-15); (4) was there any empirical, historical, scientific evidence to the contrary? has any evidence come to light for the last two thousand years to contradict the Gospels? did anyone present the dead body of Jesus to prove he had not arisen? did anyone show his dead body in the tomb after the third day of his burial? The surest way for the enemies of Christianity to have destroyed it would have been to present the dead body of Jesus at the time the apostles began to preach his resurrection (Acts 2:1ff.). The only record we have of the response made to the preaching of the resurrection of Jesus Christ (Acts and Epistles of the New Testament) is that the enemies of Christianity slandered, persecuted and killed its proclaimers. The enemies offered not one iota of scientific, historical evidence to refute the gospel. There have been many *theories* over the centuries, suggesting alternatives to accepting Christ's resurrection as a fact; *but there has been no evidence*! The reader is here urged to add to this a thorough study of *The Gospel of Luke*, by Paul T. Butler, College Press Publishing Company, pp. 476-605.

Finally, Paul lists *himself* as an eyewitness to the fact of Jesus' resurrection (15:8-11). He was not with the other eleven apostles during the forty days Jesus appeared to them in his resurrected body (Acts 1:3). But Paul *saw* the Lord (Acts 9:27; 26:16, 19; I Cor. 9:1). Jesus appeared to him some years later as he journeyed on

CHAPTER 15   FIRST CORINTHIANS 15:12-34

the road to Damascus. If ever there was a person set against the proposition that Jesus of Nazareth arose from the dead it would be Paul (formerly called, Saul of Tarsus)! If ever there was a person who would have demanded visible, empirical evidence before becoming a believer in Jesus, it would have been Paul! He was thoroughly convinced to do everything he could to oppose Jesus of Nazareth and Christianity (see Acts 22:3-5; 26:9-11). In all good conscience, he actually believed he was serving God by opposing Christ and executing Christ's followers (see I Tim. 1:13). If ever there was a person with the best opportunities and capabilities to *prove* that Jesus of Nazareth had *not* arisen from the tomb, it would be Paul! So, how do we account for the greatest enemy Jesus and the Church ever had, becoming the greatest apostle, persuader of others, and missionary the Church ever had? And the list of enemies converted does not stop with Saul of Tarsus (Paul). Three thousand Jews on the Day of Pentecost, some of whom had probably been at Passover, crying, "Crucify him, crucify him," were converted (Acts 2:1ff.). A great company of Hebrew priests became obedient to the faith (Acts 6:7). Some of Caesar's Praetorian Guard probably became Christians (Phil. 1:13) and some of Caesar's own "household" were converted (Phil. 4:22)! If there had been any good evidence to contradict the resurrection of Jesus Christ, some of these people would have *known* it and would have *brought it forward* for the whole world of that day to acknowledge.

Any person today who says Jesus of Nazareth was not raised from the dead is obligated to produce proof. It is the burden of the unbeliever to produce evidence. It must be historical, empirical, scientific evidence. He must produce authentic, accurate, credible eyewitnesses with evidence. Theories will not do! Christians believe on the basis of the written documents of those who saw, heard and touched the resurrected Jesus (I John 1:1-4). The argument is not *whether* a resurrection *could* or *could not* occur. The case in point is, *did* a resurrection occur or *did it not*. The case is not to be resolved philosophically, but historically, legally, on the basis of evidence and testimony. The answer is, YES! beyond any reasonable doubt!

SECTION 2

Its Holiness (15:12-34)

    12 Now if Christ is preached as raised from the dead, how can some of you say that there is no resurrection of the dead?

FIRST CORINTHIANS

13 But if there is no resurrection of the dead, then Christ has not been raised; 14 if Christ has not been raised, then our preaching is in vain and your faith is in vain. 15 We are even found to be misrepresenting God, because we testified of God that he raised Christ, whom he did not raise if it is true that the dead are not raised. 16 For if the dead are not raised, then Christ has not been raised. 17 If Christ has not been raised, your faith is futile and you are still in your sins. 18 Then those also who have fallen asleep in Christ have perished. 19 If for this life only we have hoped in Christ, we are of all men most to be pitied.

20 But in fact Christ has been raised from the dead, the first fruits of those who have fallen asleep. 21 For as by a man came death, by a man has come also the resurrection of the dead. 22 For as in Adam all die, so also in Christ shall we be made alive. 23 But each in his own order: Christ the first fruits, then at his coming those who belong to Christ. 24 Then comes the end, when he delivers the kingdom of God the Father after destroying every rule and every authority and power. 25 For he must reign until he has put all his enemies under his feet. 26 The last enemy to be destroyed is death. 27 "For God has put all things in subjection under his feet." But when it says, "All things are put in subjection under him," it is plain that he is excepted who put all things under him. 28 When all things are subjected to him, then the Son himself will also be subjected to him who put all things under him, that God may be everything to every one.

29 Otherwise, what do people mean by being baptized on behalf of the dead? If the dead are not raised at all, why are people baptized on their behalf? 30 Why am I in peril every hour? 31 I protest, brethren, by my pride in you which I have in Christ Jesus our Lord, I die every day! 32 What do I gain if, humanly speaking, I fought with beasts at Ephesus? If the dead are not raised, "Let us eat and drink, for tomorrow we die." 33 Do not be deceived: "Bad company ruins good morals." 34 Come to your right mind, and sin no more. For some have no knowledge of God. I say this to your shame.

15:12-19 Cleanses From Defilement: Paul asks, "If I am preaching Christ as raised from the dead, what do some of you expect to gain by saying there is no resurrection for believers?" He proceeds to

CHAPTER 15 — FIRST CORINTHIANS 15:12-34

answer his own rhetorical question by saying, in essence, "You can't have the hope if you don't have the history!" If Christ was not raised from the dead, then hoping in him for anything else is vain. If Christ is not raised, and if there is no resurrection for those who trust in Christ, then the whole Christian religion is in vain.

First, apostolic preaching would be vain if there is no resurrection. All Christian preaching for two hundred centuries would be vain if Christ is not historically, actually, factually raised from the dead. Why, then, do men who do not believe the historical resurrection of Christ preach the Christian religion? For money (Jesus predicted there would be hirelings, John 10:10-13; Paul predicted there would be some from among the "Christian" religion who would exploit it, Acts 20:29-30); for position or fame—there are those who love the praise of men more than the praise of God. There are some who do not want the moral implications which the historical resurrection of Jesus would force upon them, but they want the "Christian religion" to try to *soften* by euphemistic (but useless) verbiage the cruel, stark, reality of injustices never to be righted, of tribulations and sacrifices never to be repaid or vindicated, to soften the utter defeat of human death. An existential philosopher said, and without the resurrection he is correct, "Life is never more absurd than at the grave." But, hallelujah, because of the fact of the resurrection life is never absurd!

Second, all faith would be void without the resurrection. Faith in God, Christ, the Bible, faith that truth is better than falsehood, faith that goodness and love is to be preferred over evil and hate, faith in today and tomorrow, faith that life is worth living—all is useless if there is no life beyond the grave, no heaven, no eternity, no truth, no God. The apostles were false witnesses, the most despicable charlatans or ignorant dupes who ever lived, if the resurrection of Christ is not historically valid. But are we to believe they have gotten by with such a monstrous hoax, having duped millions of the best minds for almost two millenniums? Could what their testimony produced for all these centuries have been produced by the cruelest, most preposterous lie ever perpetrated upon the human race?

Third, and *most crucial,* if Christ has not been raised, those who have believed in him are not forgiven—they are still *in* their sins. The cross, the vicarious, substitutionary atonement of Christ's death, is invalid without the resurrection. The only hope we have that Christ did what he promised to do by the cross is his resurrection (see II Cor.

1:20; I Peter 1:3-5; Luke 24:44-48). If Christ's promise of atonement for man's sin is not validated by his resurrection from the dead, he is simply another crucified Jew, and his death has not as much efficacy to atone for my sins as an animal sacrifice. Study the sermons of the apostles and evangelists in the book of Acts. They did not wait until the "annual Easter services" to proclaim the resurrection. They never preached the death of Christ without preaching his resurrection! Too much modern preaching is depending upon the sentimentalism aroused by portraying the shocking violence of Jesus' death. The mental decisiveness brought about by the persuading evidence of the resurrection, without which there is no true conversion, is seldom made the focus of either edificatory or evangelistic proclamation. If we are going to restore the church of the New Testament, we must restore the *gospel* of the New Testament!

If Christ is not raised, then those who have "fallen asleep" (died) have *perished*. Are we to believe that all the millions of Christians who have poured out their lives upon the altars of love, usefulness and goodness have *perished* and will not be raised from the dead? That includes some of my very dear ones, and yours! Will faith, and love, and goodness perish, and wickedness, falsehood and dissolution win, after all? Is there no wiping out of defilement? No forgiveness of sin? No vindication of faith? Without the resurrection there is none!

If a man's hope in Christ and his teachings is to be restricted to this life on earth only, he is, of all men, most pitiful. The word *eleeinoteroi,* from the Greek word *eleos* (mercy, pity), is translated in the KJV as "miserable." It means, "to be pitied." If this life is all there is, Christians are pitiful fools to be hoping in Christ. They would be better off to abandon the teachings of Jesus which insist on "counting others better than self," or "turning the other cheek," or "not pleasing oneself, but pleasing one's neighbor, for his good," or giving up one's liberty and rights for the sake of others. If this life is all there is, people would be better off following Buddha or Mohammed, or Darwin or Marx, or no one! Certainly, if there is no resurrection, and Christ is not who he claims he is, and this is all the life there is, those who still maintain allegiance to the Christian faith are either "putting us on" or self-deceived, living in a dream world of their own creation; see Special Study entitled, "On Cloud Nine."

15:20-28 Conquers Dissolution: This is *not* the only life there is! Christ has, in fact, been raised from the dead. He is the "firstfruit" of resurrection from the dead. The Bible record documents the fact that there were persons resurrected from death, chronologically, before Jesus. In fact, Jesus raised three people (Jairus' daughter; the widow's son at Nain; and Lazarus) before his own resurrection took place. But Paul is not speaking chronologically here, unless he is denoting the uniqueness of Christ's resurrection over those preceding his. All others resurrected from death died again. Their bodies have suffered the same decay and dissolution all other human bodies suffer. But when Jesus rose from the grave, he did not die again. He ascended, after forty days, to heaven in the body which came out of the tomb. The apostles were eye witnesses to this ascension (Acts 1:9-11). From heaven Jesus has appeared to some (Paul, John). But Paul's figure of speech "firstfruit" (Gr. *aparche,* akin to *aparchomai* which means, "to make a beginning") is from Old Testament times. In the Law of Moses the first portion of the harvest was to be given to the Lord as an indication the worshiper understood that *all* the harvest was, in reality, the Lord's (Deut. 26:2-11). Whatever "firstfruit" was, the rest of the harvest was. Christ's resurrection was "firstfruit" of all the dead. Adam was, because of his sin, "firstfruit" of the death of humanity; Christ was, because of his sinlessness, "firstfruit" of the resurrection of humanity. All mankind dies bodily because of Adam's sin; all mankind is to be resurrected bodily because of Christ's victory over sin. That is all Paul is saying here. He is not teaching "original sin" and "total depravity," and he is not teaching "universal salvation." All creation, man and matter, belongs to God. He will resurrect it all. Temporarily, God has subjected all his creation to futility, hoping it will hope, and one day be set free from its bondage to decay (Rom. 8:18-25). But only those who trust Christ as their "firstfruit" will be adopted as sons. *All* of dead humanity will be resurrected, but only those who have trusted Christ will be given eternal life; those who have not trusted Christ will be imprisoned forever in torment (see John 5:25-28; Luke 16:19-31; Rev. 14:9-13; Rev. 20:11—22:5).

"Each in his own order" does not mean there are going to be two or three increments to the resurrection of humanity, separated by time. Paul clears up any misunderstanding about that in his epistle to the Thessalonians (I Thess. 4:13—5:3). When Jesus comes again to resurrect humanity, it will be one complete, final resurrection. No segment of humanity, physically alive or dead, will "precede" the other. Paul uses the Greek word *tagmati* in 15:23 and it is translated "order." *Tagma* is a Greek military term meaning "a rank, a company, a group." Paul explains what he means by "order" in the last half of verse 23. Christ's resurrection *ranks* first and is "firstfruit"—then, at his second coming, the *second ranking* resurrection of the whole harvest of humanity, including those who belong to him. It is *rank* of resurrection emphasized, not chronology, to *prove* there will be a second rank because there was a first.

At Christ's coming is the end. The KJV italicizes the word *cometh* in verse 24, indicating it is a supplied word. And that is more to be desired than the RSV translation which is: "Then comes the end...." The Greek text is: *eita to telos,* literally, "then, the end." Christ's second coming and the end are *simultaneous.* God's redemptive program will find its *telos,* its goal, its completion, when Jesus comes to resurrect all the dead. Then will come to an end this world and all its powers. There will be no more pretending powers, no more powers temporarily granted by God to human beings. God alone will exercise sovereignty. All others will be willing servants, or banished, incarcerated enemies. In the meantime the Son reigns until he has established all that God has spoken by the mouths of his prophets (see Acts 3:17-26), both Old and New Testament prophets. The Bible clearly teaches that no human being is going to know when Christ is coming back (see our comments, *The Gospel of Luke,* College Press Publishing Company, pp. 467-519). How long Christ will take to "put all his enemies under his feet," and who those "enemies" are, we do not know. But the fact of his resurrection makes it *certain* that day will come (see Acts 17:30-31). The last "enemy" is death (cf. Rev. 20:9-15). Death will be *abolished* (Gr. *katargeitai,* "destroyed")—it will not exist anymore.

God has subjected this world and all creation to the Son (Christ) (John 5:19-29) in order that the Son might carry out his redemptive and mediatorial work. This work began with his incarnation and continues through his high priesthood (cf. the book of Hebrews). But when the Son finishes this work and returns to consummate redemption and judgment, there will be no more need for mediation. The person of Son will be the person of eternal Father, that God may be everything to every one.

15:29-34 Conserves Decency: Only by the power of faith in the resurrection will man be able to preserve moral goodness. Only those who hope to be welcomed to heaven and become as Jesus is will have the power to desire holiness (I John 3:1-3).

The discussion of the purifying power of the hope of resurrection is begun by questioning the Corinthians on their reason for having been baptized. The RSV translates: "Otherwise what do people mean by being baptized on behalf of the dead?" The Greek preposition, *huper*, may be translated either "on behalf of" or "with reference to." In the light of the context, and the following evidence, we believe the second translation is the correct one. The Corinthian Christians were being asked, "If the dead are not actually raised, why are people still becoming Christians and being baptized *with reference to* the resurrection from the dead?"

Some commentators think this verse (15:29) is a reference to an ancient practice among Christians where the living is baptized as a "proxy" on behalf of someone who has already died. Such a ritual is practiced in modern times by a large religious sect. The context is clear that Paul is focusing on the *foolishness* of engaging in any rite or activity that pretends faith in a bodily resurrection which the pretender disbelieved. Second, there is *no documented* practice such as this among Christians of the first century. It would be unlikely that *only Paul* would mention, in *only this one place,* such a radical practice if it were settled doctrine. Third, the most natural understanding of Paul's question would be to associate it with the initial baptism of a Christian believer. A fundamental rule of hermeneutics is to always interpret a passage according to its most natural meaning. Baptism is the action of a believer which confirms his trust in the vicarious death of Christ and the vicarious resurrection of Christ to new life (see Rom. 6:3-5; Gal. 3:26-27; Col. 2:12-13). In faithfulness to Christ's command to be baptized, the believer receives the forgiveness of sins (cf. Acts 22:16; Acts 2:38; I Peter 3:21). If Christ is not raised, and there is no resurrection for those who believe in Christ, baptism as to form and purpose is meaningless. What is the point in being baptized (immersed) "in reference to being dead in sin" if there is no resurrection? Fourth, the Bible teaches that each man is responsible for his own faith and obedience to Christ (cf. Ezek. 18:1-24; 33:1-20; Luke 16:19-31; II Kings 14:6; Deut. 24:16; Jer. 31:30; Matt. 16:27; Rom. 2:6; Rev. 20:12). The Roman Catholic Church teaches that works of "proxy" may be done by the living for the dead (masses for the dead, prayers for the dead, etc.), but such teaching has no basis in scripture and is rejected by all evangelical Christendom. It is absurd to think that the spiritual, moral choices of one human being would be accepted by God as willingly made by another human being when the second person made no such choices. Fifth, there is only one mediator between God and man, and that mediator is Jesus Christ (I Tim. 2:5). Only *he* could accomplish a redemptive deed vicariously (for someone else). To think that this passage teaches the possibility of one human being baptized "by proxy" for another human being, dead or alive, is to fly in the face of the exclusive mediatorship of Jesus Christ. Sixth, to take verse 29 to refer to vicarious baptism being practiced at Corinth but stating that Paul would not have approved of it, is dodging the issue of all five propositions above. To think the practice was going on and that Paul would not renounce such a *crucial contradiction* of apostolic revelation is naive. Baptism by proxy strikes at the very heart of the gospel: ". . . *you* will die in *your* sins unless *you* believe that I am he" (John 8:24); ". . . but unless *you* repent *you* will all likewise perish . . ." (Luke 13:3, 4). Had proxy-baptism been a practice at Corinth, Paul would have devoted more than two questions to the issue! If proxy-baptism was widely practiced in the first century church, why is there total silence about it in the writings of the apostle John (John's Gospel, his epistles, and Revelation, were all written near the end of the first century, circa. 95-100 A.D.)?

Already in Paul's day, Christians were being arrested for sedition against the Roman empire and thrown into arenas to be slaughtered by wild beasts. The "fourth seal" opened in the Revelation written by the apostle John predicts the fact that great numbers of human beings would be killed "by wild beasts of the earth" in the struggle between Christ's church and the Roman empire (Rev. 6:7-8). Paul now says (15:30-32), "If there is no resurrection from death, why do I allow myself to be imperiled almost every hour of my life?" Some circumstances of life Paul could not control, of course, but those threats, persecutions and murderous attacks upon his person because he was a Christian missionary (cf. II Cor. 1:8-10; 4:11; 11:23-29) he could have foregone by simply renouncing Christ and the resurrection. Did Paul fight with beasts? This may be simply a figurative expression describing his struggles with "beastly" human beings when he was at Ephesus (cf. Acts 19:23-30). Had Paul literally fought with beasts in the Roman arena it is probable that he would have listed the experience in II Corinthians 11:23-29. It would not be unusual to speak of the enemies of God as "beasts." The prophet Daniel did; John the apostle did (Revelation). John even categorizes all idolatrous heathen who worshiped the Roman emperor as "those with the mark of the beast."

The only logical *alternative* to believing the bodily resurrection and practicing Biblical Christianity is *hedonism*. The religious person who

CHAPTER 15   FIRST CORINTHIANS 15:12-34

repudiates the historicity of Christ's bodily resurrection but advocates (and is even willing to endure suffering for) trying to practice the teachings of Jesus is a *fool*! He is either a gullible moron or a masochist! Paul is scrupulously honest in saying, "If the dead are not raised, 'Let us eat and drink, for tomorrow we die'" (15:32).

The bodily resurrection from death is *the absolutely crucial doctrine* of Christian faith. Christian theology, Christian evangelism, and Christian ethics are vain without it. Liberal "Christian" theology repudiates the bodily resurrection. As a result liberalism is insipid, powerless and useless (see Special Studies, "On Cloud Nine," and "The Existential/Neo-Orthodox Philosophy of History"). Frighteningly, even some "evangelical" Christianity (the existential-feelings-first kind) dismisses the critical necessity of the bodily resurrection in its proclamation and practice. One of the "new Christian songs" is a classic example. In a popular song by Andrae Crouch, entitled, *If Heaven Never Was Promised to Me,* these are the lyrics:

> You may ask me why I serve the Lord, Is it just for heaven's gain, Or to walk those mighty streets of gold and to hear the angels sing? Is it just to drink from the fountain That never shall run dry, Or just to live forever and ever In that sweet old by and by?
>
> But if heaven never was promised to me, Neither God's promise to live eternally, It's been worth just having the Lord in my life, Livin' in a world of darkness, He brought me the light.
>
> If there were never any streets of gold, Neither a land where we'll never grow old; It's been worth just having the Lord in my life, Livin' in a world of darkness, He brought me the light.

Dear reader, this may have a lovely tune, it may have "soul," it may have "the beat," and pragmatically, it may draw crowds of people to a religious concert, but its lyrics deny the very cardinal, focal, fundamental issue Paul addresses in I Corinthians 15! If heaven never was promised to *you,* neither God's promise to live eternally, then *you* are, of all men, most to be pitied if you are practicing the Christian gospel. You should eat and drink, for tomorrow you will die and perish, if there is no resurrection and no heaven. If my hope is "just having the Lord in my life" here, in this existence, I am a fool for thinking I walk in "light"!

If there is no bodily resurrection and heaven, we should be writing "Christian" songs with lyrics like these:

FIRST CORINTHIANS

a. Brief and powerless is man's life; on him and on his race the slow sure doom falls pitiless and dark. Blind to good and evil, reckless of destruction, omnipotent matter rolls on its rentless way; for man condemned today to lose his dearest, tomorrow himself to pass through the gate of darkness, it remains only to cherish, ere the blow falls, the lofty thoughts that enoble his little days. . . .
—*Bertrand Russell*

b. Life has become in that total perspective which is philosophy, a fitful pullulation of human insects on the earth, a planetary eczema that may soon be cured; nothing is certain in it except defeat and death—a sleep from which, it seems, there is no awakening. . . .
—*Will Durant*

c. In spite of all my desperation to a brave looking optimism, I perceive that now the universe is bored with him (man), is turning a hard face to him, and I see him being carried less and less intelligently and more and more rapidly, suffering as every ill-adapted creature must suffer in gross and detail, along the stream of fate to degradation, suffering and death.
—*H.G. Wells*

Verses 33 and 34 confirm our comments on 15:12-19. The moral muscle of the gospel rests ultimately in the preaching of the historicity of the bodily resurrection. Paul quotes the Greek poet, Meander. The KJV translates it, ". . . evil communications corrupt good manners." The RSV translates it, ". . . Bad company ruins good morals." The Greek word *homiliai*, is the word from which the English words *homiletics* and *homily* come. The word is most often used to mean, "communication, conversation, discourse, talk." Certainly in this context Paul is talking about some of the Corinthian Christians who were *"saying* that there is no resurrection." Evil *preaching* and *teaching* corrupts good morals. And teaching that there is no bodily resurrection is *evil teaching*. The entire second epistle of Peter is a treatise on the fact that false teaching about the Lord Jesus and his deity is the source of the corruption of morality. When Paul wrote "good" morals, he did not use the most common Greek word for "good" which is *agathos*; he used the word *chresta*. *Chresta* means "good" in the sense of "that which is right because it produces good" —practical or useful goodness. The word *chresta* is used by Matthew

CHAPTER 15   FIRST CORINTHIANS 15:12-34

in recording Jesus' great invitation, ". . . for my yoke is *easy* (*chresta,* usefully-good)" (Matt. 11:30). Paul says in 15:33, evil, anti-resurrection, preaching is morally impractical. Liberalism is not only philosophically dishonest, it is ethically useless. It is worse than that, it is ethically corrupting! The fundamental cause of human immorality is the repudiation of the gospel facts—specifically, the historical resurrection of Jesus Christ. That is the essence of Paul's statement in 15:33-34. Anyone who aspires to search for, defend, and lead mankind to the *truth* must surrender to this! Philosophers, scientists, educators, preachers, lawyers, politicians and artists are under obligation to learn, believe and proclaim the bodily resurrection of Jesus Christ as the source of all morality and goodness. Paul called the philosophers at Athens to moral conversion and repentance by the power of the resurrection of Jesus (see Acts 17:30-31).

To sin, in light of the historicity of the resurrection, is insane. Essentially that is what Paul meant by his statement, "Come to your right mind, and sin no more." The Greek word Paul uses is *eknepsate,* is literally, "sober up." He is using it here to exhort the Corinthians to shake off the seductive moral stupor into which they have fallen by believing those who are saying there is no resurrection. False teaching about the resurrection has confounded their mental abilities like drunkenness confounds the brain. They are not thinking *right* (Gr. *dikaios,* rightly, correctly, truly). First, they are *philosophic schizoprenics.* They are not facing reality. They are repudiating the resurrection and at the same time pretending the Christian faith is valuable. Second, since the resurrection is true, as Paul has logically demonstrated, no matter how much they deny it they are going to face the judgment of God in the next life and to sin in light of this is insanity! Paul has appealed to incontrovertible evidence and irrefutable logic throughout this treatise on the resurrection. Now he *commands* (Gr. *eknepsate* is in the imperative mood) the Corinthians to start thinking as they should. Faulty thinking is a sin! Christians are not permitted the insanity of deliberately ignoring facts (see John 8:31-32; 8:43, 45, 46, 47; II Thess. 2:9-12; II Peter 3:5). Christians must constantly guard against the tendency to subvert clear, logical thinking by the selfish desire to follow feelings and urges of the flesh. Christians are continually urged by the scriptures to set their *minds* on God's word (Rom. 8:5-8; Col. 3:1-4; and Peter urges Christians to "gird up" or put-to-work their "minds" I Peter 1:13). To choose to be a Christian is to choose to apply one's mental processes in conformity to the sovereign word of God. To choose to be a Christian is to allow one's every thought to be brought into captivity to obedience of Christ (II Cor. 10:3-4). To choose to be a Christian is to choose to see nothing any more from a human point of view but through the perspective of Christ's constraining love (II Cor. 5:14-21). There is only one hope for changing men's morals into that classified "good" (useful) by God, and that is to persuade them to believe the bodily resurrection.

"For shame to you I am speaking" says Paul (literally, in Greek). They were listening to "some" of those within the congregation who were saying there is no resurrection. Paul is apparently pointing to the anti-resurrectionists when he says, "some" are ignorant of God. Denial of the resurrection, especially by those posing to be Christians, is worse than a shame, it is a tragedy, a spiritual catastrophe!

SECTION 3

Its Heavenliness (15:35-57)

35 But some one will ask, "How are the dead raised? With what kind of body do they come?" 36 You foolish man! What you sow does not come to life unless it dies. 37 And what you sow is not the body which is to be, but a bare kernel, perhaps of wheat or of some other grain. 38 But God gives it a body as he has chosen, and to each kind of seed its own body. 39 For not all flesh is alike, but there is one kind for men, another for animals, another for birds, and another for fish. 40 There are celestial bodies and there are terrestrial bodies; but the glory of the celestial is one, and the glory of the terrestrial is another. 41 There is one glory of the sun, and another glory of the moon, and another glory of the stars; for star differs from star in glory.

42 So is it with the resurrection of the dead. What is sown is perishable, what is raised is imperishable. 43 It is sown in dishonor, it is raised in glory. It is sown in weakness, it is raised in power. 44 It is sown a physical body, it is raised a spiritual body. If there is a physical body, there is also a spiritual body. 45 Thus it is written, "The first man Adam became a living being"; the last Adam became a life-giving spirit. 46 But it is not the spiritual which is first but the physical, and then the spiritual. 47 The first man was from the earth, a man of dust; the second man is from heaven. 48 As was the man of dust, so are those who are of the

CHAPTER 15 FIRST CORINTHIANS 15:35-57

dust; and as is the man of heaven, so are those who are of heaven. ⁴⁹Just as we have borne the image of the man of dust, we shall also bear the image of the man of heaven. ⁵⁰I tell you this, brethren: flesh and blood cannot inherit the kingdom of God, nor does the perishable inherit the imperishable.
 51 Lo! I tell you a mystery. We shall not all sleep, but we shall all be changed, ⁵²in a moment, in the twinkling of an eye, at the last trumpet. For the trumpet will sound, and the dead will be raised imperishable, and we shall be changed. ⁵³For this perishable nature must put on the imperishable, and this mortal nature must put on immortality. ⁵⁴When the perishable puts on the imperishable, and the mortal puts on immortality, then shall come to pass the saying that is written:
 "Death is swallowed up in victory."
 ⁵⁵"O death, where is thy victory?
 O death, where is thy sting?"
 ⁵⁶The sting of death is sin, and the power of sin is the law. ⁵⁷But thanks be to God, who gives us the victory through our Lord Jesus Christ.

15:35-41 It Is Manageable: Questions about the mechanics of bodily resurrection have been raised throughout the history of mankind. Alleged absence of observed demonstration of such mechanics has been put forward repeatedly as proof that bodily resurrection is impossible. People want to know how human bodies that have died and returned to dust, have been consumed by fire, or have been eaten by animals or sea-life, which in turn have died and dissolved, may be raised from the dead. How can this be possible?
 First, we must accept the revelation of God that he can manage it. "When God reveals, by special enlightenment through his Spirit, things which eye has not seen . . . (I Cor. 2:6-16), it is folly and irreverence to try to prove whether God told the truth. It is unreasonable to expect the scope of human experience and reason to provide the proof of things reaching so far beyond both reason and experience. . . . No method of science or of philosophy can prove some statements which are of central importance in the Bible. . . . These . . . must be accepted upon the authority or reliability of the one who says it is so. . . . The demand that all Bible statements must be discovered by scientific method, proved by rational processes, or confirmed by results in practice, before they can be regarded as authoritative or established truth, is simply a demand that God must not be greater

than man and must not reveal anything man could not find out for himself with his own closely limited, earthbound senses." (Seth Wilson, in, "Reflections" *Christian Standard,* June 17, 1984).

Second, in the light of all the evidence of resurrection in the "natural" creation surrounding him, it is *foolish* for man to question the manageability of it. Paul uses the Greek word *aphron,* literally, "mindless, without sense." Those who cannot believe in a resurrection of the human body because it dissolves back into dust after death are *not very observant.* The miracle of resurrection occurs every time a seed falls into the ground, dissolves, and produces a new green plant. It is no accident that the bodily resurrection of Jesus Christ took place in the Spring season of the earth.

There are two important lessons about resurrection taught in nature. (1) Death is necessary. It is not an obstacle to resurrection. In fact, if there is no death, there will be no resurrection. That which does not die shall never be resurrected (John 12:24-26). Any farmer or gardener knows a seed must "die," rot and dissolve (and yet it is the seed which has the "life" in it) before the new and completely different form of life can be "raised up." (2) The new life from the dead seed is different in form, much more grand, and actually the fulfillment of the purpose of the dormant seed itself. Put a bean seed into the ground and what comes up is a green plant. The plant is from the seed, and inseparably linked to it, but much better and alive, producing. It is significant that Jesus, in the parable of the growing seed (Mark 4:26-29), said that when a farmer plants a seed it produces a plant *of itself* (Gr. *automate,* automatically). The seed is planted in the earth and those two elements together *automate* the new life. If we had never seen the seed-to-earth-to-death-to-different-life process before, and someone said it happens, we would have our doubts. But since God has made it possible for us to see it over, and over, and over again, for us to say we do not believe a resurrection after death is manageable is foolish. We might as well say now, we do not believe a bean plant will grow from a bean seed because it is dead when it is put into the earth. Which of us fully understands the process of bean seed—to bean plant? If God has resurrected plants for centuries, "Why should it be thought a thing incredible that God should raise the dead?" (Acts 26:8)

Third, God is not locked into managing only one kind of body. God has created, as nature well attests, many different kinds of bodies. Scientists know there is such a difference they are able to

CHAPTER 15　　　　　FIRST CORINTHIANS 15:35-57

tell whether a single cell comes from a human, an animal, a bird, or a fish! How did Paul know this before modern science "discovered" it? Paul knew it directly from the Creator, by revelation. Furthermore, God is not limited to just four or four-million kinds of bodies. He "gives it a body as he has chosen, and to *each kind* of seed its own body." There is a correspondence between what the body looks like and what the entity inside is like. If we trust God, we will be satisfied with what we look like!

Fourth, there are two major divisions of bodies; there are celestial (heavenly) bodies, and terrestrial (earthly) bodies. Celestial bodies have a different glory, a different purpose, than terrestrial ones. God managed to create and managed to sustain bodies as different in time, space, size and function as the human mind is able to imagine. Since Paul has already listed the terrestrial bodies (15:39), he now delineates the celestial as sun, moon and stars. And each of the celestial bodies are different! And how many stars are there? And God manages each of them! Assuredly, then, God can manage the resurrection of human bodies and even give each human a different body if he wishes!

It is breathtaking to contemplate. God makes bodies to fit the multitudinous differences in the entities inhabiting them! No two snowflakes are alike—no two entities are the same. So is the resurrection of the body. The differences that exist in human personalities here will exist forever in glory. Human personality is not wiped out by disaster and the grave. Human personality goes on in all its uniqueness, even if the earthly body goes back to dust. And, wonder of wonders, God has promised to give that unique human personality a new, different, body to *fit it,* different from all other bodies, but eternal. We *will* know one another in heaven!

We have seen this demonstrated in the Lord Jesus Christ himself, "the firstfruit" of the resurrection from the dead. He was in a different body after his resurrection; yet it was similar to the old body that had died and been buried. It retained some of its old essence while also having new attributes. In its new form it was not subject to the old limitations of time and space—not touched by exhaustion and pain. But he was the same pure, true, loving Jesus. And they recognized him. But bodily he could go through walls of a building, materialize and dematerialize.

15:42-50 It is Mandatory: The destiny of humankind is immortality. The transformation (or, recreation) of a body fitted for

FIRST CORINTHIANS

eternality is, therefore, mandatory. Once again, even the natural order of things tells us the body of this life is *perishable* (Gr. *phthora,* corruptible, decomposable). As the physical body ages, it slows down, weakens, deteriorates. Eventually, and inevitably, it must die and disintegrate. Just like the bean seed, it must rot and decay, *but* one day it will become a new plant, gloriously designed for its eternal existence, imperishable. It is "planted" in the earth in *dishonor* (Gr. *atimia,* valueless, worth nothing) because we have sinned and perverted its created glory. Whatever is good or to be desired in the body of this existence inevitably decays and becomes valueless. God has subjected it to futility and the bondage of decay (Rom. 8:19-23), he brings the whole creation to dishonor, for a purpose. He wants it to "groan" for redemption, (see Gen. 3:17-19; 5:29; Eccl. 1:2ff.). The physical body is "planted" in *weakness* (Gr. *astheneia,* without strength) and will be raised in *power* (Gr. *dunamei,* dynamically, "dynamite"). Men like to boast of the strength of their bodies, yet a tiny, almost invisible, microbe can devastate it and even kill it. The physical limitations of our present bodies are frustrating. But the body God raises after this one is planted will never be ravaged by disease, sickness, pain, time, space, or decomposition. It will suffer no weaknesses!

The human body of this existence is *physical* (Gr. *psuchikon,* natural, "soulish," or psychical). Ray C. Stedman calls it his "earth suit, or time suit."

> But this "earth suit" is designed only for this life. It is not designed for anything else. It works fairly well in this life, but something could happen to this "earth suit" while I am talking or walking around. I could fall over and somebody would come along and say, "He's dead!" But it would not be so. I would not be dead. The "earth suit" would have died, but I would be as much alive as I have ever been, and already enjoying the new body, the "heaven suit," the "eternity suit." Paul's argument is, there is a body designed for the heavens, as well as one for the earth. What the apostle is saying throughout this whole chapter is that there is a definite link between the two.

(*Expository Studies in I Corinthians,* by Ray C. Stedman, pub. Word, p. 315)

Man has his "earth suit" from the *first* Adam (the word *Adam,* in Hebrew, means, "man"). Man may have his "heaven suit" from the *last* Adam, Jesus Christ, if man believes him and obeys him. There

CHAPTER 15   FIRST CORINTHIANS 15:35-57

are only two Adams; the first Adam and the last Adam, Jesus. The only other person beside Adam to become the *father* of a race is Jesus. Human beings are all sons of the first Adam by physical "soulish" procreation; human beings may be sons of the last Adam by spiritual regeneration. Adam, the first man, was made from the *dust* (Gr. *chiokos,* from *cheo,* lit. "to pour," hence, "loose earth or dust"). The first Adam became a living *soul* (Gr. *psuchen,* psyche), the last Adam became a *life-giving spirit* (Gr. *pneuma zoopoioun).* What is the difference between soul-life and spirit-life? There must be a difference as Paul is thinking of it here. Soul-life is the animating life. Animals are said to have souls (see Gen. 1:20 where the Hebrew word *nephesh,* "soul" is used for animal life; and Gen. 2:7 where man became a live-soul, *nephesh).* Evidently, the difference between *soul* and *spirit* is that the soul is not an entity which exists apart from the body.

Stedman explains that when God breathed into Adam's body of clay the divine Spirit, the "joining together of spirit and body produced another phenomenon called the 'soul,' the personality." The soul animates the body and allows that body to function. When man sins, and all men sin, God's *Spirit* is quenched and he withdraws and that "soul" and body is condemned to eternal death. That is the destiny of all who have sinned *like* the *first* Adam (and all men have). But, all praise to God, the *last* Adam, Jesus Christ, *became,* by living a perfect, sinless life in the flesh (Rom. 8:1-8; Heb. 2:14-18, etc.) *a life-giving spirit.* Any human being who wants, may now be reborn a spiritual being, by faith and obedience to Jesus Christ. That is what Peter means in I Peter 1:3-9; what Paul means in II Corinthians 5:1-21. Without Christ's vicarious atonement, without his conquest of sin and death, in the flesh, without his resurrection as "first fruit" from the dead, there would be no resurrection for any man for there would be no *spiritual rebirth* possible. This passage casts great light upon all that is taught in the scriptures about the necessity of the new birth and indwelling presence of the Spirit of Christ (the Holy Spirit). Do not fail to notice that Paul calls Jesus the *last* (Gr. *eschatos*) Adam. There is no redeemer of mankind yet to come. Those who do not join the "race" fathered by Jesus Christ, by being born again, will not see eternal life. They will be resurrected to eternal death as offspring *only* of the *first* Adam.

In man's experience it is the *physical,* natural order (Gr. *psuchikon* "soulish" body) first, and the *spiritual* (Gr. *pneumatikon,* spiritual body) afterward (Gr. *epeita*). The destiny of soul will also be the destiny of body (I Thess. 5:23-24). If the soul of man has been sanctified by the recreation of God's Spirit within him, then the spirit and soul and body will be kept sound and blameless at the coming of our Lord Jesus Christ!

The soul-spirit is separated from the body for a little while at the time of physical death. The soul-spirit returns to God who gave it and the body returns to the dust of the earth (Eccl. 12:7). But the nature of your soul-spirit determines what the nature of your resurrected body will be. The corruptible body is put aside in the grave, but it will be raised incorruptible if it has, in the course of this life, been the temporary residence of a Spirit that is incorruptible—the Spirit of Christ. If, therefore, you would like one day to bear the *image* (Gr. *eikona,* icon) of the heavenly body, you must possess the heavenly life now. What must be happening is the will of God being lived out in your life now, on earth, as it is in heaven (Matt. 6:10).

All of the foregoing Paul has said to substantiate the divine fiat, "... Flesh and blood cannot inherit the kingdom of heaven!" Beyond the grave, only that which is spiritual (heavenly) can enter heaven. What is highly esteemed among men is abomination in the sight of God (Luke 16:15). All the trappings of this life, fame, money, physical beauty, self-righteousness, can never survive the grave. They rot along with the physical body. God does not want them—will not have them! He has something far better for those who trust him. Nothing in this world has any value, in itself, in the sight of God. Only as it enobles the spiritual in man is it to last beyond our funerals. Flesh and blood cannot do anything of value in the kingdom of God. This is what shocked Nicodemus when Jesus told him, "Truly, truly, I say to you, unless one is born anew, (or from above), he cannot see the kingdom of God" (John 3:3-5). All those descended from the first Adam, who have sinned as he did (and all have), must start all over again. They must be *born* again. They must be born of water (baptism, an expression of our penitent, receiving, faith) and the Spirit (the grace of God shed abroad in our hearts), (John 3:5).

15:51-57 It is The Mark (Goal): The "mystery" (actually, the gospel is very often called the "mystery" Eph. 1:7-10; Col. 1:24-27) is *not* that "we shall not all sleep," but that "we shall all be changed." He goes ahead and explains, the "mystery" is the dead being raised "imperishable." The Greek word used here for "changed" is not *metamorphou* (or, metamorphosis, transformation), but *allagesometha*

CHAPTER 15   FIRST CORINTHIANS 15:35-57

from *allasso,* meaning, "made to be *other* than it is." The change will be complete. The word is also used of the final change of the material creation (Heb. 1:12). This is the goal of God for all who believe in his Son, Jesus Christ.

This change, upon the bodily form of all humanity occurs at Christ's second coming—"at the last trumpet." Some will not "be asleep" (dead) at that time—some will still be living in this existence. It is to occur *in a moment* (Gr. *en atomo,* English, *atomic,* minute); in the "twinkling of an eye" (Gr. *en hripe,* in a glance) refers to the twinkle of light that occurs when you blink. It is one of the fastest speeds known to human observation. It will be instantaneous—it will be a miracle. God will be in a hurry to give his saints what Christ has earned for them and that for which they have "kept the faith."

The Greek word *dei,* beginning the sentence in verse 53, emphasizes that this change *must* occur. This mortal nature *must* put on immortality because "Death is swallowed up in victory!" Those who have believed that Christ has defeated death must not be imprisoned again in a state of corruption, held bondage by the fear of death (Heb. 2:14-15). They must not have their abiding place any more in a body that is dying, afraid of death, and testifies of death. Death and Hades are to be thrown into the lake of fire and brimstone, forever banished from the believer's presence (Rev. 20:14). There is a sting to death. The very nature of our physical life (its nature that is doomed to destruction) makes death sting. Even in full view of Christ's victory over death, we still wince at it. We shudder at its appearance because it is an unknowable quotient. It is something over which we have no control—it is inexorable, inevitable. We fear it because of our sin in the light of God's absolute law. But the glad tidings, coming from the historical resurrection of Jesus Christ, are, *the power of sin is broken.* It no longer has dominion over us (Rom. 6:14; 8:2; 7:6; 5:17, 19). Thanks be to God who *is giving* (Gr. *didonti,* present tense verb, "continuing to give") us the victory over our corruptible "man" through our Lord Jesus Christ. There is nothing more precious in the whole scheme of redemption than this promise that every day the Christian can lay hold afresh of the *grace* of Jesus Christ. Every day, though reminded of the weakness and mortality of the flesh by his faults and failures, the Christian can grasp by faith, again, the renewing and refreshing power of his immortality imputed to him by Christ. The victorious life is God's goal or mark for all men. Sin is the life of defeat. Sin is missing God's mark because the life of sin bears the image of the man of dust, doomed to corruption and eternal death.

SECTION 4

Its Helpfulness (15:58)

58 Therefore, my beloved brethren, be steadfast, immovable, always abounding in the work of the Lord, knowing that in the Lord your labor is not in vain.

15:58a In Steadfastness: What a helpful, practical, glorious conclusion. Who said Christianity is impractical? Why else would anyone have any desire to be steadfast and immovable in this life? What other philosophy would produce stability in this life? Only the perspective based on the historical resurrection of Jesus Christ will do that! Paul uses the Greek words *hedraioi* and *ametakinetoi*; they are translated, "steadfast" and "immovable," respectively. *Hedraioi* means "seated, settled-in, fixed"; it is used to form one of our English suffixes e.g. "tetra*hedron*" denoting a crystal having a specific number of facets or surfaces. It also forms the second half of the English word "cathedral" which also means, "seated above." Christians have the power of the resurrection to help them live stable, fixed, settled lives. *Ametakinetoi* means "motionless, unexcitable, not given to passion." Part of the word, *kinetoi,* is the word from which the English words *kinetic, kinematics, kinescope* come. These English words all have to do with "motion." The alpha-privative and the prepositional-prefix, *ameta,* would cause the word to be translated, "absolutely, completely, immovable." The only way to be steadfast and immovable in this world of dissolution and mortality is to believe the resurrection! The resurrection is the key-stone of the arch supporting moral immovability in the storm of temptation.

15:58b In Service: The resurrection is the impetus for *abounding* in the *work* of the Lord. Preaching is work! Evangelism is work! Shepherding the flock is work! Teaching the saints is work! Learning God's Word is work! Loving is work! Being a "good Samaritan" is work! Believing is work (John 6:29); repenting is work (Rev. 2:5). To be a Christian a person must exhaust himself, his talents, his resources, his time, his soul and his body in the work of the Lord, (see Eph. 4:12; II Thess. 1:11; II Tim. 4:5; John 9:4). Let's face it,

CHAPTER 15　　　　　　　　FIRST CORINTHIANS 15:58

there are times when the devil will tempt us to perceive doing the will of God is a *chore,* or worse, *repressive* and *futile.* Even Jesus cried, "Father, if it be possible, let this cup pass from me." But Jesus, in his moments of temptation to depression "offered up prayers and supplications, with loud cries and tears, to him who was able to save him out of death, and he was heard for his godly fear" (Heb. 5:7). Jesus did the work of God through the power of trusting in the resurrection!

15:58c In Security: There is nothing which will bring to the human soul the feeling of security and satisfaction as completely as the knowledge that one's *labor is not in vain!* So very much of everything written, painted, built, said, done, applauded, acquired, attained in this world is doomed to disappear. Only that which has been done in the name of Christ will be transferable (in different form) into the kingdom of God to come (heaven). Everything else has perished, is perishing, or shall perish. "Vanity of vanity, all is vanity" (Eccl. 1:2). The Christian whose hope is in the resurrection is the only person in this world who can find true, complete, abiding satisfaction and fulfillment. His labor is not in vain in the Lord. When he passes from this life to the next, his works follow with him (Rev. 14:13). If a man believes in God and his Son, his prayers and alms go up before God as a "memorial" (Acts 10:4). Every act of kindness in the name of Jesus and for his sake (even a cup of cold water) is remembered and will be rewarded by the Lord (Matt. 25:31-46). So, let us lay up for ourselves treasures in heaven (Matt. 6:19-21) where they are eternally secure and fulfilling.

APPLICATIONS:

1. The gospel gives salvation only to those who "hold it fast"— God's offer of salvation is free, but conditioned on loyalty.
2. The *facts* of the gospel are important *first*—even *before* what we feel about it, or before its usefulness.
3. The *terms* in which the gospel is to be preached are objective, not subjective. It is history not autonomous human decisiveness.
4. Proof of the historicity of Christ's resurrection follows all the canons of legal, scientific evidence—can you name them?
5. There is significance to Paul's listing of himself as a witness to the bodily resurrection of Christ—what is it? Does it convince you? Would it convince others? A Jew?
6. What do you think of the moral honesty of those who deny the

bodily resurrection of Christ and still want to practice Christianity? Would you?
7. What kind of life would you live if you did not believe in the bodily resurrection of the dead? Why?
8. Would you like to be baptized for someone who is dead? Would you be able to trust a God who allowed righteousness "by proxy"?
9. How often is the resurrection of Christ preached and taught at your congregation?
10. Do you see liberalism and modernisn (now, it is neo-orthodoxy) as "corrupting good morals"?
11. Are you resigned to the fact, as nature teaches, that there is no new life unless death comes first? Has it been easy to be reconciled to the inevitability of death?
12. What kind of body do you think you will have in eternity?
13. Do you expect to recognize in eternity people you have known here? Why? How?
14. What of this life are you expecting to take with you to heaven?

APPREHENSIONS:

1. What was the "form" of the apostolic gospel proclamation?
2. Why does Paul say Christ died, was buried and arose, all *according to* the scriptures? What scriptures?
3. What evidence is offered by those who deny the resurrection of Christ? How do they explain the gospel accounts of it?
4. How many "enemies" of early Christianity became advocates of it? Why?
5. Why are we still in our sins if Christ has not been raised from the dead?
6. Why are men to be pitied if they have hoped in Christ only for this life?
7. Isn't there some value in practicing Christianity even if Christ was never raised from the dead?
8. Why is Christ "firstfruit" of the dead? Which dead?
9. What is "baptism for the dead"? Is it practiced today—by whom?
10. Why are people who are sinning *not* in their right minds?
11. Why do men say, "How are the dead raised"?
12. What is the answer?
13. What is the difference between the *first* Adam and the *last* Adam?
14. Why can't flesh and blood inherit the kingdom of God?
15. What difference does believing in the resurrection make in how we feel about Christian works?

Special Study

ON CLOUD NINE

"Man, you are really out there on cloud nine!" This is one of the favorite "slanguage" expressions used by some to categorize ideas which they believe to be unrealistic, unreasonable and irrational. Over the years liberal theologians and liberal preachers have built up and bowled over their straw-men of conservative-Christianity. They have relegated all fundamental, historical views of the Bible, God, Christ, man, conversion and the church to "cloud nine." Conservative Christianity, they say, is too much concerned with doctrines to be realistic or relevant.

We believe that the opposite is true. We believe that liberalism (even in its latest form—Neo-orthodoxy) is "out there on cloud nine." We believe that history, reason, experience and revelation all combine to prove that liberal theology is unrealistic and irrelevant.

Both the apostles Peter and Jude state unequivocally that any theology which denies that the written record contained in the Bible is a God-breathed, historically infallible, revelation of the supernatural redemption in Christ is "cloud nineism." Any such theology is like a cloud without water . . . it is unrealistic and irrelevant. II Peter 2:17-21, "These are springs without water, and mists driven by a storm; for whom the blackness of darkness hath been reserved. For, uttering great swelling words of vanity, they entice in the lusts of the flesh, by lasciviousness, those who are just escaping from them that live in error; promising them liberty, while they themselves are bondservants of corruption; for of whom a man is overcome, of the same is he also brought into bondage. For if, after they have escaped the defilements of the world through the knowledge of the Lord and Saviour Jesus Christ, they are again entangled therein and overcome, the last state is become worse with them than the first. For it were better for them not to have known the way of righteousness, than, after knowing it, to turn back from the holy commandment delivered unto them." Jude 11-13, "Woe unto them! for they went in the way of Cain, and ran riotously in the error of Balaam for hire, and perished in the gainsaying of Korah. These are they who are hidden rocks in your love-feasts when they feast with you, shepherds that without fear feed themselves; clouds without water, carried along by winds, autumn trees without fruit, twice dead, plucked up by the root; wild waves of the sea, foaming out their own shame; wandering stars, for whom the blackness of darkness hath been reserved for ever."

FIRST CORINTHIANS

It is unrealistic to attempt a complete rebuttal of liberalism in so brief an essay. Nevertheless, the following outline will hopefully produce enough light to show the irrelevancies and irreparable weaknesses of an unrealistic liberal theology.

Antecedents of Liberalism

1. *Rationalism*: Rationalism had its modern birth as reaction against the extreme dogmatism, anti-intellectualism and authoritarianism of the medieval Roman Catholic Church. This philosophical revolution brought about the Renaissance with its extreme swing to rationalism and freedom from all authority. This resulted in the "autonomous man." Man's ability to reason became the sole criteria of judging a thing to be true or valuable. All that is non-conceptual, or empirically non-repeatable is untrue, according to rationalism.

2. *Materialism or Empiricism*: Materialism or Empiricism says that all we can know is sensory knowledge or all that is, is matter. It denies the supernatural . . . it denies miracles and arbitrarily assigns them to the realm of superstition; it denies spirit. Man becomes a creature and captive of environmental influences and may be conditioned or manipulated by empirical stimuli. This philosophy is far from being dead. Behavioristic psychology is founded upon it. It is being taught in the majority of our state colleges and universities.

3. *Evolutionism*: All life originated by chemical processes . . . that which is organic came from inorganic. This is the only recourse for man in explaining his being and the universe when he refuses to have God in his knowledge—he can only worship the creature and the created if he rejects the Creator. Evolution is irrational, unscientific, unrealistic. It creates hundreds of unanswerable questions, problems and inconsistencies. Evolution solves no real problems and answers no real questions! Evolutionism did not start with Charles Darwin. It started as far back as the ancient Greeks, Aristotle, Democritus and perhaps even earlier (cf. Romans 1).

4. *Scientism*: "It seemed that science was always proved right and religion wrong. The idea began to arise that science could solve all of man's problems, that it was only ignorance and inertia, particularly the ignorance and inertia of the Churches, which were holding back the forward march of science, the new savior."[1]

---

1. *A Layman's Guide to Protestant Theology,* by Wm. Hordern, p. 47.

SPECIAL STUDY: ON CLOUD NINE

This is scientism, the worship of science. Science became the sacred cow! Natural law (which is only man's description of what he has observed) became God!

Nietzsche, the German philosopher, said, "God is dead!" With such a "philosophical annihilation" of God came the death of all moral standards and out of Nietzsche's teachings came Nazi Germany under his most infamous disciple—Adolf Hitler.

5. *Humanism*: "Scientific Humanism is the doctrine that men, through the use of intelligence, directing the institutions of democratic government, can create for themselves, without aid from supernatural powers, a rational civilization in which each person enjoys security and finds cultural outlets for whatever normal human capacities and creative energies he possesses."[2] Without a supernatural standard just who is going to decide what are the "normal human capacities" and the "creative energies," who is going to decide what "security" is and who is going to decide between "cultural outlets" and non-cultural outlets? With only relativistic standards society must ultimately either become completely subjected to dictatorship of the most powerful or it must end in chaotic anarchism.

Humanism is an unrealistic "optimism in man's ability to provide for himself all that is needed to have a life that is consistent with his being." All this actually results in determinism and mechanistic materialism or anarchism, and neither determinism nor anarchism is freedom!

6. *Subjectivism*: Some humanistic theologians found such strict materialistic and animalistic views to be inconsistent with man's real nature. Materialism led only to an incoherent, unrealistic outlook and practice of life. So the theologians, acceding to the so-called scientific destruction of the historical accuracy of the Bible, attempted to base religion on subjective feeling alone . . . value and truth was to be felt and not arrived at from the facts.

They said science knows that the Bible is untrue, but that has nothing to do with truth . . . for truth or value has to be felt! And although the Bible is inaccurate and full of superstition, God can speak to us through it.

"In Schleiermacher religion found an answer to many of the problems of his age. For one thing religion was made independent of

---

2. *Living Issues of Philosophy,* by H. H. Titus, p. 216.

philosophy and science. Religion, based on the individual's personal experience, had a realm of its own; it was its own proof; it bore its own validity. Furthermore, the center of religion is shifted from the Bible to the heart of the believer. Biblical criticism cannot harm Christianity, for the heart of the Bible message is that which it speaks to the individual, and it speaks even more clearly because the critics have enabled us to understand it."[3] Could there be any philosophy more unrealistic, unscientific, unreasonable?!

And so, modern liberalism in the form of existential neo-orthodoxy, seeking to reconcile "lies" as truth, seeking to get answers from a book they admit is full of error, is more unrealistic and incoherent than all its predecessors!

Results

1. *Agnosticism*: Unbelief—no eternal verities or values. Truth is "becoming" . . . man is making truth as he experiments. Truth is created pragmatically. That is, if an action works it is true; if not, false.

But again, who's to be the judge as to its workability? What's workable for one may not be for all, or, what's workable today may not be tomorrow.

If man is the result of accidental inorganic chemical clashes, if God is dead, if there is no truth except what is rational and empirical, then there is nothing eternal and nothing valuable but animalistic satisfaction of the flesh!

2. *Socialism*: The governments of men become the Beneficient Father . . . the Savior of the race. Men's philosophies (outlook on life) permeate every avenue of their existence. Religious philosophy and political philosophy cannot be separated. You cannot compartmentalize life! All that you think affects your whole life. Religious liberalism has brought on political liberalism and socialism. It has placed *worshipful* emphasis on material results in the assumption that a particular standard of living brings "salvation" and governmental paternalism brings the "kingdom of God" upon earth. Statement after statement by the liberals to this effect may be found in the little book, so vehemently denounced by the religious liberals themselves, *None Dare Call It Treason*.

---

3. Hordern, *op. cit.*, p. 59.

SPECIAL STUDY: ON CLOUD NINE

All the evils of immorality, greed, kick-back, favoritism, paternalism, waste, exploitation in big government are a direct result of the religious philosophy of liberalism which says man himself and his material well-being . . . is heaven: the philosophical or political method of bringing this about is their "God."

3. *Immorality*: If there are no eternal values, no God, no hereafter, how can there be any morality? All good is relative only to individual desires or the desires of one who can, by force, control thoughts and deeds through fear or brain-washing. This is why we have "sun, suds and sex" on the Florida beaches. This is why we have cheating on television quiz shows. This is why we have more divorce and adultery than ever before. A liberalism which says there is no God, no true Bible, no heaven, no hell, that a great society may be built without them is "cloud nineism"! Such a philosophy is unrealistic, irresponsible, demonical!

4. *War*: The liberal theological schools of Germany taught philosophies which spawned Marx, Lenin, Hitler and many of the present and past leaders of American education and politics. When there is no God and when the Bible is renounced as merely the invention of ignorant, fallible men, then all values are relative. The values of a man like Hitler become relative to building the Third Reich. Marx's values were relative to the glorification of the State. Liberal theology breeds greed, lust for power, prejudice, exploitation of humanity, and war.

5. *Eclecticism*: Syncretism in religion, ecumenism of the World Council of Churches, one world governmentalism is another result. Liberalism reduces Christ to a mere human in whom may be found the highest human attainment of what is good and right. Christ becomes a mere teacher of ethics . . . simply another religious philosopher or prophet like Mohammed, Buddha, or Confucius. Such a religious philosophy absorbs all which is supposed to be good and valuable from each of the "great" world religions. How can truth, *absolute truth* (that is what Christianity claims to be), absorb that which is not true either historically or pragmatically? Christianity and all other religions are diametrically opposed.

It is totally unrealistic to build one's religious beliefs and philosophy of life upon a conglomeration of teachings which are contradictory! Pessimism or a schizophrenic fear and anxiety follows from such a "mixed up" religion.

FIRST CORINTHIANS

This pessimism and anxiety is not only evident by the living of many people today, but it is stated in our songs, art, literature, and contemporary philosophers.

History and reason demonstrate that liberalism, anti-supernaturalism and unbelief are responsible for our sensual, schizophrenic, suicidal society!

Peace, joy and fruitfulness which are absolutely necessary for a balanced life are all based upon trust and faith and a coherent philosophy of life. The only coherent philosophy of life is one that is centered on and saturated with the love of God demonstrated in history in Christ (God Incarnate) and experienced by a personal fellowship with the Holy Spirit as He lives in men through His Word!

Yes, liberal theology is unrealistic. It is worse than that! It is ungodly, impotent and damning!

Answers

1. *Know the truth*: Every Christian must know why and what he believes. The study of evidences for belief in Christ must not be reserved for only a few of the so-called "theologians." The apostles and Christians of the first century made this the bed-rock basis of all they believed, taught and practiced. Every sermon recorded in Acts is built upon historical evidence for the deity of Jesus Christ.

All of life's motivations have their origins in either truth or lie. If we desire to move men to live true to God's purpose for them we must know God's truth and why it is true, and be able to present it to others. Parents should be teaching their children NOW why they believe. Men and women should be steeping their own minds and hearts in evidences for belief.

2. *Preach the truth*: Let the church and Christians be more concerned with revealed truth than with programs. Let the church be more concerned with regenerating the hearts of individuals by the power of the Holy Spirit through His Word rather than with social reform or raising living standards, and the slums will disappear. Let the church and Christian people have the courage to preach the truth with their lives. Let them live up to what they teach in their Sunday School classes on Sunday, letting Christ live His life in them, and racial injustice will cease.

3. *Pray daily*: We do not really believe in prayer per se as the psychologists do for a "release" but we believe in the Lord Jesus who

SPECIAL STUDY: ON CLOUD NINE

promised to answer prayer. But we really do not act like we believe in the Lord who promised or we would pray more! It is the Lord's will that truth be victorious over lie . . . liberalism is a lie, pray that it may be defeated on every hand.

4. *Send laborers*: Support colleges and churches which train men and women to declare the truth. I never cease to be amazed at parents who look down their noses at the Bible Colleges. They act as if life consists in just a living. And of course, in order to learn how to make a living one must go to a college where atheistic, Communistic, immoral teachers teach infidelic philosophies. God have mercy upon us.

5. *Warn people*: Romans 16 tells us to "mark those who cause divisions and disputings among us." The Scriptures are emphatic in their exhortations to warn people, to point out *by name and doctrine* those who are contrary to revealed truth. John says that the only way we know the Spirit of Truth and the spirit of error is to compare all that is taught with what the apostles recorded in the New Testament.

LIBERALISM IS CLOUD NINEISM. IT IS UNREALISTIC IN:

1. *Its approach to or view of God.* Nature proves God exists. Men must deny reason to deny the *facts* connected with the relevation of God in Christ.

2. *Its view of man.* Man is more than flesh and bone. Man is a spirit . . . he is a person. But not if the liberal view is to be accepted.

3. *Its view of sin.* Sin is more than the unfortunate conditioning of an unfortunate environment. Sin is of the will, and of the heart regardless of ones environment.

4. *Its view or approach to salvation.* It has no supernatural power. Why strive for social improvement if there are no eternal verities, no Almighty Judge, etc.

5. *It is even unrealistic in its view of social reform*: Without divine power of regeneration there is no lasting social reform.

Any religion that does not answer the human predicament is worse than useless. Death, and the sin which causes it, is the human predicament. There have been many religious and metaphysical theories for its cure, but only one way of fact! This was when God entered history, time, and space, and said, "This is what I have done with sin and with death . . . I punish sin upon the cross in My Son . . . I conquer death in the resurrection of My Son from the tomb."

FIRST CORINTHIANS

Purposes

(Why bother with a polemic against Liberalism?)

1. *Men are lost in it.* There is futility and hopelessness in this life without Christ. There is no hope of eternal life in a Christless Liberalism.

2. *Men and women are seeking to be loosed from its tyranny.* Many people thirst for the historical Christianity. People are beginning to awake to the tyranny and hopelessness of Liberalism. Many unbelievers use the unrealistic and contradictory nature of Liberal Christianity to scoff at all religion. They do not know there is a real Christianity of fact and life in the Holy Spirit.

3. *We have the power.* What has been said before is sufficient to show that the battle is basically a battle of ideas. What we believe will ultimately control and direct what we do. Paul says, "For though we walk in the flesh, we do not war according to the flesh (for the weapons of our warfare are not of the flesh, but mighty before God to the casting down of strongholds); casting down imaginations, and every high thing that is exalted against the knowledge of God, and bringing every thought into captivity to the obedience of Christ"; (II Cor. 10:3-5). Peter points out that through a knowledge of Christ we have granted unto us the divine power of God which gives us all things that pertain to and are relevant for life and godliness, (II Peter 1:3-4).

Christianity is more than a way of life. It is the only coherent, consistent, realistic and relevant life possible! The divinely inspired Christianity of the New Testament in all its pristine purity is intensely practical. It is intensely relevant and contemporary to all men in every situation and forevermore. But it is all of this only if it is historically and infallibly true. It is true! Its truth makes all other philosophies of life inconsistent, irrelevant, powerless and untrue. The most insane, incoherent, schizophrenic existence that man can bring upon himself is to attempt to live a coherent life which is based upon an incoherent philosophy. Any philosophy of the universe and man's purpose and destiny which is bereft of divinely revealed truth is powerless and insane. Paul says that the power and relevance of Christianity is due to its divine truthfulness and this divine truthfulness was demonstrated when God intervened in time and space and history and by the bodily resurrection of Jesus Christ showing that the supernatural is just as real, if not more real, than the natural.

SPECIAL STUDY: ON CLOUD NINE

Hear, then, the conclusion: "Wherefore my beloved brethren be ye stedfast, unmovable, always abounding in the work of the Lord for ye know that your labors are not in vain in the Lord" (I Cor. 15:58).

Special Study

THE EXISTENTIAL / NEO-ORTHODOX PHILOSOPHY OF HISTORY

An attempt will be made, in this comparatively brief study, to focus on the Neo-Orthodox / Existential philosophy of history. To this end we shall endeavor to show a few of the antecedent influences leading to this particular view of history; a definition of this philosophy of history; results of this philosophy of history. Basic to an understanding of any aspect of the Existential theology (if indeed it may be called a theology) is recognition of its reactionism toward a religion that presents itself to man's reason for verification. The Crisis theology is also a reaction against what its adherents call, "immanentism." To them the orthodox theology of a God revealing Himself in the realm of the phenomenal (ordinary history) means an immanentistic, pantheistic theology and restricts God. It claims to be an enemy of rationalism but in our opinion it enthrones rationalism more authoritatively than any of the rationalists and restricts God as orthodoxy could never do. Their constant demand is for a "wholly Other" God —beyond the realm of reasonableness and human history and in so doing they make man's emotions the exclusive point of contact with a God that, by their own declaration, cannot be contacted.

By their arbitrary, authoritarian and dogmatic postulate that a revelation from God is not verifiable by the logical processes of man they have enthroned their "inability to know" which is really enthroning rationalism. Basically, Existentialism is nothing more than a modified agnosticism all dressed up in the robes of religious terminology.

We hope, in all fairness, that we have represented their position correctly. With our background of orthodoxy and ordinary view of history it has not been easy to follow their thinking to clear conclusions.

Antecdents

The antecedents of the existential philosophy of history may be traced back with certainty to Immanuel Kant and other rationalistic philosophers, and perhaps even further back into the age of Platonism. But we shall not go beyond Kant. We feel rather reluctant to criticize Kant; considering our very brief acquaintance with his work, but it is necessary to do so to see his influences upon modern theological

EXISTENTIAL / NEO-ORTHODOXY PHILOSOPHY

trends. We therefore accept the interpretations of other writers concerning his epistemological and metaphysical presuppositions. The educational background of Barth (German school of rationalism) and the ethnic relationship of Barth and Kant (both German) lead us to believe that Kant had a strong influence upon Barth's theology.

There is no doubt that Kant's ideas concerning the way man arrives at and interprets his natural experiences contain some truth. But when it comes to the metaphysical (that which is beyond the natural) Kant becomes an agnostic. He maintains that metaphysical knowledge about the general characteristics of reality is *impossible* to attain. If we seek inside ourselves for what is the Cause (caps mine) of, or the basis of, our mental machinery of forms and categories, we are unable to discover anything. Similarly, when we try to move beyond the phenomenal world (ordinary history), to the realm of "things-in-themselves" (brute fact), we are again unable to discover the Cause.

Kant believes that "the difficulty which prevents us from developing any metaphysical knowledge is that we have no way of determining if our mental apparatus is applicable to anything beyond the world of possible experience, the phenomenal world. We possess no concepts, no forms of intuition, no logical schema, that we have any reason to believe apply to the Self, or to the 'things-in-themselves', the real objects that may exist beyond the world of appearance."[1] Thus Immanuel Kant aribtrarily decides that God, if there is a God, could not reveal Himself to man for man has no way of categorizing or understanding that which is beyond the phenomenal (brute fact). Either this or Kant believes that God has not the ability to communicate the noumenal (that is, non-empirical world) through the phenomenal.

Kant further posited that "our logical forms and our categories are organizing principles . . . which allow us to acquire *a priori* knowledge about the world of appearance," but ". . . cannot be extended to tell us about a possible transempirical world, unless we could discover some means of determining whether the metaphysical realm can and must be thought of in the same way as the phenomenal one."[2] In other words, our own reason becomes the criteria of judgment as to whether God is able to reveal Himself to man in man's own categories or not.

---

1. *Philosophy Made Simple,* Popkin & Stroll, Doubleday & Co., Inc., p. 97.
2. *Ibid.,* p. 98.

There is that element of truth within Kant's philosophy that ought to be appreciated. It is true in a certain sense that man could not know God by reason alone nor through his experience with the world about him. But that does not preclude the possibility of God revealing Himself to man in man's categories to a degree sufficient for man to accept by faith what is unknowable but revealed. It appears that Kant has written revelation off as impossible simply by making his own reason the judge. And thus Kant gives to the existentialists the first faint echoes of the necessity for the "wholly Other" God and the autonomous man.

Dialecticism is the other important antecedent with the Crisis theologians. This form of rationalism had its beginnings in Plato but Hegel is responsible for organizing the dialectical philosophy into its influential position among philosophers. The dialectic proceeds: All change, especially historical change, takes places in accordance with the law of the dialectic: a thesis is produced, it develops an opposition (its antithesis), a conflict between them ensues, and the conflict is resolved into a synthesis which include both thesis and antithesis. "Hegel believed that in discovering the dialectic he had discovered a *necessary law* of nature."[3] Men and nations are merely pawns of historical necessity—it is really the dialectic which controls the course of events. Hegel's philosophy is very near pure pantheism. His "Absolute Mind" (God) becomes the real universe, manifesting itself outwardly as world history, and inwardly as the rational dialectical process, "marching toward full self-realization."

For Hegel the historical process proceeds from level to level through the dialectic movement from thesis to antithesis to synthesis. All change, all thinking and all life proceed from affirmation to denial, or from claim to counter claim to a new integration which later develops a new opposition. Development takes place in "Waltz-time" —"One, two, three; one, two, three."

Hegel holds that fundamental principles of law, morality, and social institutions of art, religion, and philosophy are connecting stages in the logical evolution of the rational will. The dialectical movement of progress through conflict runs through everything he wrote. This dialectical movement is observable in things and in thought, in the human mind and in all history. His idea of conflict is very apparently carried over into the existential ideas of negation and

---

3. *Ibid.,* p. 65.

EXISTENTIAL / NEO-ORTHODOX PHILOSOPHY

crisis. To Hegel, the "Absolute" was the sum total of all things in their development—it was reason itself, it was Mind, and it was the metaphysical definition of God.

Kierkegaard, father of existentialism, was influenced by the Kantian epistemology and the Hegelian dialectic. Kierkegaard vehemently opposes Hegel's "System" and pretends to set off his forms of dialecticism in sharp distinction from those of Hegel. But SK is a dialecticist, nevertheless. Both Hegel and SK deny that all facts are under the control of the logic of an antecedent God. "With respect to the theologian's (SK's) concept of God as an eternal and unchanging Being, we can see that it would be logically impossible for God to be part of the historical world. By definition, no historical or temporal properties apply to God. If one believed that God existed in time, that God was able to act in human historical situations, one would be believing something that is logically absurd."[4]

God cannot make Himself known. Man cannot reach God from any point in history. Yet man must contact God. Thus we have the dialectical conflict and we must take the irrational leap trying to reach the synthesis. The Unknown is a torment to man—yet it is also an incitement. "God is the wholly Unknown, yet Reason may prepare for His coming."[5] As one writer has said, Kierkegaard has "improved on Kant's concept of correlativity and Hegel's concept of mediation (both assumed that phenomenal logic and fact are independent of God) by making timeless logic more timeless, by making brute fact more brute, and by developing new speeds for the shuttle train service (SK's "Inwardness" and "Leap") between them,"[6] (parentheses mine). Both SK and Hegel reject the Christian concept of a self-sufficient God—both reject the idea of the counsel of God, according to which history is simply, what it is. Such concepts to them destroy true "inwardness" and require men to accept that which is alien to them because it is above them. History as the Christian knows it petrifies subjectivity according to these theologians. Objective proof is taken to be an enemy of true faith because it claims to deal with certainties and finished quantities. But the true subjective thinker, the dialecticist, is constantly occupied in striving—seeking the conflict or arriving at the Crisis. Finality at any point must at all costs be

---

4. *Ibid.,* p. 188.
5. *The New Modernism,* by C. Van Til, Presbyterian & Reformed Pub. Co., Phila., Penna., p. 61.
6. *Ibid.,* p. 62

avoided. "Dialecticism is irrationalistic in its assumption of "brute fact" and rationalistic in its virtual ascription of legislative power to the human mind over the whole field of possibility (dialectical process),"[7] (parentheses mine).

In his commentary on Romans, Barth simply carries on where Kierkegaard left off in the dialectic. According to Barth, every attempt to come to God directly by means of ordinary history must be condemned. The relation of man to God must be dialectical subjectivity. Truth is to be found by "inwardness." Unable to find universality (reality) by means of external history, Barth's Individual finds it in himself by means of "inwardness." The Individual is said to be dependent on nothing outside himself. The Individual which disowns all rationality and universality outside himself claims to have these qualities within himself. Barth says on one hand that faith cannot hold on to any content that comes to it from without itself and thus shows his irrationality. But when on the other hand he says, "faith is, as it were, creative of divinity," then he is relegating to man the ability to conjure up his God dialectically, and he shows his rationalism. This coincides with Kierkegaard's idea that truth exists solely in the subjective, personal certainty of the believer.

Thus the Crisis theologians have built their theology upon two assumptions of humanistic philosophy. First, the "wholly Other" God, the "Unknowable" realm of "brute fact" which is beyond rationality. Secondly, the autonomous Individual who finds truth subjectively—who comes to true "inwardness" and self-realization through the rational, dialectical process which leads to the conflict and the "leap." These assumptions directly affect the New-orthodox/ Existential philosophy history.

Philosophy of History

Some philosophies of History:

> Providential view of History: The Hebraic/Christian view - History and civilization are viewed as under the control and moving toward the purpose of the Divine Being, God.
>
> Theory of world cycles: Seneca - believed that human life is periodically destroyed and that each new cycle begins with a

---

7. *Ibid.*, p. 64.

EXISTENTIAL/NEO-ORTHODOX PHILOSOPHY

golden age of innocence and simplicity. The arts, inventions and later the luxuries lead to vice and deterioration. Fate or, the fixed order of the universe, must be accepted with resignation.

Corrupting influence of Civilization: Rousseau - human nature is good, yet men and human society are evil. Mankind deteriorates as civilization advances. The soul of man is corrupted as the science and the arts become more perfect. Misery has increased as man has departed from the simpler, primitive conditions.

History as the expression of reason or spirit: Hegel - worked out an elaborate metaphysics of history in terms of monistic idealism. He believed that reality is spirit manifesting itself in nature, in human history and in the actions of man. History is the development of spirit which expresses itself through successive stages. When spirit reaches the stage of rational freedom, it is fully conscious. World history does not belong to the realm of matter but to the realm of spirit. Whereas the essence of matter is gravity, the essence of spirit is rational freedom. Reason in history, rather than providential interventions marks the transition from Augustine to Hegel.[8]

There are other philosophies of history which may have affected the Neo-orthodox philosophy of history:

Historical nihilists: Those who deny that there is any meaning, pattern or purpose in history.

Historical skeptics: Those who assert that we do not know whether or not there is a pattern or purpose in history.

Historical subjectivists: Those who claim that any pattern which seems to be present in historical development is not actually present in history but is merely a creation of human minds or imaginations.[9]

The foregoing philosophies of history are introduced merely to show that the Neo-orthodox concept of history is absolutely foreign to the Christian or Biblical concept of history. As we shall see the Neo-orthodox philosophy of history is more anti-historical, Kantian-critical, Hegelian-pantheistic than anything else. Barth's usage of the

---

8. *Living Issues in Philosophy,* H.H. Titus, 2nd ed., American Book Co., 1953, pp. 457-459.

9. *Ibid.,* p. 456.

idea of what he calls "primal history" has its origin in Kant. Barth's ideas of the Individual and of "primal history" are inseparable. The Individual, according to Barth, has true universality within himself. That is, he is not dependent upon anything external. God, therefore, does not speak to the Individual directly through history. If God is to appear to man in history (and He must, for even Barth is able to see that man cannot save himself), it must be in another sort of history. This other sort of history is called "primal history."

Kant's critical system begins with the assumption of the non-createdness of man. The Self is wholly free or autonomous. Human thought is creative in character. The world of history becomes the training ground of the Self. In history the Self attempts to make a never-ending progress toward its self-chosen or created Ideal. Of course, Kant is not speaking here of the "empirical-self." The empirical-self must be thought of as subject to nature and history. BUT THEN, THE EMPIRICAL-SELF IS NOT THE *REAL* SELF, according to Kant. The Autonomous-self is the *real* self. And to be the real self, it must be free.

It is with this notion of the *homo noumenon* that Kant approaches historic Christianity. Naturally he cannot accept historic Christianity as final—if he did the idea of the *homo noumenon* progressing toward its self-chosen Ideal would be lost. In historic Christianity it is God who creates nature and history; in Kant's critical philosophy it is the autonomous man that creates both. Kant accepts the accounts of historical Christianity as being merely figurative, symbolic pictures made by the free moral Self. "Christ is merely the archetype of man's disposition in all its ideal purity."[10] Christ, for Kant, is not simply the revelation of God Incarnate affecting the "empirical self" of man. He is the Ideal which reason sets before itself. For Kant, no historical revelation, whether by word (Scripture) or by fact (Christ), can be taken at face value. Revelation is basically no more than a figure of speech by which reason (the autonomous man) goads itself toward its self-chosen Ideal. Because of the limits of the reach of reason, reason therefore must resort to what Kant calls the "schematism of analogy." It is this "schematism of analogy" that Kant finds in Scripture. Now it is quite incomprehensible how mankind should have set such a perfect Ideal for itself as Christ—therefore it is quite proper for the Bible to speak "analogically" of this Ideal as "coming down" to man.

---

10. *The New Modernism,* by C. Van Til, p. 85.

EXISTENTIAL/NEO-ORTHODOX PHILOSOPHY

We must look briefly at the philosophies of Franz Overbeck concerning history, for Barth urges his followers to listen to what Overbeck has to say on the idea of "primal history." Overbeck sees the realm of primal history as the realm of origins. It is the realm where the Individual is confronted with pure contingency (that is, where no distinctions are discernable between the universal and the particular). When the subject operates (through the subjective leap) in the field of primal history, he is said to stand outside of empirical history and to be functioning in the realm of pure contingency. Ordinary, empirical history is the realm of relativities and correlativities. If we are to have contact with the Absolute (God) it must be in non-historical or super-historical dimension. The true man in man is, according to Overbeck, above the passage of time and unaffected by an empirical historic Christianity. The true man (the real man, the soul) is, like Plato's man, a member of an ideal world. True Christianity, says Overbeck, appears in the realm of primal history. To seek true Christianity in the realm of empirical history is to make it subject to the manipulations of men, for in the realm of empirical history man is supreme. Here he makes his distinctions and differentiations relative to himself. It is the territory which he may call his own. He is lord in this realm because in it he merely deals with himself. All historical interpretation must be subjective because the relations of things as they appear to us in time (ordinary history) concern that side of things which belong to us and which are, in fact, our own creation. It is only when we turn to primal history that man can really meet God. These men simply deny that God influences the history of the world, as we know it, at all.

Empirical history, says Overbeck, tells no consistent tale. "It is full of sound and fury without intelligible meaning." The world simply is what it is without any reason in it that we can see. But man as a living organism is always subject to the ambiguities of the temporal, while man as the subject of thought (the real man) is able to transcend time itself and thus the ambiguities disappear. Man just thinks all the ambiguities of history away through the subjective process. To bring Christianity into alliance with empirical history is, to Overbeck, to admit that it is of this world and that it partakes of the ambiguities of this world. If history as a whole tells no intelligible tale, it follows that there can be no special turning-points in it that have particular meaning. Thus in Overbeck's system there is no sense in asking about the origin of temporal history or about the end of history, or about the Christ of history. For him, in history, nothing is ever finished.

Now let us see how these agnostic and rationalistic ideas are further developed in Barth. Barth's conception of primal history is very similar to that of Overbeck. Both negatively criticize ordinary, empirical history and follow with a "gospel" of hope through primal history. "But Barth gives far greater emphasis to the positive element than Overbeck did . . . as a traffic director he beckons vigorously, lest men go down the road of historical relativity."[11] Barth says of temporal history that "for all its competence it is not history, but photographed and analyzed chaos." To think of Christianity or salvation as apprehensible within historical relativities (ordinary history) would inevitably bring Christianity or truth to an ultimate death. In history we can never expect to meet God. At least, we shall never meet a God who is really other than ourselves. Barth argues that to think of God as creating the world in time is to "reduce God's transcendence to the level of a mere link in the chain of immanent causes."

"The gospel is not merely other and higher than history; it is the contradiction of history."[12] The righteousness manifested to the world in Christ-Ideal is timeless and transcendental and unambiguous; the history of relativities—of the world—is ambiguous. The Christ-Ideal through whom sin is removed from the world has no historical existence. Within history, Jesus as the Christ can be understood only as Myth, or as Kant would say, "schematic analogy."

It is just here that Barth's dialecticism begins to show itself. He believes that "it is the idea of pure contingency (primal history) as the correlative to the idea of absolutely comprehensive rationality (empirical history) that must do the saving work."[13] In other words, there is no way to God from history by way of negation, and, on the other hand, the only way to God is the way of negation. The very meaninglessness of history constitutes its meaning. By the contradictory and ambiguous character of history, the Individual is driven to despair; just because he is driven to despair; he sees the exit, or, ". . . minus times minus equals plus," and we have the Crisis. "He beholds the marvelous fact that the contradictory (the nature of ordinary or phenomenal history) which held him encased in the mazes

---

11. *Ibid.*, p. 89.
12. *Ibid.*, p. 90.
13. *Ibid.*, p. 92.

EXISTENTIAL/NEO-ORTHODOX PHILOSOPHY

of correlativity is the power by which he breaks through to the realm of the incommensurable."[14] Notice where the *power* is said to reside! The power unto salvation is in man's capacities to discern and reason (apart from a revelation of God). When the Individual has sensed the true meaninglessness of history and sought with passion the God of pure negation, he has also found the positive relation of God to the world.

When we have stressed the meaninglessness of history with all our power, we begin to understand that the positive relation between God and man, which is the absolutely paradoxical, exists. It is hopeless to reach the Christ by ordinary history. But we reach Him easily when, by faith(??), we are ready to leap into the void. "The true Christ, the Christ not subject to history, the Christ of paradox, is seen with the eye of faith alone . . . and faith deals with that which is beyond all the differentiations of history."[15]

The value of history lies beyond history, in primal history. It lies in the CRISIS within which all history stands, in the "sickness unto death." In primal history our relationship with Christ becomes contemporary. It is a relationship or contact with Him which lies beyond the scope of man's empirical self. Thus fundamentalists need not defend the historicity of the gospel narrative, and critics accomplish nothing by trying to destroy it; by faith we are always contemporary (face to face) with the Christ-Ideal by living within the Moment.

According to Barth, there may or may not have been a resurrection of Jesus in empirical or ordinary history. But he is not concerned with this primarily. It is the true resurrection (in the realm of primal history) that we must see. The true resurrection must be found in the subjective Moment. It is in the Moment—the subjective leap which Barth equates with faith—that we become contemporary with Christ's resurrection. As Van Til says, "by faith the believer (according to Barth) enters as it were into an airplane and by means of it transcends the mediation of history." But anyone, wherever he may be, can take to the air in this wholly subjective airplane. If no one is dependent upon any historically mediated gospel content, all men are equally unable and equally able to come to Christ in the airship Subjectivity.

"The oracles of God are the comprehensible signs of the incomprehensible truth that, though the world is incapable of redemption,

---

14. *Ibid.,* p. 94.
15. *Ibid.,* p. 95.

yet there is a redemption for the world."[16] Any man anywhere may hear these oracles through the Moment (subjective leap). These oracles of God are not dependent upon objective testimonial reporting. The truth reached through the "leap" can neither be taught nor handed down by testimony. The past is, as it were, dead, and has no message for us, for "the meaning of every epoch in history is directly related (or contemporary) to God."

Notice how Barth's philosophy of history contradicts orthodoxy's concepts of history. According to Orthodoxy, nature and history reveal the mind of God; for Barth nature and history are the results of the creative mind of man. For Orthodoxy God reveals Himself directly in history; for Barth, history is primarily the revelation of the ambiguities of mankind. Orthodoxy believes the Scriptures contain the direct revelation of God and His will made known to sinners; for Barth, the Scriptures contain a necessarily mythological statement of the ideas of primal history. For the believer in historic Christianity, Adam was the first historical man who first truly knew and loved God and then forsook Him; for Barth, Adam is an idea by which every man may picture to himself his existence as it comes into being through the Moment. For Orthodoxy redemption was accomplished by Christ in history; for Barth, redemption is not a matter accomplished *for* man in history, but *by* man in utter freedom from history.

Barth's adoption of the Kantian and Hegelian philosophies did not lead him to a really transcendent, wholly-Other God, but instead, his dialectical theology inevitably led him to a religion which was immanentistic and a God which was merely the self-chosen Ideal of the would-be autonomous man.

Barth contends that all history is, strictly speaking, no more than a promise. The apostles were no closer to the fulfillment of revelation than the prophets. The witnesses of the resurrection still deal with the promise only. To be a true witness of the resurrection is not to preach matters of historical tradition, but to point beyond history to primal history. A true faith will not build its house upon the quicksands of ordinary history. Since there is no objective revelation within phenomenal history, Barth contends, there is no historical subject that might receive such a revelation. The empirical man is not the real man. Barth contends whole heartedly for the distinction

---

16. *Ibid.,* p. 102.

between the empirical, temporary self and the real Individual, the man within man. This is the Self that believes and obeys the revelation of God (which is reached in the Crisis—the Moment) and consequently this Self cannot be a historical self. Barth does not deny, of course, that there is such a thing as an empirical self. What he contends is that this empirical self or historical-consciousness has nothing to do with the Word of God. The empirical self turns about in this world of surface phenomena (relative History) as a rat in a maze.

Here is how Van Til explains Barth's dialectical philosophy of history:

> It is in the realm of primal history that the dialectical union between God and man takes place. Revelation is primal history . . . this means that history (ordinary history) is not revelation. Primal history is a dimension that lies as it were between super-history and ordinary or surface history, while yet it impinges on both. Revelation is super-history in the sense that there is eternal happening in God Himself. On the other hand, revelation is also ordinary history. Yet it is neither in super-history nor in ordinary history that God meets man. It is in the tension between the two that revelation takes place, and it is this tension that constitutes the realm of primal history. It is here that God meets man in person. Ordinary history points to primal history and primal history constitutes the meaning of ordinary history. Primal history is the realm of meaning inasmuch as it is the realm of the Logos (what Barth does with John 1:1-18 must be neat). This realm is free from ordinary historical continuity; its unity is that of contemporaneity. It is history but it works directly on men of nearest and farthest times. Men become partners in primal history and, when they are such, they are members of the Church of Christ.[17]

And so the great rationalism of Barth stands out prominently in all that he says. Barth's Individual is after all saved by a revelation that is exclusively internal and subjective in character. His wholly-Other God proves not to be so wholly-Other as he would have us believe, but is contingent with the consciousness of the autonomous man.

---

17. Cornelius Van Til, *The New Modernism* (Philadelphia: Presbyterian and Reformed Publishing Co., 1947), pp. 154-155.

FIRST CORINTHIANS

That Barth's successors maintain the same philosophy of history, may be established by a few quotations from Reinhold Niebuhr.

Theological literalism also corrupts the difficult eschatological symbols of the Christian faith. In these the fulfillment of life is rightly presented, not as a negation but as a transfiguration of historical reality. If they are regarded as descriptions of a particular end in time, the real point of the eschatological symbol is lost. It ceases to symbolize both the end and the fulfillment of time, or to point to both the limit and the significance of historical development as the bearer of the meaning of life.

In the same manner a symbolic historical event, such as the "fall" of man, loses its real meaning when taken as literal history. It symbolizes an inevitable and yet not a natural corruption of human freedom. It must not, therefore, be regarded either as a specific event with which evil begins in history nor yet as a symbol of the modern conception of evil as the lag of nature and finiteness.

In a similar fashion the affirmation of the Christian faith that the climax of the divine self-revelation is reached in a particular person and a particular drama of his life, in which these particular events become revelatory of the meaning of the whole of life, is falsely rationalized so that the Jesus of history who is known as the Christ by faith is interpreted as an inhuman and incredible personality with alleged powers of omniscience within the conditions of finiteness. In this way the ultimate truth about God and His relation to men, which can be appropriated only in repentance and faith, is made into a "fact" of history.

These errors of a literalistic orthodoxy tend to obscure the real issues between Christianity and modern culture as surely as the premature capitulation of liberal Christianity to modern culture. The Christian truth is presented as a "dated" bit of religious fantasy which is credible only to the credulous and which may be easily dismissed by modern man."[18]

The points of reference for the structure of the meaning of history in the Christian faith are obviously not found by an empirical analysis of the observable structures and coherences of

---

18. *Faith and History,* by Reinhold Niebuhr, Scribners, 1949, pp. 33, 34.

EXISTENTIAL/NEO-ORTHODOX PHILOSOPHY

history. They (the points of reference) are revelations apprehended by faith, of the character and purposes of God. The experience of faith by which they are apprehended is an experience at the ultimate limits of human knowledge; and it requires a condition of repentance which is a possibility for the individual, but only indirectly for nations and collectives.[19]

Niebuhr ridicules the faith that seeks to be founded upon the testimony of "revelatory facts" within ordinary history. He says of the resurrection that it was not empirical fact, but the subjective interpretation of the meaning behind the death of Jesus (cf. page 147-148 of "Faith and History" by Niebuhr). He says of the orthodox faith that it is a "faith not quite sure of itself," and ". . . always hopes to suppress its skepticism by establishing the revelatory depth of a fact through its miraculous character . . . this type of miracle is in opposition to true faith."[20]

Some Results of the Existential Philosophy of History

This rationalistic theology has devastating effect on all aspects of historic Christianity. Hear what it has to say concerning the Christian hope!

The question of hope naturally involves our concept of the future and so the whole question of time and its meaning and the outcome of history is affected. Universalism finds its most striking expression in Barth's discussion of the Christian hope. Barth couches his theology in orthodox terms when he contends that our hope is to be fixed not on some Platonic idea but on solid historical fact. BUT WHAT HAVE WE LEARNED THAT BARTH CALLS A GENUINE HISTORICAL FACT? This is the all-important question. "Time and place are a matter of perfect indifference. Of what these eyes see it can really be equally well said that it was, is and will be, never and nowhere, and that it was, is and will be, always everywhere possible."[21] Indeed a fact of history is, according to Barth, not genuinely such unless it is everywhere and always possible. It is this sort of fact that is everywhere and always happening. This is to say, the resurrection of Christ stands, in Barth's case, for the Idea of the general progress of the

---

19. *Ibid.*, p. 136.
20. *Ibid.*, pp. 147-148.
21. *The New Modernism*, p. 339.

human race toward Ideal perfection—the resurrection is everywhere and always happening.

Barth claims that fundamentalism has, by means of its doctrine of the direct revelation of God in the Incarnation of Jesus, limited God. We have bound God to His own revelation; He is no longer free, or wholly-Other. Barth speaks of God as being *contingently* present with man and it is only when God is thought of as contingently present with us that God Himself may become true history in us and with us. BUT DOES THIS FREE GOD OR DOES IT LIMIT HIM MORE THAN THE ORTHODOX THEOLOGY? To Barth we do not really exist except to the extent that we are contemporaneous with God. With such a philosophy as this it must also be true that God does not really exist except to the extent that He is contemporaneous with us. God is not Object—He is Subject. A real historical fact, according to Barth, therefore takes place only as an event, as a process of contingent contemporaneity of God with man and of man with God and that, subjectively.

Barth argues that history as such "is dumb"; it speaks with a chaos of voices mutually contradictory of one another. The space/time world is a world of no meaningful significance. Kant reduced the teachings of historic Christianity one by one to the level of illustrations of "eternal truths," truths of reason. Barth does virtually the same thing. If there is to be a genuine resurrection, a resurrection that shall be everywhere and always possible to all men, there must be a burial in which the God of orthodoxy is buried. THERE MUST BE NO ANTECEDENT BEING OF ANY SORT IN THE THEOLOGY OF CRISIS! A fact, to be a real fact for Barth as for Kant, must be ultimately constructed by the autonomous mind. Only then can it ever be reconstructed, ever re-experienced by the dialectic. Thus the antecedent God must be buried.

The resurrection as a genuine historical fact then is, according to Barth, a process and such a process as includes the whole race. Moreover, the process is only beginning. It has not been finished at any point, nor will it be finished at any point in the future. It must always be a contemporaneous fact. For Barth, any fact that may possibly be finished at some future time on the calendar is no true historical fact. It would be a fact that could be fully revealed without being at the same time fully hidden. This simply destroys the Christian hope of the Second Coming. The existentialist can never say "Maranatha" as we say it.

EXISTENTIAL/NEO-ORTHODOX PHILOSOPHY

Does not Barth wed the very rationalism and scientism that he professes to divorce? Scientism will recognize no facts as facts unless they are universally verifiable, unless they can be tested by experience at any time. Barth holds that facts are not allowed as facts unless so pronounced by would-be autonomous man after the principle of an exhaustive, rational, dialectical process.

In all his irrationalism and subjectivism, Barth, like his philosopher predecessors, has but cleared the ground for a rationalism in which all difference between God and man is finally removed. Barth's theology leaves us without hope and without God.

The existential theology has come full circle in Reinhold Niebuhr and Rudolph Bultmann from its original reaction against rationalism and liberalism to a liberalism all its own. It is clearest, perhaps, in Bultmann's "demythologization" of the Scriptures. In view of the pervading spirit of scientific realism of our age, it becomes necessary for us, says Bultmann, to interpret the Christian message in terms that are relevant. All pre-scientific myths must be cut away such as the myth of the pre-existent Lord, the myths of heaven, hell, angels, miracles, virgin birth and the empty tomb and resurrection.

The death of Jesus of Nazareth, according to Bultmann, is not to be understood as the expiatory death of a substitute. That an incarnate divine being should cancel out the sins of men through his blood is, to Bultmann, "primitive mythology." However, one can believe in the cross of Christ, says Bultmann. "Its decisive, history-shaping significance is made apparent by the fact that it is effectual as an eschatological event; that is, it is not an event of the past, to which one looks back, but it is an eschatological event in time and beyond time, so far as it is understood in its significance, and insofar as it is always present for faith."[22]

Bultmann also denies that the resurrection of Christ is an actual event. For Bultmann the existentialist interpretation of the New Testament is entirely independent of historical factuality. One must make a sharp distinction between "historical facts" and "historic encounter." The Christian *kerygma* of God's salvation in Jesus Christ has nothing to do with facts which may have happened in Palestine between A.D. 1 and 30. The "kerygmatic Christ" calls men "here and now" to the decision of faith. Faith is not to be

---

22. "Dare We Follow Bultmann?" by J. Schneider, in *Christianity Today*, June 5, 1961.

understood as faith in the personal Saviour but means "emancipation from the past" and to come to true self-realization, true individuality.

"The existentialism of Bultmann is nothing more than a modern variation of that anthropocentrism which, beginning with the Enlightenment, has continued to plague theology, and according to which the standard of validity is seen in existential significance."[23] In other words, Bultmann is merely a modern extension of the Kantian, Hegelian, Kierkegaardian and Barthian enthroning of the Individual or autonomous man.

To Bultmann the cross of Jesus is merely a sign for the fact that it is worthwhile to bear one's own suffering willingly. The resurrection is merely the knowledge of the "meaning of the cross." For him the Second Coming of Christ is "rationally inconceivable."

For Bultmann the name Jesus Christ represents not a personal living reality of God's saving revelation in the sphere of history but merely a concept, an ideogram, a symbol or a principle for the event of contemporary preaching."[24]

Bultmann's theology is no theology at all, but rather a philosophical wisdom in Christian garb. His "revelation" of God becomes a synonymous concept for the attainment of a new self-consciousness or understanding; but in no way does it mean the reality of an actual intervention of God in the historical world of space and time.

He strips the New Testament of all its power and authority and then sets out to transform society with the "real Jesus," the "demythologized New Testament." His philosophy, like the philosophies of his predecessors, is able to offer only the ego-centric, autonomous, empirical-Self which may, through the subjective leap become contingent with the Christ-Ideal. This is essentially the same thing that Liberalism offered and which the world found hopeless and powerless to transform men. The existential philosophy is doomed to failure for it lacks the only enduring and all-sufficient foundation, Jesus Christ, who is both historic man and at the same time the resurrected and transcendent Lord. It lacks that which is basically fundamental to a transforming power—trust in a Divine Personality who reveals Himself to man within the historic relativities of man's dimensions. It lacks also that other essential element of transforming power—

---

23. "Dare We Follow Bultmann?" by W. Kunneth, in *Christianity Today,* October 13, 1961.
24. *Ibid.*

EXISTENTIAL/NEO-ORTHODOX PHILOSOPHY

authority resident and available in a Personality higher and wiser than man himself.

In their efforts to overcome the rationalism of 19th century European theologians with irrationalism, the existentialists have become neo-rationalists rather than neo-orthodox. They do not *openly* deny the existence of God. They simply swing the pendulum of theology to the opposite extreme of rationality and irrationally demand a wholly-Other God who, because He must remain non-phenomenal to remain free, cannot reveal Himself in phenomenal history. Therefore the real man must contact God through an irrational leap—wholly subjective faith. Man's contact with God therefore must stand dependent upon man's inherent capabilities. So we have the autonomous man "creating" faith through the dialectical process moving toward his "self-chosen" Ideal.

Jesus of Nazareth was not God Incarnate for these theologians, but a symbolic picture, a "schematic analogy," of the self-chosen Ideal. The existential theology is as much of the spirit of anti-Christ as modernism, liberalism, agnosticism or the Gnosticism which was contemporary with John, who wrote, "Beloved, believe not every spirit, but prove the spirits, whether they are of God, because many false prophets are gone out into the world. Hereby know ye the Spirit of God: every spirit that confesseth that Jesus Christ is come in the flesh is of God: and every spirit that confesseth not Jesus is not of God and this is the spirit of the anti-christ, whereof ye have heard that it cometh; and now it is in the world already" (I John 4:1-3).

The existential theology is in direct contradiction to the New Testament witness concerning the Incarnation. "And the Word became flesh, and dwelt among us (and we beheld his glory, glory as of the only begotten from the Father), full of grace and truth" (John 1:14). Any sensible exegesis of this passage will not allow for the existential philosophy of history.

The existential theologians, by implication, call the New Testament writers liars . . . "That which was from the beginning, that which we have heard, that which we have seen with our eyes, that which we beheld, and our hands handled, concerning the Word of life . . . declare we unto you . . ." (I John 1:1, 3).

Hopelessness is the progenitor of pessimism, epicureanism, materialism and all manner of sin while it goes about paralyzing any kind of transforming and enduring faith. Existentialism is father and mother of HOPELESSNESS!

Chapter Sixteen

THE PROBLEM OF AIDING CHRISTIAN BRETHREN (16:1-24)

IDEAS TO INVESTIGATE:

1. Why were the saints to "put something aside" each first day of the week if Paul would not pick it up until 6 months later?
2. What is "prospering"? What percentage of one's "prosperity" should he give to the Lord's work?
3. Did Paul expect the Christians at Corinth to help him financially with his missionary work?
4. Is there other aid, besides financial, called for in this chapter? What kind? Is that still relevant for the church today? How accomplished?
5. What is a "holy kiss"? Would it be good to practice that now?

SECTION 1

Endow (16:1-9)

16 Now concerning the contribution for the saints: as I directed the churches of Galatia, so you also are to do. ²On the first day of every week, each of you is to put something aside and store it up, as he may prosper, so that contributions need not be made when I come. ³And when I arrive, I will send those whom you accredit by letter to carry your gift to Jerusalem. ⁴If it seems advisable that I should go also, they will accompany me.

5 I will visit you after passing through Macedonia, for I intend to pass through Macedonia, ⁶and perhaps I will stay with you or even spend the winter, so that you may speed me on my journey, wherever I go. ⁷For I do not want to see you now just in passing; I hope to spend some time with you, if the Lord permits. ⁸But I will stay in Ephesus until Pentecost, ⁹for a wide door for effective work has opened to me, and there are many adversaries.

16:1-4 Ministering: The Corinthian Christians had a problem with giving. In an earlier communication with them Paul apparently mentioned the need for a contribution to relieve the suffering of their

CHAPTER 16　　　　　FIRST CORINTHIANS 16:1-9

brethren in Judea. Now he writes to set forth apostolic directions on how to best collect that contribution. Evidently, between this letter (I Corinthians) and the next (II Corinthians) (a period of 4 or 5 months —Spring to Fall of 57 A.D.), the Corinthians had some misunderstandings and misgivings about this collection for the saints in Jerusalem. In I Corinthians 16:1-4 Paul sounds as if he is *ordering* the people to give, whether they want to or not. Someone may have taken offense at his bluntness, so he wrote II Corinthians, chapters 8 and 9, to explain that all giving must be done willingly, as each man has purposed in his own heart, and not out of coercion. But it is a fact, that both of these are scriptural motives for Christian stewardship. Paul uses the Greek word *logeias* (lit. "something counted, a collection") to describe what he had "*directed*" (Gr. *dietaxa,* given orders for as in the military) to the churches of Galatia. Now he *commands* the church at Corinth (Gr. *poiesate,* 2nd, pl. 1 aor., imperative, "You do!") to take up offerings, and tells them how to do it. They started to do what he ordered (see II Cor. 8:10), but then they stopped. So he wrote later holding before them the example of the Macedonians and telling them they must not give as if it were an *exaction.* Jesus taught his stewardship lessons under the same two principles. First, Jesus is the Master, our King. He has every right to give his servants orders about the conduct of their stewardship. On the other hand, the obedience of the servant is to be done under an attitude of willingness and cheerfulness. If obedience has to be coerced and is resented, the servant of Christ is no better than the "elder brother" who stayed home but hated every minute of it, (see Luke 15:25-32).

This chapter is the crown of all the teaching of the first Corinthian letter. The epistle started with the reminder, "God is faithful, by whom ye were called unto the *fellowship* (Gr. *koinonian,* "communion") of his Son Jesus Christ our Lord" (I Cor. 1:9). Because of that *fellowship* with Jesus Christ, Christians have been called into partnership or communion with the whole church of Christ everywhere in the world. The Corinthians needed to know that their relationship to Christ also involved brotherhood with the whole world-wide church whether in Corinth, Macedonia, Galatia or Jerusalem. They must be led to *share* in supplying material needs and spiritual needs of all the brethren "called unto" the same fellowship ("communion") as they—no matter where those brethren were. Perhaps Paul is *ordering* this lengthy and regular collection for benevolence as part of the therapy for their self-centeredness. Whoever would save his life shall lose it, but whoever would lose his life for Christ's sake and the Gospel's, shall secure it.

Giving is not optional for the Christian. Every place Paul established a congregation of believers he taught them they must give. Jesus taught that to be his followers a person must be willing to give when one has hardly anything at all (the poor widow with two mites, Luke 21:1-4; Mark 12:41-44) and to give all when one has everything (the rich young ruler, Luke 18:18-30; Matt. 19:16-22; Mark 10:17-22). Giving is the very essence and breath of Christianity.

There were two reasons the Christians in Judea were needing financial help. First, a famine (Acts 11:28) had devastated the area; second, many of the Jews who had become christian in Judea were being persecuted and their "goods were being plundered" (Heb. 10:34) by their Hebrew persecutors. It is instructive to note the different Greek words the apostle uses to describe this "contribution":

a. *logeias* - "a thing that has been counted, a collection." (I Cor. 16:1)
b. *charin* - "a gracious gift" (I Cor. 16:3)
c. *koinonia* - "a taking part, a fellowship, a communion" (II Cor. 8:4; 9:13)
d. *diakonia* - "a ministry, a deaconship" (II Cor. 8:4)
e. *hadroteti* - "bountiful, abundance, liberal gift" (II Cor. 8:20)
f. *eulogian* - "well-counted, blessed-counting" (II Cor. 9:5)
g. *leitourgia* - "serviceable gift, a gift to serve, a liturgy" (II Cor. 9:12)
h. *eleemosune* - "alms, gift of mercy, gift for the poor" (Acts 24:17)
i. *prosphora* - "a sacrificial offering" (Acts 24:17)

From all these synonyms we get a picture of Christian giving as systematic, liberal, willing, and purposeful. Stedman (*op. cit.*) notices the following outline in Paul's instructions here:

1. Giving is to be a universal Christian practice - "as I directed the churches of Galatia, so you also are to do . . ."
2. Giving is in celebration of Christ's resurrection - "On the first day of the week . . ."
3. Giving is personal - ". . . *each* of you is to put something aside . . ."
4. Giving should be planned and with regularity - ". . . put something aside and store it up . . ."

CHAPTER 16   FIRST CORINTHIANS 16:1-9

5. Giving is not to be measured by amount but by motive - ". . . as he may prosper . . ."
6. Giving should be done without special pressure - ". . . so that contributions need not be made when I come . . ."
7. Giving should be applied faithfully to that for which it has been given - ". . . I will send those whom you accredit by letter . . ."

The Greek syntax of verse 2 is interesting: *kata mian sabbatou hekastos humon par heauto titheto thesaurizon ho ti ean euodotai . . .,* "Upon the first of the week each of you by himself is to deposit the things being stored up however he is prospered . . ." You see, they were storing up their offerings constantly—every day—then on Sunday they took their personal collection and *deposited* it in the congregational offering. In the culture of the first century, most people were paid at the end of every day for their labor (see Matt. 20:8). Every day they "stored up" part of their daily wages, according to how much they were paid, and deposited it on the Lord's Day (first day of the week). This is clearly an assertion that in the first century church there was a time (first day of the week) and a responsible administering (deposit) for money given by Christians to the Lord's work. It is also a clear indication that the early Christians met on the first day of the week to worship and share in the Lord's work.

The Greek word *euodotai* is a combined word from *eu,* meaning "well or good," and *hodos,* meaning "road or journey or path." It is translated in verse 2, "prosper." Christians are to give according to "the goodness of the road" they travel. If God has given a man a "hard row to hoe" (hard times, poverty) he should give whatever he is able to give. He must give something, but it may be very little compared to what others have to give. But that is all right with God. It does not need to be a tithe (10 percent) There is nowhere in the New Testament that tithing is commanded for the Christian. The Christian's relationship is on a much higher level than tithing. The expectation for a Christian is loving, self-sacrificing, responsible stewardship of 100 percent of all with which he has been entrusted. He will give as he believes the Lord has given to him, and what he retains he will not consider his own but he will use it wisely and frugally to serve Christ in the best manner possible and bring glory to his name. We cannot give more than we have. God knows that (II Cor. 8:12), and accepts it. God is singularly interested in the "readiness" of mind and heart to give. With God, motive is all important (see Matt. 6:2, 3, 4, 19, 20, 21). Great sums of money may be given (see

FIRST CORINTHIANS

Luke 21:1-4; Mark 12:41-44) but if the motive is self-righteousness, it is an abomination with God, (see Isa. 1:10-17; Micah 6:6-8).

Paul anxiously guarded against exacting contributions for the Lord's work through special pressures. He said, ". . . so that contributions need not be made when I come . . ." He really said, in Greek, *hina me hotan eltho tote logeiai ginontai,* "lest whenever I come then collections there are." Why this instruction?

> Because the apostle knew that when he was personally present he had a tremendous impact on people. He did not want their giving to be because they were moved by his preaching or by his stories of what God had done, or in any other way to be pressured. No professional fund raisers would have been permitted in the early churches. Paul says, in effect, "Do not bring out the thermometer; do not put on a three-ring circus, with people running down the aisle bringing pledges to meet a predetermined goal. I do not want that." Your giving is to come out of a heart that has been moved by the grace of God. God does not want giving on any terms other than those. Giving must be without special pressure.
>
> (Ray C. Stedman, *op. cit.,* p. 327)

Finally, Paul advises the church at Corinth of its responsibility to insure that the collection for the needy gets to Judea as intended. The apostle offers to *help* deliver the money if he is needed, but he will let the Corinthian congregation decide who the messengers shall be.

These are principles, based on apostolic authority, the church will do well to follow closely in every age. They are never outdated or irrelevant. We have so much in America! We are so prosperous, in comparison with the rest of the world. God has certainly given Americans, considering our liberties as well as our material endowments, an "easier row to hoe" than the majority of the world's people. Of course, we do not expect unbelievers in America to give to the Lord's work as they have been prospered. But it is doubtful that most Christians in America give as they have been prospered. Let us repent, and do it!

16:5-9 Missions: If we did not know the humble nature of Paul, and did not know his passion for being self-supporting by plying his trade of tent-making, we would think him a bit presumptuous

CHAPTER 16　　　　　　　　　　FIRST CORINTHIANS 16:1-9

to invite himself to be the guest of the Corinthians. Paul undoubtedly has another motive for inviting the Corinthians to support him in his intended missionary work. He would want to allow them the privilege of sharing in the fruits of his labors (see Phil. 4:17; II Cor. 11:7-11; 12:13).

Paul established the church in Corinth (Acts 18:1ff.) in A.D. 51 on his 2nd missionary journey. He remained there a year, and returned to Palestine via Syria (Acts 18:18-22). He began his third missionary journey in A.D. 54 going first through Galatia and Phrygia (Acts 18:23), then to Ephesus (Acts 18:24). During a three-year stay at Ephesus (Acts 18:24—19:41) he wrote I Corinthians. Leaving Asia Minor (Acts 20:1-4) he went to Macedonia. From Macedonia he wrote II Corinthians. Then he went on down into Greece where he spent three months, visiting Corinth again after about a six-year absence. While at Corinth, in 57 A.D., he wrote the epistle to the Romans. In our text here (I Cor. 16:5) Paul writes from Ephesus of his plan to visit Corinth "after passing through Macedonia."

Paul *intended* to stay with the Corinthians. He was "passing through" Macedonia *toward* (Gr. *pros,* preposition denoting direction) Corinth. He intended to stay at Corinth *in order that* (Gr. *hina,* conjunction denoting purpose, aim or goal) they might *speed him on his journey,* (Gr. *propempsete,* aorist imperative active verb, meaning, "you will furnish me with things necessary for a journey"— see Titus 3:13; III John 6). He did not want to see them "just in passing." He intended to spend some time with them, "if the Lord permits." He would need to be housed, fed, perhaps even given financial assistance (even though he usually earned his own living— Acts 20:33-35; I Cor. 4:9-18; II Cor. 11:7-12; 12:14-18; I Thess. 2:5-9; and he taught other Christians to do the same—I Thess. 4:9-12; II Thess. 3:6-15). There were certainly times when Paul did take financial aid (Phil. 4:15-19) and he said he had a right to take such aid in his ministry (I Cor. 9:1ff.). Some preachers, evangelists and missionaries, in this affluent twentieth century, are forced to surrender full-time ministries because of lack of financial support. Perhaps the major reason for insufficient financial pay to ministers of the gospel is that many Christian people do not believe a minister works hard enough to deserve pay equal to those who do manual labor, or equal to those professionals who have invested in years of training and apprenticeship. Most ministers of the gospel today are being paid a salary about equal to janitors and public school teachers—most of whom must take a "second job to make ends meet." Ministers with families have difficulty staying out of debt and conducting a full-time ministry on that kind of pay. Most preachers and missionaries never complain. They go right on struggling, feeling the psychological pressures of living each day on the edge of insolvency. They do it because they have a servant's heart. But even the ox (let alone the human servant) is worthy of his hire (I Cor. 9:8-12).

The apostle intended to stay at Corinth. He needed assistance. He was going to be put to the test in Ephesus. He would be run through the "psychological grinder" there. As he was writing he could see a "wide door for effective work" opening for him but there were many adversaries. It would be *hard work*, taxing every mental and emotional fiber of his being. The financial aid he might expect from Corinth would boost his spirit. But he would also be looking for some spiritual encouragement through his stay in Corinth. Even the greatest of the apostles needed human comfort. Some of the most pathos-filled words in all the Bible are those of Paul in the Roman prison awaiting death when he asked Timothy to "do your best to come to me soon" (II Tim. 4:9-18). Paul may have also had in mind the same reason he took financial aid from Philippi. He may have wanted Corinth to have the blessing of participating in the future "fruits" of his ministry (see Phil. 4:17). Whatever his reasoning, it appears he *did not* receive financial aid from Corinth. He apologizes (II Cor. 11:7-11; 12:13) for having done them a disservice for not having demanded it! Any group of Christians that *does not pay* its preacher sufficient wages to relieve him of financial anxiety, does not help him prepare for retirement, and does not encourage him by understanding how hard he labors, is *doing itself a disservice!* Such a church could never realize the satisfaction of sharing in the fruits of his labor.

SECTION 2

Endorse (16:10-18)

10 When Timothy comes, see that you put him at ease among you, for he is doing the work of the Lord, as I am. 11 So let no one despise him. Speed him on his way in peace, that he may return to me; for I am expecting him with the brethren.

12 As for our brother Apollos, I strongly urged him to visit you with the other brethren, but it was not at all his will to come now. He will come when he has opportunity.

13 Be watchful, stand firm in your faith, be courageous, be strong. 14Let all that you do be done in love.

15 Now, brethren, you know that the household of Stephanas were the first converts in Achaia, and they have devoted themselves to the service of the saints; 16I urge you to be subject to such men and to every fellow worker and laborer. 17I rejoice at the coming of Stephanas and Fortunatus and Achaicus, because they have made up for your absence; 18for they refreshed my spirit as well as yours. Give recognition to such men.

16:10-12 With Reassurance: Paul sent Timothy (and Erastus) from Ephesus to Macedonia (Acts 19:22) and thence to Corinth. After these two helpers had departed on their journey, news came from Corinth that was very disturbing. People from Chloe's household brought a letter and news by word of mouth that the church was struggling in the throes of schismatism, immorality, indifference, disorderliness, and false teaching. Paul knew how easy it would be for such behavior to *ruin* a young preacher by making him discouraged and cynical. The apostle charges the Corinthian church (Gr. *blepete,* imperative mood), "*See* that you. . . ." give Timothy every reassurance possible for his ministry among you. Paul says, in Greek, *blepete hina aphobos genetai pros humas,* or, "See that you aim to make him be without fear among you." They are not to just let Timothy "shift for himself" in this matter of finding strength and assurance for his work. They are to make it their purpose to relieve him of all that would dishearten and depress him.

The Greek word *aphobos* is translated in RSV as "put him at ease" but is literally, "without fear or phobia." What would Timothy have to fear in Corinth? Pretended sophistication, intellectualism, Gentile cultural differences (shocking enough in themselves to a Jew), all in addition to the problems within the church itself. Paul hopes the Corinthians will conduct themselves toward Timothy according to the principles he has enumeratered in chapters 8 through 10. Paul said, "Let no one despise him. . . ." The Greek word *exouthenese* means, literally, "to erase from an account-ledger," or, "to make of no account." Timothy was young, and a Jew. Timothy had no training in Greek literature as Paul had. Sophisticates from the great cities of Greece might tend to show contempt for a young Jewish lad like Timothy. But Timothy was "doing the work of the Lord" and he was important to Paul, so he directed the Corinthians not only to support him while he was there, but also to speed him on his way back to him.

Old and young can become close and intimate companions in the work of the gospel. The young person should be respectful and heedful of wise guidance (I Tim. 5:1-22; II Tim. 2:24-26), and the older person is not to think of youth as "of no account." Young people need to feel secure through being encouraged, strengthened, and built up.

Evidently, the Corinthians had requested Paul to insist that Apollos, an eloquent man, and a favorite teacher of the Corinthians, return for a visit. It is apparent the Corinthians thought Paul had not transmitted their request to Apollos. What did the Corinthians think—that Paul, out of jealousy of Apollos' superior oratorical ability and his popularlity at Corinth, spitefully ignored their request? Paul replies, "I strongly *urged* (Gr. *parekalesa,* exhorted, encouraged) him to visit with the other brethren." But the more Paul urged, the more Apollos declined. The Greek would literally say, "And *altogether* it was not his will to come now." Apollos was spiritually-minded and loving enough to reject even something he most probably would have enjoyed rather than give any occasion, or appearance, of "competition" among Christian co-workers. Apollos did not wish his name or his abilities to be abused in support of schismatism or any of the other aberrations of the Corinthian church. He told Paul he would visit Corinth later, when a good opportunity offered itself to him. Whether he did or not, we do not know. His and Paul's actions in these circumstances are exemplary. Let all Christians "doing the work of the Lord" reassure one another in the same kind of conduct.

16:13-14 With Righteousness: All Christians should endorse the gospel and give aid to those who labor full-time in its proclamation by living righteously. That is the best endorsement and aid that may be given to those who work so hard and with little reward in this life. Paul said of the Christians at Thessalonica, "For you are our glory and joy" (I Thess. 2:17-20). He wanted these Corinthians to be "epistles of his, to be known and read by all men" (II Cor. 3:1-3).

He exhorts them to be *watchful* (Gr. *gregoreite*). It is in the imperative mood, thus a command. The male name, *Gregory.* is from this Greek word, and means "vigilant, alert, awake, on guard." The Christian cannot afford to be inept, unaware, careless, unmindful, mesmerized, hypnotized, manipulated and seduced! Paul was afraid for the Corinthians that "as the serpent deceived Eve by his cunning, their thoughts would be led astray from a sincere and pure devotion to Christ" (II Cor. 11:3). What was happening to the church with all its problems (especially the false teaching about the resurrection) was not amusing or insignificant. It was evil, destructive, spiritual-insanity.

Next, Paul says, "Be standing in the faith." The Greek verb, *stekete,* is present tense, imperative mood. Once again, it is a command for them to continue their posture before the world in the faith. Paul used the definite article (Gr. *te,* "the" faith), so he is not talking here about personal subjective faith as a virtue, but *the* faith as a body of doctrine. He wanted the Corinthians to take a constant stance upon a knowledge and practice of *the* revealed faith (the teachings and writings of the apostles). Standing fast in *the* faith or in the Lord is something which can be determined in an objective way. We can know whether we are keeping *the* faith if we are keeping Christ's (and the apostle's) word (I John 2:3-6; 2:24; 3:24, etc.). Standing in *the* faith gives unimaginable aid and encouragement to teachers of *the* faith. It is the kind of aid and reward that will never pass away.

Third, Paul says the Corinthians will give aid and comfort to their Christian allies (brethren) by being *courageous.* Actually, the Greek word is *andrizesthe,* and literally means, "act like a man." They are exhorted (the Greek verb is present tense, imperative mood) to continue maturing, growing up, behaving like adults who learn from experience. All marks of mature adulthood (self-control, caution, sensibility, courtesy, firmness, cool-headedness, consideration for another's opinions and trials, tenderness) is what Paul says will contribute to strengthening their fellow Christians. Mature men do not let peer-pressures or vanities of the world seduce them away from the truth. Mature men are able to endure persecution and tribulation without giving in to falsehood. Some of the Corinthians had behaved like immature babies (see I Cor. 3:1ff.). It goes without saying that the church today needs members who "act like men."

Fourth, they are ordered to *be strong* (Gr. *krataiousthe,* again, present imperative). The Greek word is from a root word which means "to be forceful, dominating, mighty." There is no place for any kind of weakness in the Christian life—neither intellectual, moral or spiritual. To be a Christian one must "swim against the tide" of human opinion and worldly lifestyle. To be a Christian one must endure a constant war between his flesh and the things of God's Spirit (Gal. 5:17; Rom. 7:13-25). All the world is on the side of the evil one. The Christian will get no help from the worldly-minded people in this world! Do not expect any. What may seem like help from the world is only deception and seduction. To be a Christian demands the best, the strongest, and the most mature. And the Christian who wishes to aid his brother must be forceful (not overbearing) in his support of the gospel.

Finally, Paul says, "Let all that you do be done in love." Love is the supreme virtue (see comments on ch. 13). Without it everything else is wrong. With it (true, agape-love) everything is right. It is that virtue which validates every other professed virtue. Love is the power that sculptures all talents, circumstances, and characteristics of the human personality into a monument reflecting and praising the glory of the Son of God. When all is done in love there is no problem with aiding Christian brethren, (see I Peter 4:8).

16:15-18 With Respect: When Paul wrote to the Christians at Rome he said, "Pay . . . respect to whom respect is due, honor to whom honor is due" (Rom. 13:7). He said the same to the Christians at Philippi (see Phil. 2:29) and Thessalonica (see I Thess. 5:12).

Paul deals first with the motive for respecting fellow-workers. The household of Stephanas, first converts in Achaia (Gr. *aparche,* lit. "firstfruit"), *devoted* (Gr. *etaxan* "addicted" KJV) themselves to the *service* (Gr. *diakonian*, deaconship) of the saints. Respectful attention to and emulation of such people is a strong Biblical theme (see Heb. 11:1—12:2; I Peter 5:1-5; II Tim. 1:13; 2:1-2; 3:10-17; Heb. 13:7, etc.). Respect in the service of the Lord is earned, not inherited.

Next, Paul says, "be subject to such men and to every fellow worker and laborer. . . ." The Greek word is *hupotassesthe*. This comes from the same root word (*tasso*) as the word *etaxan,* translated "addicted" or "devoted" in 16:15. The prepositional prefix, *hupo,* means "under." Thus, the word *hupotassesthe* means, literally, "be addicted or devoted under," or, "subjected to, subordinated to." It is the same word used by Paul in Ephesians 5:21 to deal with attitudes and behavior of husband and wife toward one another. The most practical spiritual help we can give to a Christian ally or brother is to subordinate ourselves in service to him. You will note that "subordination" is not just to a select few, but "to every fellow worker and laborer" (16:16). This substantiates Jesus' example and apostolic teaching throughout the New Testament (see Matt. 20:25-28; Luke 22:24-27; John 13:1-20; Gal. 5:13; Eph. 5:21; Phil. 2:3; I Peter 5:5). There is no "ruling class" in the kingdom of God. Christ is the only King—everyone else is a servant who is to subordinate himself to his brethren. We are to "outdo one another in showing honor" (Rom. 12:10). It is interesting that Paul uses the Greek conjunction, *hina* ("in order that") to connect the *devotion* of Stephanas' ministry with the *subordination* of the Corinthians to emulate his example. In other words, Stephanas devoted himself to ministry *in order that* the Corinthians might surrender to his guidance in living the Christian life! That is the way it must be with all "leaders" in the Church—wherever they wish others to follow, they must lead! They will never bring others to submit to their leadership unless they devote themselves ("become addicted to") ministering!

Finally, Paul directs, "give recognition to such men." The Greek word *epiginoskete* does *not* mean what we usually think of as "recognition" (applause, flattery, hero-worship). *Epiginoskete* means, "to know thoroughly; to recognize a thing to be what it really is, to be perceptive." The element of expressing gratitude and encouragement is involved, but not braggadocio or adulation. All that is very dangerous to a person's relationship to God. It was said of Jesus, ". . . you are true, and teach the way of God truthfully, and care for no man; for you do not regard the position of men" (Matt. 22:16). Jesus said of himself, "I do not receive glory from men" (John 5:41). We must be careful to be sincerely grateful for every brother in Christ, expressing it without setting any Christian above another by bragging about him or fawning over him. When Paul wrote this about his fellow laborers, he did not intend the Corinthians to call these fellows before the congregation and give them plaques or put their names in periodicals as if they were the *only* co-laborers who ever helped him. He simply wanted the Corinthian church to be hospitable, kind, *perceptive,* and appreciative. Christians should get acquainted with and *get to know thoroughly* such men as Stephanas and Fortunatus and Achaicus; their devotion in service to Christ and his Church might "rub off on" those who get to know them.

SECTION 4

Embrace (16:19-23)

19 The churches of Asia send greetings. Aquila and Prisca, together with the church in their house, send you hearty greetings in the Lord. 20 All the brethren send greetings. Greet one another with a holy kiss.

FIRST CORINTHIANS

21 I, Paul, write this greeting with my own hand. 22 If any one has no love for the Lord, let him be accursed. Our Lord, come! 23 The grace of the Lord Jesus be with you.

16:19-20 Dearly: Paul wanted Christians in every nation, culture, race and language to acknowledge their common citizenship in the eternal kingdom of God. Wherever he went, whenever he wrote, he promoted Christian unity and fellowship. Christians *are* united. The fellowship or communion of believers is an accomplished work which took place in the redemption Christ finished. Unity *is* the Christian calling because Christ "created in himself one new man in place of the two. . . ." Christ broke down the dividing wall of hostility and reconciled all who will accept this reconciliation as *one* body, (Eph. 2:11-22). Now, it is the responsibility of Christians to "give diligence to maintain the unity of the Spirit in the bond of peace . . . " (Eph. 4:1-16).

The oneness of the universal brotherhood in Christ was not dependent on material things. The first century church did not have church buildings but usually met in people's houses for congregational worship. Aquila and Prisca had a church in their house. This does not mean, of course, that church buildings are not good. Anything in God's creation which can be used to honestly and faithfully further the preaching of the Gospel should be used to its best advantage. But we must never think we have to have "things" to follow Christ. We must never think that one culture and people has to use the same methods or tools another one uses to follow Jesus.

Paul wanted the Corinthian church to know that the churches (Christians) of Asia Minor ("foreigners") sent them *hearty* (Gr. *polla,* "much") greetings in the Lord. Politically and socially, the people of Asia Minor and Greece were enemies, and had been for centuries. But Paul expects the power of Christ's love to make them brothers, eager to love one another and eager to be "one body" in the Lord.

He orders them, "*You greet*" (Gr. *aspasasthe,* imperative mood, meaning, "salute, embrace") one another with a *holy kiss* (Gr. *philemati hagio*). This is the kind of warm embrace brothers and sisters in the flesh often give one another. It is not the kiss of passionate lovers. It is an exhortation for Christians to break down the walls of formality and hypocrisy, to free themselves of prejudice and partiality, and *embrace* one another as brothers. We are to *receive*

CHAPTER 16   FIRST CORINTHIANS 16 19-23

one another as Christ has received us (Rom. 15:7); we are to be kind to one another, tenderhearted, forgiving one another, as God in Christ forgives us (Eph. 4:32); we are to have a *sincere* love of the brethren, loving one another from the heart, *fervently* (I Peter 1:22); we are to do good to all men, and *especially* to those who are of the household of faith (Gal. 6:10). And a *proper* display of emotions toward Christian brethren is always in order! Telling and showing our love aids our Christian brethren.

16:21-24 Discreetly: This is an ominous way to close a letter! He writes, "If anyone has no love for the Lord, let him be accursed." The Greek word is *anathema,* literally, "let him not stand"; the word came to mean, "let him be cursed or damned," (see Gal. 1:8-9; I Cor. 12:3; Acts 23:14; Mark 14:71; Acts 23:12, 21). Christians are to give aid to all men, especially the brotherhood, but with *discretion.* Paul does not pronounce this curse upon unbelievers, but upon those who *profess* to be Christians. It is interesting that Paul uses the Greek word *philei,* "affection, friendship" here instead of *agape* for *love. Phileo* is the word Jesus used to challenge Peter's profession of love for his Master (John 21:15ff.). It is the word to denote a love involving personal, emotional affection. Paul is challenging the reality of love professed but not expressed. Christianity is not merely a series of philosophies or doctrines to be taught and learned—it is a Person to know and love. If anyone knowing Christ, has not developed an affection for him, something is seriously wrong in his life. He is, in fact, on his way to being "damned." This was the damnation of the Pharisees. They professed a love for God but did not have it (cf. John 5:42; 8:39-47). Christian love is discerning. It will not aid hypocrisy or anti-christs. It will not condone apostasy or immorality. Christian love *will* give aid to honest seekers and those making honest errors, because that is what Christians, themselves, are.

In what appears to be a play on words, Paul follows the Greek word *anathema* with the Aramaic word *marana tha. Marana tha,* according to the *Didache* ("Teaching of the Twelve," written between 80 and 120 A.D., not written by the apostles, but held in high regard by the early church), was a word used in the early Christian observance of the Lord's Supper and meant, "Our Lord has come!" Thus, it would refer to the Lord's first advent, not his second coming. Anyone who has no affectionate love for Jesus Christ is damned because there is no other redemption to be offered. Redemption has already come in the person of Jesus Christ. Love him or be damned!

FIRST CORINTHIANS

And that is how Paul concludes this letter to Corinth. That is how he sums up all he has taught them. This is what he desires they remember above all else. "If any one has no love for the Lord, let him be damned!" It may seem rather an ugly tone with which to finish a letter, but how else can you interpret the impact of the Christian gospel? The unique feature of the Christian faith is that it requires a resolute adherence and a constant devotion to the Lord Jesus Christ. Merely to use a title, to call him "the Lord" and yet have no personal love or devotion, to show no regard for him in one's life, is the worst form of hypocrisy. When a man truly loves the Lord Jesus, his emotional attachment is always matched by readiness to obey Christ's revealed word. "He that hath my commandments, and keepeth them, he it is that loveth me" (John 14:21). Why do men call him "Lord, Lord," and do not the things which he says? (Luke 6:46).

So this is what Paul would underline: the secret of a happy life, a holy life, a victorious life, a Christian life, is a personal, real devotion to the Lord Jesus Christ. If you do not have that, you have nothing, and you will stand condemned on the Judgment Day.

Not to love the Lord Jesus means that in one's heart he is in rebellion against the highest throne in all the universe. Not to love the Lord Jesus is to reject the loveliest character of all history. In Christ is every possible beauty; there is nothing lacking in him. Not to love the Lord Jesus is a refusal of the greatest Lover of one's soul. Not to love Jesus is to curse oneself and be under the curse of Almighty God.

There was another church, working hard, patiently enduring persecution, orthodox in doctrine, bearing up for Christ's name-sake, and not complaining. But it had abandoned the *love* it had at the first. It was threatened that its "lampstand" would be removed unless it repented (Rev. 2:1-7). That was Paul's warning also to the church at Corinth.

The apostle's last words of this letter to the saints in Corinth are "The grace of the Lord Jesus be with you. My love be with you all in Christ Jesus. So be it!" The KJV italicizes the word *be,* to show it is supplied by the translators. In both sentences, the Greek preposition *meta* would literally be translated simply, "with." Could Paul not be inferring, "The grace of the Lord Jesus *is* with you; My love *is* with you all in Christ Jesus," instead of inferring he is wishing it to be so? The Christians at Corinth were having some serious problems; they had made serious errors; but they were mostly honest errors (not with a high-hand). Some of them were wanting apostolic guidance in order to repent and correct their sins. So Paul addresses them as "the church of God . . . those sanctified . . . called to be saints" (I Cor. 1:2). The grace of the Lord Jesus *was* with them even when they were in error, so long as they did not deliberately continue in the error after the apostle gave them divine direction. The love of Paul *was* with them even though their immaturity, jealousy, ignorance, and indifference to immorality troubled his soul.

So closes the immortal letter of the apostle Paul to the church of God at Corinth. It analyzes most of the problems that plague the saints. Times and cultures may differ through the centuries, but human nature never does. Problems that plague the saints remain essentially the same; causes of the problems and manifestations of the problems remain practically the same. And, because this apostolic letter, sanctioned by the Holy Spirit, is the revealed word of God as to the source and implementation of principles which will resolve the problems, it is forever relevant. It is imperative that today's church regularly study this epistle in its entirety. Christians must read this letter; preachers must feed their congregations through expository sermons from this book; congregations must put into practice the divine directions, because I Corinthians is a book in the imperative mood.

APPLICATIONS:

1. Do you "store up" *constantly*, either literally or mentally, what you intend to give to the Lord's work?
2. Do you "deposit" regularly (weekly or monthly) what you have "stored up"?
3. What are the reasons for regular or systematic giving?
4. Does your congregation try to get contributions by pressure tactics? What tactics does it use?
5. Does it make any difference what methods are used to get offerings just so long as the church's needs are met? Why?
6. Should the church be concerned about the administering of collections? How?
7. What does your congregation think about the preacher's salary? How much should it be? Does he really work hard enough for it?
8. What other ways may a congregation support those who are doing the work of the Lord (elders, deacons, Sunday School teachers, communion preparers, janitors, etc.)? Does your congregation? What can you do about it?

FIRST CORINTHIANS

9. Have you ever considered righteous living as being an aid to those who labor in the Lord's work?
10. Do you think members of your church "act like men"? Why?
11. Do the "leaders" in your congregation "addict" themselves to ministering to the members? Do they have difficulty getting people to follow their lead? Why?
12. Do you agree with Paul, "If anyone has no love for the Lord, let him be damned"? Why?

APPREHENSIONS:

1. What is a "contribution"?
2. How much should a Christian contribute?
3. Why did Paul say to deposit their contributions on the "first day of the week"?
4. Why were they sending the contribution to Jerusalem?
5. Why did Paul invite himself to spend the winter in Corinth?
6. Why did he insist they "speed him on his journey"?
7. What were the Christians at Corinth to do for Timothy?
8. What is "standing firm in the faith"?
9. What is "being courageous"?
10. Why should Christians be subject to men like Stephanas?
11. How should we give recognition to such men?
12. What is "greeting one another with a holy kiss"?
13. Do the problems of Corinth still exist in the church today? Are the solutions Paul directed to Corinth workable in today's technological age? Why?

Index of Scriptures

Old Testament
Genesis

Reference	Page
1	59
1:10-31	107
1:20	343
1:27-28	121
1:28	125
2	59
2:7	343
2:18	124, 202, 204
2:18-25	121
2:21-22	203
3:1-7	28
3:15	39
3:17-19	342
5:29	342
9:1	125
14:23	188
39:1-9	188
41:45	138

Exodus

Reference	Page
12:14-20	90
13:1—17:16	179
17:1-7	25
17:7	184, 313
20:1	41
20:3-23	183
20:6	292
32	183

Leviticus

Reference	Page
18:16-18	82
18:22	207
19:15	65
20:2-13	185
20:10-11	82
20:13	207

Numbers

Reference	Page
14:1-26	185
14:22	25
16:41-49	185
17:5-10	185
21:4-6	184
22:25-30	244
23:19	15
24	183
25	183

Deuteronomy

Reference	Page
1:6	41
1:17	65
5:7	183
6:4	14, 154
6:16	184
8:3	180
8:11-20	185
9	183
10:12	293
13:1-5	245
16:9-20	65
18:15	180
18:18-19	25
18:22	245
22:5	207
23:15-16	136
23:17-18	207
24:16	333
25:4	165
26:2-11	331
27:20	82

I Samuel

Reference	Page
15:29	15
19:18-24	244

II Kings

Reference	Page
2:3-15	304
4:1	304
4:38	304
14:6	333

Ezra

Reference	Page
4:7	308

Nehemiah

Reference	Page
7:2	66

II Chronicles

31:4-19	167

Job

2:6-7	87
2:9-10	188
5:13	71
13:10	65

Psalms

16:1-11	325
17:4	10
17:7	71
22:1	325
22:16	325
30:2	218
31:5	325
33:9	41
33:10	71
49:6	71
51:10-11	114
94:4	71
97:10	293
115:3-8	183
118:22-23	55
119:4	10
127:1	55

Proverbs

1:10	188
4:14	188
5:8-11	112
6:24-32	112
7:24-27	112
24:23	65
27:1	71
28:21	65
31	208

Ecclesiastes

Reference	Page
1:2	342,347
8:11	88
9:3	29
12:7	344

Isaiah

1:5	218
1:10-17	380
5:20	83
6:5	29
8:20	245
10:15	71
14:21	312
17:13-26	12
25:6-9	90
26:9-10	88
28	23
28:7-13	25
28:11-12	312
28:16	55
29	23
29:14	71
33:24	218
40:8	15
42:1-4	213
42:6	213
44:3	233
48:16	14
49:8	213
52:13—53:12	28
53:1-2	29
53:4-11	325
53:5	218
54:4-8	120
54:13	23
55:1-2	90,233
55:11	15,35
58:11	233
59:21	180
62:1-5	120
63:11-13	180

INDEX OF SCRIPTURES

(Isaiah)

Reference	Page
64:4	71
65:13	90
65:17	71
66:18-23	61

Jeremiah

6:14	218
7:4-11	180
7:13	41
8:11	218
9:1	29
9:23-24	29,30,71
14:4	41
16:1-4	142
17:5-10	29
17:9	49,69
18:13	65
20:7-12	29
29:1-8	135
31:30	333
35:5-6	188

Ezekiel

16:1-34	120
18:1-24	333
22:11	82
33:1-20	333

Daniel

1:8	188
6:4	66

Hosea

1	120
2	120
3	120
5:13	218
9:10	183

Micah

6:6-8	380

Zephaniah

Reference	Page
1:8	207
11:12-13	325
12:10	325
13:7	325

Malachi

2:9	65
3:1-5	56

New Testament
Matthew

1:5	138
1:18	143
1:23	308
3:11-12	232
4:1-11	187,188
4:21	16
5:4	84
5:6	90
5:13-16	92
5:27-30	89,232
5:31-32	129
5:32	81,128
5:43-48	65
6:1-6	49
6:1-18	282
6:2-21	379
6:10	344
6:19-21	347
6:25-34	165
7:1-27	67
7:16	70
7:22	245
9:1-8	241
9:10-11	92
10:1-8	224,228
10:10	167
10:39	281
11:1-30	22
11:7-11	241
11:16-19	37

(Matthew)

Reference	Page
11:19	92
11:20-24	25
11:25-30	37,38,223,286,337
12:18-21	213
12:30	58,281
12:30-31	190
12:38	25
12:39	313
12:41-44	378
13	275
13:1-23	56
13:1-53	11
13:5-6	55
13:20-21	55
13:31-32	28
13:33	92
13:55	164
15:1-20	108,159
16:4	313
16:13-19	55
16:17	223
16:20	256
16:25	281
16:27	333
18:1	51
18:7	83
18:15	171
18:17	86
18:20	216
19:1-12	123,129,144
19:3-12	127
19:8	126
19:9	81,128
19:16-22	378
20:8	379
20:11	185
20:20-28	67,235,386
20:24	65
20:27	52
20:28	29,51
21:16	286,387
21:18-19	241

(Matthew)

Reference	Page
21:42	55
22:1-14	90
22:30	141
22:39-40	173
23:1-39	49
23:5-12	51
24:1-34	139
24:24	245
24:35	41
25	276
25:1-13	90
25:31-46	299,347
26:6-12	142
26:28	29
27:30	158
27:41-44	25
28:11-15	326
28:18-20	92,103
28:19	19

Mark

Reference	Page
1:19	16
4:1-34	11
4:26-29	35,340
5:41	308
7:1-13	159
7:14-23	108
7:18-19	156
7:21-23	29
8:35	281
9:34	65
9:35	59
9:38-41	51
10:2-12	129
10:17-22	378
10:35-45	51
10:44	192
12:41-44	380
13:1-31	139
14:3	142
14:71	389

INDEX OF SCRIPTURES

(Mark)

Reference	Page
15:19	158
15:22	308
15:34	308

Luke

Reference	Page
1:27	143
2:5	143
4:1-13	187,188
5:14	126
5:30	185
6:133-135	218
6:46	390
8:1-3	208
8:4-18	11,56
8:11	25,77
8:15	37
8:56	126
9:24	281
9:46	65
9:49-50	51
10:1-20	25
10:7	167
10:29-37	282
10:38-42	142
11:32	99
11:41	156
11:50-51	66
12:1	218
12:13-31	103
12:42-43	66
12:48	66
12:49	56
13:3-4	334
13:20-21	92
13:22-30	25
14:1	90
14:7-14	51
14:25-33	103
15:22-32	90,377
16:10-15	103
16:15	344

(Luke)

Reference	Page
16:18	129
16:19-31	331,333
16:30-31	25,259
18:9-14	69,283
18:18-30	378
19:7	92
19:11-27	65
21:1-4	378,380
21:1-33	139
22:24-27	59,65,386
22:24-28	51
22:31-32	87
22:44	175
23:34	39
24:25	325
24:44-48	330
24:49	232

John

Reference	Page
1:1-18	14,115,369
1:14	375
1:38	308
1:41-42	229
1:42	308
2:3-4	51
3:2	222
3:3-5	344
3:16	280
3:21	38
4:1-2	20
4:10	233
4:13	233
4:25-30	51
4:31-34	49
4:34	90
4:36-38	53
5:17-46	14
5:19-29	268,332
5:25-28	331
5:41	387

(John)

Reference	Page
5:42	389
5:44	37
6	267
6:15	51
6:25-71	49
6:29	346
6:32-33	180
6:35	233
6:35-63	90
6:38-40	268
6:41-43	185
6:45	14,23
6:61	185
6:63	41,49,152,213
6:66	57
7:3-4	51
7:16	268
7:17	39,50,153
7:24	67
7:32	185
7:37-39	233
7:38	244
7:49	69
8:24	334
8:25-30	14
8:26-28	268
8:31-32	163,337
8:31-36	298
8:37	37
8:39-47	292,337,389
8:43-47	37
8:58	14
9:4	346
9:7	308
9:28	74
9:35-41	37,38
10:7-18	166
10:10-13	329
10:17	269
10:22-39	14

(John)

Reference	Page
10:24-38	241
10:37-38	222
10:41	241
12:6	224
12:20-25	103
12:24-26	340
12:27-43	37
12:49	268
13	169
13:1-20	386
13:5-11	51
13:6-9	152
13:34-35	173
14	41
14:1-11	14,271
14:1—16:33	223
14:11	222
14:15-23	39,114
14:18-24	14
14:21	86,390
14:23	86,233
15	41,276
15:1-5	270
15:1-11	114,232
15:7	86
15:7-11	14
15:10	86,241
15:11	86
15:12-14	103
15:12-17	173
15:21	39
16	41
16:13	36,42
16:15	14
16:27	280
17	41,276
17:1	210,232
17:1-5	14
17:3	152
17:4	268
17:13-26	29
17:14-17	41

INDEX OF SCRIPTURES

(John)

Reference	Page
17:15-19	92
17:17	10
17:19	10
17:21	264,268,269,270
20:22	41,232
21:15	389
21:15-19	49,280

Acts

Reference	Page
1:3	326
1:8	222
1:9-11	331
2	250,252,253
2:1	231,326,327
2:1-21	232
2:8	229
2:14-21	41
2:17	185
2:22	14
2:25-32	325
2:38	19,20,103,114,308,333
2:42	273
3:17	39
3:17-26	332
4:12	19
4:36	164
5	274
5:5-10	241
5:28	126
5:32	114
6:1	185
6:1-6	65,254
6:7	327
7:58—8:3	9
8	254
8:5	254
8:14-24	287
8:17	254
8:20	188
8:31	38

(Acts)

Reference	Page
9:1-2	9
9:1-31	9
9:19-23	9
9:22	44
9:26-27	164,326
9:36	208,308
10	249
10:4	347
10:9-16	157
10:14	172
10:15	107
10:34	64
10:44-48	244
10:44—11:18	232
10:47-48	253
10:48	19
11:22-30	164
11:28	378
13	137
13:1-3	163
13:2—15:35	9
13:2	164,255
13:8	89,308
13:11	241
13:27	39
13:33-35	325
15:1	135
15:19-20	108
15:20	149
15:29	149,164
15:36—18:22	10
16	137
16:1-4	172
16:10	44
16:14-15	20
16:19-34	20
16:24	126
16:35-39	173
16:37	160
17	172

FIRST CORINTHIANS

(Acts)

Reference	Page
17:6	28,73
17:16-21	32
17:16-34	148,173
17:22-23	37
17:28	9,33
17:30-31	33,39,332,337
18	5
18:1	381
18:1-4	164
18:1-11	323
18:3	74
18:4-19	151
18:8	19,20,50,76,77,103,232
18:9	34
18:17	10
18:18-22	381
18:23	381
18:24-28	208
18:24—19:31	381
19	254,255
19:1-7	249
19:22	77,383
19:23-30	334
19:37	172
20:1-4	381
20:3	10
20:7	214
20:28	115
20:28-32	49
20:29-30	70,329
20:33-35	381
20:35	115
21:19	208
21:21-24	151
21:25	108
21:26	172
22:1-21	9
22:3	9
22:3-5	327
22:16	19,20,103,333

(Acts)

Reference	Page
22:28	9
23:4	74
23:6	9
23:12	389
23:14	389
23:21	389
24:5-21	172
24:17	378
25:10	100
26:2-8	172
26:4-5	9
26:8	340
26:9-11	327
26:16-19	326
26:26	14

Romans

Reference	Page
1	59,266,350
1:1	9
1:1-16	208
1:5	54
1:11	256
1:11-12	255
1:18	107
1:18-32	23,37,38,183
1:19-20	152
1:21	185
1:22-25	191
1:24-27	207
2	59
2:6	333
2:11	64,65
2:20	333
2:24	65
3:21	66
3:27-28	30
4:1	77
5:17-19	345
6:1-11	20
6:3-5	333

INDEX OF SCRIPTURES

(Romans)

Reference	Page
6:5	103
6:12-23	173,176
6:13	188
6:14	345
6:15-23	115
7:3-4	129
7:6	345
7:13-25	69,87,385
8:1-11	114,343
8:1-17	223
8:2	345
8:5	114
8:5-8	49,337
8:5-11	176
8:5-17	235
8:18-25	331
8:19-23	342
8:29	11,163
8:32	60
10:1	35
10:17	25,113
12:1-2	28,151
12:1-8	176
12:1-13	245
12:3	68
12:4-13	124
12:5	261,274
12:6	228,229,303
12:9	295
12:10	173,387
12:14-21	13
12:14—13:7	107
13:1-7	26,131,135
13:7	386
13:14	176
14	15,149,154,157
14:1-4	108,171
14:5	155
14:7-9	196
14:14-15	152
14:15-21	159

(Romans)

Reference	Page
14:19	192
14:20	158
14:23	155,156
15	154
15:1	173
15:1-2	106,192
15:1-7	271
15:2	106,192
15:3	158
15:5-6	18
15:7	389
15:18-19	256
15:26-27	163
16	355
16:13	110
16:17-18	219
16:25-27	38

II Corinthians

Reference	Page
1:1	9
1:3-11	87,187
1:8-10	334
1:15	78
1:16	78
1:20	213,330
1:23	78
2:5-11	58
2:5-17	11
2:17	34,169
3	165
3:3	384
3:11	385
3:17-18	163
3:18	11,152,244
4	165
4:2	34,59,169
4:3-6	58
4:11	334
4:16-18	58,140,141
4:16—5:1	60

(II Corinthians)

Reference	Page
4:16—5:21	88
5:1-21	343
5:11-21	29,169
5:14	173,282
5:14-17	153,219
5:14-21	103,213,235,338
5:16-17	58
5:19	14,213
7:12	82
7:14-15	168
8	377
8:4	378
8:7	13
8:10	377
8:12	379
8:20	378
9	260,377
9:5	378
9:12	378
9:13	378
10:1	78
10:3-4	338
10:3-5	23,78,356
10:10	34
10:12	29,67
11:1-33	30
11:3	59
11:7	164
11:7-11	170,381,382
11:7-12	381
11:21-33	73
11:23-29	334
11:33	77
12:1-10	87,187
12:1-21	30
12:7	34,257
12:9	30
12:10	285
12:11-18	170
12:12	13,35,41,68,222

(II Corinthians)

Reference	Page
12:13	381,382
12:13-17	167
12:14	6
12:14-18	77,381
13:1	6
13:5	217
13:11	16,18

Galatians

1:1	9
1:6-9	245,272
1:8-9	267,389
1:10	196
1:14	199
1:20	219
2:1-21	173
2:3	172
2:3-5	159
2:6	65
2:11	65
2:11-14	159
2:20	103
3:20	14
3:23-29	103
3:23—4:7	287
3:25-29	20
3:26-27	103,333
3:28	136,201
4:9	152
4:16	292
5:1	166
5:1-12	151,159
5:1-26	103
5:6	163
5:7	175
5:13	103,173,386
5:14	173
5:17	87,385
5:19-21	16,52
5:20	149

INDEX OF SCRIPTURES

(Galatians)

Reference	Page
5:22	280
5:22-25	244
5:23	175
5:24-26	103
6:1	67,326
6:1-5	285
6:10	389
6:14	30

Ephesians

Reference	Page
1	242
1:1-23	38
1:7-10	344
1:22-23	274
2:11-22	12,388
2:19-22	57
2:20	55
2:21-22	273
3:10	99
3:16-19	244
3:17	114
4	267
4:1-16	49,274,388
4:3	16
4:3-13	261
4:4-6	271
4:7	13,229,246
4:11-13	242
4:11-16	285,287,312
4:12	346
4:13	18
4:13-16	257
4:14	51,59
4:15	291
4:15-16	231
5:16	44,50
4:18	39
4:22	29
4:32	389
5:3	85

(Ephesians)

Reference	Page
5:3-14	218
5:11-12	85
5:18	90
5:19	310
5:21	122,125,316,386
5:21-23	110
5:21-27	85
5:22-23	119,120
5:23-32	274
5:26	103
6:1-4	208
6:4	76
6:5-9	136
6:9	64,65
6:10-23	176
6:13	188

Philippians

Reference	Page
1:1	9
1:13	327
1:21	60
1:27	18,271
2:1-11	53
2:2	18
2:3	386
2:3-4	102
2:3-8	214
2:4	106
2:5-11	169
2:14	185
2:29	386
3:1-16	170
3:2	135
3:3-7	30
3:4-6	172
3:5	9
3:14	174,175
3:17	77
3:19	110
4:1	57

(Philippians)

Reference	Page
4:8	151
4:9	77
4:11	134
4:11-13	74, 283
4:14-18	163
4:15-18	166
4:15-19	381
4:17	381, 382
4:22	327

Colossians

Reference	Page
1:1	9
1:18	274, 275
1:19	14
1:24-27	231, 344
1:24-29	38, 49
1:27-29	34
2:2	44
2:8	199
2:9	14
2:12-13	103, 333
2:16-23	159
2:18	71
2:18-23	176
2:19	44, 274
2:20-23	108
3:1-4	337
3:1-24	26
3:12-13	102
3:14-15	173
3:15	13, 174
3:18	316
3:18-19	120, 122
3:22—4:1	65, 136
3:25	64

I Thessalonians

Reference	Page
1:1	9
1:9	149
2:5-6	196

(I Thessalonians)

Reference	Page
2:5-9	381
2:9	164
2:9-12	77
2:11	76
2:13	38, 77, 199
2:17-20	384
2:19-20	57
4:2	126
4:3	10
4:3-8	130
4:4	10, 119
4-9-12	381
4:11	164
4:13	140
4:13—5:3	331
5:12	386
5:14	173
5:21	67
5:23-24	344

II Thessalonians

Reference	Page
1:9	170
1:11	346
2	138
2:1-12	139
2:1-15	87
2:9	245
2:9-12	37, 337
2:10	291
2:13	232
2:13-15	77
3:6	86, 92
3:6-15	67, 219, 228, 381
3:8	164, 170
3:14	58, 86, 91, 92
3:14-15	87
3:15	86

I Timothy

Reference	Page
1:2	76
1:5	126, 173, 244, 289

INDEX OF SCRIPTURES

(I Timothy)

Reference	Page
1:8	100
1:8-9	127
1:8-11	26,131
1:12-16	54
1:12-17	9
1:13	9,39,327
1:15	9,69
1:18	126
2:5	202,334
2:12-14	208
2:15	10
4:1-4	108
4:1-5	138,192
4:3	125
4:4-5	59
4:5	119
4:14	254
4:15	107
5:1-22	384
5:8	140
5:9-16	144,208
5:14	130
5:17-18	165,167
5:21	65
5:22	255
5:23	241
6:1-2	136
6:6-19	140
6:13	126
6:17	126

II Timothy

Reference	Page
1:6	255
1:13	77,386
2:1-2	386
2:1-7	164
2:5	175
2:24-26	384
3:6-7	37
3:10-17	386

(II Timothy)

Reference	Page
3:16-17	228,288
4:1-3	176
4:1-8	138
4:5	346
4:7-8	175
4:9-18	382
4:10	57
4:20	241,257

Titus

Reference	Page
1:4	76
2:3-5	208
2:9-10	136
3:5	103
3:10	219
3:10-11	92
3:13	381

Philemon

Reference	Page
v. 1	9
v. 10	76

Hebrews

Reference	Page
1:1	66
1:12	345
2:1-4	89
2:3-4	25,222,256
2:4	13,41,229
2:5-18	60,298
2:10	77
2:14-18	343
2:18	188
3:7-19	180,184
3:14	60
4:12-13	69
4:14-16	188
5:7	347
5:11-13	49
5:11-14	50,54,218
5:11—6:12	287

(Hebrews)

Reference	Page
5:12-14	90
5:13	286
6:1	90
6:4	233
6:17	213
7:2	308
9:12	115
10	138
10:5-10	29,115
10:19-25	104
10:22	103,155
10:32-34	140
10:32-39	187
10:33	73
10:34	378
11:1	77
11:1—12:2	389
11:7	27,99
11:35-40	241
12:1	175
12:1-17	187
12:11-12	292
12:14	10
12:14-15	345
12:22-23	90
13:4	119
13:7	386
13:15-16	61

James

Reference	Page
1:2-11	187
1:4-5	243
1:13-15	187
1:14-15	218
1:17	14
1:18	77
1:19-20	29
1:22-25	28,289
1:25	243
2:1	64
2:8	173

(James)

Reference	Page
2:9	64,65
2:11-12	99
2:15	99
2:19	282
3:8	18
3:13-16	70
3:13-18	41,151,245
4:1	274
5:14	255
5:19-20	67,285

I Peter

Reference	Page
1:2	232
1:3-5	330
1:3-9	343
1:4	233
1:7	56
1:9-12	61
1:13	337
1:13-25	12
1:18-19	115
1:22	389
1:22-25	77,163
1:23	77
2:2-3	90
2:4-8	55
2:13-14	135
2:16	173,181
2:20	102
2:20-23	55
3:1-2	128
3:8-15	102
3:21	103,333
4:3	149
4:8	386
4:9	185
4:12-13	55,56
4:12-19	138
5:1-5	386
5:2	49
5:5	386

INDEX OF SCRIPTURES

I Peter

Reference	Page
1:2-4	288
1:3-4	28,152,213,356
1:3-5	105
1:3-11	243
1:3-21	11
1:6	174
1:16-21	41,325
1:20-21	42,308
2:1-22	92
2:4	99,205
2:9	188
2:10	99
2:17-21	349
2:20-22	104
3:1-7	37
3:3-7	323
3:5	337
3:17	188,218

I John

Reference	Page
1:1-3	375
1:1-4	327
1:5-8	244
1:8—2:6	104
2:3-6	385
2:5-6	86
2:15-17	293
2:16	187
2:24	49,86,233,385
3:1-3	28,332
3:1-6	244
3:14-24	173
3:18	291
3:19-21	156
3:24	49,86,114,233,285
4:1-3	375
4:1-6	41,44,87,233,228,245,288
4:7-21	173
4:10	278
4:12	114

(I John)

Reference	Page
4:16	289
4:19	152,278,299
4:20	153
5:3	293
5:21	149

II John

v. 4	57
v. 6	293
v. 10	92
v. 11	92

III John

v. 3	57
v. 4	57
v. 6	381
v. 9	57

Jude

v. 3	42,175,272,288
v. 6	99,205
v. 11-13	349

Revelation

2	57,83,277
2:1-7	390
2:2-4	281
2:5	346
2:14-15	183
2:20-23	183
2:26-27	99
3	57,83,277
3:1	219
3:15-17	219
3:19-21	114
3:21	99
5:9	115,304
6:7-8	334
7:9	304
9:11	304

(Revelation)

Reference	Page
9:20-21	149
10:11	304
11:9	304
13:7	304
13:14	245
14:6	304
14:6-7	99
14:9-13	331
14:13	347
16:14	245
16:16	304
17	183
17:2	81

(Revelation)

Reference	Page
17:4	81
17:5	304
18	183
18:3	81
18:9	81
18:9-19	140
19:20	245
20:6	231
20:11—22:5	331
20:12	333
20:14	345
22:10-11	281
22:17	233

Index of Places

A
Achaia 1,2,10,19,374
Acrocorinthus 1
Acropolis 1,3,4
Aegeon Sea 3
Africa 307
Agora 3
America 306,307,380
Asia Minor 9,57,83,183,381,388
Athens 1,3,5,34,175,206,337

B
Babylon 25,87,137

C
Canaan 138
Cilicia 9

D
Damascus 9,326

E
East Africa 307
Eden 16,17,28,39,60,187,294,300
Egypt 60,82,90,137,179,307
England 12,206
Ephesus 6,10,18,77,78,332-336, 381-383

F
France 203

G
Galatia 292,378,381
Germany 203
Gethsemane 175,206
Greece (Greek) 1,2,9,10,12,15,25, 32,33,40,54,69,73,74,82,98,102, 106,135,149-151,165,174,175,196, 202,205-207,232,307,381,388
Guatemala 296

I
Iconian Sea 3
Italy 2

J
Japan 306
Jerusalem 139,254,273,287,294,374

Jew (Hebrew, Israel, Judea) 2,3,6, 9,14,25,28,33,55,56,60,61,69,73, 82,86,89,90,92,109,135,138,149-151,154,155,159,165,167,172,173, 179,180,182-185,196,203,205-207, 209,222,232,242,251-253,255,269, 284,287,288,292,307,312,313,325, 326, 330,342,378,380,383

M
Macedonia 10,77,374,381,383
Mars Hill 34
Mediterranean Sea 1,9,65
Missouri (St. Louis) 2
Maoh 138

N
Naim 331

P
Palestine 19,373,381
Pelogonneasus 1,174
Pantheon 3
Perea 123
Persia 25,88,137
Philippi 100,151,163,382,386
Phoenicia 307
Phrygia 381
Pompeii 148,193,223
Poseidan 3

R
Rome 2,4,5,19,25,55,74,98,100, 120,135,137-140,149,183,203,205, 207,210,273,281,287,332-336

S
Samaria 254
Sparta 175,206
synagogue 6,209
Syria 203,381

T
Tarsus 9,326
Thessalonica 6,331,384,386
Troas 214,215
Turkey 9

409

Index of Subjects

A
adultery 81
angel 99,100,204,205,245,281
ascetism 92
atonement 13,22,24,27,29,33,38, 39,76,90,104,115,211,213,216,265, 298,329,330,343

B
baptism 8,19-21,33,76,77,103,104, 129,179-181,189,232,233,249,250, 252,253,255,256,259,287,333,334, 344
brass 4

C
carnal 49,51,83,84,87
collection 6
communion 6,89,90,92,188,189, 210-219
conscience 65,150,154,155,158,159, 171,192-195,327
copper 98
creation 38,59,60,121,135,144,162, 163,165,181,183,204,205,207,275, 280,331,332,342,388

D
debauchery 4,5,102,103
Declaration & Address 15
dichotomy 16
discipline 57,76,84,88,93,95,96, 100,107,187,208,274,291,293
dissension 15,51
disunity 12
division 11,12,14,16,18,19,22,53, 58,68,69,70,72,79
divorce 6,82,126-132,137,144,353, 373
drunkenness 52,83,102

E
enmity 51
envy 52,55,223,281,283

Epicurianism 150
excommunicated 86-88,93
Existentialism 267,320-323,329, 335,352,358,360,362,372-375

G
gentleness 13,88,105,106,116,151, 183,288,321,375
gift 6,13,14,25,38,42,53,55,66,72, 123,124,131,184,221-224,226,227, 229,230,232-237,242,244,246,248, 254,255,257,260,280-282,286,288, 303,305,308,310,314,317,318
gluttony 157
Gnosticism 13,88,106,108,116,151, 183,288,321,375

H
harlotry 28
heresy 16,21
homosexuality 4,83,102,107,116, 120,207

I
idolatry 4,51,83,92,102,108,113, 148-150,153,155,156,181-183,186, 189,190,193,195,223
immorality 4,6,11,14,51,55,81,82- 85,89,91-93,97,102,105,109,112, 150,173,181,182,184,196,223,274, 337,353,383,389,391
immortality 88,265,341,345,391
impurity 51
incest 81-85,90,98
incorruptible 88
integrity 6
Isthmean Gameo 3,175

J
jealousy 11-13,53,55,57,70,86,229, 232,245,283,391
judgment (day) 13,38,51,56,68,69, 99,185,244,312,332,337,390

INDEX OF SUBJECTS

K
kingdom 10-13,22,23,26-28,51,58, 64,65,67,79,88,89,97,101-104,106, 123,124,153,159,172,185,201,218 252,253,344,347,352,386,388

L
law court 97,100,101,106,114
licentiousness 51,58
litigation 98
luxury 4

M
marble 4
marriage 6,55,83,110-112,119-130, 132,134,137-142,144,145,148,152, 164,166,184,202,208

N
Nazarene 206
Nazarite 206
Nemean 175
Neo-orthodoxy 265,267,349,352, 358,362,363,375

O
Olympic Games 3,174,175

P
papyri 13
parable 11,28,56,89,247
party 12,51,57,58,65,69,73,74,83
Passover 89,90,211
Pentecost 19,20,55,78,185,231,250, 252,253,256,327
persecution 56,57,162
Pharisee 9,69
pottery 4
polygamy 121
profligacy 4
promiscuity 4,84,106,107,110,113, 116,130,131
prostitution 4,105,110-113,116,183
Pythian 175

Q
quarrie 18

R
rationalism 350
reconciliation 28,29,33,39,86,90, 101,128,130,213,266,388
redemption 20,21,24-29,33,38-40, 42,43,66,77,78,89,115,116,181, 185,186,216,218,231,233,260,268, 269,288,289,298,303,332,334,342, 343,345,349,367,368,388,389
repentance 11,21,25,33,76,78,79, 84,86-88,91-93,103,103,114,128-130,132,167,217,252,259,282,285, 287,334,337,344,346,370,371,380, 390,391
Restoration Movement 174
resurrection 6,20,24,25,33,35,38, 43,51,52,55,88,99,104,116,182, 231,257,259,321-341,343,345-347, 355,356,367,371-374,378,385
revelation 13,17,22,23,36,38,40,41, 43,45,49,50,53,54,104,107,112, 113,139,151,152,157,166,181,186, 194,223,224,231,245,264,266-268, 305,306,322,339,341,349,364,367-369,371,372,374
righteousness 24,26-29,83,89,98, 113,115,116,181,183,298
robbery 4,83,92,102,106

S
salvation 8,13,20,22,28,38,40,42, 43,57,86,103-105,128,152,170-173, 186,189,195,201,216,258,261,263, 265,266,268,269,287,323,352,355, 366,367,373
sanctification 8,10-12,29,85,89, 103-105,116,128,222,253,273,277, 280,288,289,344,391
Sanhedrin 119
schism 6,12,53,70,77,78,218,242, 271,383,384

schizaphrenia 16
second coming 88,139,185,216,281, 309,332,345,372,374,389
sectarianism 20,266
self-control 52
slavery 2,26,135,136-138
sorcery 51
Stocism 150
strife 51,53,57
synagogue 171

T

temptation 4,56,57,83,93,115,120, 123,134,140,142,143,150,153,180-183,186-188,193,227,296,346,347
theft 4
tradition 154,159,199,200

W

war 26,142
wealth 4,28
wine 5,149,210,211,215
wisdom 28,29,38
worship 4,6,14,149,150,154,155, 171,183,190,191,193,199-203,207, 209,210,214-216,218,219,260,313, 316,350,379

Index of People

A
Abel 77
Abraham 20,77,188
Achaicus 6,387
Adam 187,294,299,300,331,342,343,344,368
Adrian 33
Alciphro 5
Alexander 87
Alexander the Great 174,325
Allah 259
Amos 60
Ananias 89,228,241
Andocides 82
Aphrodite 4,5
Apollo 148
Apollos 19,52,55,60,70,71,384
Applebury, T.R. 24,39,99,124
Aquila 6,388
Aristophanes 5
Aristotle 350
Artemis 148
Augustine 309,363

B
Baird, W. 148
Balaam 183,244,349
Balak 183
Barclay, William 10,32,65,73,106,210,211,282,283,284,291,292,294
Barnabas 164
Barth, K. 359,362-369,371,373
Bashan, D. 249
Blos, P. 293
Boaz 138
Buddha 330,353
Bultmann 373,374

C
Caesar, Julius 2,193,325,327
Cain 283,349
Caleb 180
Caligula 82
Callias 82

Campbell, A. 214
Campbell, T. 15
Chloe 6,18,383
Chrysostom, J. 309
Churchill, W. 325
Cicero 82
Claudius 5
Cleopatra II 82
Cleopatra VII 82
Confucius 353
Conob 296
Cornelius 128,137,232,244,249,252,253
Crawford, C.C. 259
Crispus 6,19
Crouch, Andrae 335

D
Daniel 66,135,137,188,334
Darius 66
Darwin, C. 330
David 60,77,282
Demas 57
Democritus 350
DeWelt, D. 258
Dickinson, C. 294
Dionysus 210
Diotrephes 57
Dobson, J. 293
Domitian 56,138
Dorcas 286
Durant, W. 336

E
Elijah 60
Elisha 60
Elymas 89,228,241
Enoch 77
Erastus 77,383
Esther 135,137,138
Eve 59,187,384

F
Fahremkrog, L. 206
Festus 100
Fields, W. 136
Fisher, F. 145,170,204
Fortunatus 6,387
Fowler, H. 22

G
Gaius 6,19
Gallio 6
Gamaliel 9
Greenleaf, S. 323,325

H
Hananiah 66
Hegel, G. 360,361,363
Herod Agrippa 172
Herod Antipas 82
Herodias 82
Hezekiah 60,167
Hitler, A. 351,353
Hittites 309
Holy Spirit 6,7,17,39-44,49,72,74, 76,85,86,89,103,104,111-115,123, 124,145,151,163,175,177,180,183, 199,213,222-226,229,231-235,237, 244,245,247,249-260,265,268, 280,289,294,304,306,309,315,318, 343,344,354,355,385,388,391
Homer 206
Hopkins, M. 293
Horace 175
Hordern, W. 350,352
Hume, D. 240
Hymenaeus 87

I
Irenaeus 309
Isaiah 60,213,297,312
Isis 224

J
Jacob 179
Jairus 331
James 164,243,326
Jehoshaphat 60
Jeremiah 29,60
Job 188,285
John (Apostle) 55,57,281,331, 334,355
John the Baptist 113,137,241,256, 286
Joseph 66,137,188
Josephus 98,135
Joshua 60,180
Judas (Iscariot) 57,225,228,285, 291,292
Jude 349
Justin (Martyr) 215
Juvenal 207

K
Kant, I. 358-361,364,366,368,372
Ketcherside, C. 246
Kierkegaard, S. 361,362
Kildahl, J. 245,307,309
Korah 349
Kunneth, W. 374

L
Lazarus 331
Lenin 353
Lenski, R.C.H. 37,202
Lewis, C.S. 279,284,297
Lickona, T. 82
Lindsay, T. 260
Livy 207
Lucius 148
Luke 71

M
Maccabees 135
Malachi 60
Marx, K. 330,353

INDEX OF PEOPLE

Mary and Martha 142
Mary (Mother of Jesus) 164
McCartney, C. 240
McGarvey, J.W. 228
Meander 336
Melinus 82
Milligan, R. 240
Moffatt 283,284
Mohammed 258,330,353
Mordecai 137
Morrison, C.C. 265
Moses 60,77,127,164,172,180,192, 243,245,259,287,288,312,331

N
Nash, D. 279,299
Nehemiah 135,137
Nero 2,3,56,82,138,174
Newnan, A.H. 260
Nicodemus 344
Nicolaitans 288
Nida, E. 296
Niebuhr, R. 370,371,373
Nietzsche, F. 351
Noah 27,77

Onesimus 76,136
Origen 309
Overbeck, F. 365,366
Oxnam, G.B. 22

P
Pascal, B. 324,325
Penn, W. 282
Peter 19,70,87,137,157,164,172, 188,242,251,294,325,326,346
Petronius 149
Pharaoh 245
Philemon 115,136
Philip 245,254
Phillips, J.B. 66,69,72,121,140, 195,295
Philostratus 33

Plato 358,360,365
Plummer, A. 156,205,231,262
Plutarch 33
Popkin, K. 359
Potiphar 66
Praetorian Guard 327
Priscilla 6,388
Ptolemy XIII 82

R
Rahab 138
Ramsay, W. 203
Rechabites 188
Robertson 262
Rousseau, J. 363
Russell, B. 336
Ruth 138

S
Salmon 138
Samuel 60
Sapphira 89,228,241
Sassia 82
Satan (devil) 7,11,16,18,19,28,41, 58,60,85-88,100,115,116,122,123, 187,189,190,235,276,281,282,298, 347
Saul 244,282
Schleiermacher, F. 351
Schneider, J. 373
Seneca 6,362
Sergius Paulus 89,137
Silas 6
Simon 142,164
Simon Magus 245,254
Solomon 23
Sosthenes 10
Stedman, R. 342,343,378,380
Stephanas 6,19,387
Strabo 4
Stroll 359
Suetonius 82

T
Thomas 182
Thompson, F. 295
Timothy 6,71,76-78,101,119,125,
164,172,241,254,255,382,383
Titus 76,101,172
Titus, H.H. 351,363
Titus Justus 6
Trophimus 241

V
Van Til, C. 364,367,369

Vath, D. 296
Vine, W.E. 10,109
Vollmer, P. 206

W
Wells, H.G. 336
Wilson, S. 58,115,237,244,292,
317,340

X
Xenophon 98

Index of Organizations

Christian Scientists 258
Disciples of Christ 263
Mormons 258,309
National Council of Churches 263

Roman Catholic Church 159,164,
264,309,333,350
World Council of Churches 22,271,
272,353